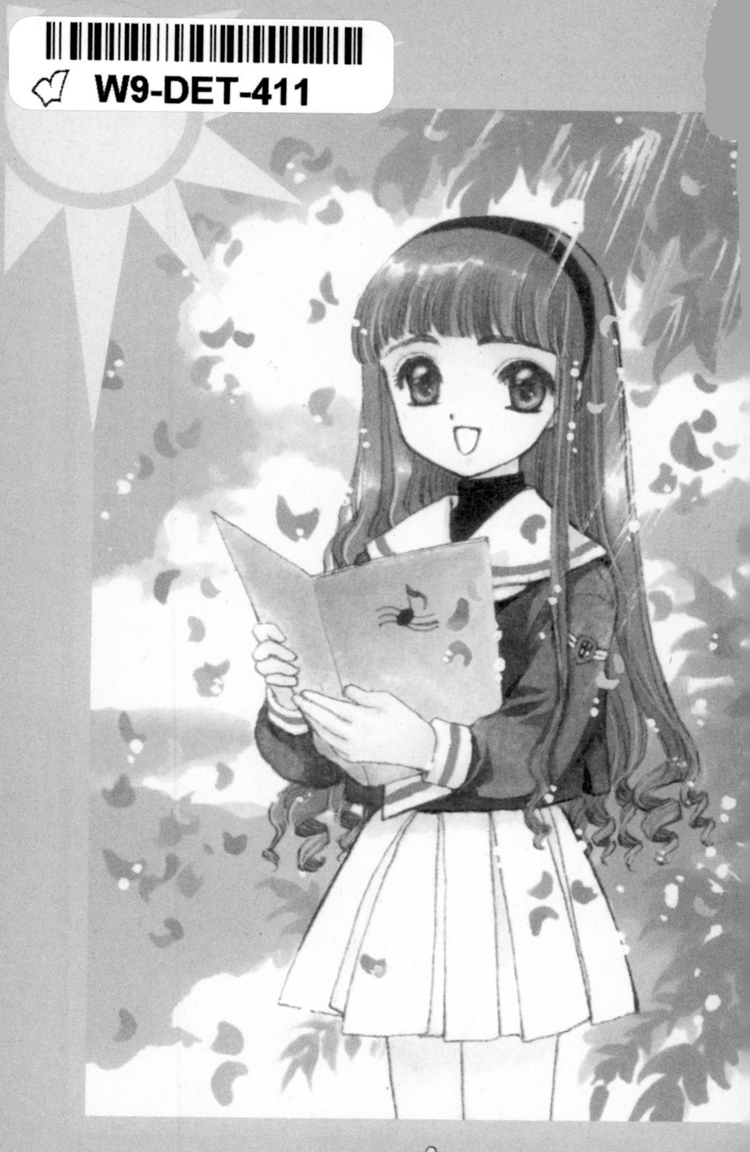

CLAMP

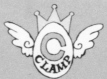

CARDCAPTOR SAKURA

▪◦▪◦▪◦▪◦▪◦▪◦▪◦▪◦▪◦▪◦▪◦▪◦▪◦▪◦▪

STAFF
SATSUKI IGARASHI
NANASE OHKAWA
MICK NEKOI
MOKONA APAPA

PLANNING AND PRESENTED BY
CLAMP

CARDCAPTOR SAKURA

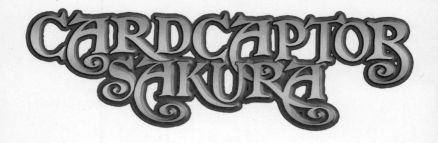

Volume 2 of 6

Story and Art by

CLAMP

TOKYOPOP®

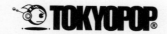

HAMBURG // LONDON // LOS ANGELES // TOKYO

Translator - Mika Onishi
Additional Translation - Athena Nibley & Alethea Nibley
English Adaptation - Carol Fox
Copy Editor - Paul Morrissey
Retouch and Lettering - Brian Bossin
Production Designers - Monalisa de Asis, James Lee, Deron Bennett
Cover Design - Aaron Suhr

Editor - Jake Forbes
Managing Editor - Jill Freshney
Production Coordinator - Antonio DePietro
Production Managers - Jennifer Miller, Mutsumi Miyazaki
Art Director - Matt Alford
Editorial Director - Jeremy Ross
VP of Production - Ron Klamert
President & C.O.O. - John Parker
Publisher & C.E.O. - Stuart Levy

Email: editor@TOKYOPOP.com
Come visit us online at www.TOKYOPOP.com

A  Manga

TOKYOPOP Inc.
5900 Wilshire Blvd. Suite 2000
Los Angeles, CA 90036

First TOKYOPOP printing: October 2003

10 9 8 7 6 5 4 3

Printed in the USA

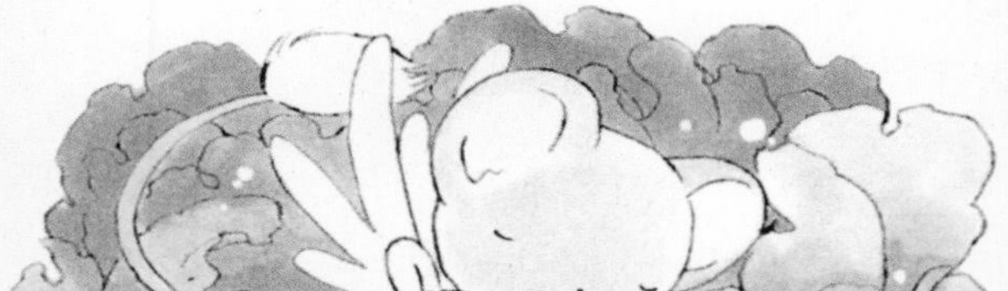

2

Table of Contents

THE STORY SO FAR...

Hello, gentle readers! Tomoyo here, Sakura's biggest fan and official chronicler of all her adventures! Since you weren't there to videotape them like I was, let me bring you up to speed on the heroic deeds of everyone's favorite card-capturing sweetheart!

It all began when Sakura-chan ran across a strange book in her father's library. When she opened it, a deck of ornate cards flew out and scattered to the winds! Then Kero-chan, a magical beast in the guise of a cute stuffed animal, emerged from the book's cover and revealed to Sakura that she had magical powers, and was the only one who could bring the cards to safety. From then on, Sakura took on the brave task of catching all the cards and bringing peace to the fair town of Tomoeda once again!

In the first volume of Sakura's adventures, she had already caught the Windy and Jump cards, but things took a turn for the positively frightening when strange things started happening in front of all of us at Tomoeda Elementary! In P.E., the Fly card almost blew us over and the Watery card threatened to drown us all in the pool! If not for Sakura's fearlessness, tragedy would surely have struck the student body. Then, in King Penguin Park, all us girls started seeing scary apparitions on the lake—I blush to confess that I saw the big penguin slide, which I had been afraid to go down—and it had the nerve to pose as Sakura's mom to draw her into the lake! Good thing Sakura showed the Illusion card who was boss, or she would surely have drowned.

And now, without further ado, let's see what happens next in the neverending drama that is the life of a Cardcaptor. I hope you enjoy following Sakura's adventures at least half as much as I do!

HEREIN LIE THE CLOW CARDS.

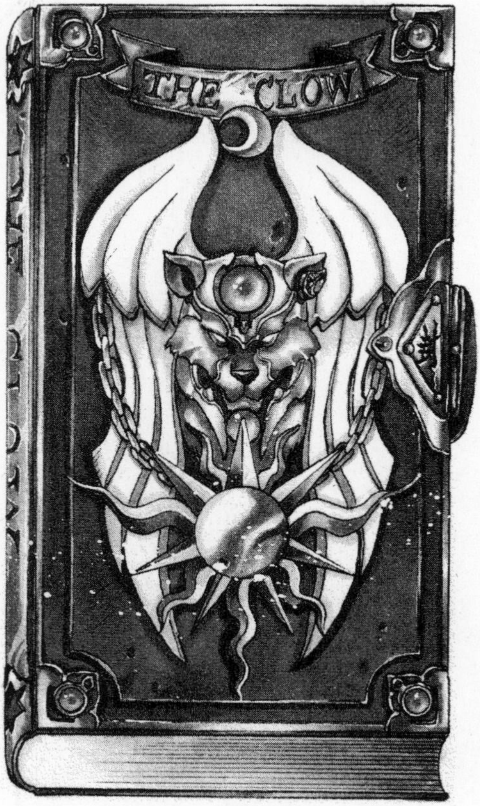
THE CLOW

IF THEIR SEAL IS BROKEN,

DISASTER WILL BEFALL THIS WORLD...

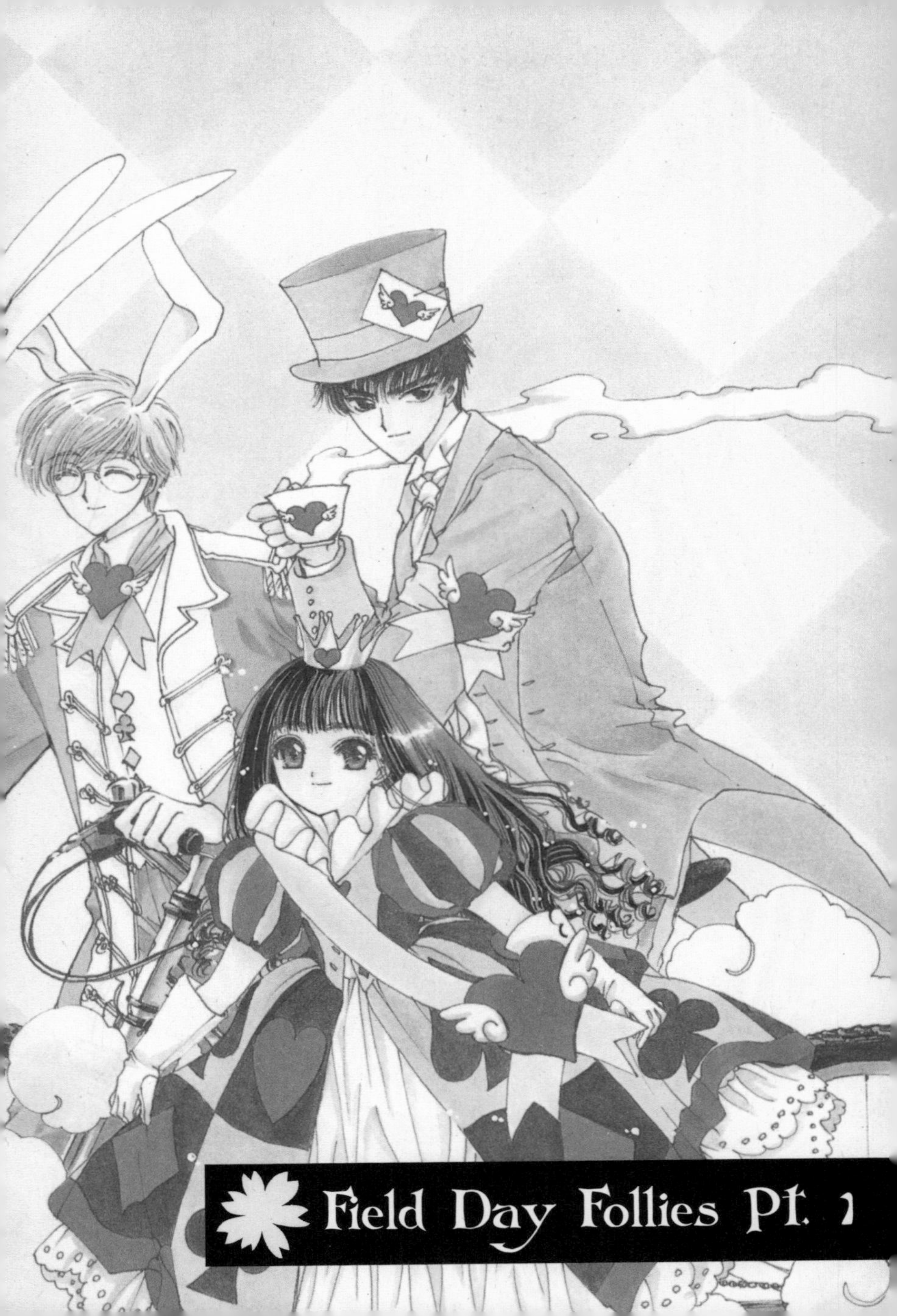
Field Day Follies Pt. 1

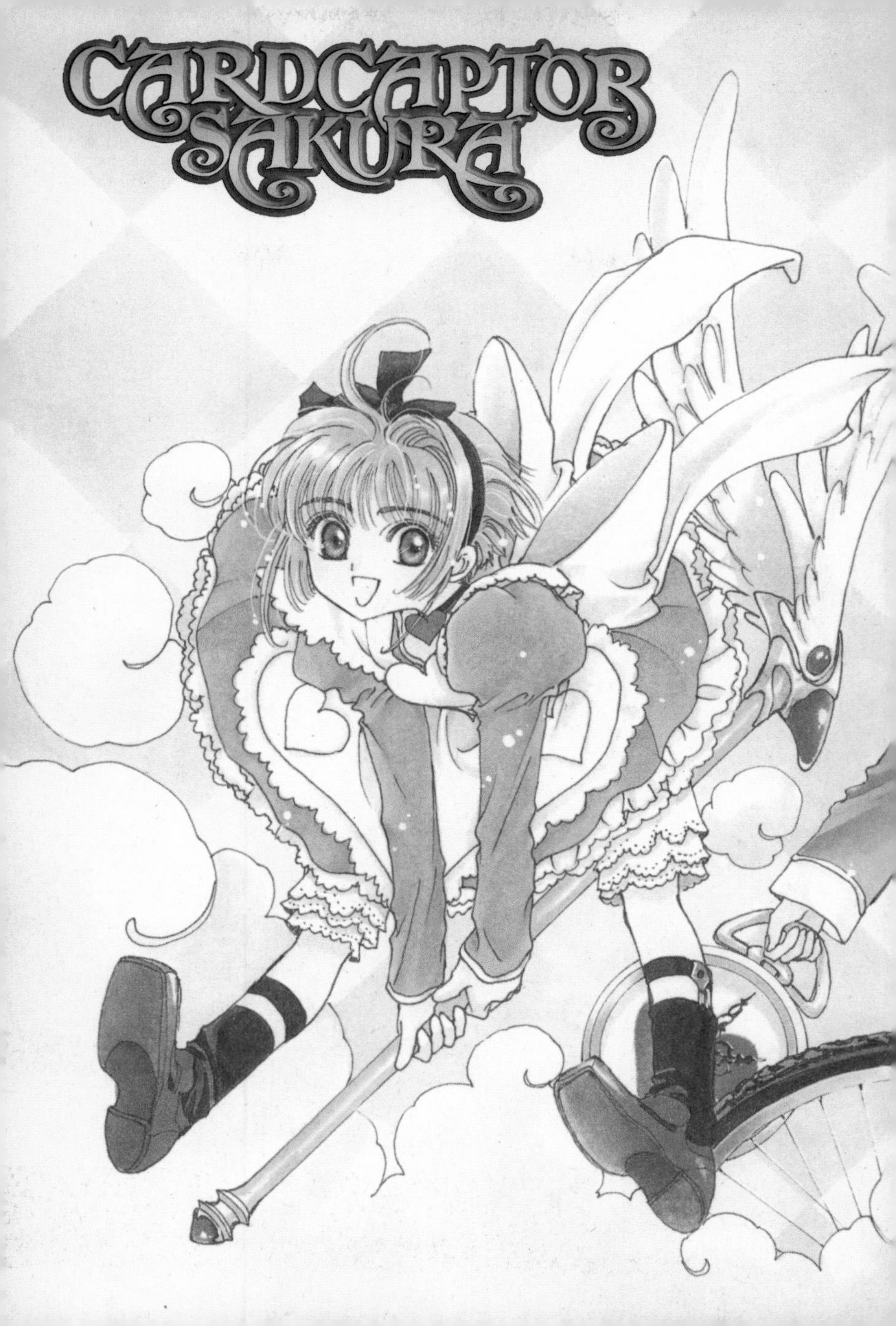
CARDCAPTOR SAKURA

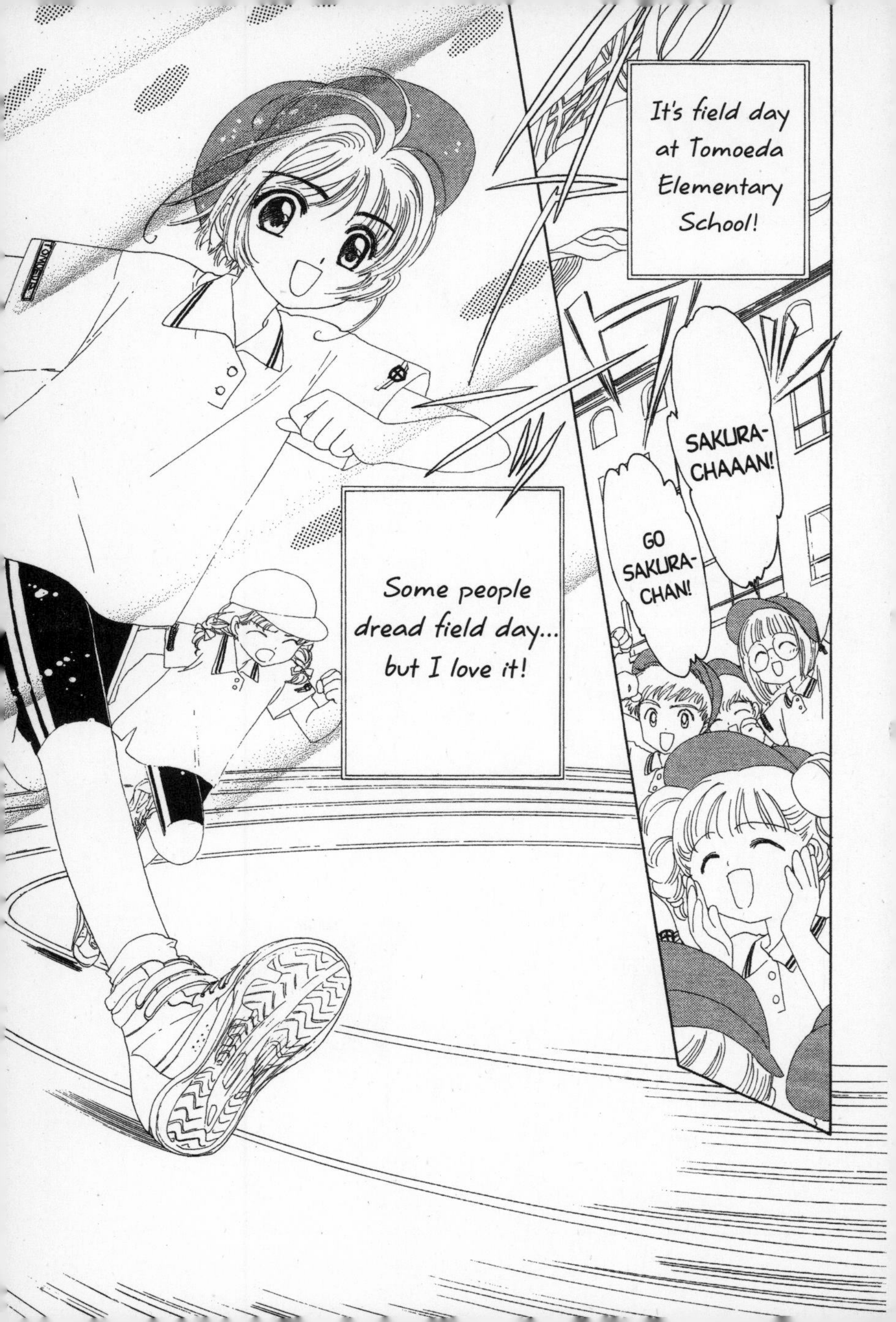
It's field day at Tomoeda Elementary School!
SAKURA-CHAAAN!
GO SAKURA-CHAN!
Some people dread field day... but I love it!

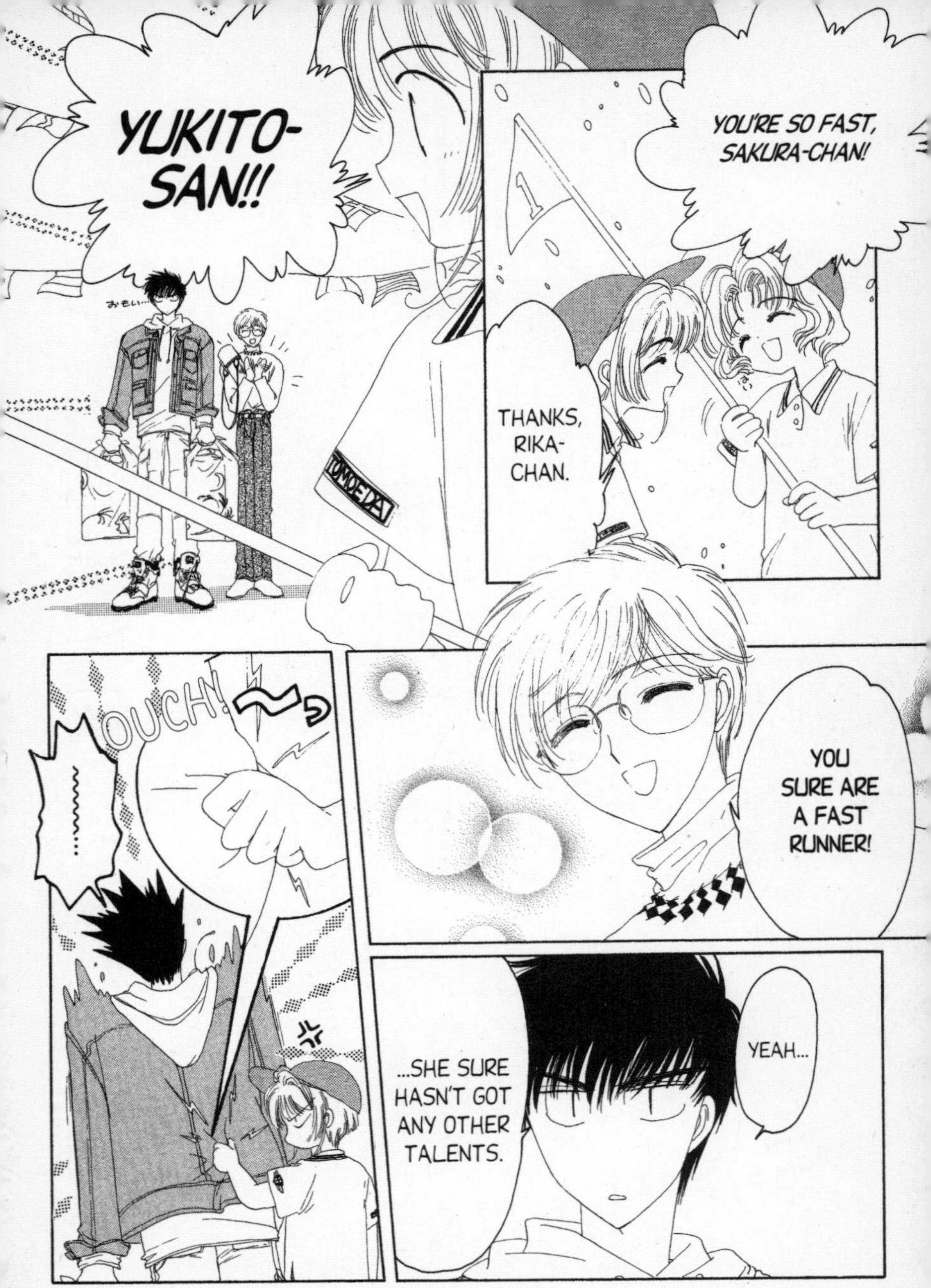
YOU'RE SO FAST, SAKURA-CHAN!
THANKS, RIKA-CHAN.
YUKITO-SAN!!
おもい…
YOU SURE ARE A FAST RUNNER!
YEAH...
...SHE SURE HASN'T GOT ANY OTHER TALENTS.
OUCH!
~っ
......

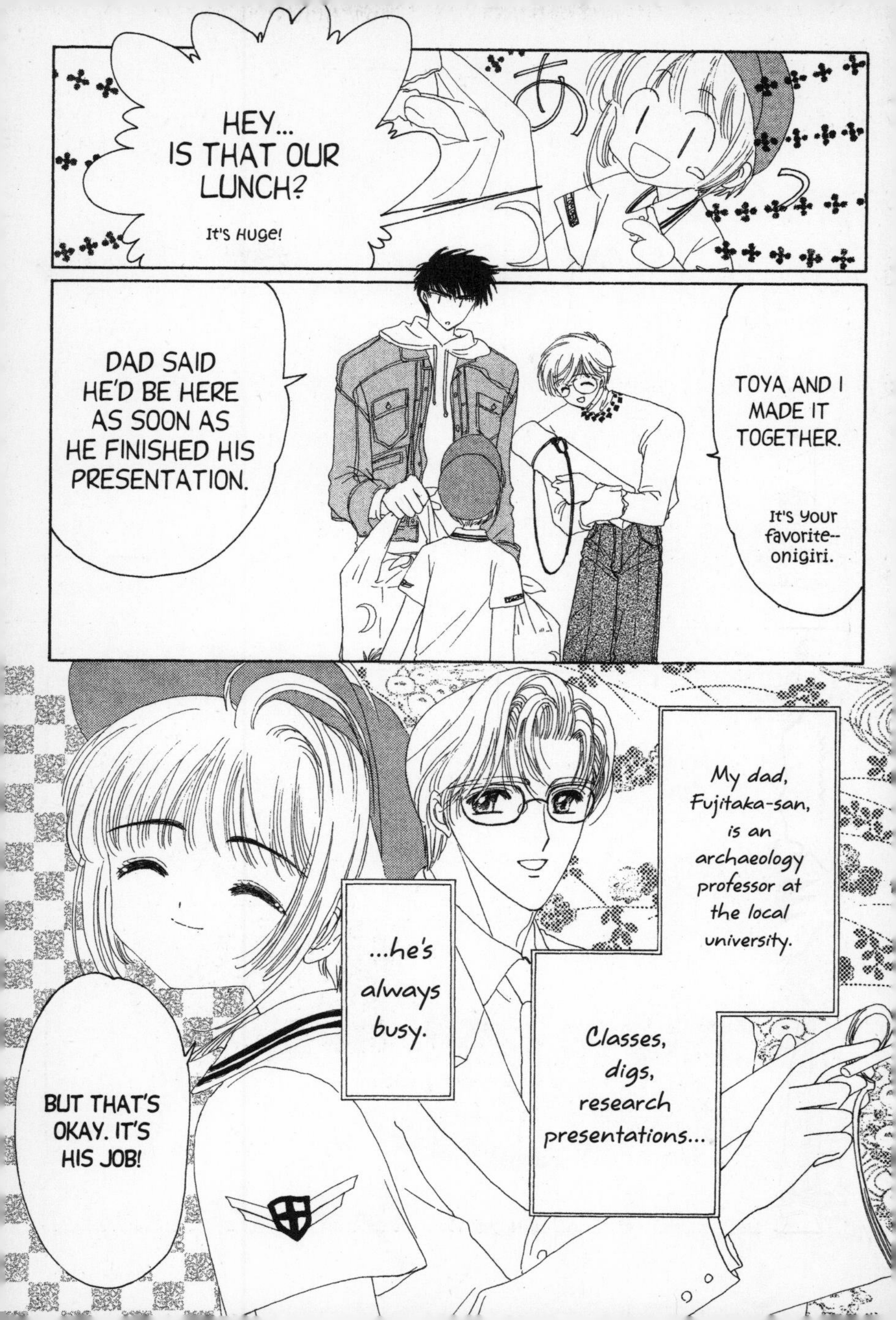
HEY... IS THAT OUR LUNCH?
It's Huge!
TOYA AND I MADE IT TOGETHER.
It's your favorite--onigiri.
DAD SAID HE'D BE HERE AS SOON AS HE FINISHED HIS PRESENTATION.
My dad, Fujitaka-san, is an archaeology professor at the local university.
Classes, digs, research presentations...
...he's always busy.
BUT THAT'S OKAY. IT'S HIS JOB!

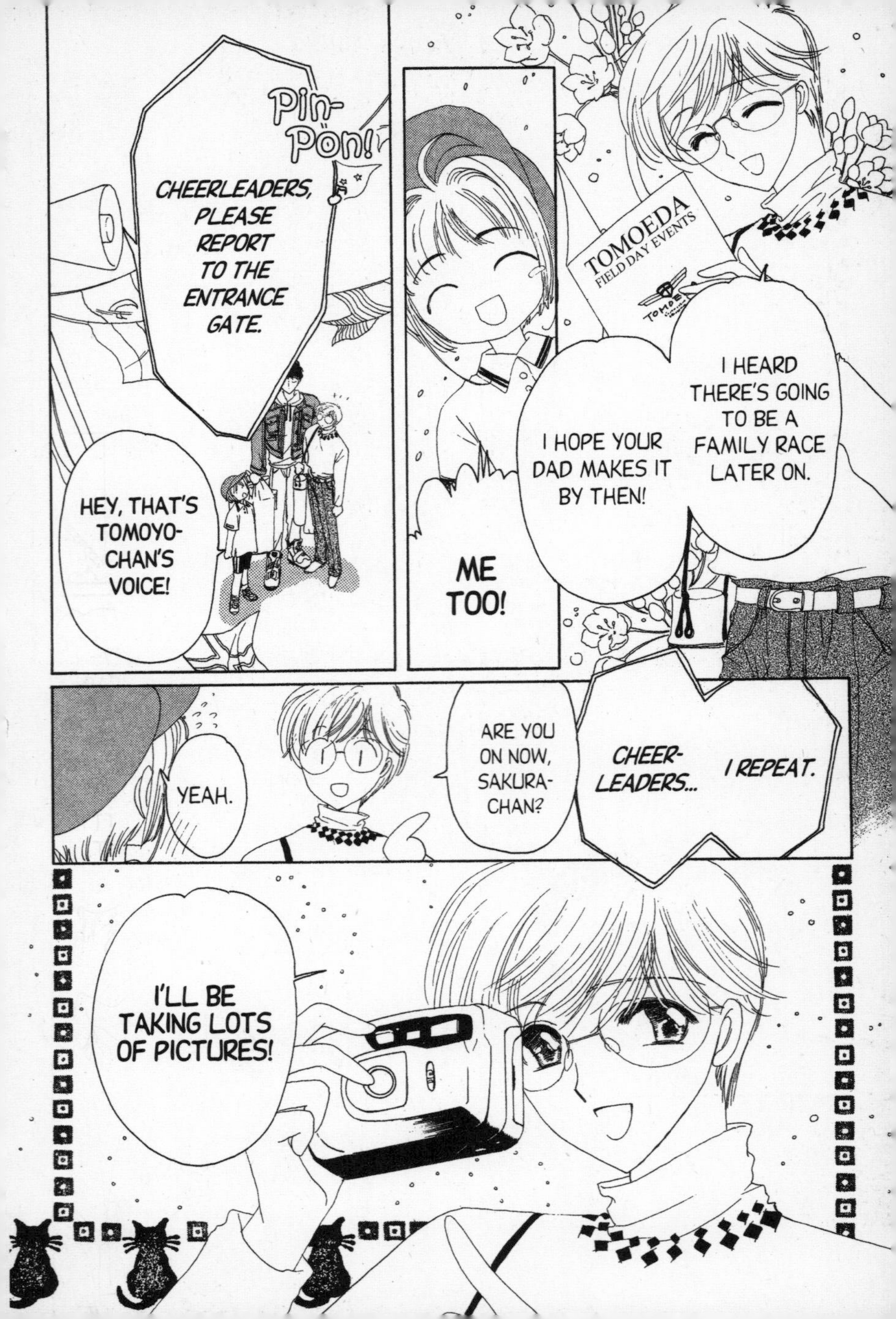
TOMOEDA FIELD DAY EVENTS
I HEARD THERE'S GOING TO BE A FAMILY RACE LATER ON.
I HOPE YOUR DAD MAKES IT BY THEN!
ME TOO!
Pin-Pon!
CHEERLEADERS, PLEASE REPORT TO THE ENTRANCE GATE.
HEY, THAT'S TOMOYO-CHAN'S VOICE!
I REPEAT.
CHEER-LEADERS...
ARE YOU ON NOW, SAKURA-CHAN?
YEAH.
I'LL BE TAKING LOTS OF PICTURES!

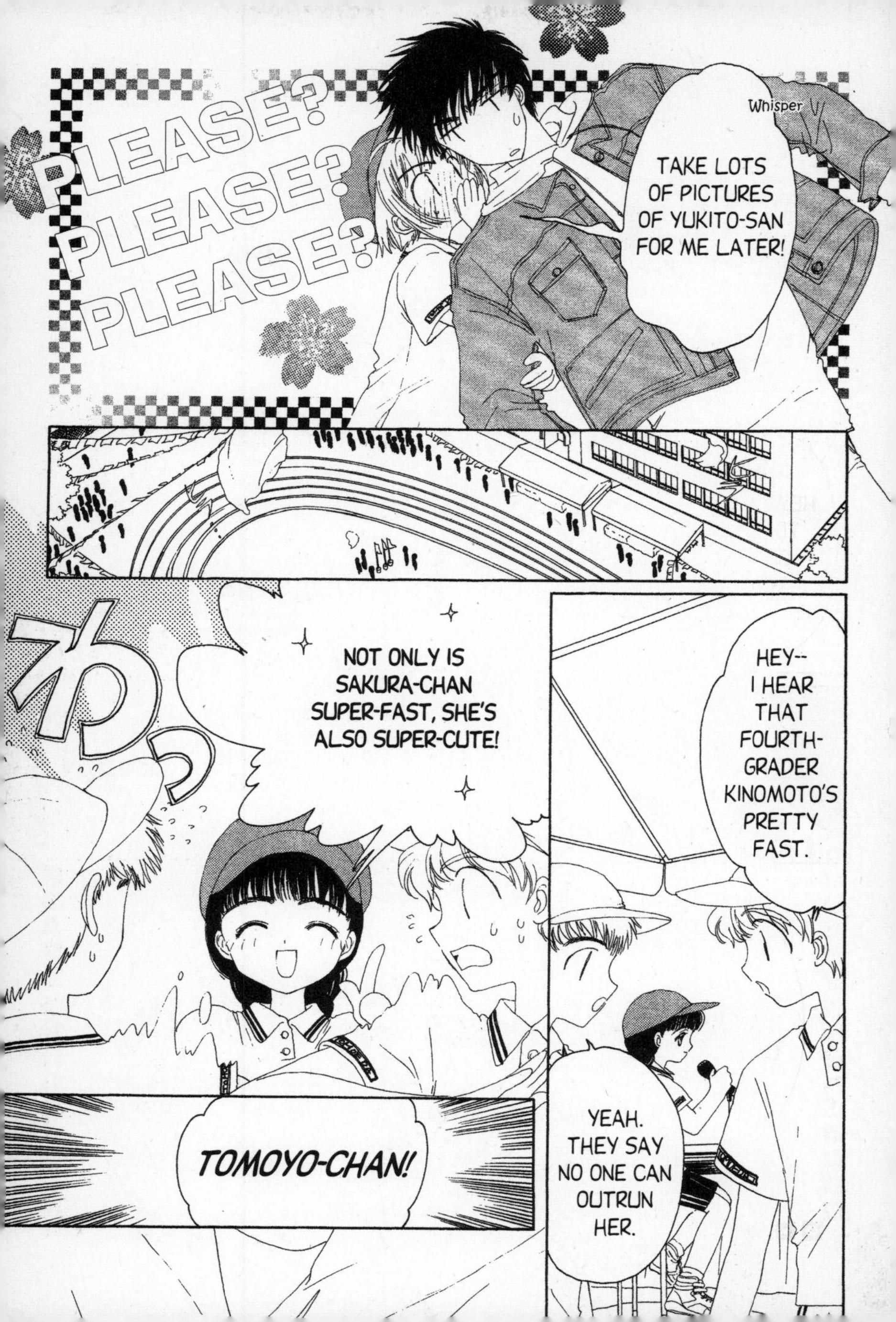
Whisper
TAKE LOTS OF PICTURES OF YUKITO-SAN FOR ME LATER!
PLEASE? PLEASE? PLEASE?
HEY-- I HEAR THAT FOURTH-GRADER KINOMOTO'S PRETTY FAST.
YEAH. THEY SAY NO ONE CAN OUTRUN HER.
わっ
NOT ONLY IS SAKURA-CHAN SUPER-FAST, SHE'S ALSO SUPER-CUTE!
TOMOYO-CHAN!

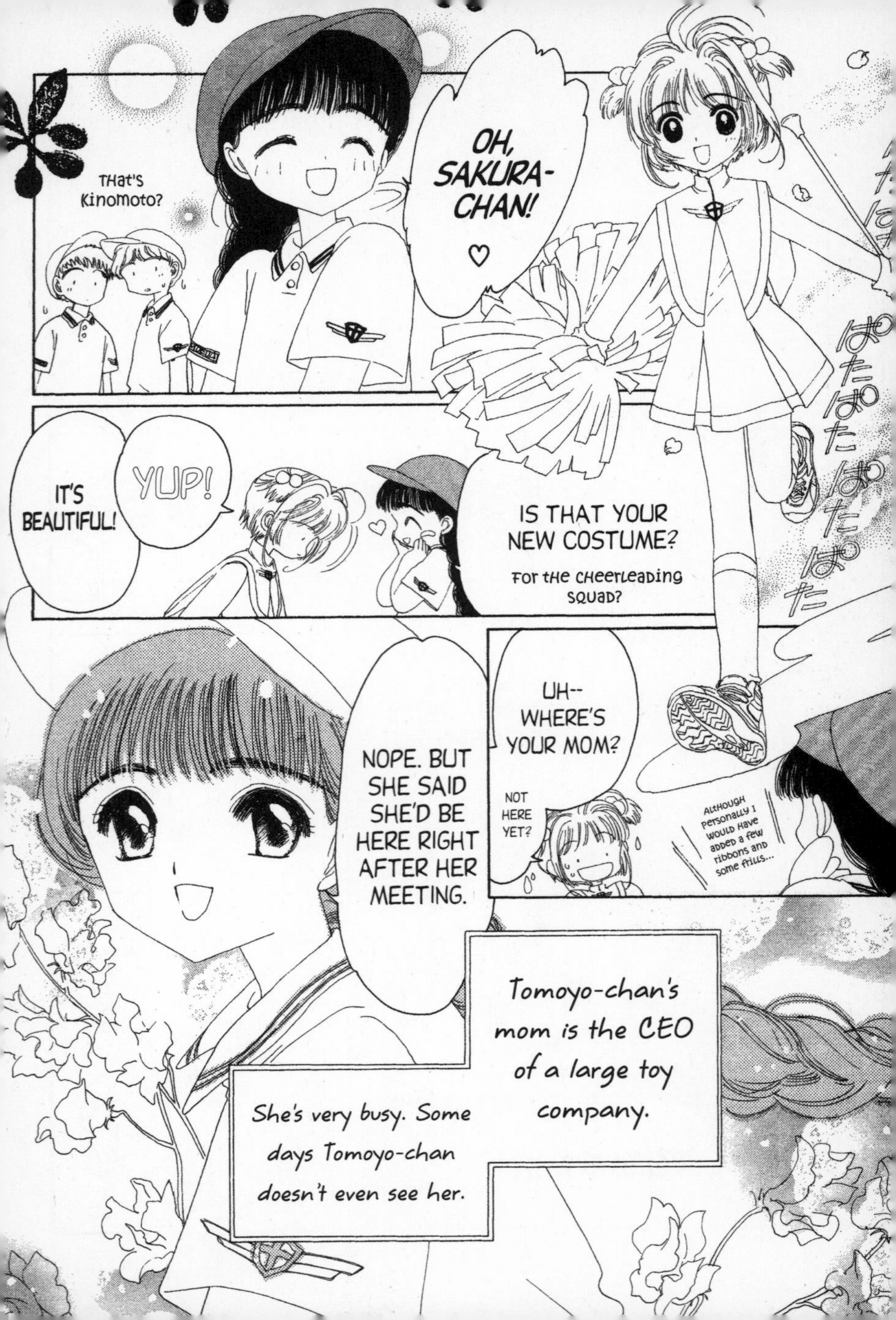

ぱたぱたぱたぱた
OH, SAKURA-CHAN! ♡
THAT'S Kinomoto?
IS THAT YOUR NEW COSTUME?
For the cheerleading squad?
YUP!
IT'S BEAUTIFUL!
UH-- WHERE'S YOUR MOM?
Although personally I would have added a few ribbons and some frills...
NOT HERE YET?
NOPE. BUT SHE SAID SHE'D BE HERE RIGHT AFTER HER MEETING.
Tomoyo-chan's mom is the CEO of a large toy company.
She's very busy. Some days Tomoyo-chan doesn't even see her.

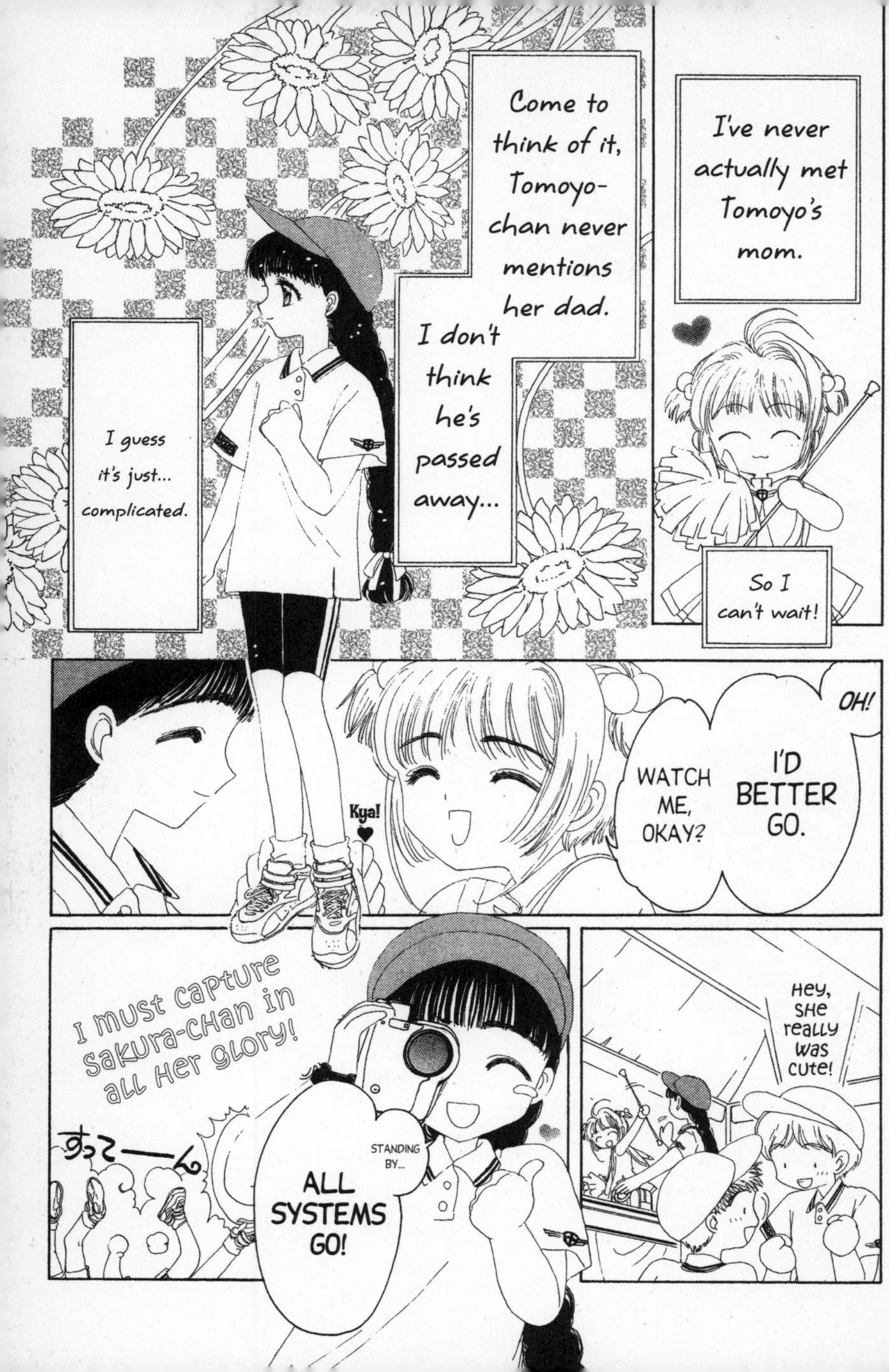
I've never actually met Tomoyo's mom.
So I can't wait!
Come to think of it, Tomoyo-chan never mentions her dad.
I don't think he's passed away...
I guess it's just... complicated.
OH!
I'D BETTER GO.
WATCH ME, OKAY?
Kya! ♥
Hey, she really was cute!
STANDING BY...
ALL SYSTEMS GO!
I must capture Sakura-chan in all her glory!
すってーん

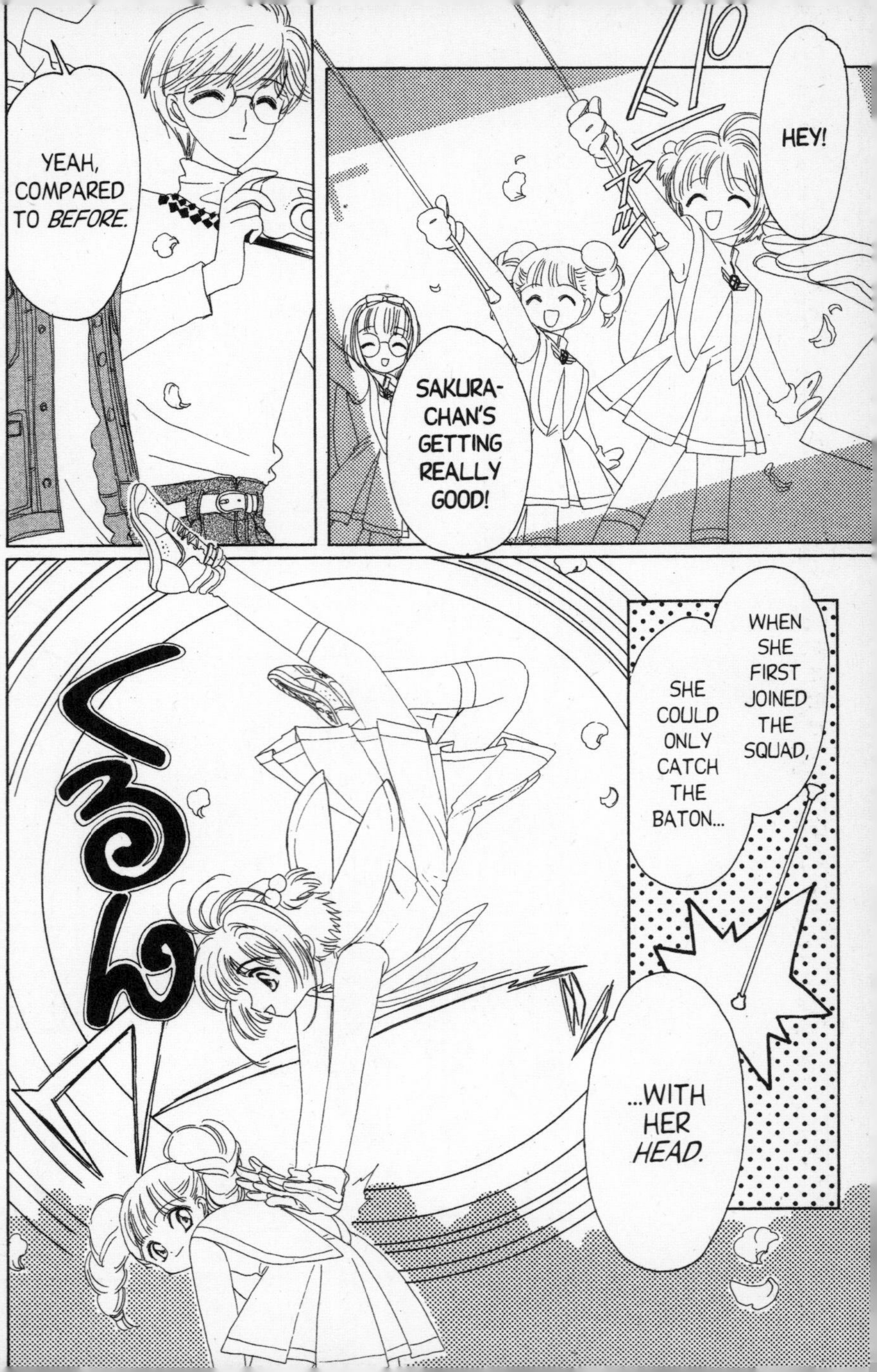
HEY!
SAKURA-CHAN'S GETTING REALLY GOOD!
YEAH, COMPARED TO *BEFORE*.
WHEN SHE FIRST JOINED THE SQUAD,
SHE COULD ONLY CATCH THE BATON...
くるん
...WITH HER *HEAD*.

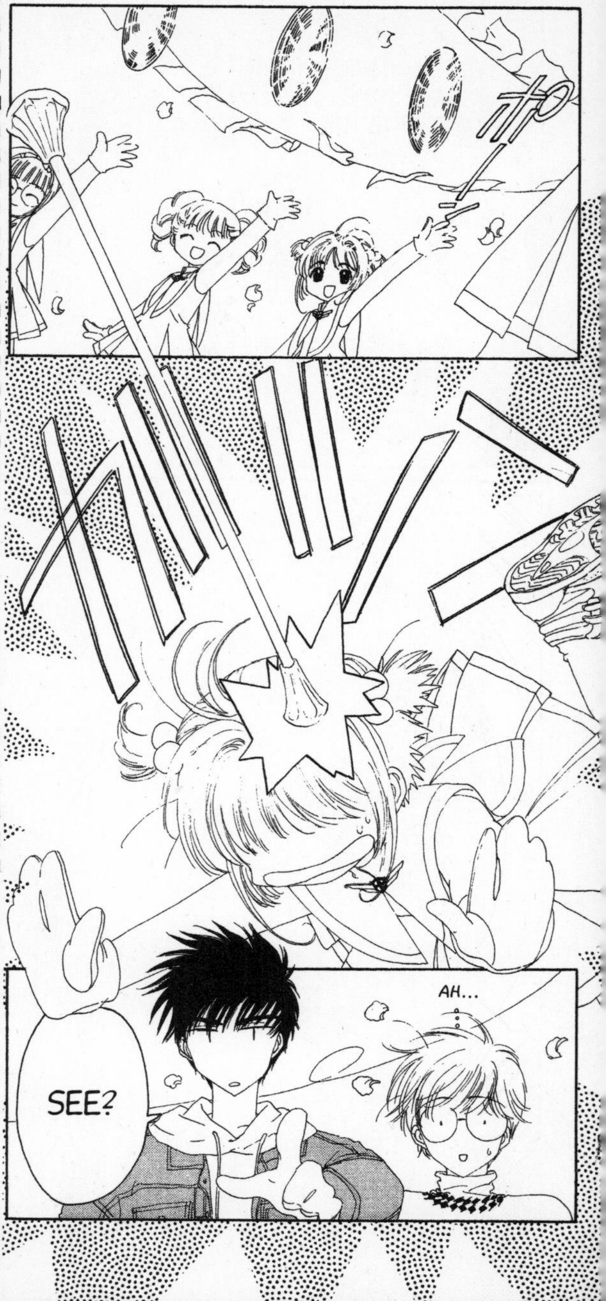
AH...
SEE?

![5]

Cerberus

Nickname:
Kero-chan
Birthdate:
Secret
Favorite Food:
Sweets
Least Favorite Food:
Anything hot and spicy
Favorite Pastime:
Video games
Favorite Colors:
Red, orange
Favorite TV Shows:
Quiz shows
Favorite Flower:
Sunflower
Wish List:
A new video game
Residence:
Sakura's room
True Form:
Unknown

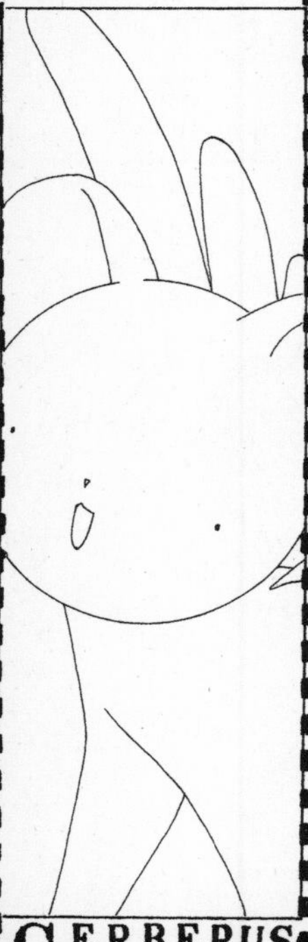

CERBERUS

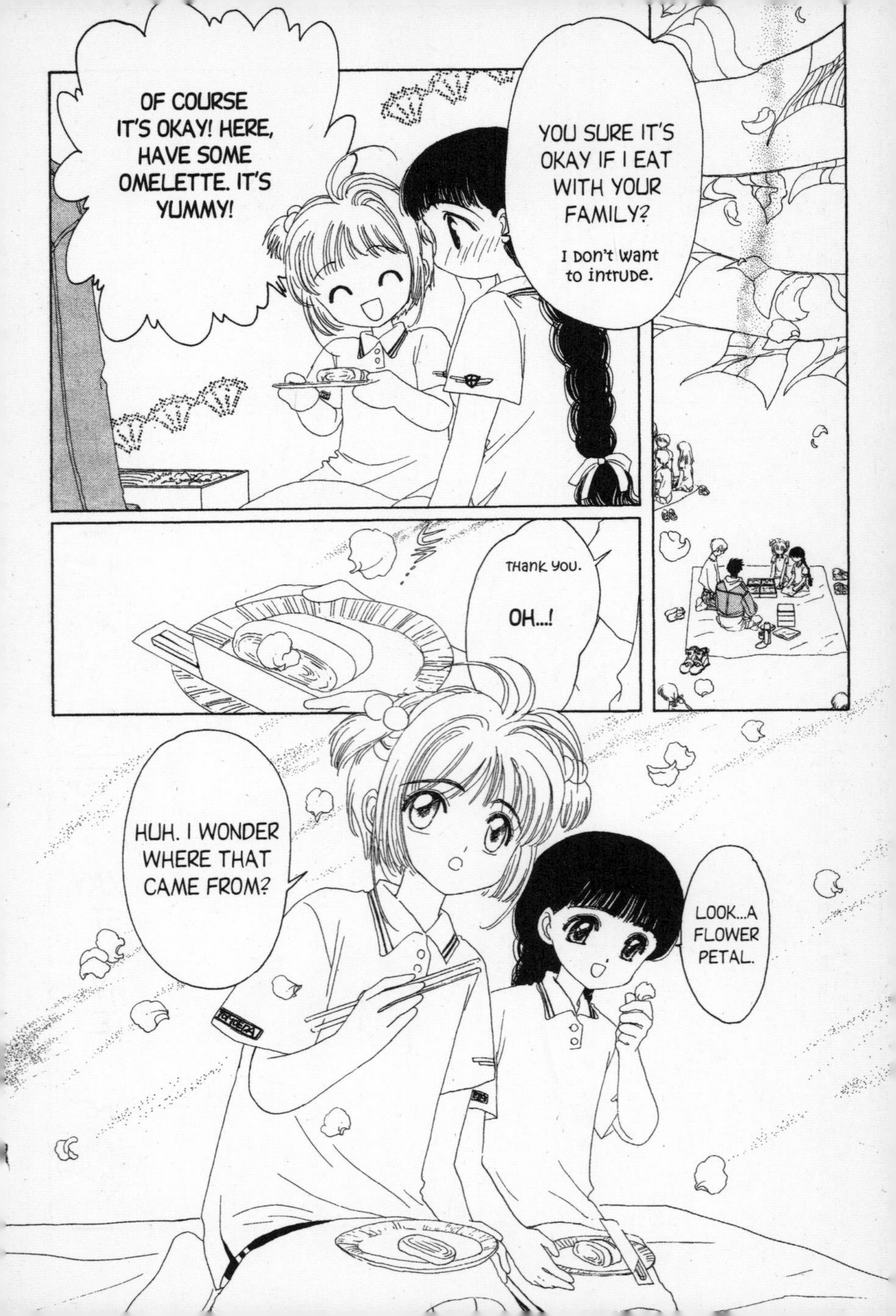
YOU SURE IT'S OKAY IF I EAT WITH YOUR FAMILY?
I don't want to intrude.
OF COURSE IT'S OKAY! HERE, HAVE SOME OMELETTE. IT'S YUMMY!
Thank you.
OH...!
LOOK...A FLOWER PETAL.
HUH. I WONDER WHERE THAT CAME FROM?

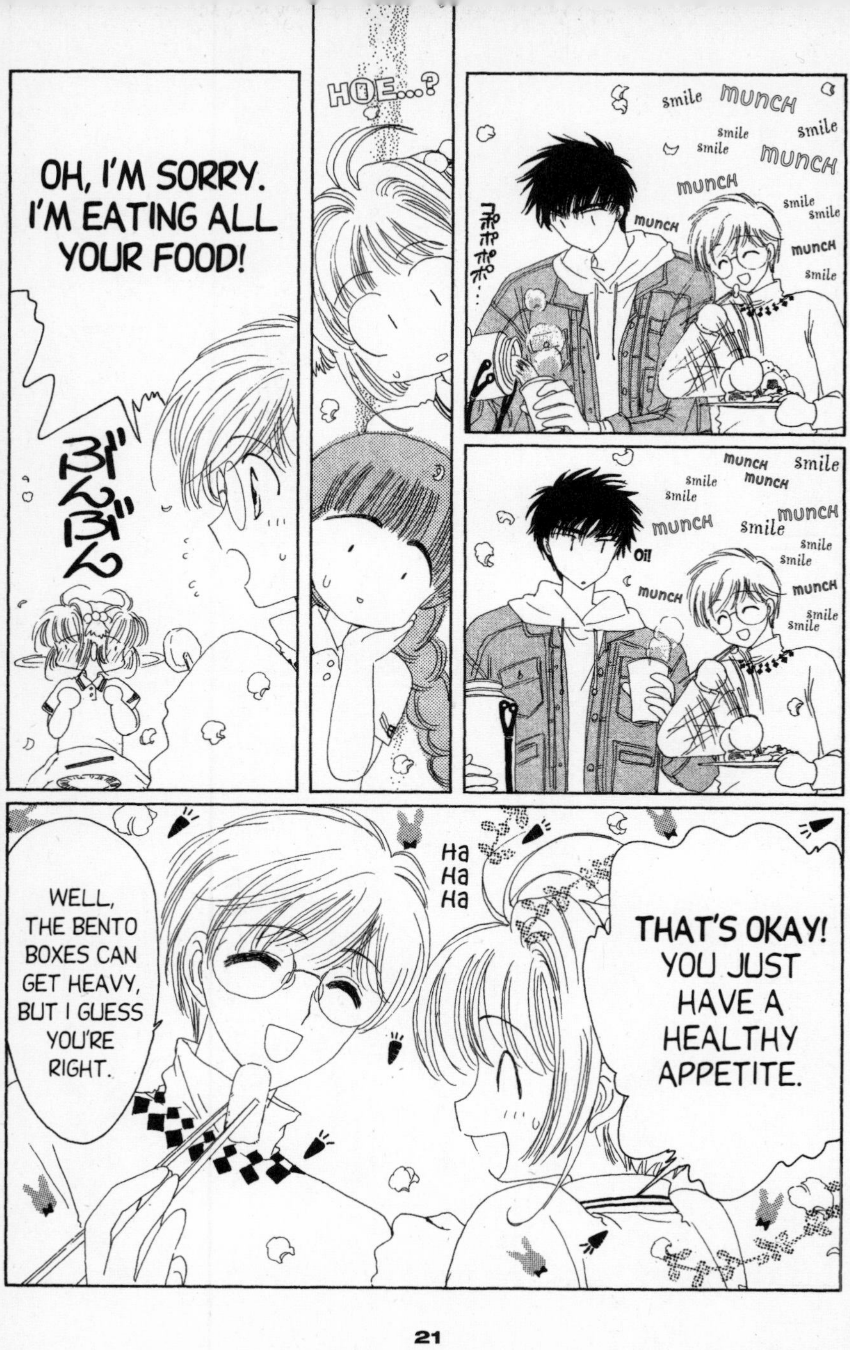
smile MUNCH smile smile smile MUNCH munch munch smile smile munch smile
munch smile smile munch smile smile munch smile munch smile smile munch smile smile
Oi!
HOE...?
OH, I'M SORRY. I'M EATING ALL YOUR FOOD!
ぶんぶん
THAT'S OKAY! YOU JUST HAVE A HEALTHY APPETITE.
Ha Ha Ha
WELL, THE BENTO BOXES CAN GET HEAVY, BUT I GUESS YOU'RE RIGHT.

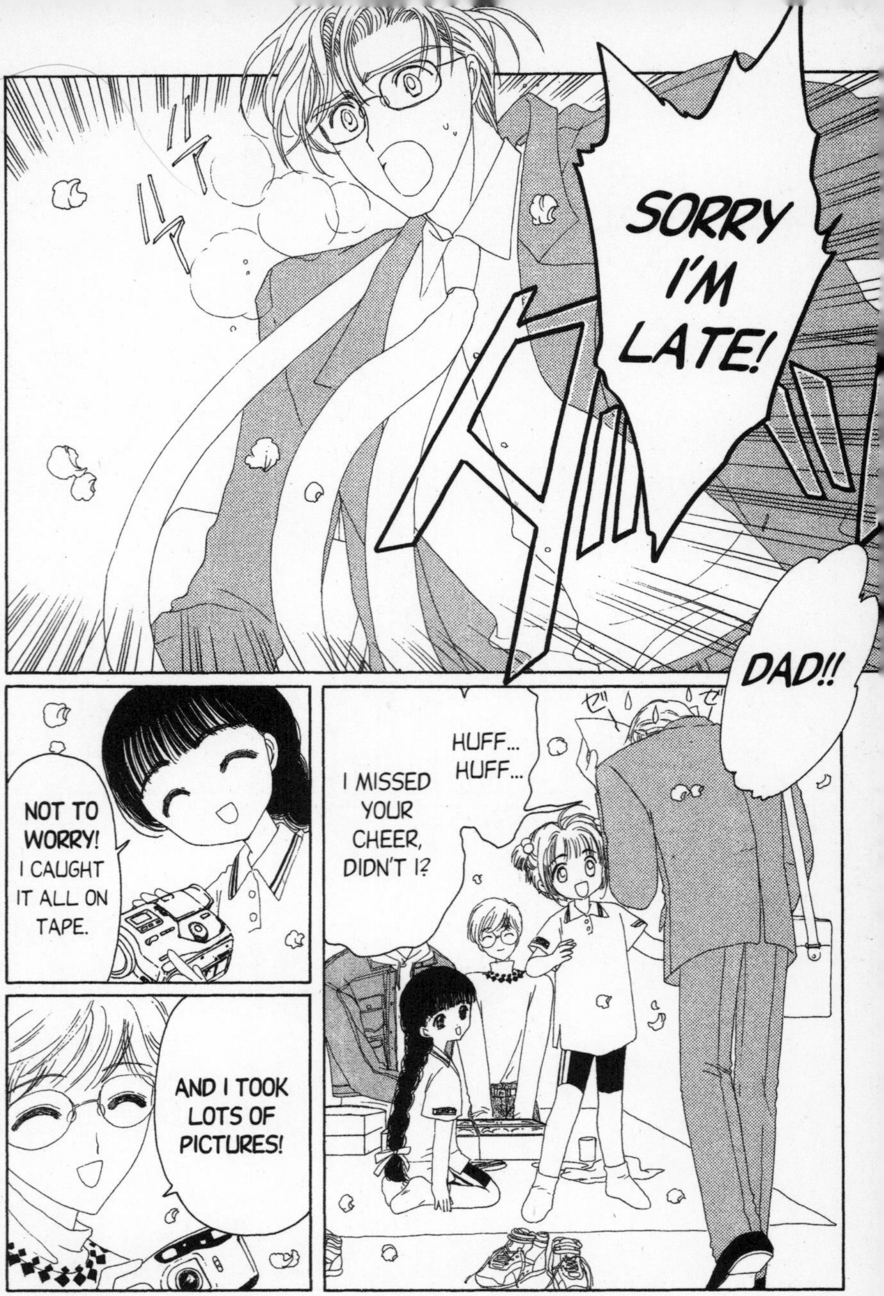
SORRY I'M LATE!
DAD!!
HUFF... HUFF...
I MISSED YOUR CHEER, DIDN'T I?
NOT TO WORRY! I CAUGHT IT ALL ON TAPE.
AND I TOOK LOTS OF PICTURES!

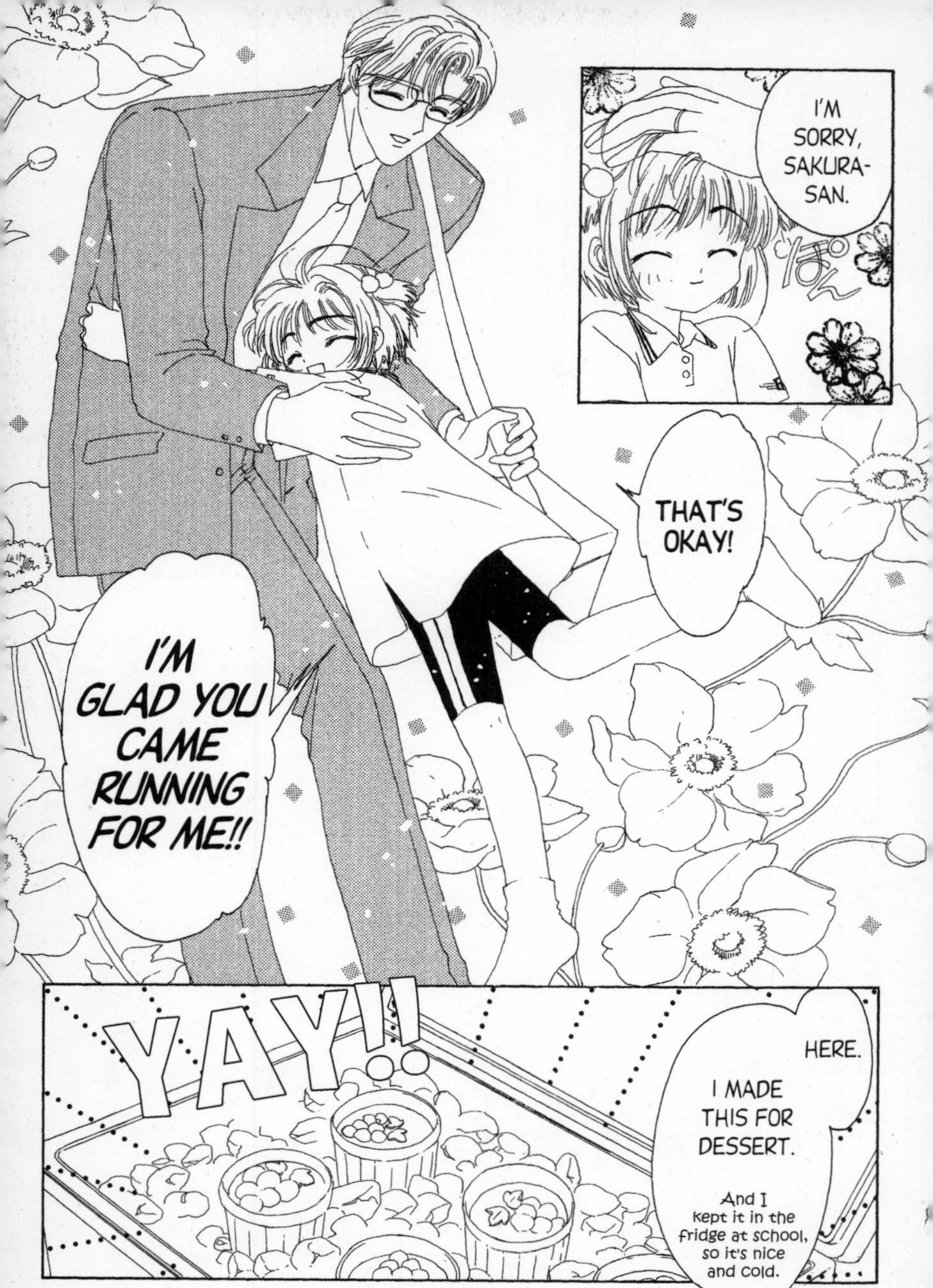
I'M SORRY, SAKURA-SAN.
ぽん
THAT'S OKAY!
I'M GLAD YOU CAME RUNNING FOR ME!!
HERE.
I MADE THIS FOR DESSERT.
And I kept it in the fridge at school, so it's nice and cold.
YAY!!

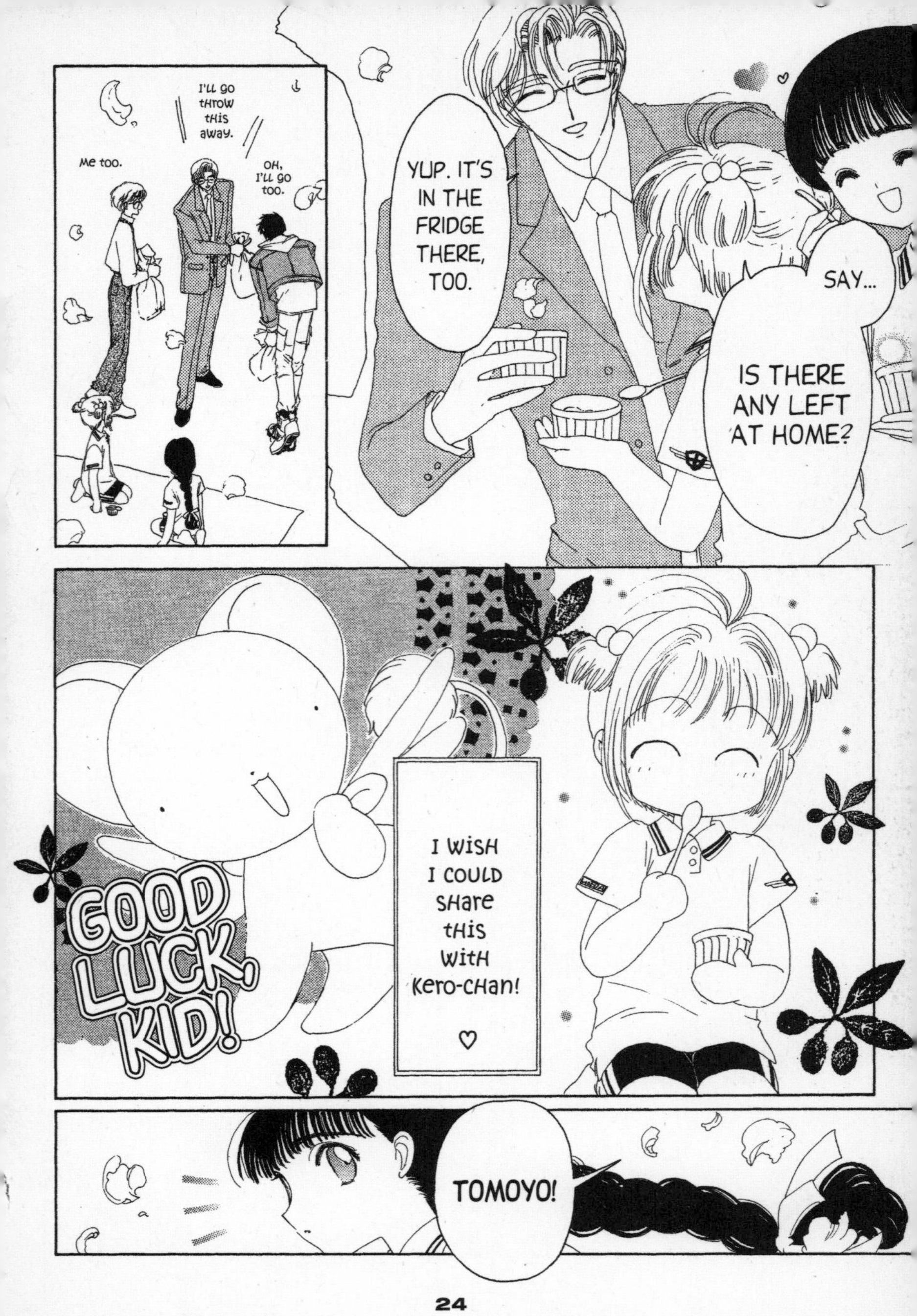
SAY...
IS THERE ANY LEFT AT HOME?
YUP. IT'S IN THE FRIDGE THERE, TOO.
I'll go throw this away.
Oh, I'll go too.
Me too.
I wish I could share this with Kero-chan! ♡
GOOD LUCK, KID!
TOMOYO!

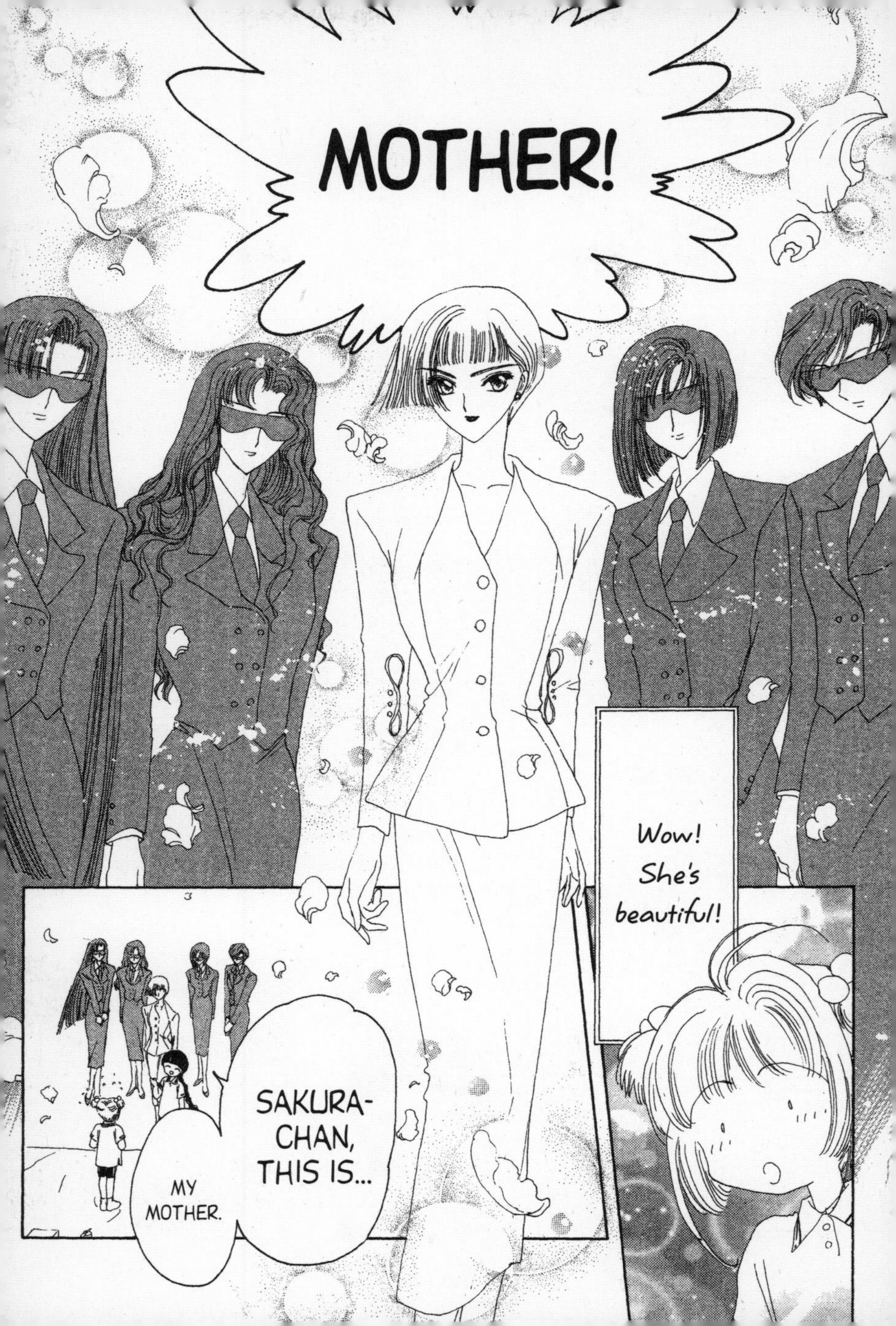
MOTHER!
Wow! She's beautiful!
SAKURA-CHAN, THIS IS...
MY MOTHER.

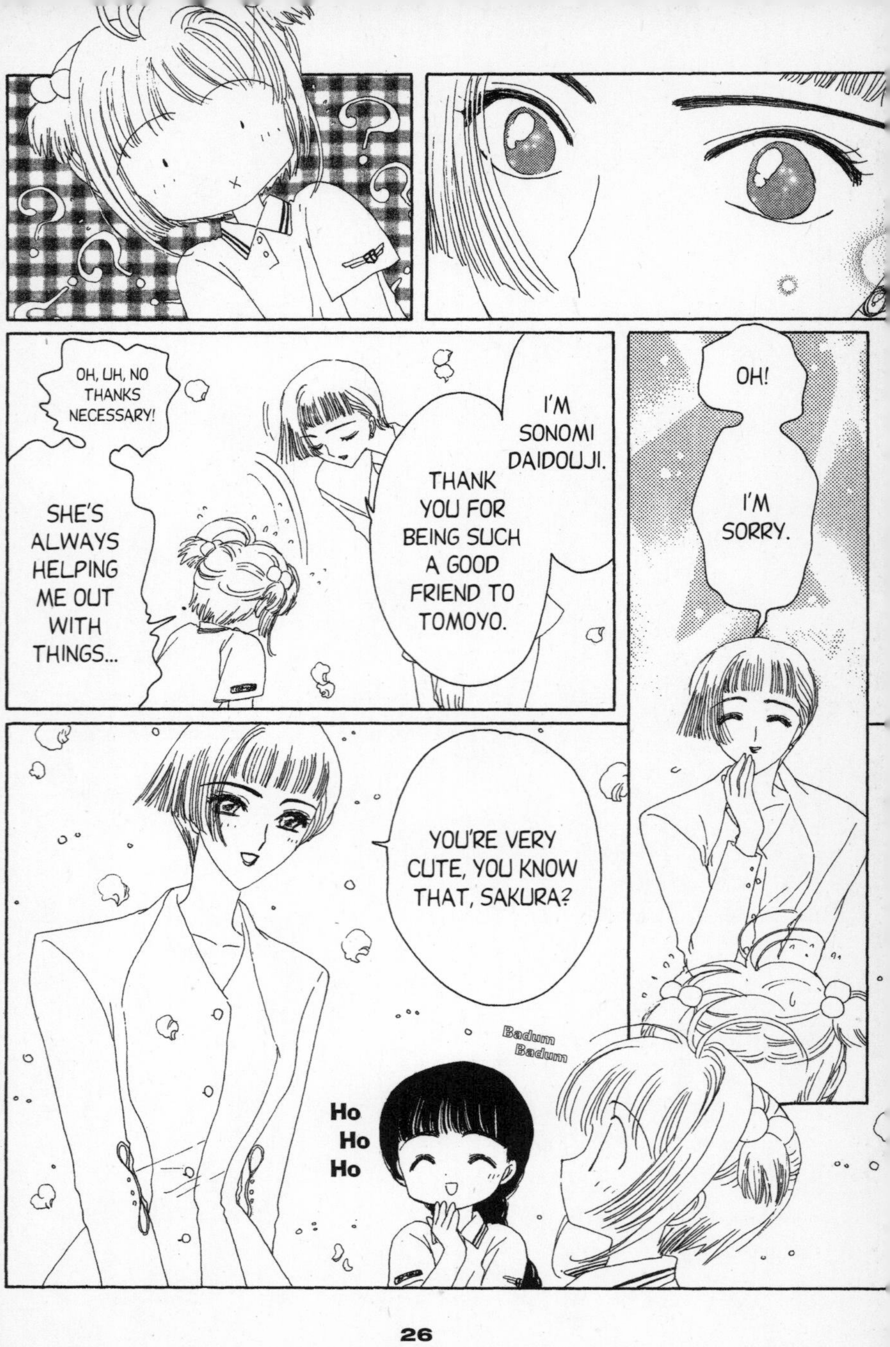
OH!
I'M SORRY.
I'M SONOMI DAIDOUJI.
THANK YOU FOR BEING SUCH A GOOD FRIEND TO TOMOYO.
OH, UH, NO THANKS NECESSARY!
SHE'S ALWAYS HELPING ME OUT WITH THINGS...
YOU'RE VERY CUTE, YOU KNOW THAT, SAKURA?
Badum Badum
Ho Ho Ho

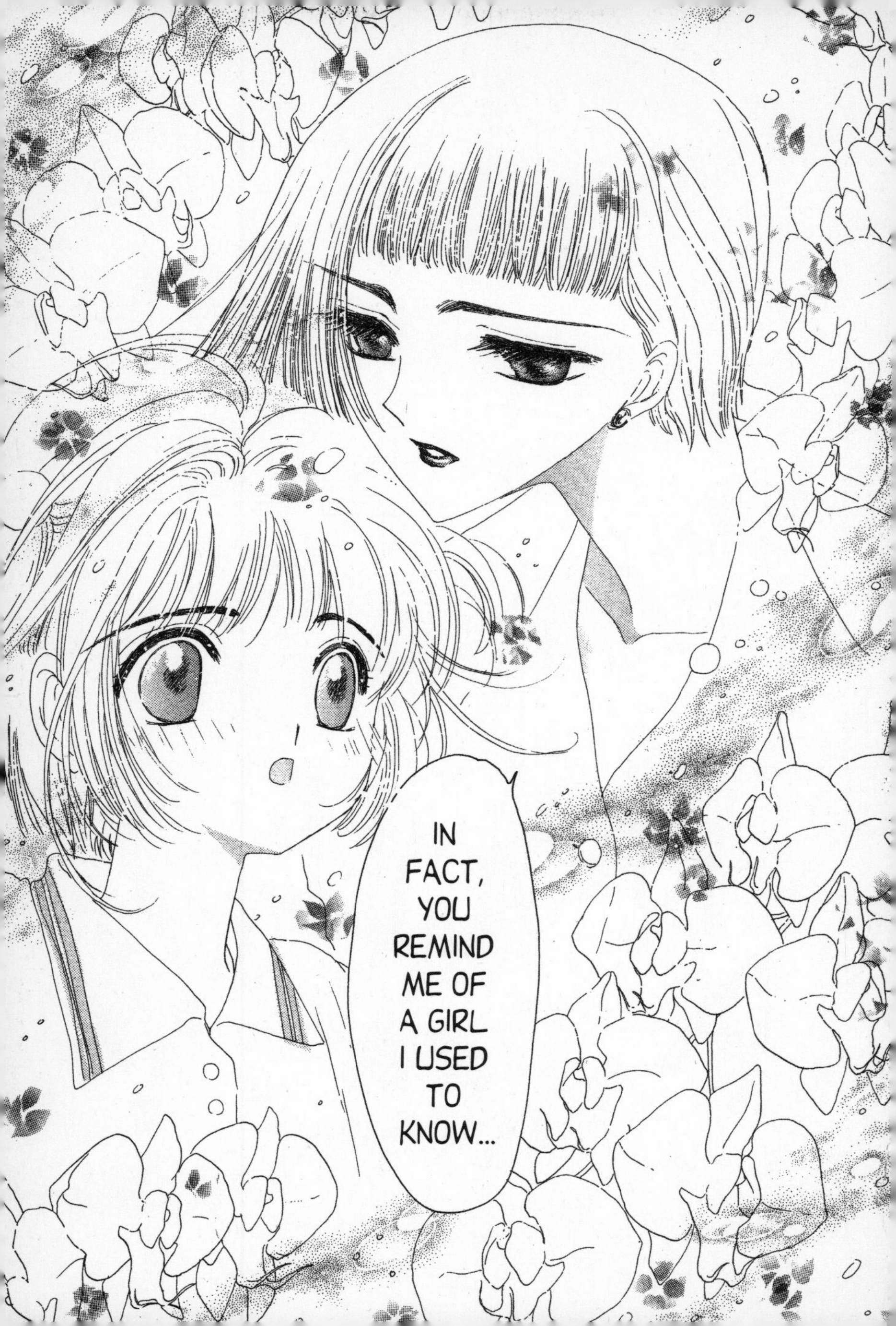
IN FACT, YOU REMIND ME OF A GIRL I USED TO KNOW...

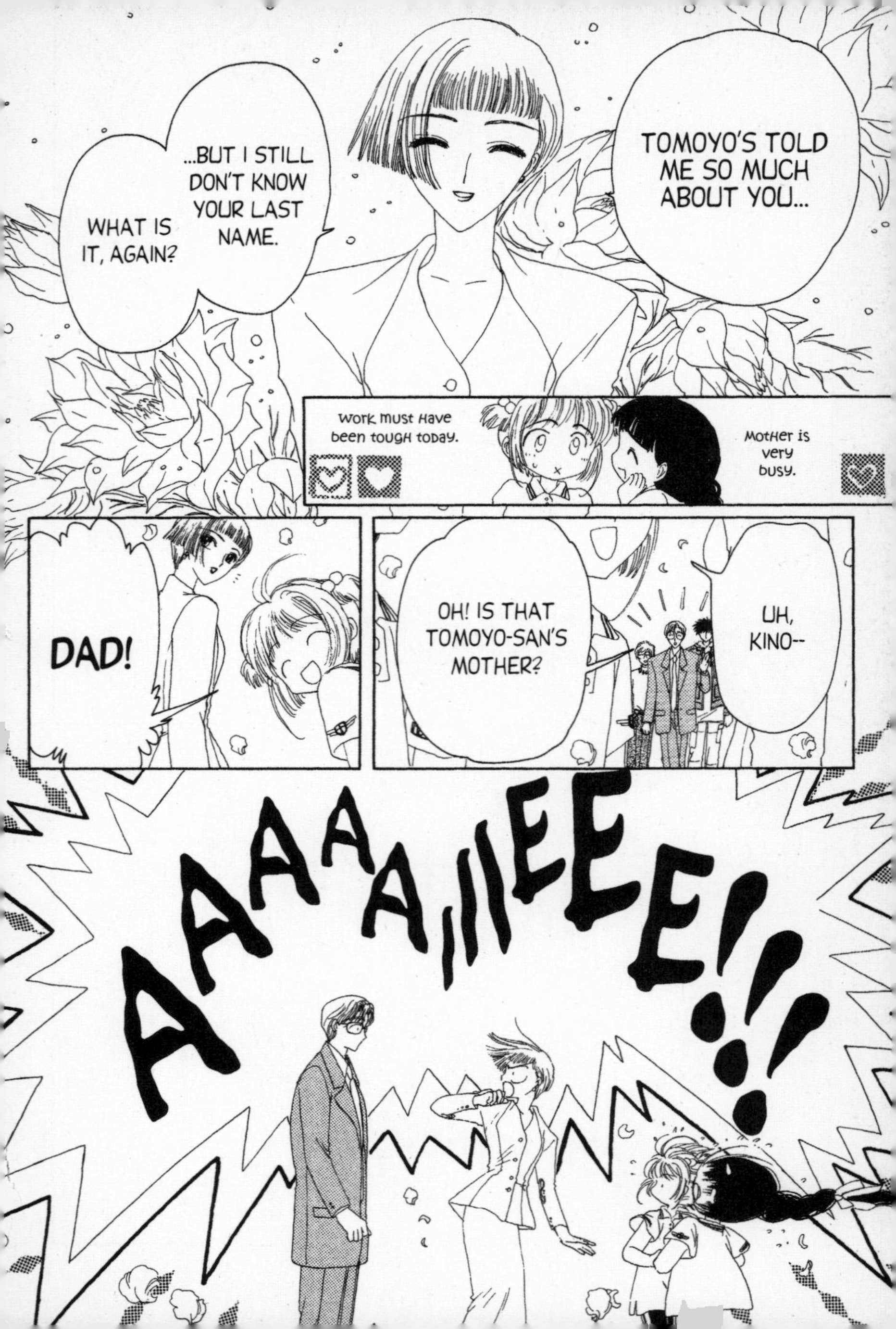
TOMOYO'S TOLD ME SO MUCH ABOUT YOU...
...BUT I STILL DON'T KNOW YOUR LAST NAME.
WHAT IS IT, AGAIN?
Mother is very busy.
Work must have been tough today.
UH, KINO--
OH! IS THAT TOMOYO-SAN'S MOTHER?
DAD!
AAAAIIIEEEE!!!

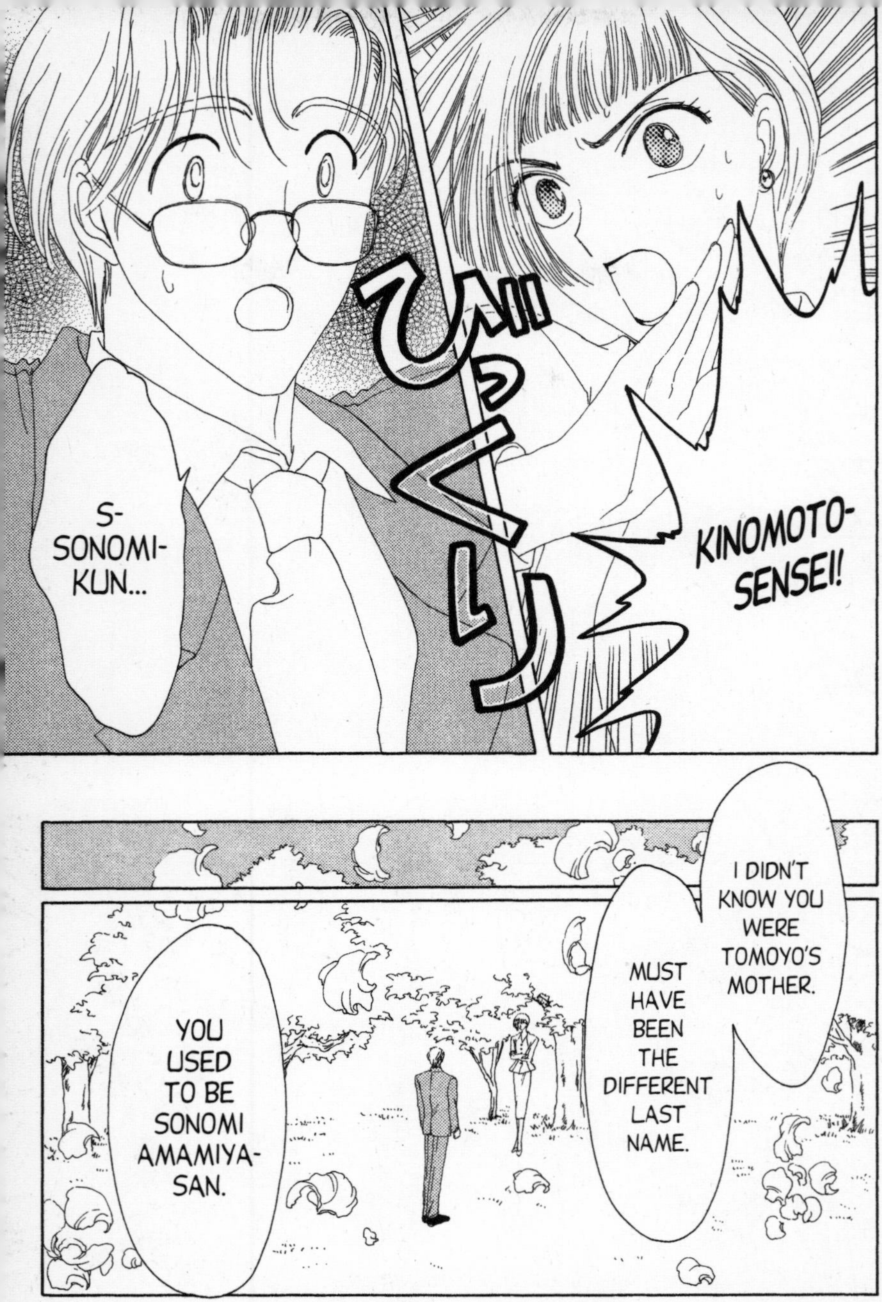
KINOMOTO-SENSEI!
ひっくり
S-SONOMI-KUN...
I DIDN'T KNOW YOU WERE TOMOYO'S MOTHER.
MUST HAVE BEEN THE DIFFERENT LAST NAME.
YOU USED TO BE SONOMI AMAMIYA-SAN.

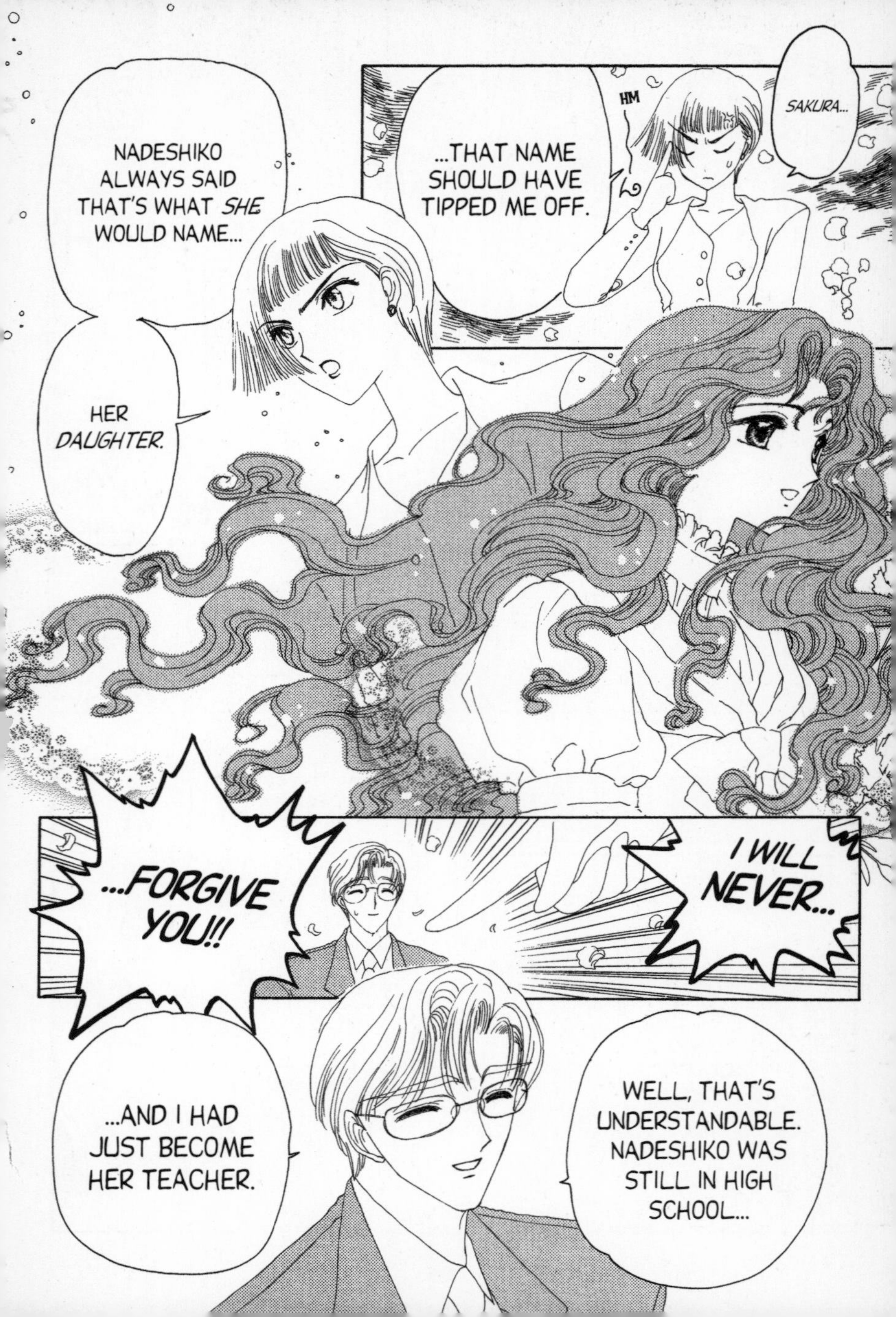

SAKURA...
HM
...THAT NAME SHOULD HAVE TIPPED ME OFF.
NADESHIKO ALWAYS SAID THAT'S WHAT *SHE* WOULD NAME...
HER *DAUGHTER.*
I WILL NEVER...
...FORGIVE YOU!!
WELL, THAT'S UNDERSTANDABLE. NADESHIKO WAS STILL IN HIGH SCHOOL...
...AND I HAD JUST BECOME HER TEACHER.

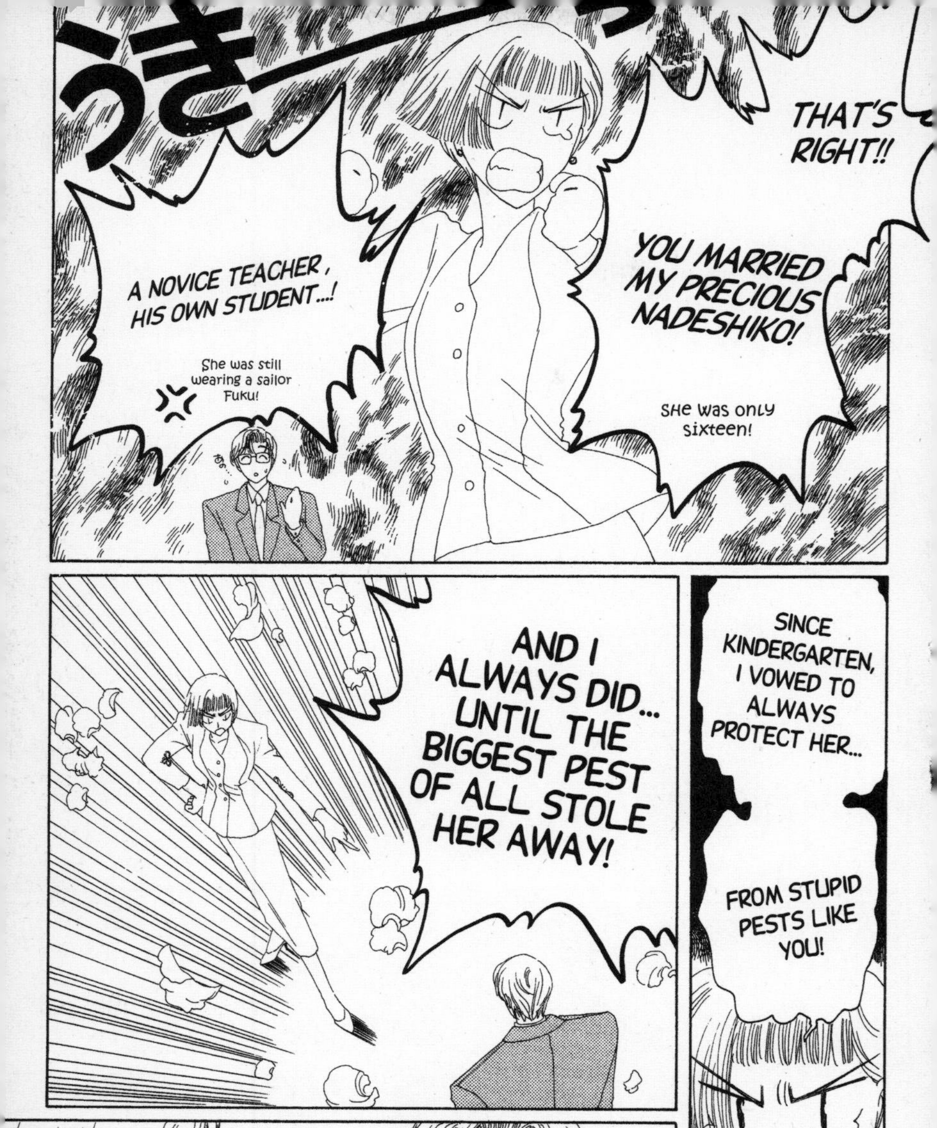
うき―っ
THAT'S RIGHT!!
YOU MARRIED MY PRECIOUS NADESHIKO!
She was only sixteen!
A NOVICE TEACHER, HIS OWN STUDENT...!
She was still wearing a sailor Fuku!
SINCE KINDERGARTEN, I VOWED TO ALWAYS PROTECT HER...
FROM STUPID PESTS LIKE YOU!
AND I ALWAYS DID... UNTIL THE BIGGEST PEST OF ALL STOLE HER AWAY!

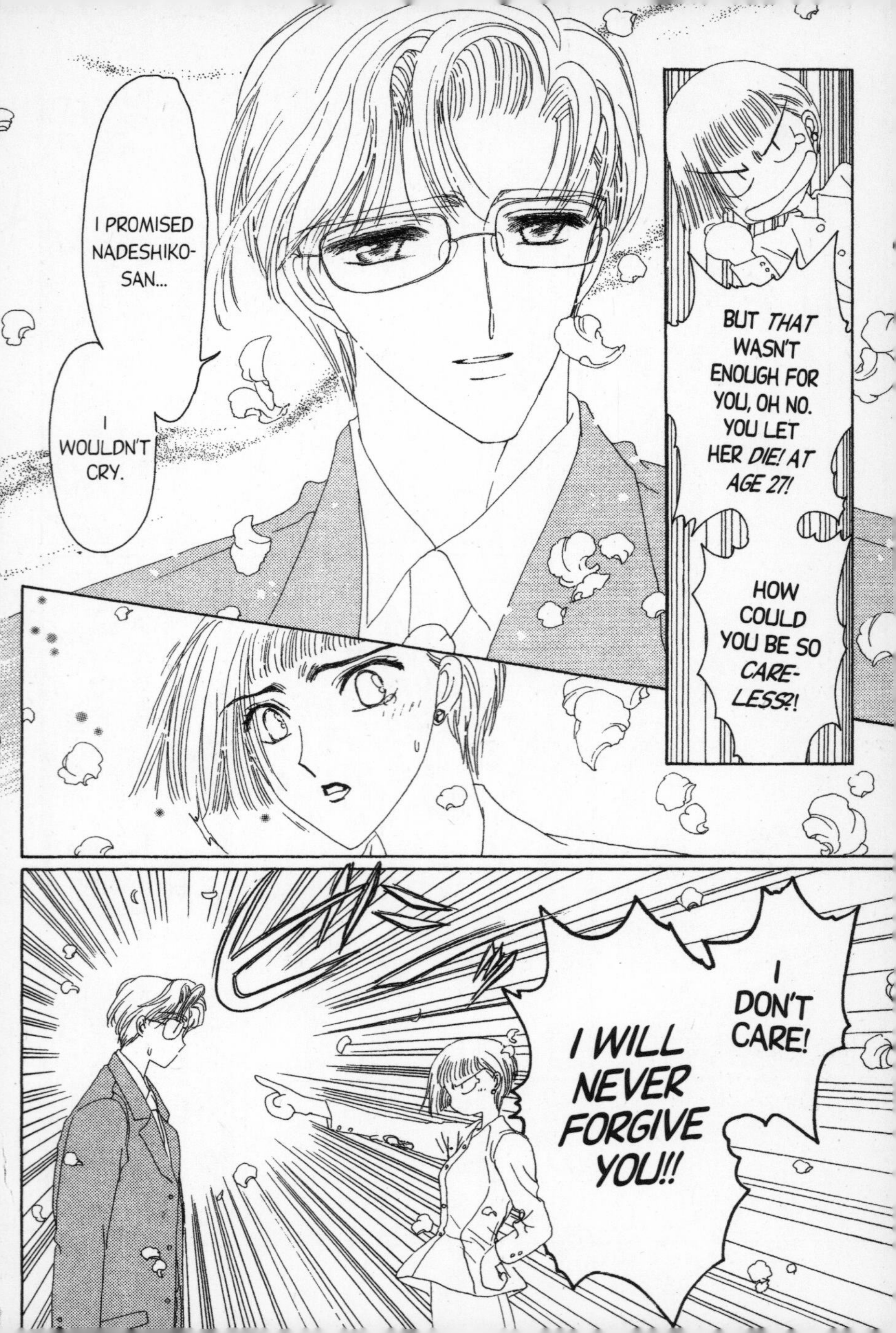
BUT THAT WASN'T ENOUGH FOR YOU, OH NO. YOU LET HER DIE! AT AGE 27!
HOW COULD YOU BE SO CARE-LESS?!
I PROMISED NADESHIKO-SAN...
I WOULDN'T CRY.
I DON'T CARE!
I WILL NEVER FORGIVE YOU!!

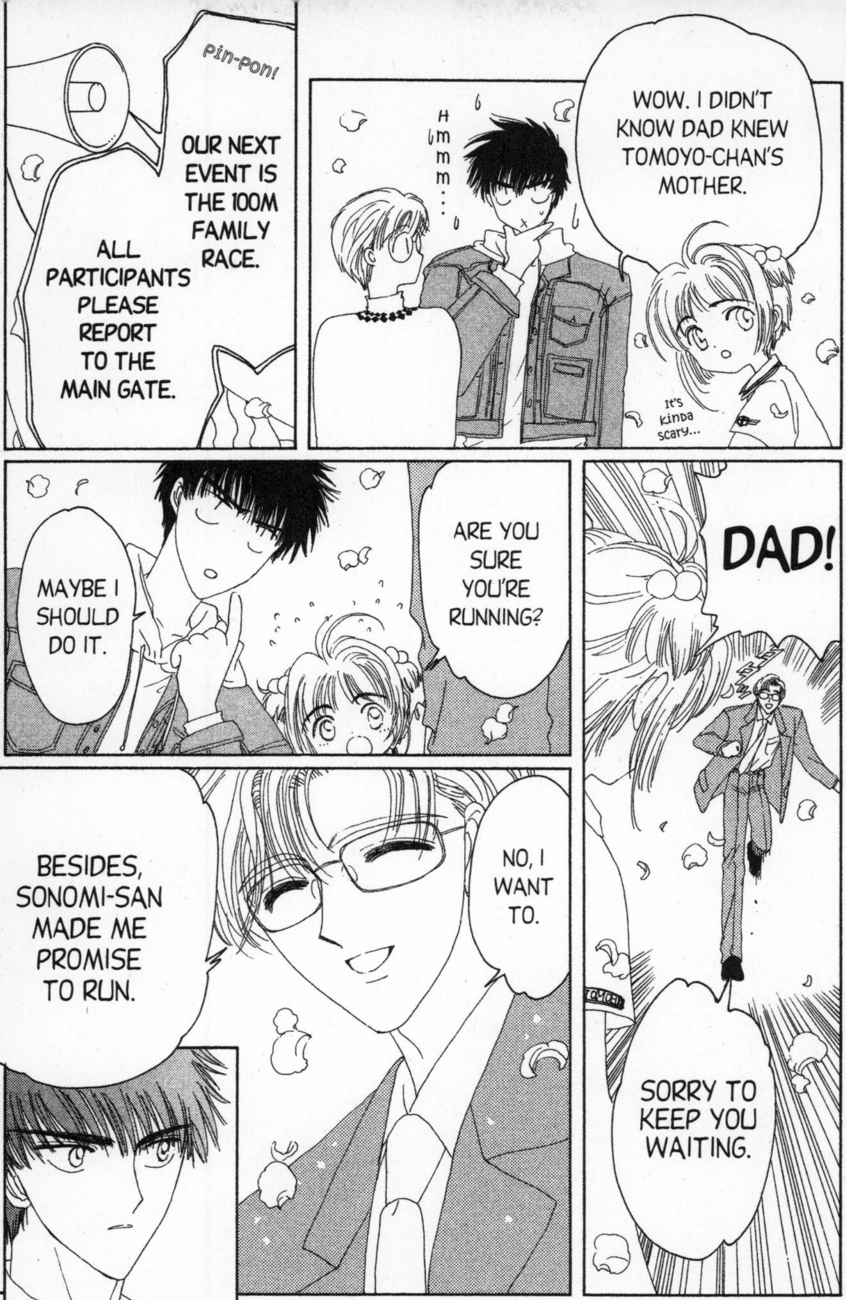
WOW. I DIDN'T KNOW DAD KNEW TOMOYO-CHAN'S MOTHER.
Hmmm...
It's kinda scary...
pin-pon!
OUR NEXT EVENT IS THE 100M FAMILY RACE.
ALL PARTICIPANTS PLEASE REPORT TO THE MAIN GATE.
DAD!
SORRY TO KEEP YOU WAITING.
ARE YOU SURE YOU'RE RUNNING?
MAYBE I SHOULD DO IT.
NO, I WANT TO.
BESIDES, SONOMI-SAN MADE ME PROMISE TO RUN.

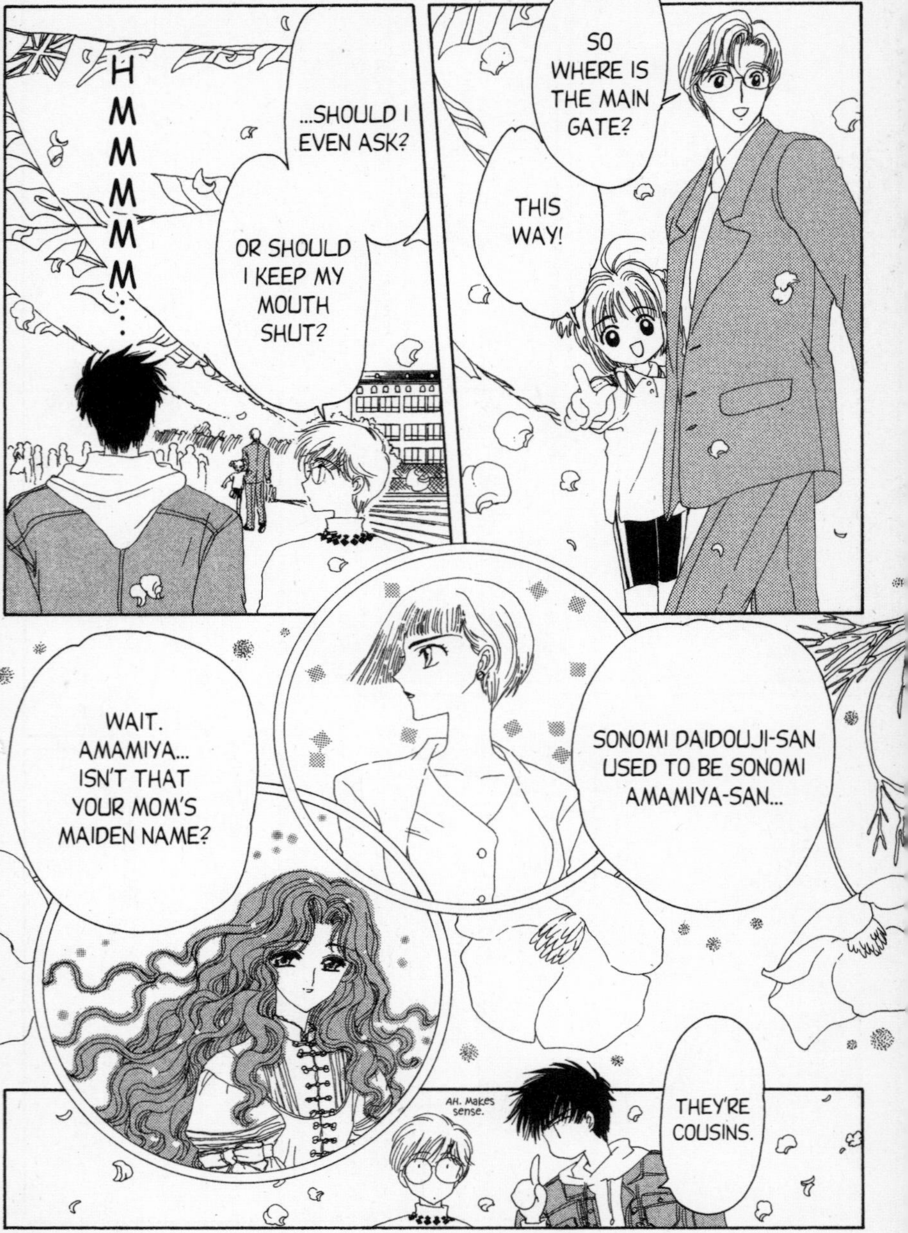
SO WHERE IS THE MAIN GATE?
THIS WAY!
HMMMMM...
...SHOULD I EVEN ASK?
OR SHOULD I KEEP MY MOUTH SHUT?
SONOMI DAIDOUJI-SAN USED TO BE SONOMI AMAMIYA-SAN...
WAIT. AMAMIYA... ISN'T THAT YOUR MOM'S MAIDEN NAME?
THEY'RE COUSINS.
AH. Makes sense.

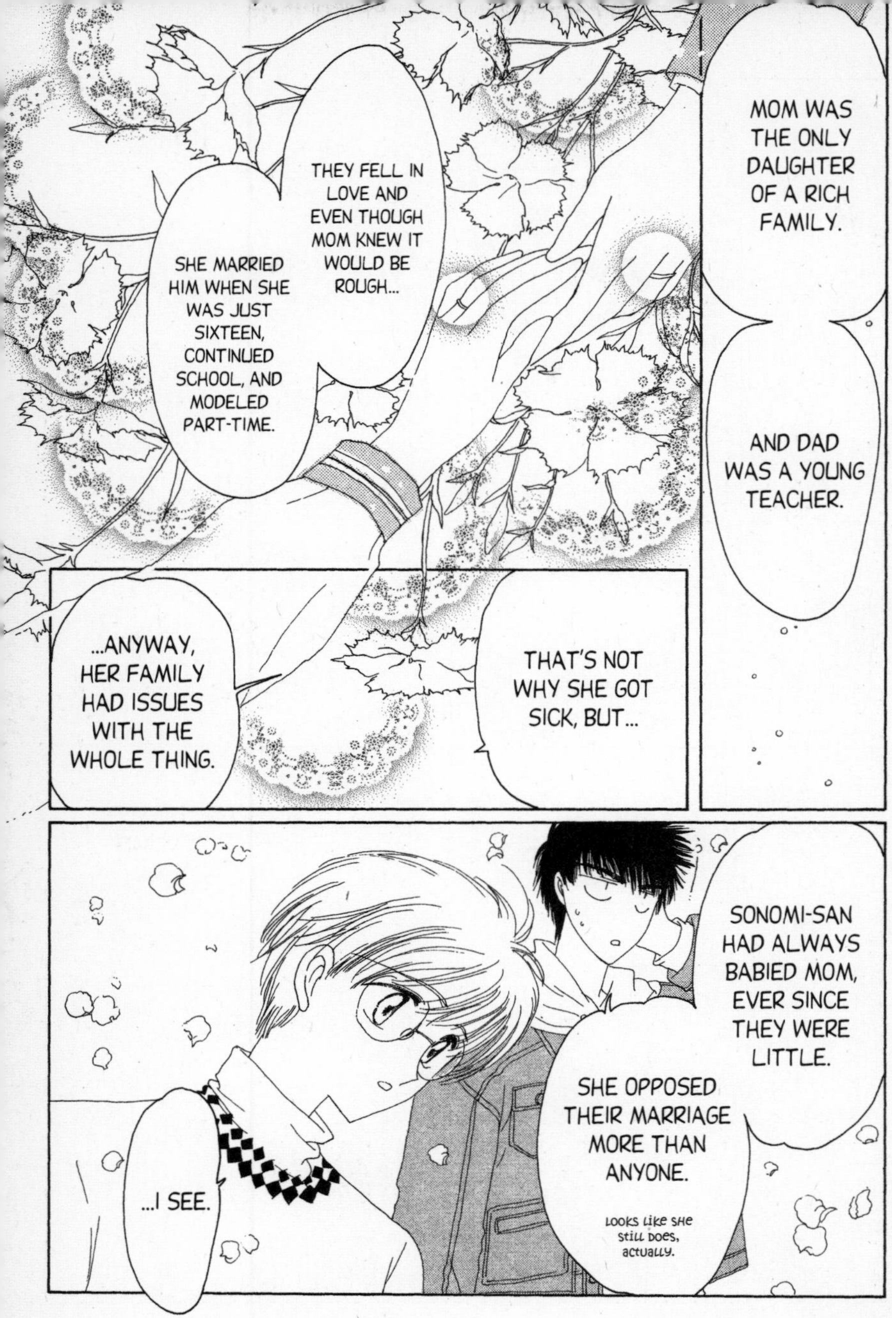
MOM WAS THE ONLY DAUGHTER OF A RICH FAMILY.
AND DAD WAS A YOUNG TEACHER.
THEY FELL IN LOVE AND EVEN THOUGH MOM KNEW IT WOULD BE ROUGH...
SHE MARRIED HIM WHEN SHE WAS JUST SIXTEEN, CONTINUED SCHOOL, AND MODELED PART-TIME.
THAT'S NOT WHY SHE GOT SICK, BUT...
...ANYWAY, HER FAMILY HAD ISSUES WITH THE WHOLE THING.
SONOMI-SAN HAD ALWAYS BABIED MOM, EVER SINCE THEY WERE LITTLE.
SHE OPPOSED THEIR MARRIAGE MORE THAN ANYONE.
Looks like she still does, actually.
...I SEE.

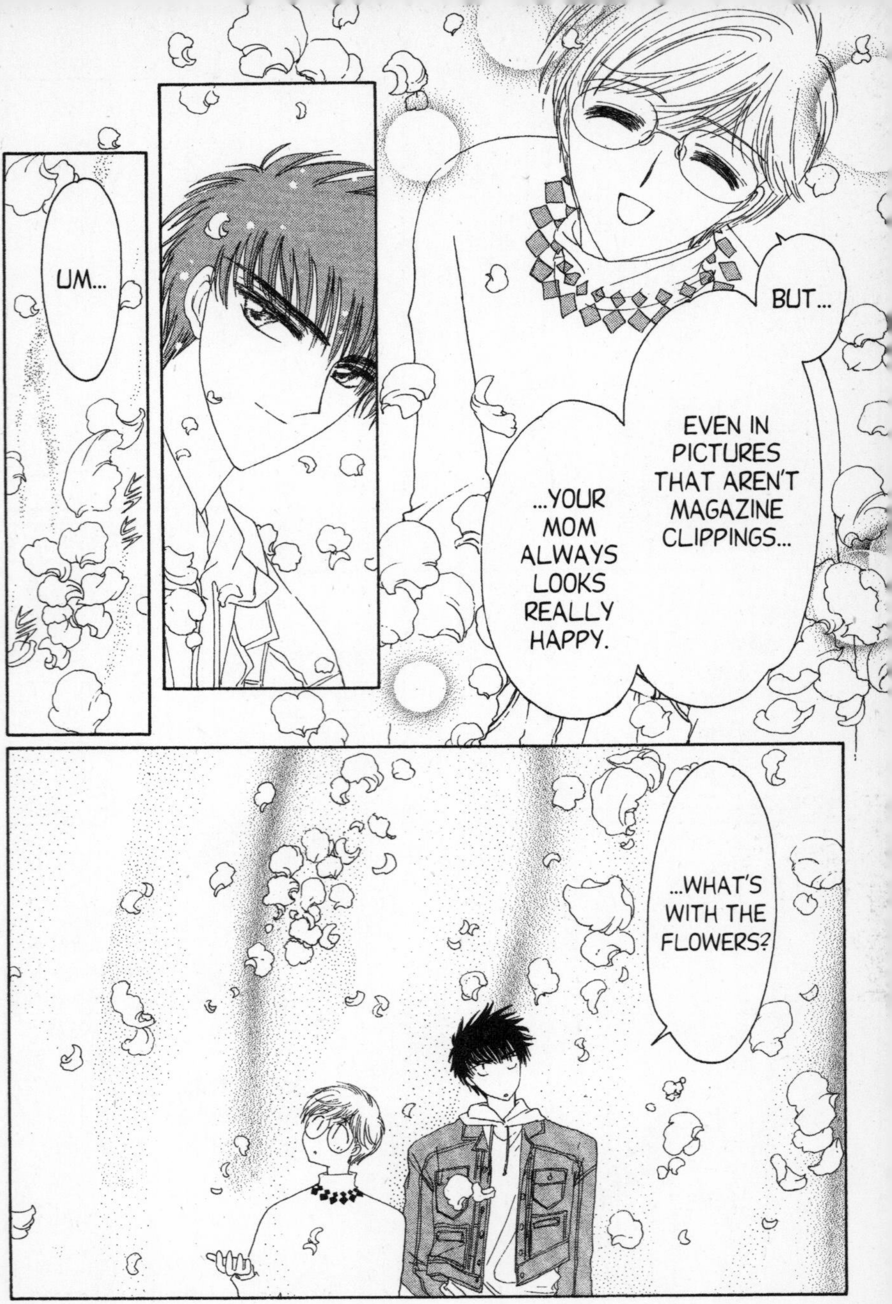
BUT...
EVEN IN PICTURES THAT AREN'T MAGAZINE CLIPPINGS...
...YOUR MOM ALWAYS LOOKS REALLY HAPPY.
UM...
...WHAT'S WITH THE FLOWERS?

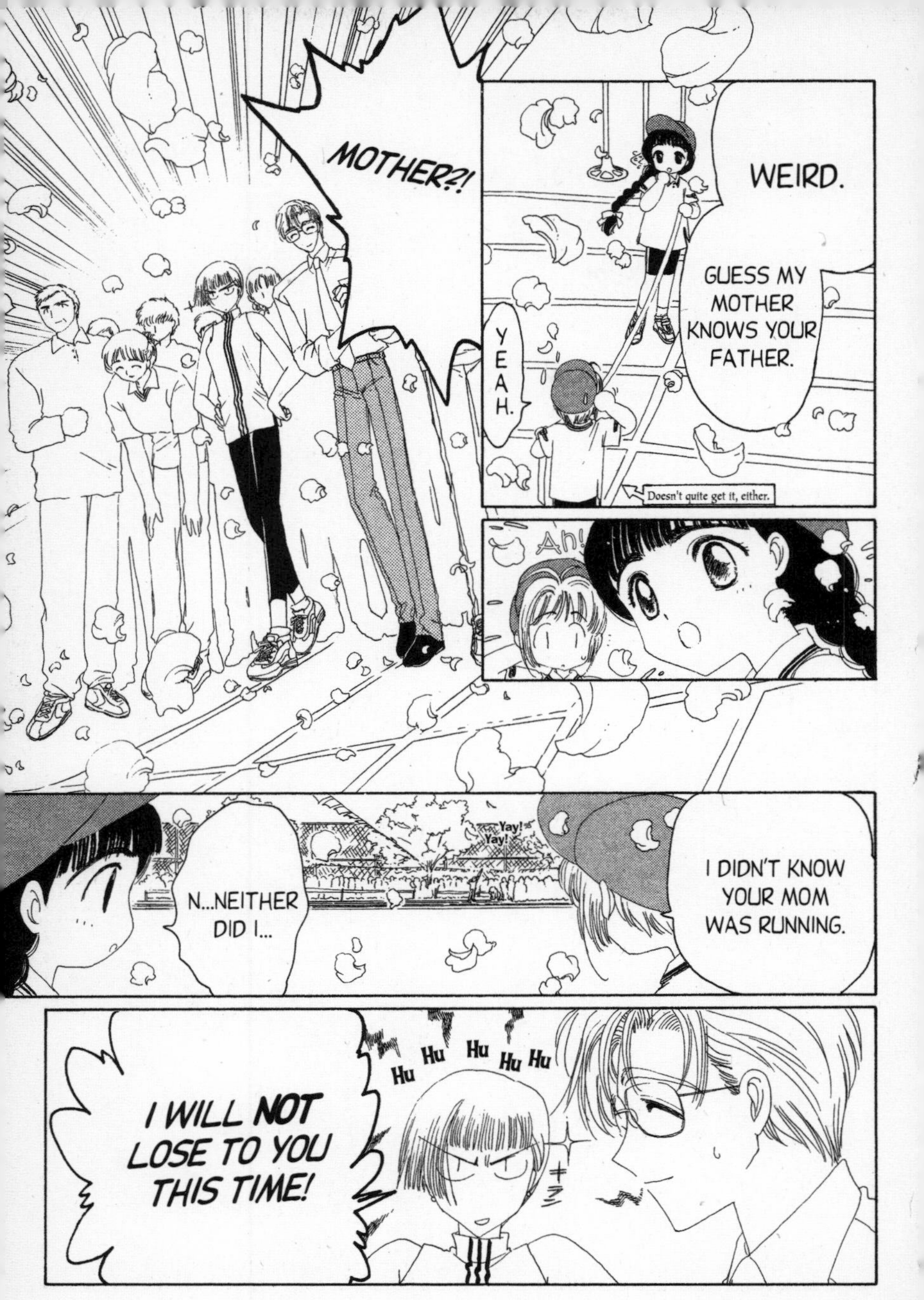
WEIRD.
GUESS MY MOTHER KNOWS YOUR FATHER.
YEAH.
Doesn't quite get it, either.
Ah!
MOTHER?!
I DIDN'T KNOW YOUR MOM WAS RUNNING.
Yay!
Yay!
N...NEITHER DID I...
Hu
Hu
Hu
Hu
Hu
キラ
I WILL **NOT** LOSE TO YOU THIS TIME!

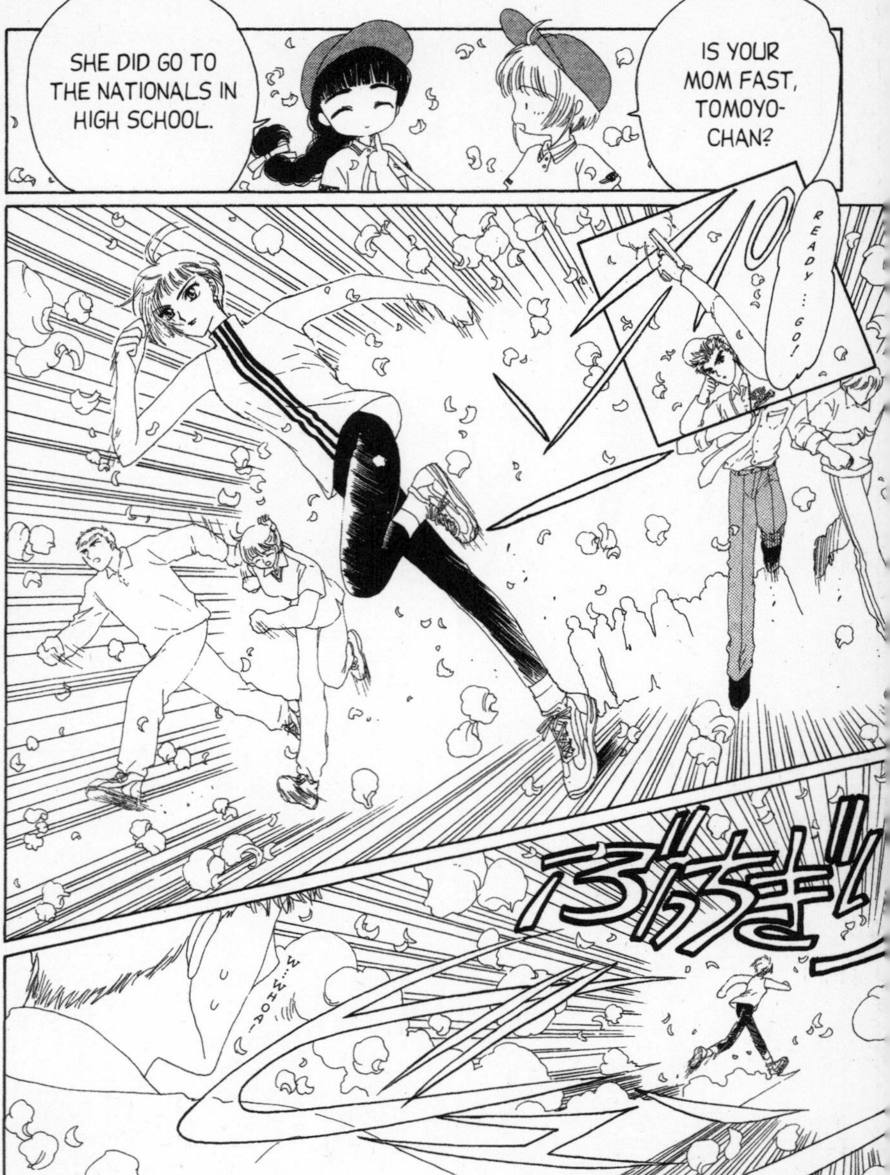
IS YOUR MOM FAST, TOMOYO-CHAN?
SHE DID GO TO THE NATIONALS IN HIGH SCHOOL.
READY... GO!
W... WHOA-!

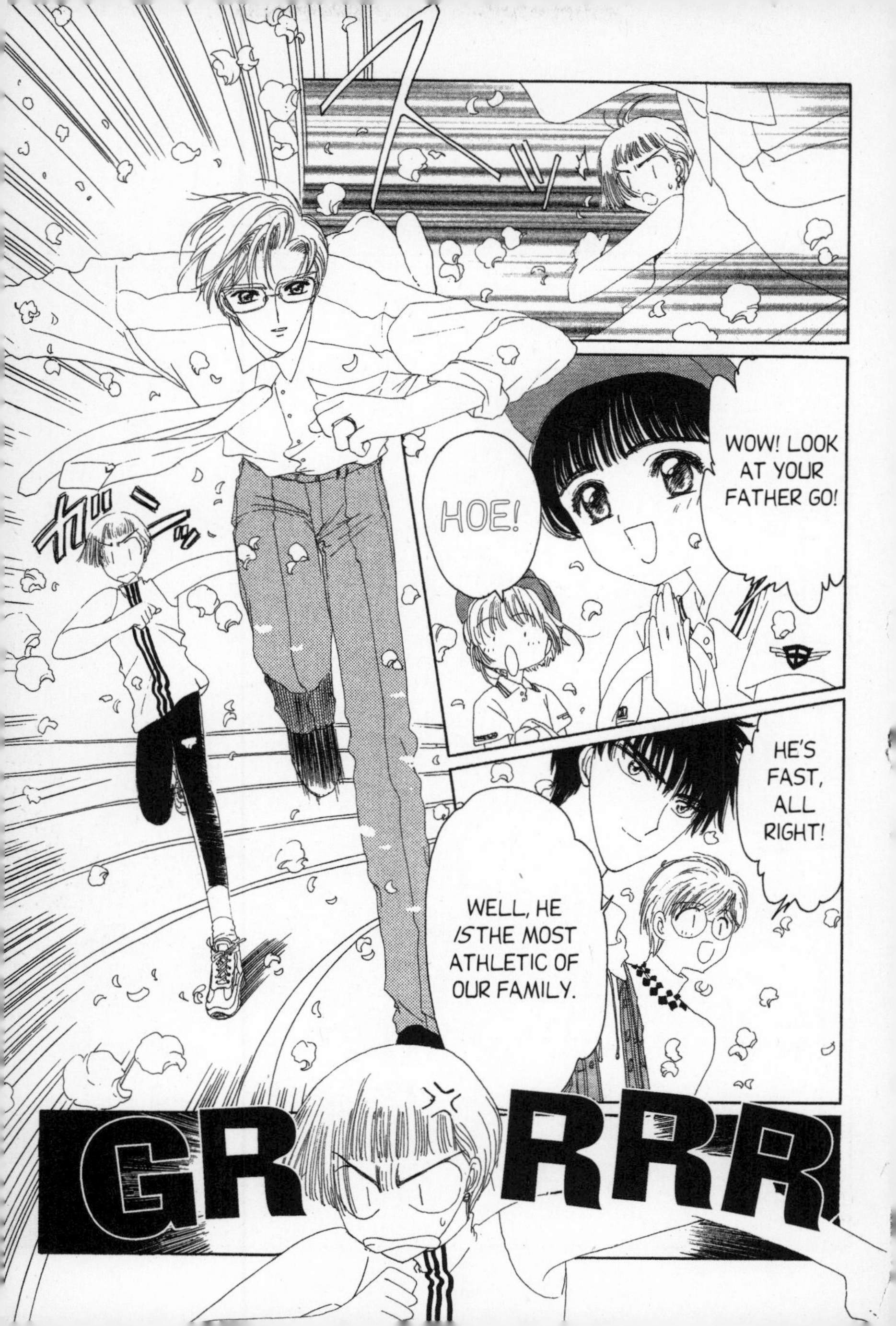
WOW! LOOK AT YOUR FATHER GO!
HOE!
HE'S FAST, ALL RIGHT!
WELL, HE IS THE MOST ATHLETIC OF OUR FAMILY.
GRRRR

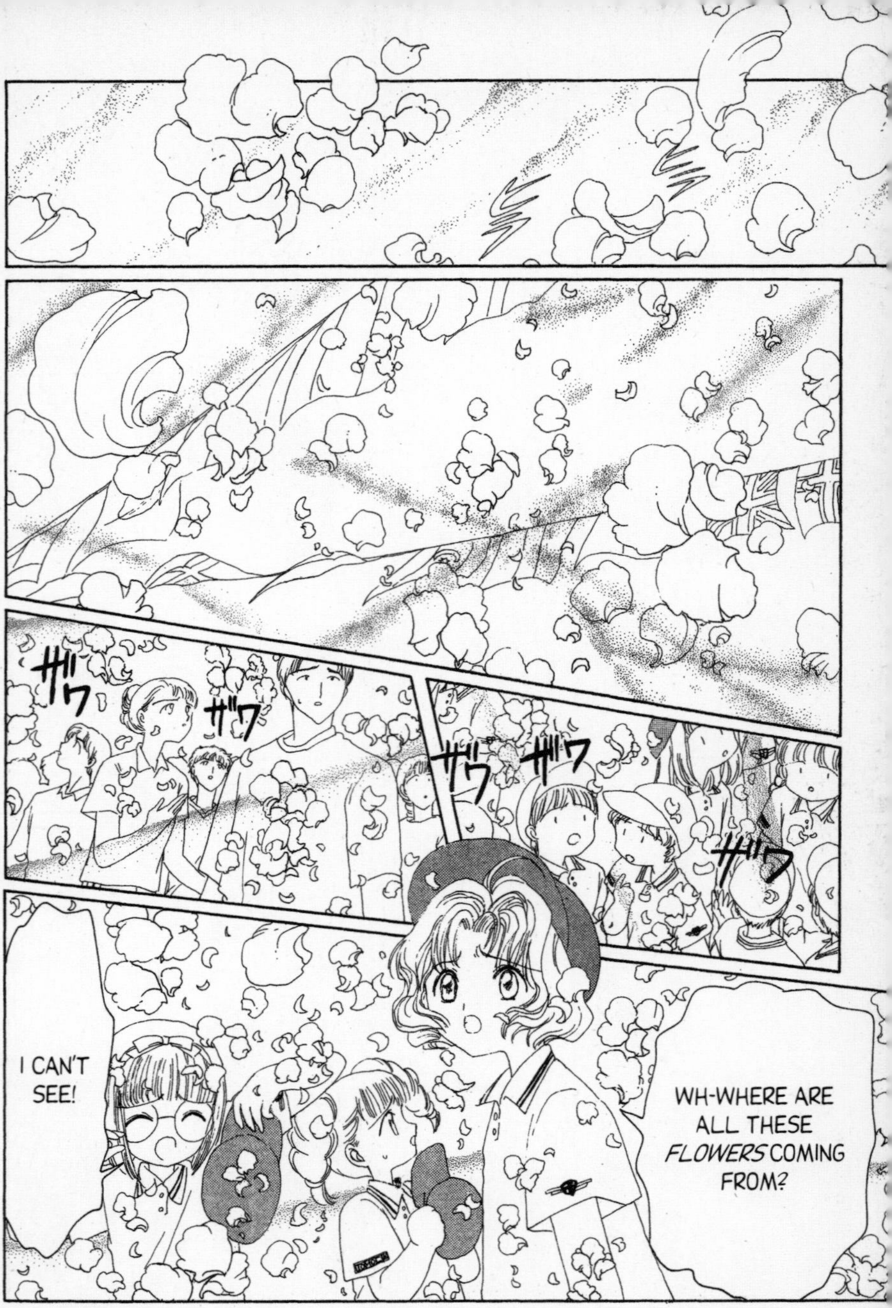
ザワ ザワ
ザワ
ザワ
ザワ
WH-WHERE ARE ALL THESE *FLOWERS* COMING FROM?
I CAN'T SEE!

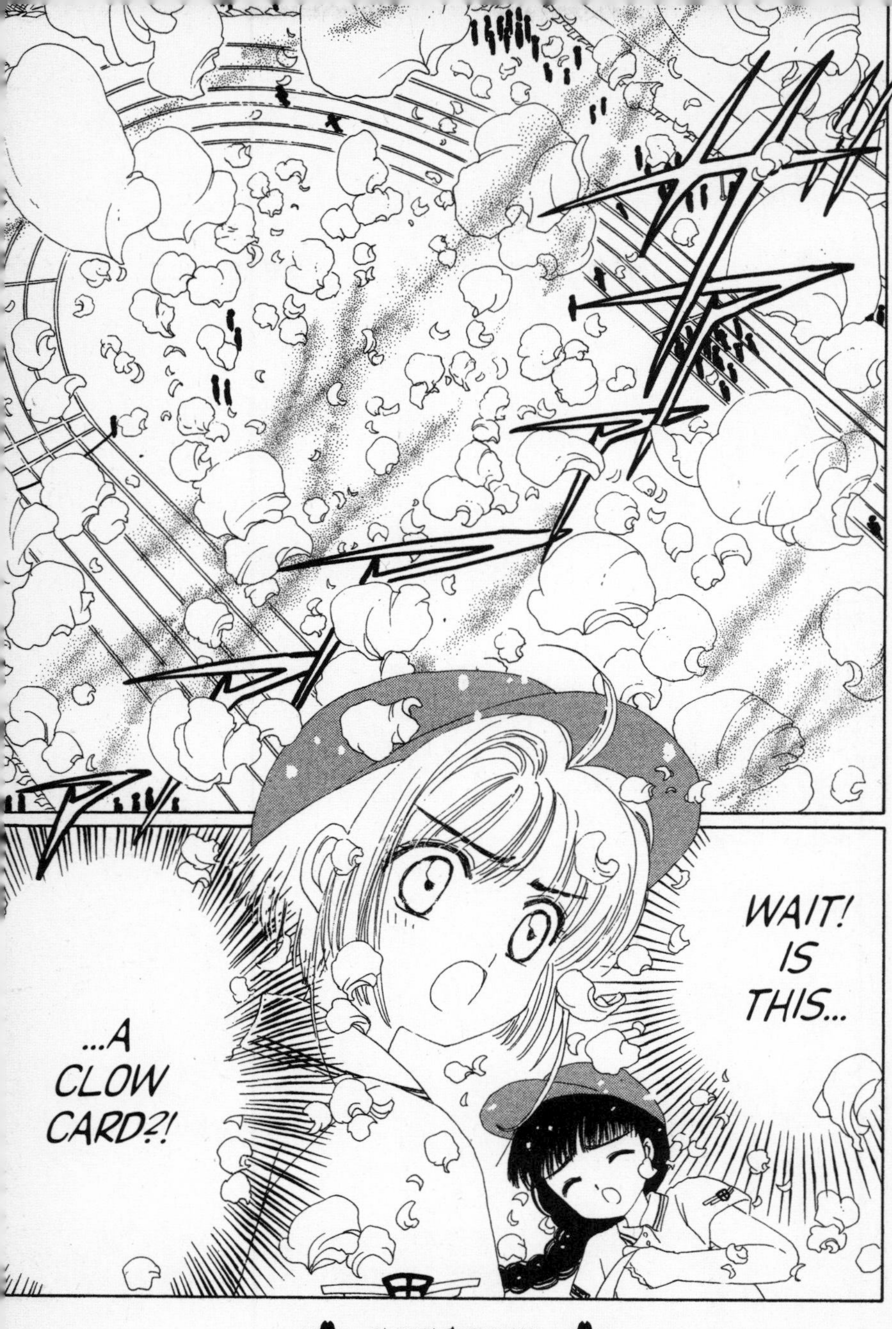
WAIT! IS THIS...
...A CLOW CARD?!

CONTINUED

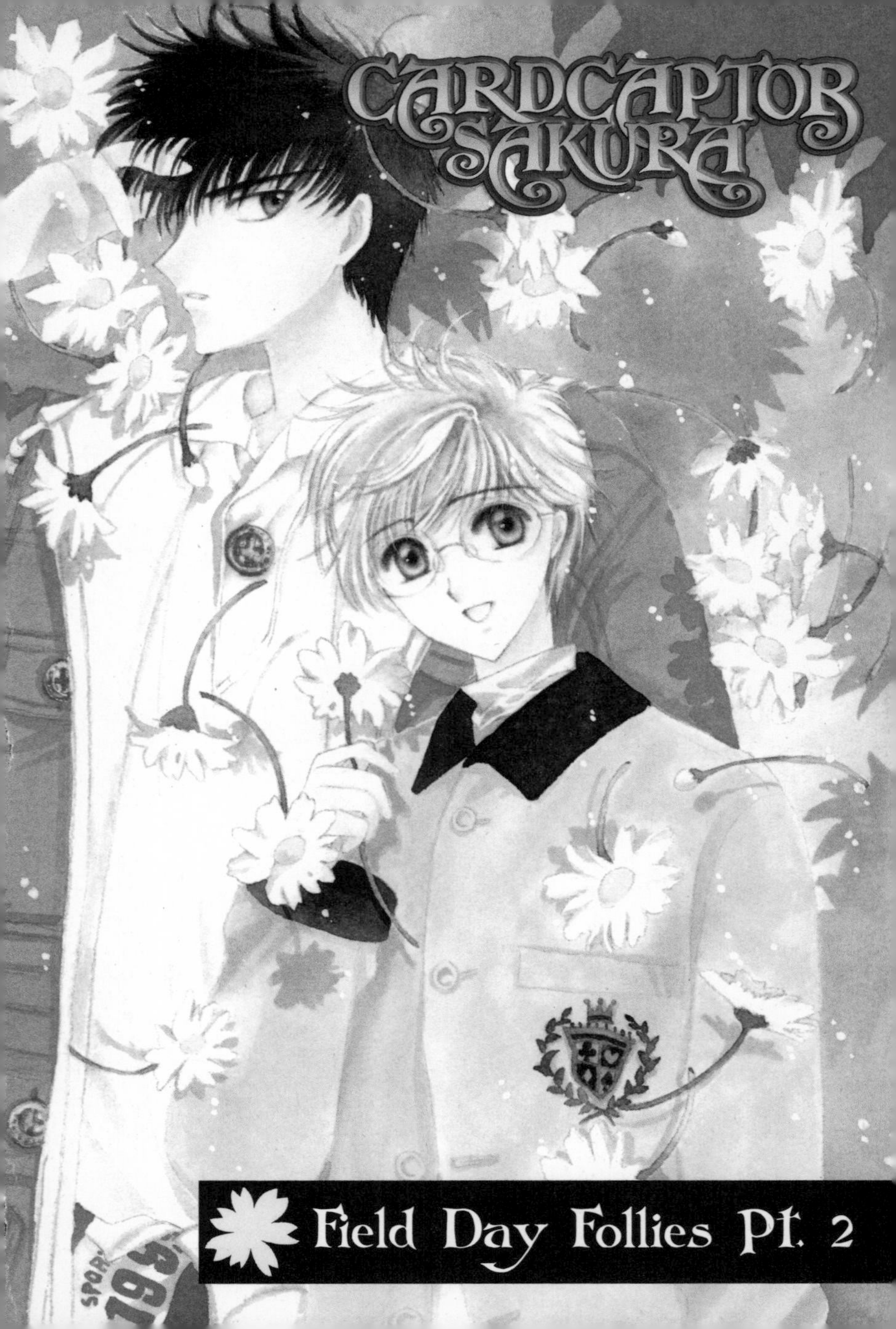
CARDCAPTOR SAKURA
Field Day Follies Pt. 2

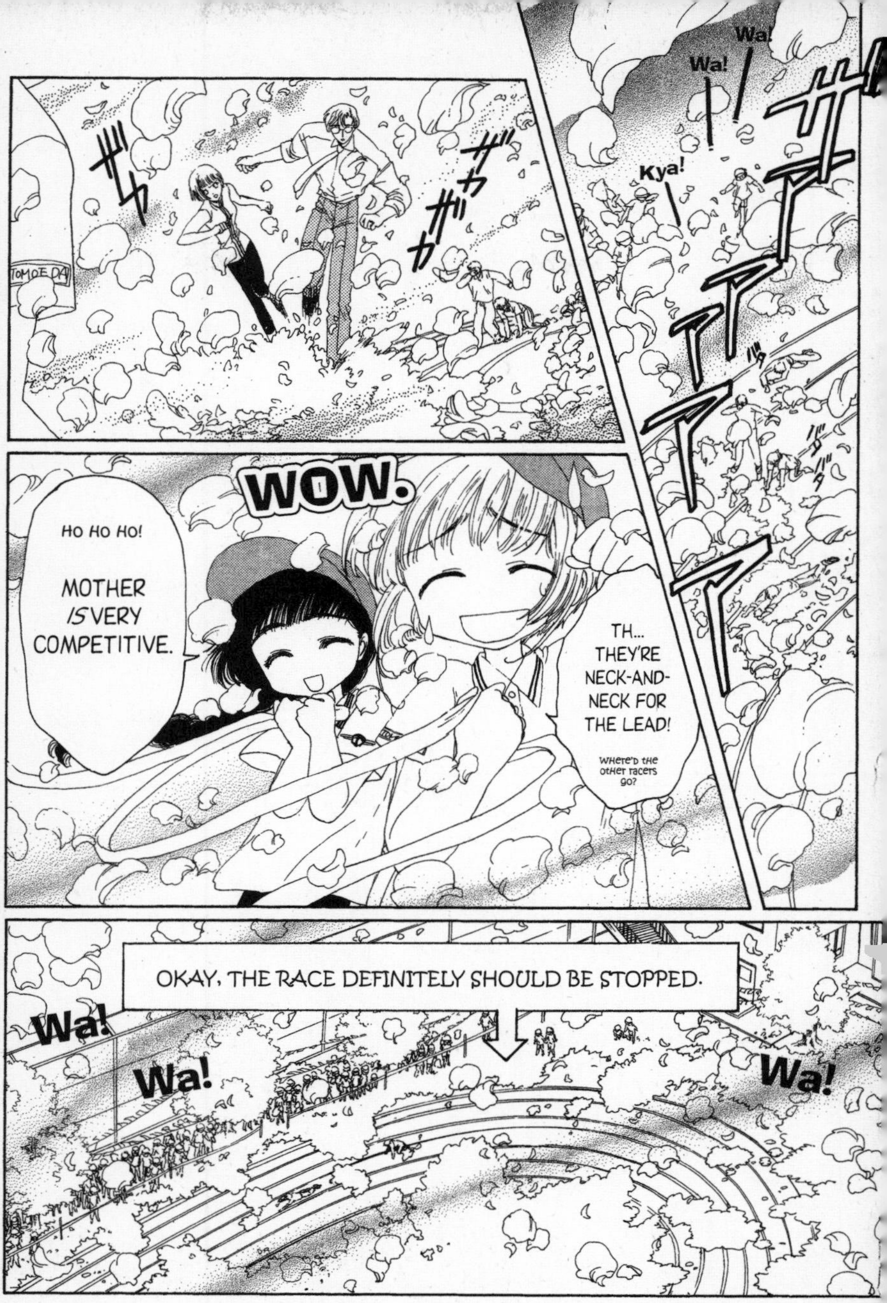
Wa!
Wa!
Kya!
WOW.
TH... THEY'RE NECK-AND-NECK FOR THE LEAD!
Where'd the other racers go?
HO HO HO!
MOTHER *IS* VERY COMPETITIVE.
OKAY, THE RACE DEFINITELY SHOULD BE STOPPED.
Wa!
Wa!
Wa!

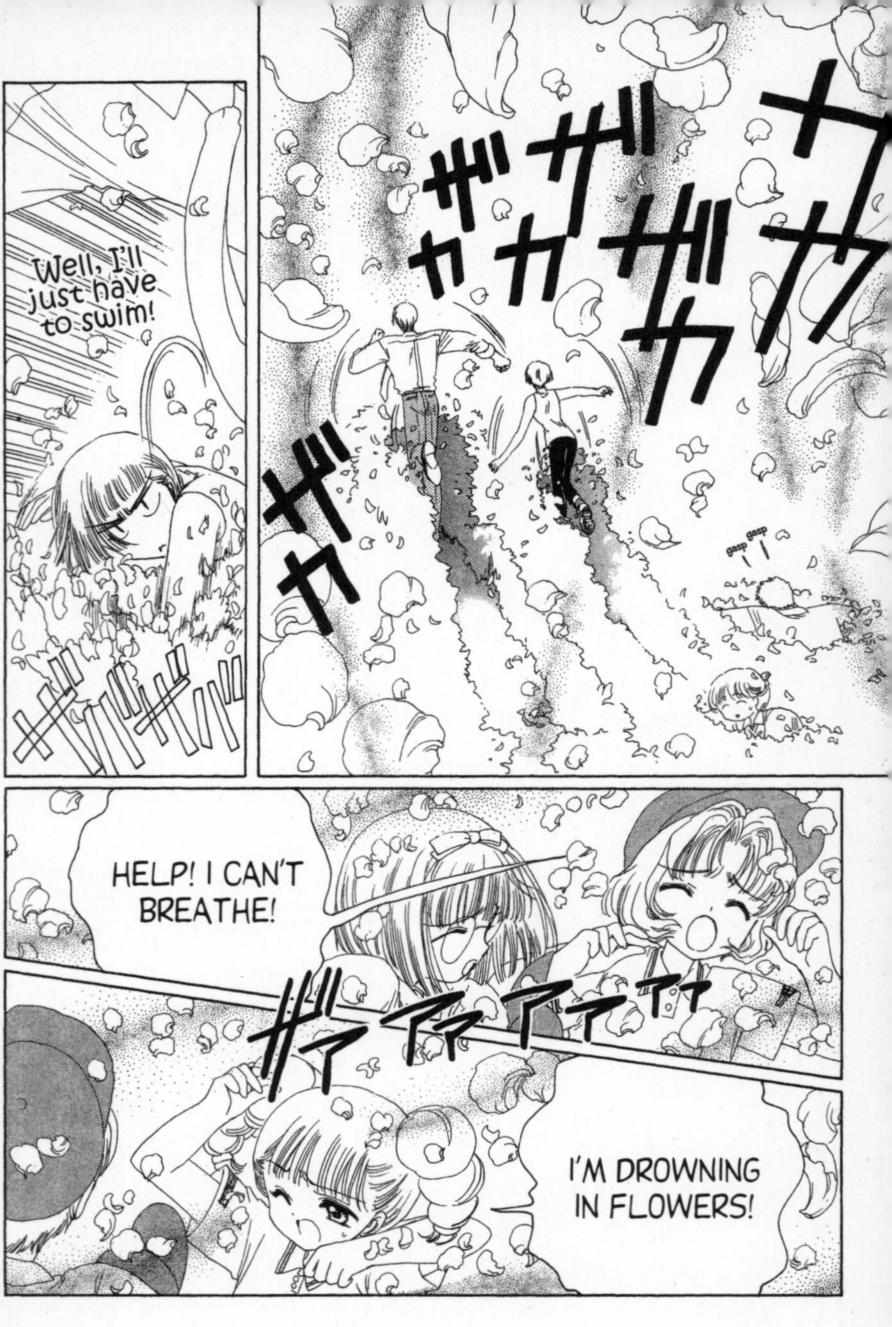
gasp gasp
Well, I'll just have to swim!
HELP! I CAN'T BREATHE!
I'M DROWNING IN FLOWERS!

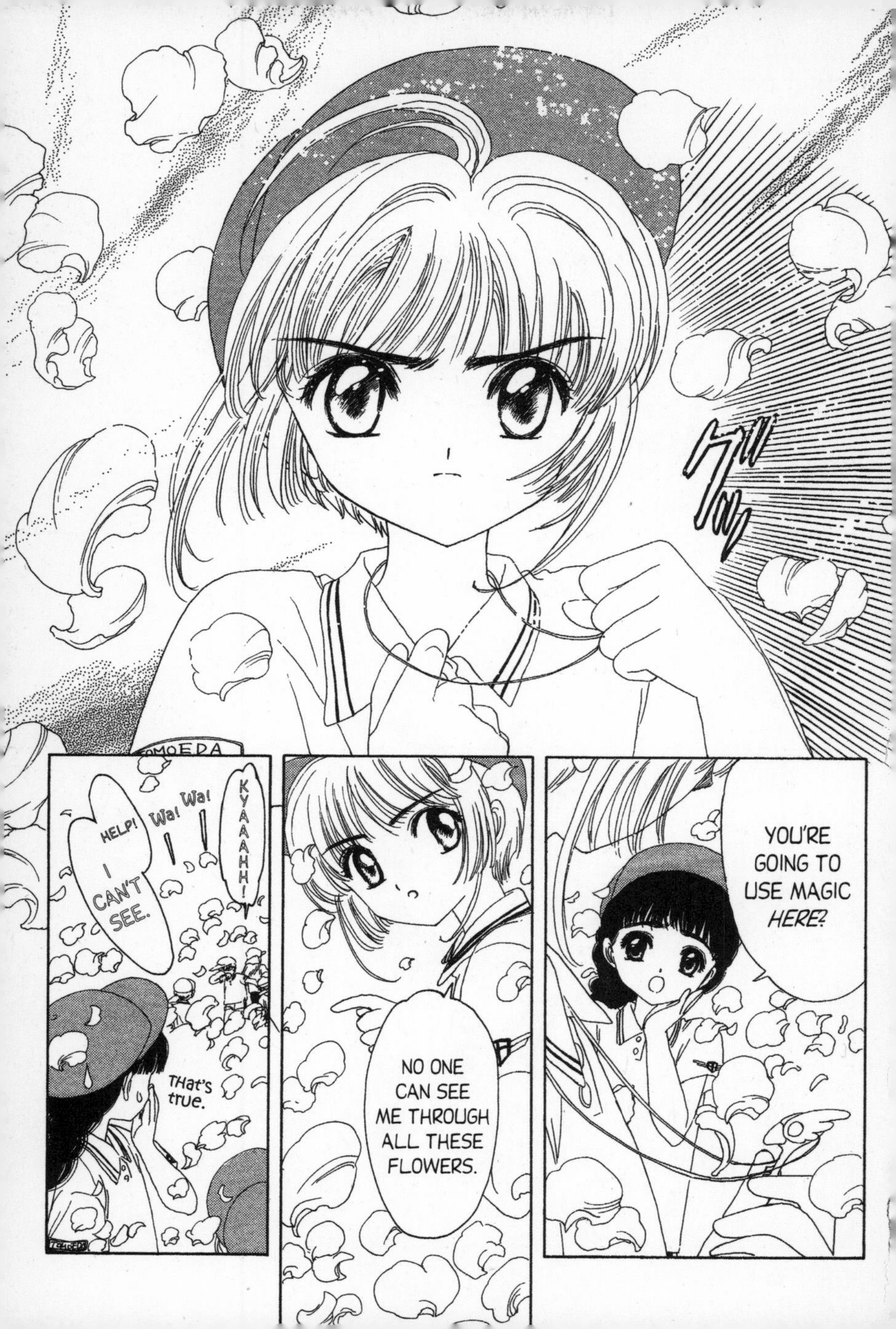
TOMOEDA
YOU'RE GOING TO USE MAGIC HERE?
NO ONE CAN SEE ME THROUGH ALL THESE FLOWERS.
KYAAAAHH!
Wa! Wa!
HELP! I CAN'T SEE.
THat's true.

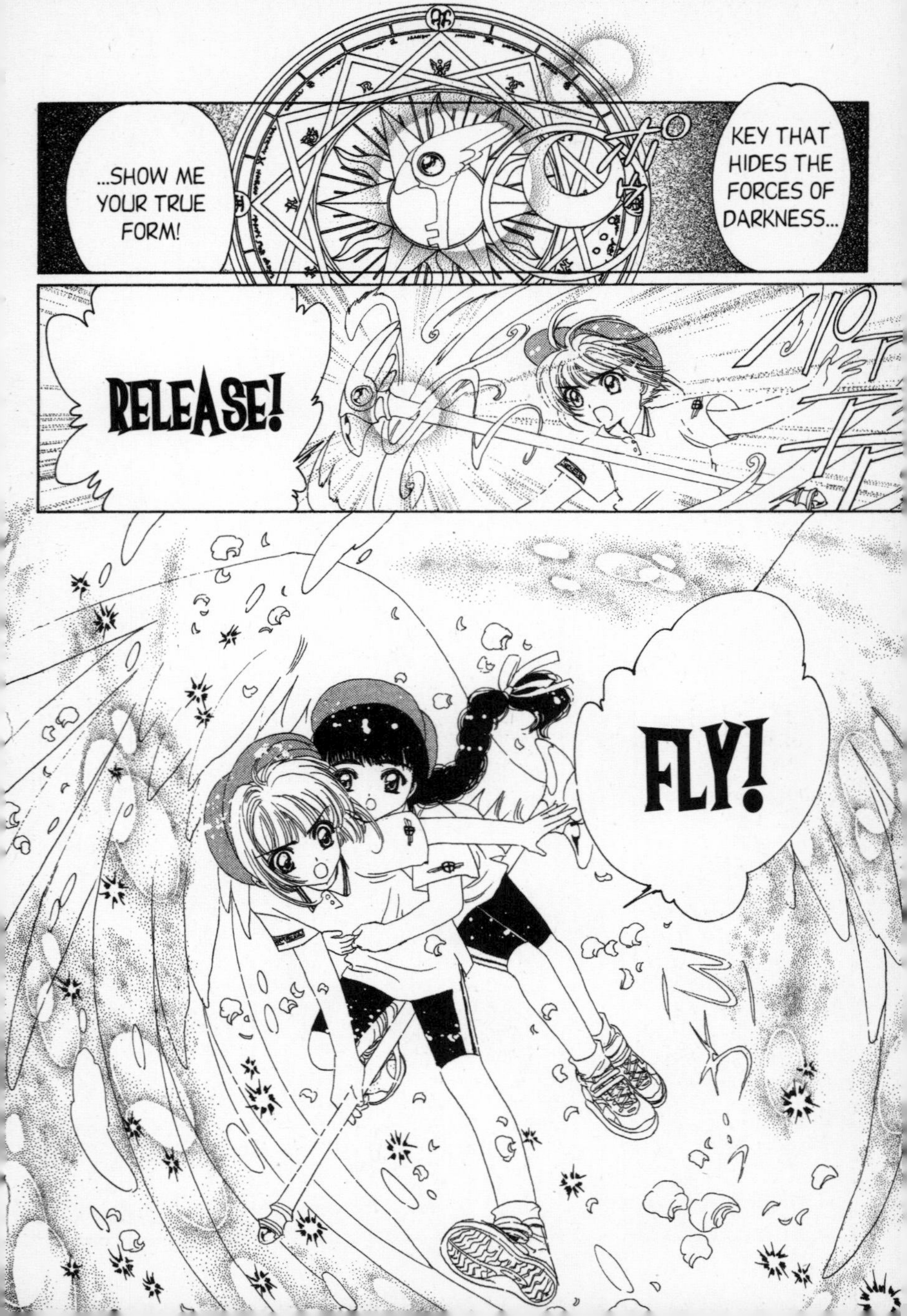
KEY THAT HIDES THE FORCES OF DARKNESS...
...SHOW ME YOUR TRUE FORM!
RELEASE!
FLY!

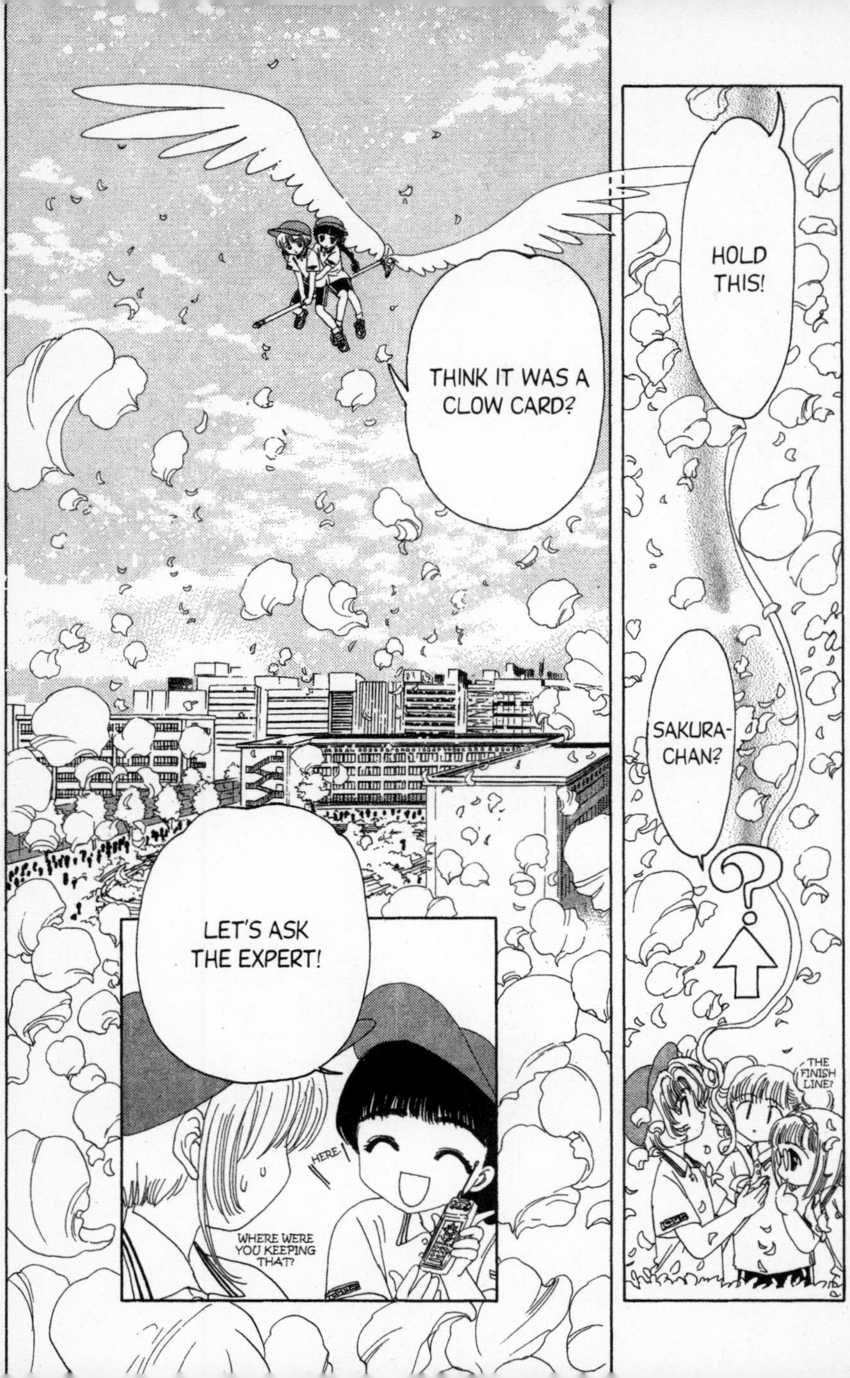
HOLD THIS!
SAKURA-CHAN?
THE FINISH LINE?
THINK IT WAS A CLOW CARD?
LET'S ASK THE EXPERT!
HERE.
WHERE WERE YOU KEEPING THAT?

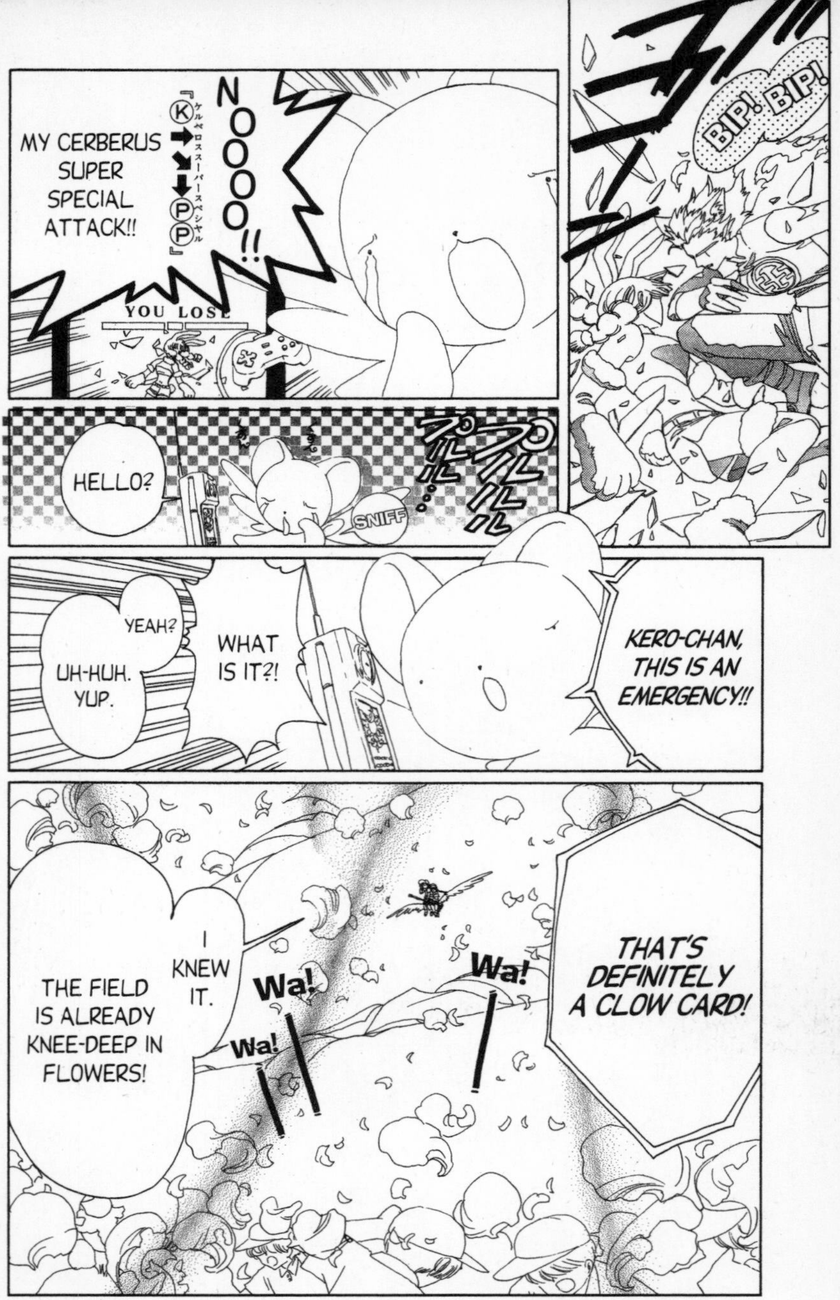
BIP! BIP!
NOOOO!!
MY CERBERUS SUPER SPECIAL ATTACK!!
『K➡↘⬇PP』
ケルベロススーパースペシャル
YOU LOSE
HELLO?
SNIFF
KERO-CHAN, THIS IS AN EMERGENCY!!
WHAT IS IT?!
YEAH?
UH-HUH. YUP.
THAT'S DEFINITELY A CLOW CARD!
Wa!
Wa!
Wa!
I KNEW IT.
THE FIELD IS ALREADY KNEE-DEEP IN FLOWERS!

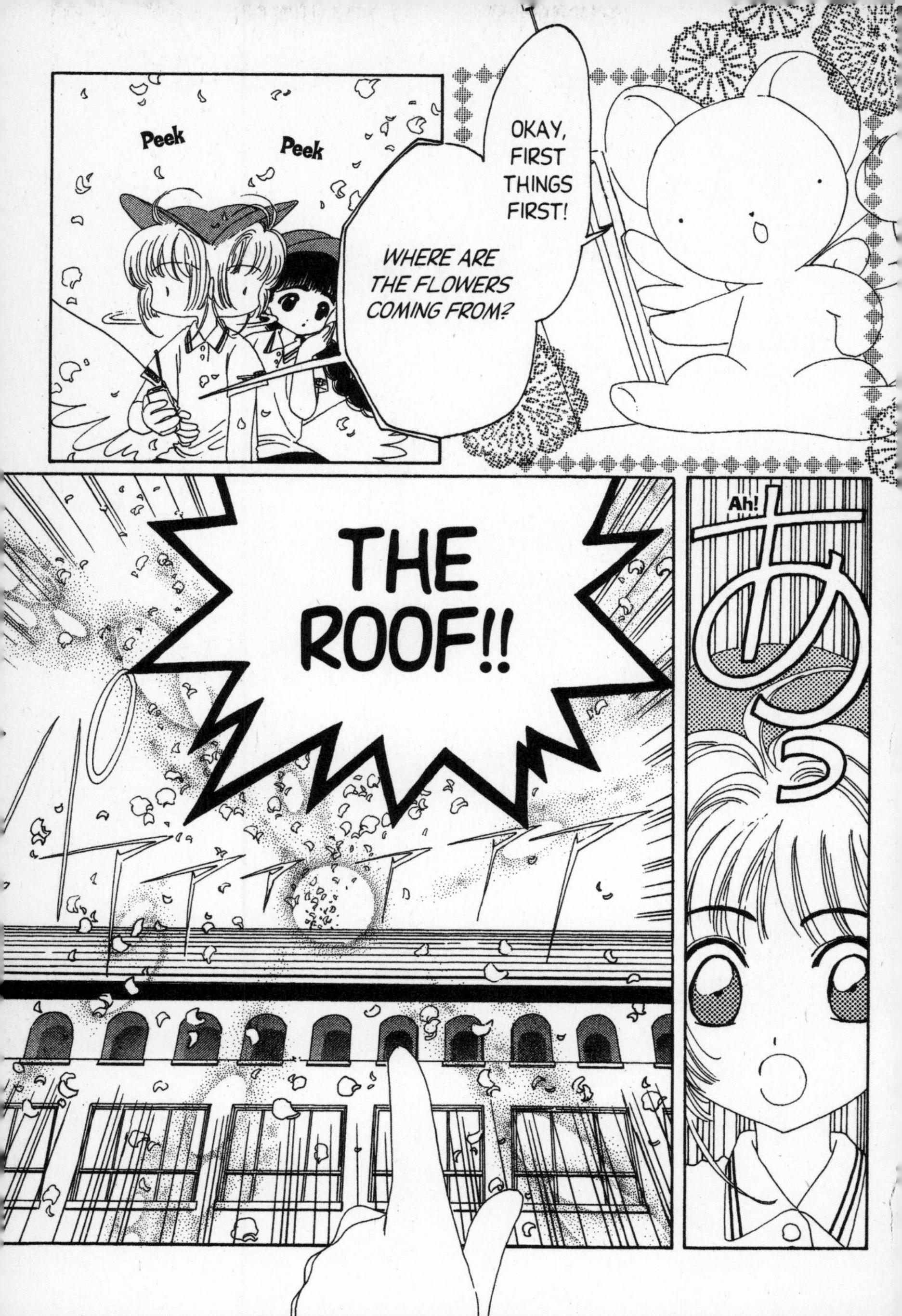
OKAY, FIRST THINGS FIRST!
WHERE ARE THE FLOWERS COMING FROM?
Peek
Peek
Ah!
THE ROOF!!

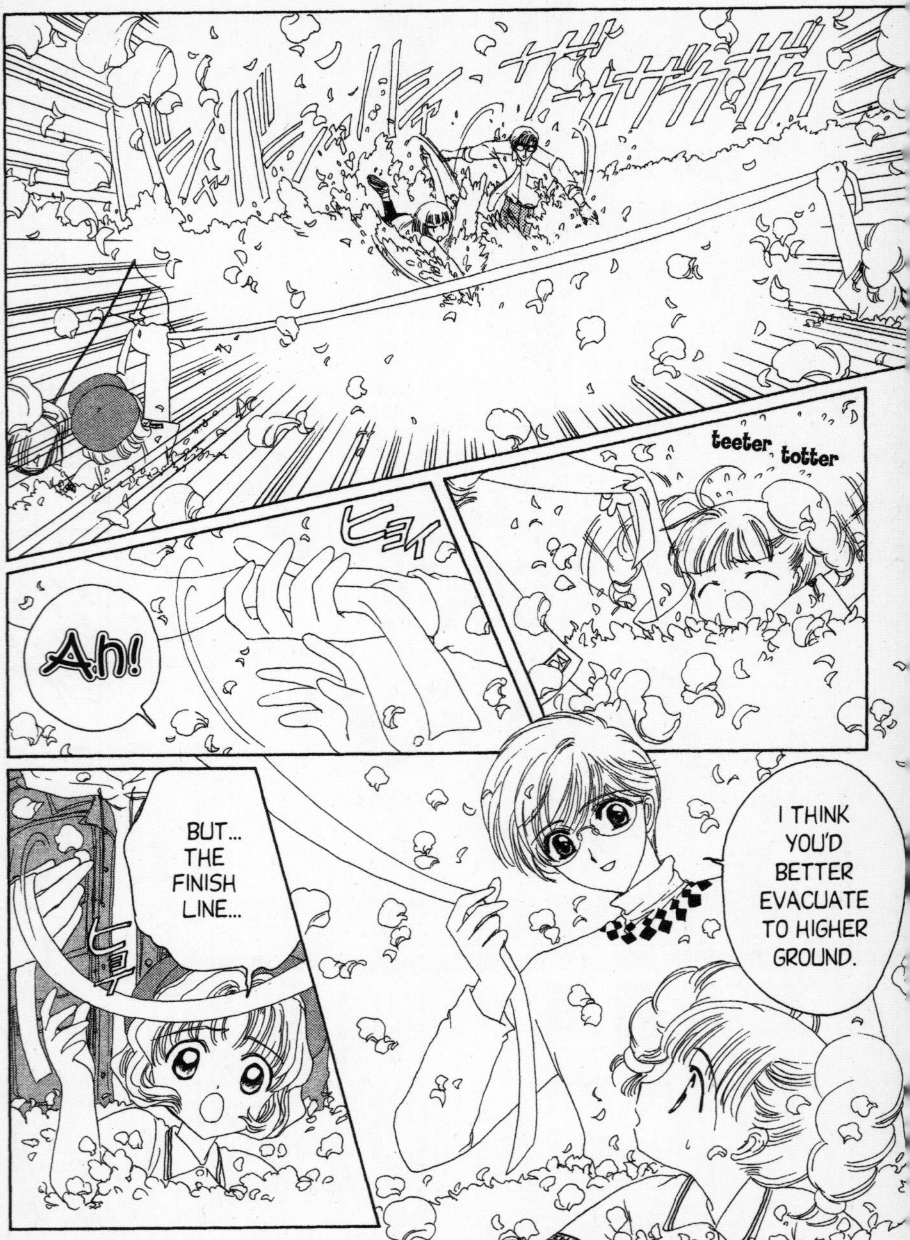
teeter totter
ヒョイ
Ah!
I THINK YOU'D BETTER EVACUATE TO HIGHER GROUND.
BUT... THE FINISH LINE...
ヒョイ

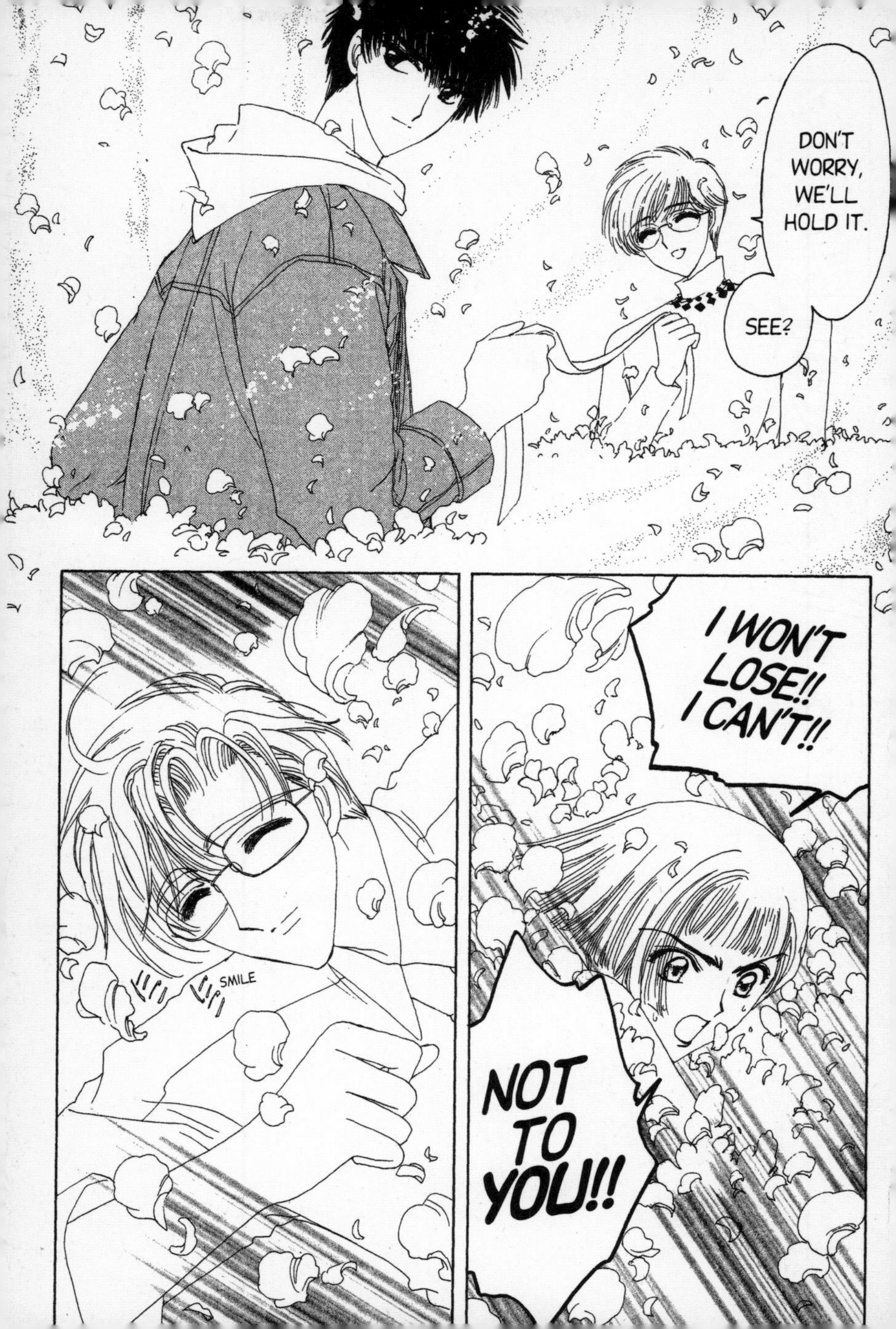
DON'T WORRY, WE'LL HOLD IT.
SEE?
I WON'T LOSE!! I CAN'T!!
NOT TO YOU!!
SMILE

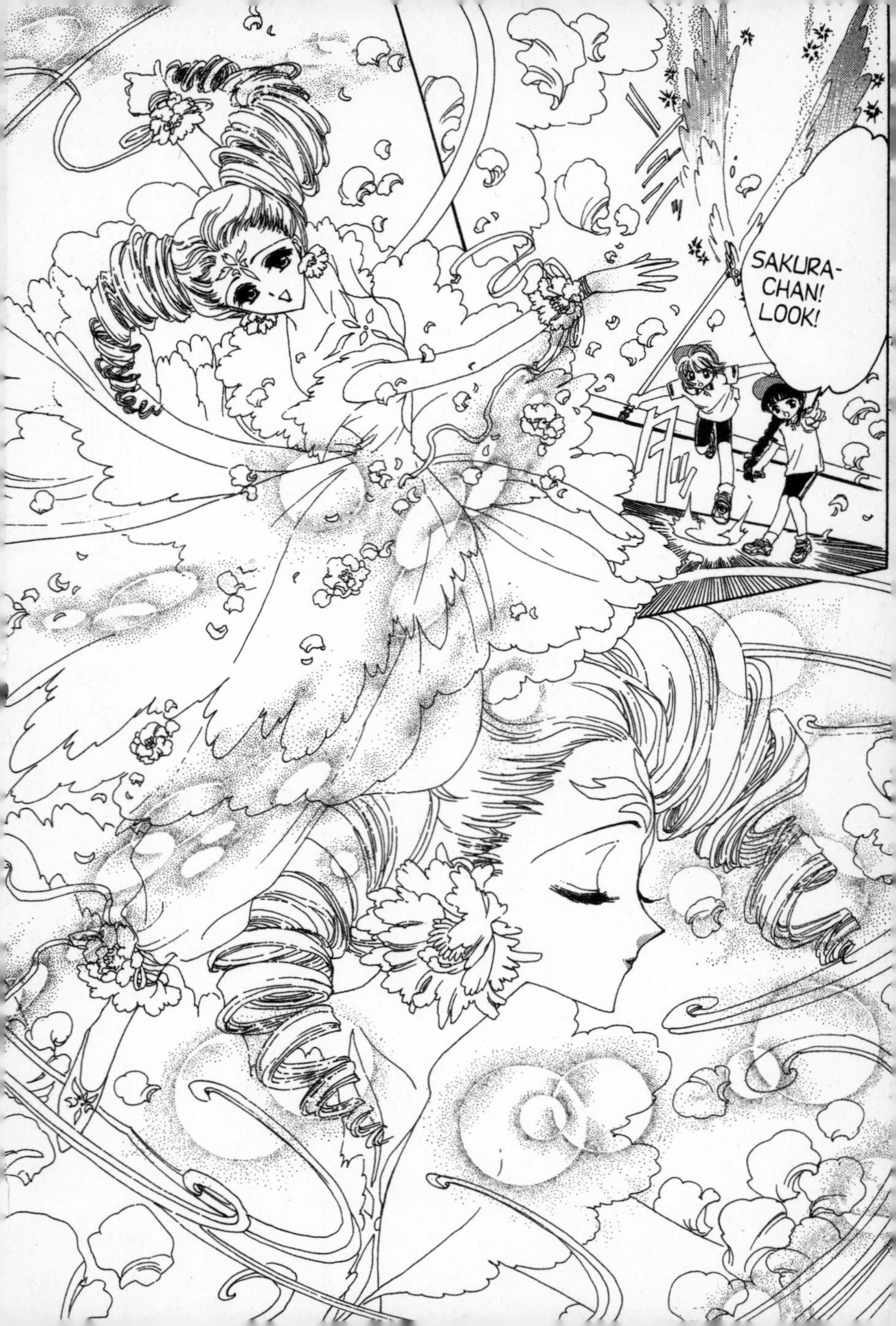
SAKURA-CHAN! LOOK!

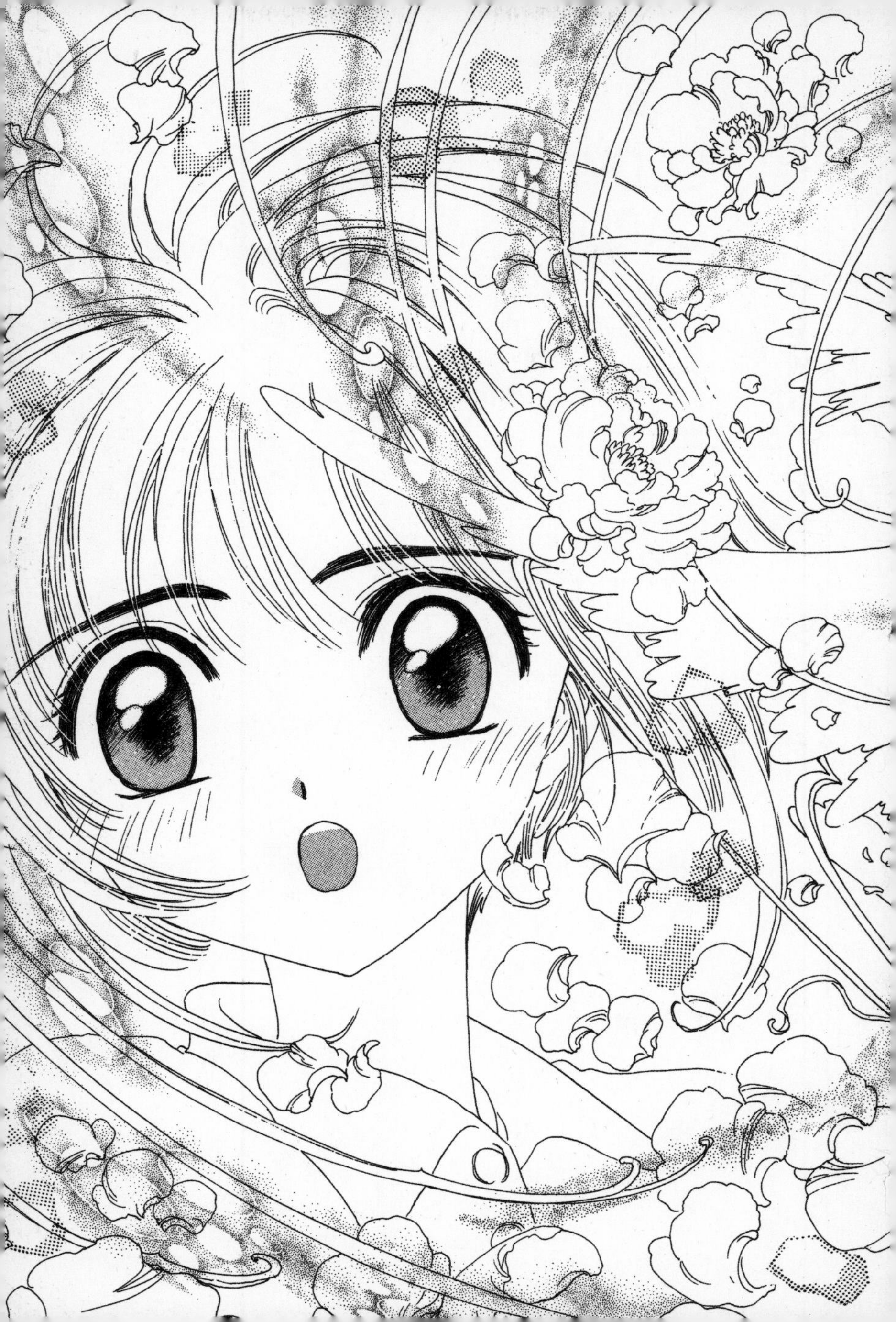

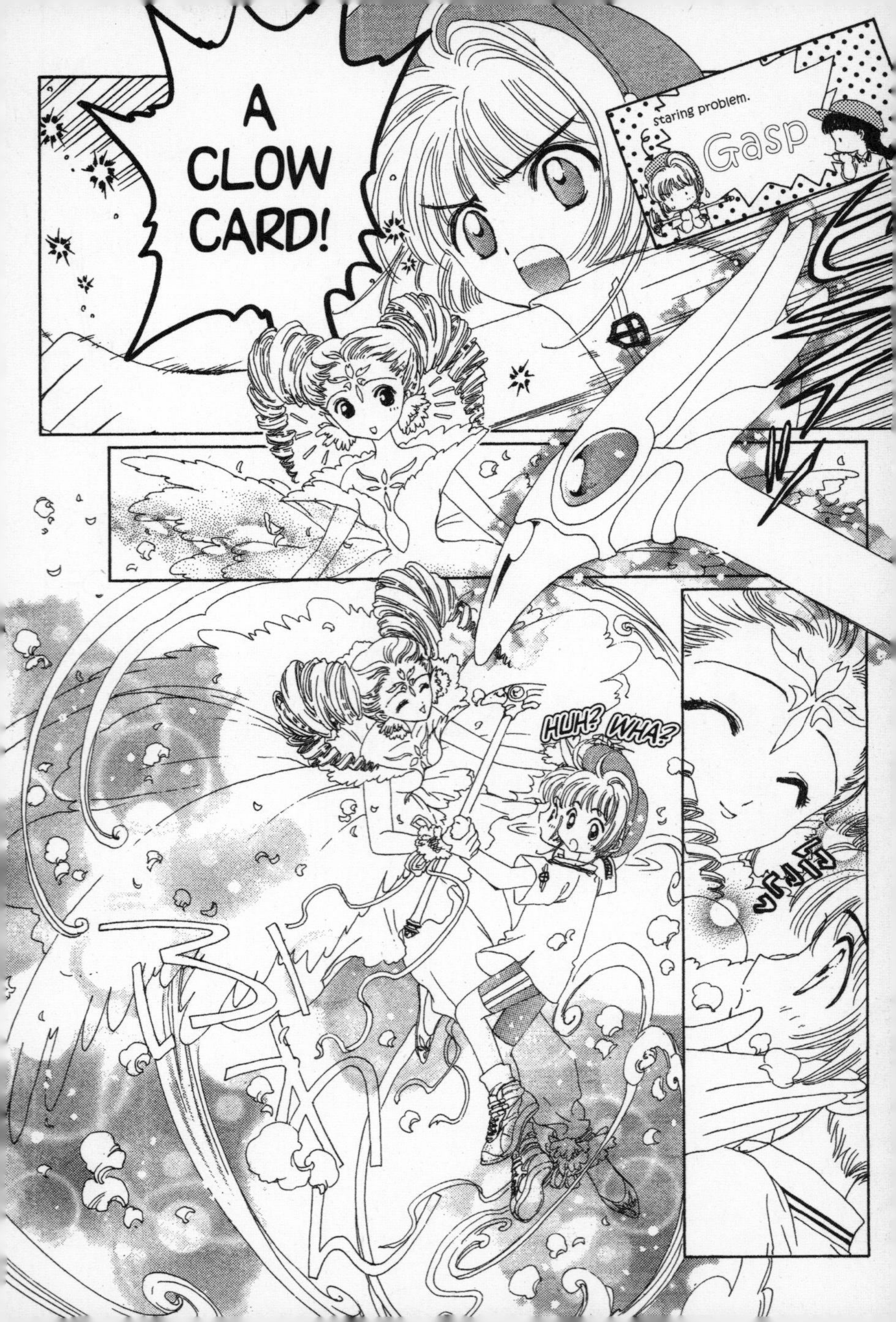
staring problem.
Gasp
A CLOW CARD!
HUH? WHA?

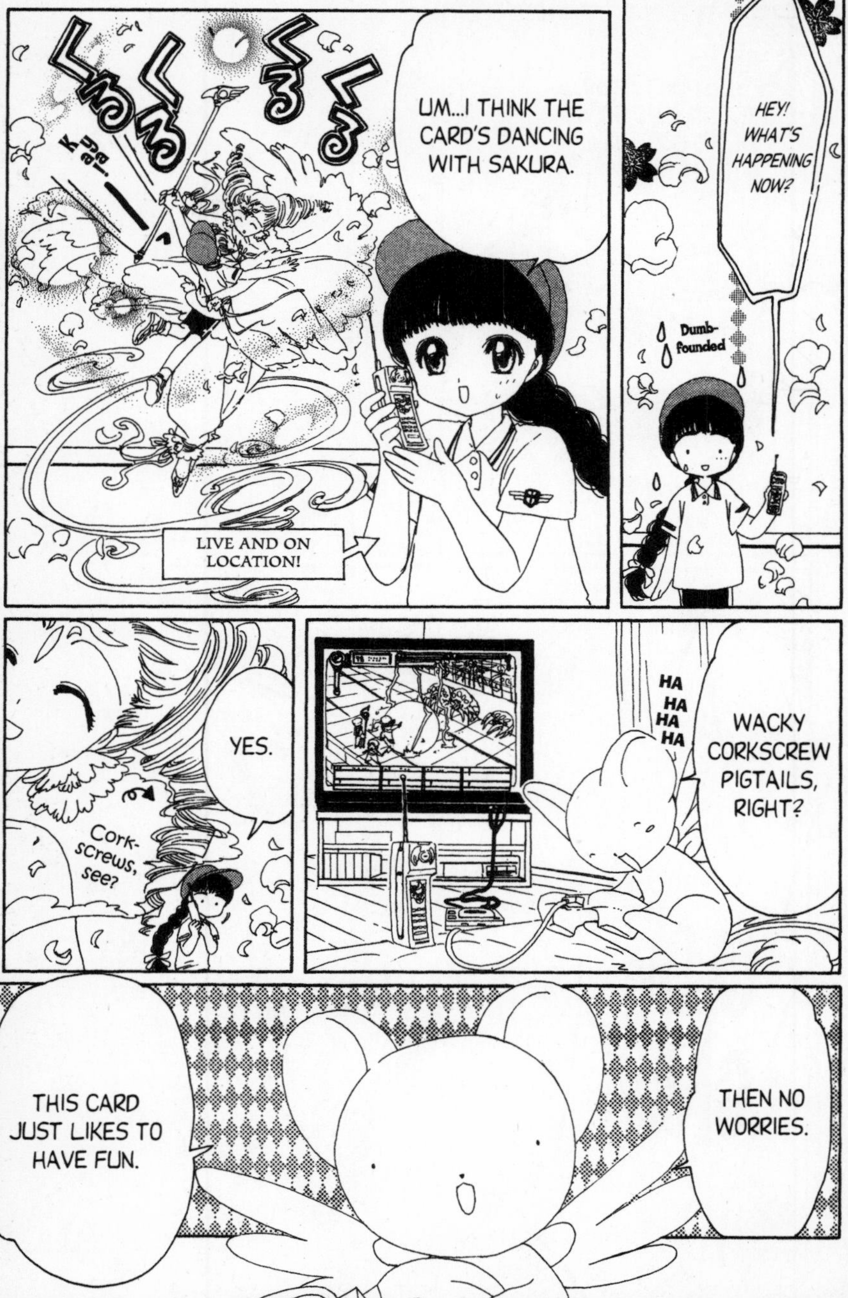
HEY! WHAT'S HAPPENING NOW?
Dumb-founded
UM...I THINK THE CARD'S DANCING WITH SAKURA.
Kyaa!
LIVE AND ON LOCATION!
WACKY CORKSCREW PIGTAILS, RIGHT?
HA HA HA HA
YES.
Cork-screws, see?
THEN NO WORRIES.
THIS CARD JUST LIKES TO HAVE FUN.

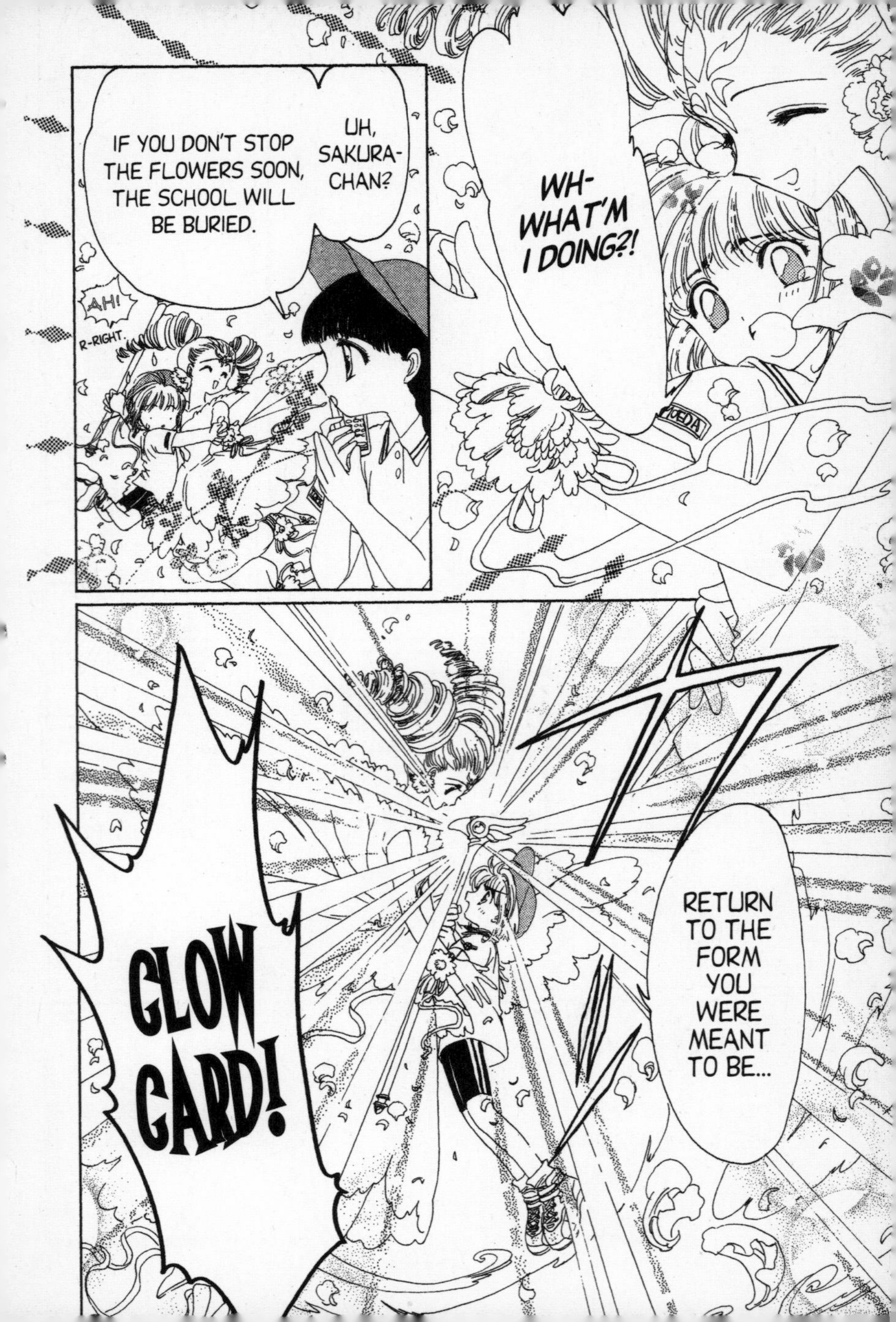
WH-WHAT'M I DOING?!
UH, SAKURA-CHAN?
IF YOU DON'T STOP THE FLOWERS SOON, THE SCHOOL WILL BE BURIED.
AH!
R-RIGHT.
RETURN TO THE FORM YOU WERE MEANT TO BE...
GLOW CARD!

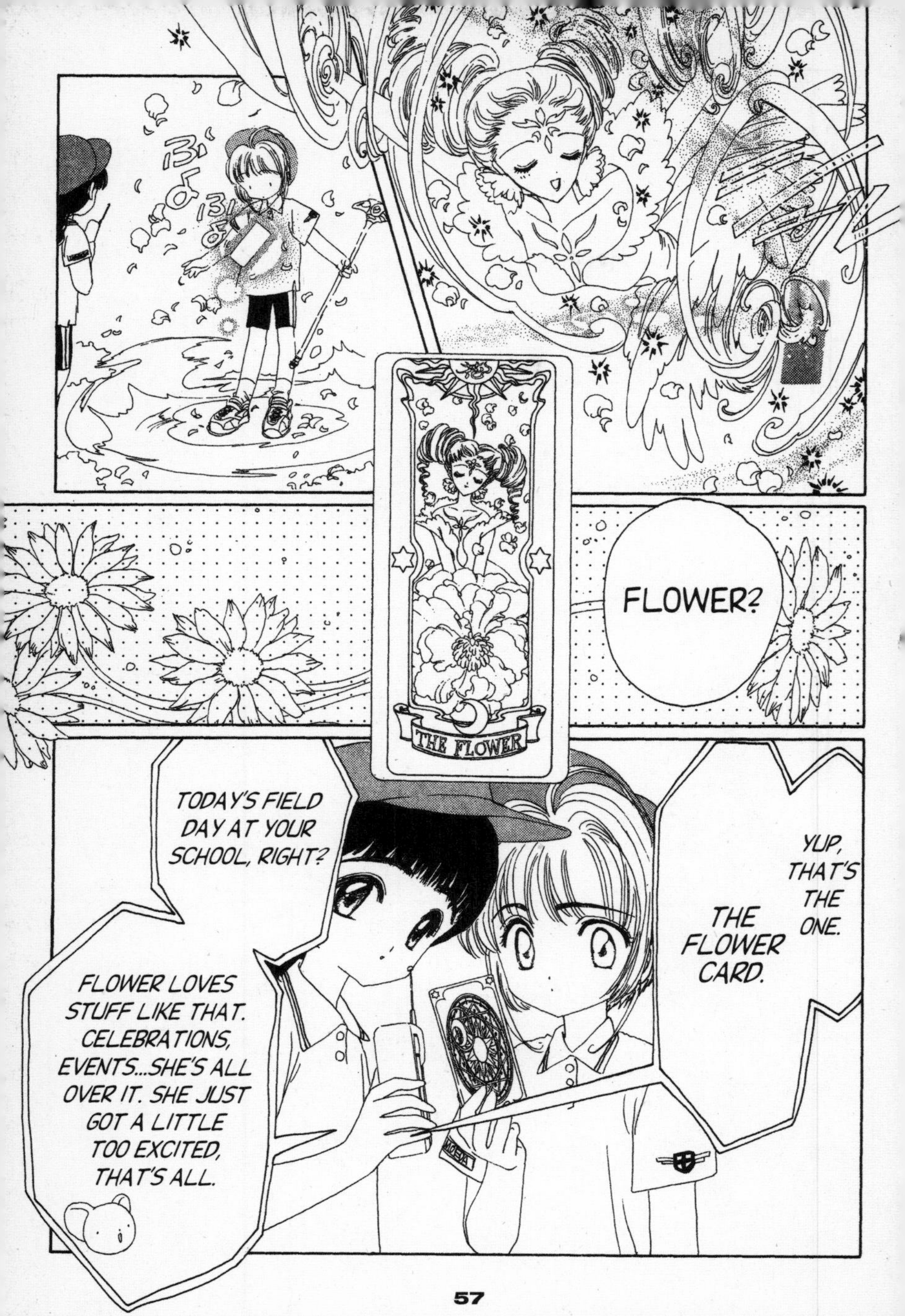
FLOWER?
THE FLOWER
YUP, THAT'S THE ONE.
THE FLOWER CARD.
TODAY'S FIELD DAY AT YOUR SCHOOL, RIGHT?
FLOWER LOVES STUFF LIKE THAT. CELEBRATIONS, EVENTS...SHE'S ALL OVER IT. SHE JUST GOT A LITTLE TOO EXCITED, THAT'S ALL.

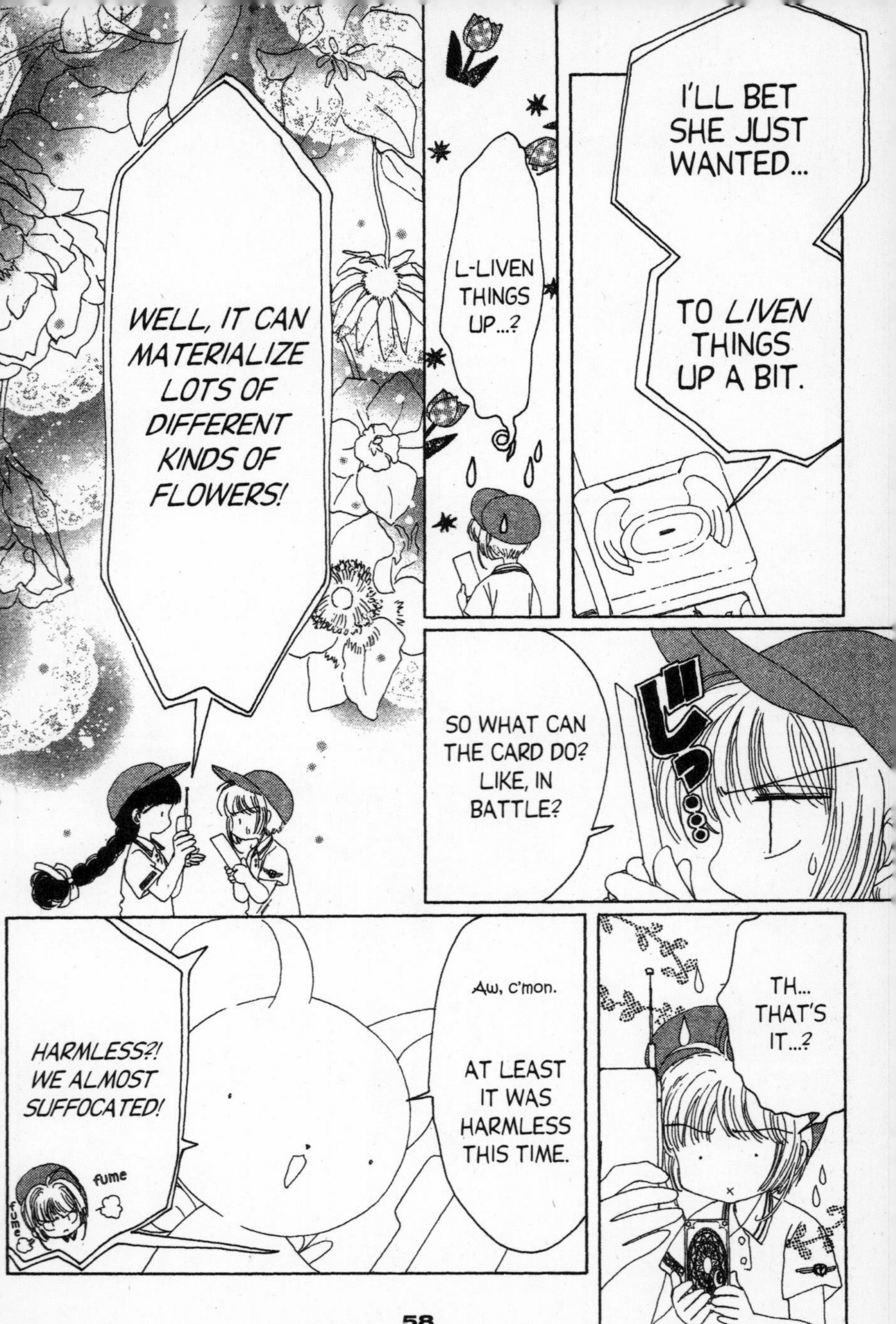
I'LL BET SHE JUST WANTED...
TO *LIVEN* THINGS UP A BIT.
L-LIVEN THINGS UP...?
SO WHAT CAN THE CARD DO? LIKE, IN BATTLE?
WELL, IT CAN MATERIALIZE LOTS OF DIFFERENT KINDS OF FLOWERS!
TH... THAT'S IT...?
Aw, c'mon.
AT LEAST IT WAS HARMLESS THIS TIME.
HARMLESS?! WE ALMOST SUFFOCATED!
fume
fume

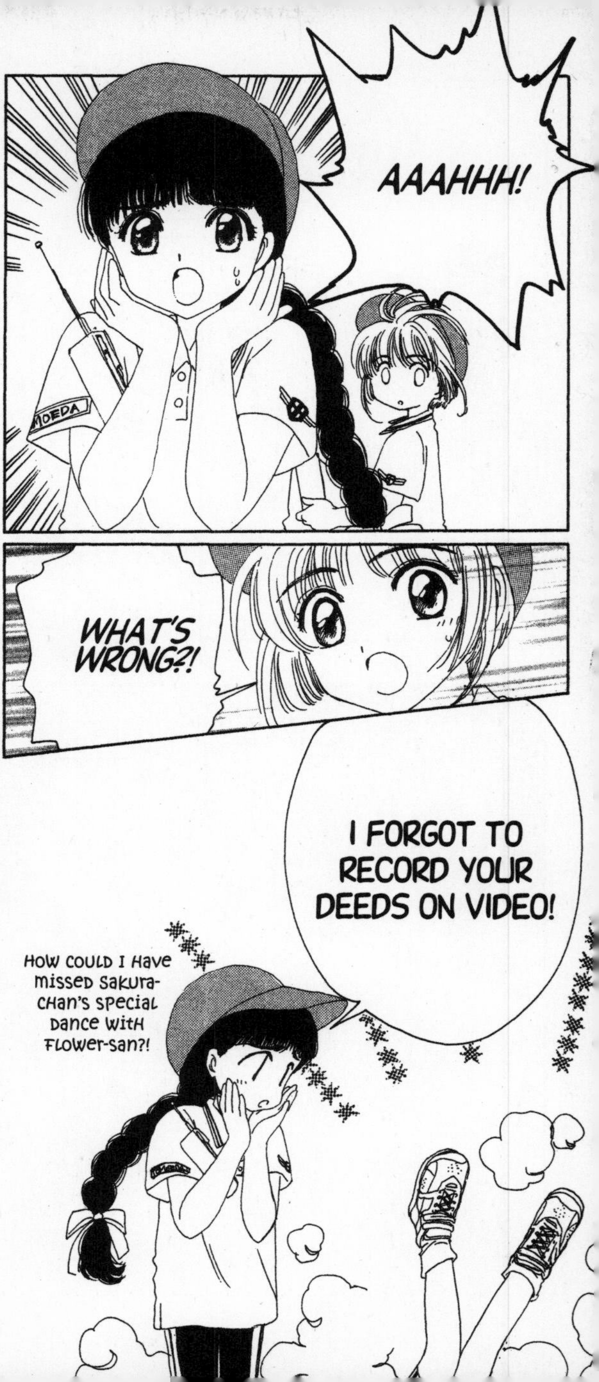
AAAHHH!
WHAT'S WRONG?!
I FORGOT TO RECORD YOUR DEEDS ON VIDEO!
HOW COULD I HAVE MISSED SAKURA-CHAN'S SPECIAL DANCE WITH FLOWER-SAN?!

6

Syaoran Li

Birthdate:
July 13
Blood Type:
O
Favorite Subject:
Physical Education, Math
Least Favorite Subject:
Grammar
Club:
None
Favorite Color:
Green
Favorite Flower:
Peony
Favorite Food:
Dim sum, chocolate
Least Favorite Food:
Konnyaku
Favorite Recipe:
None
Wish List:
Magic book written by Clow

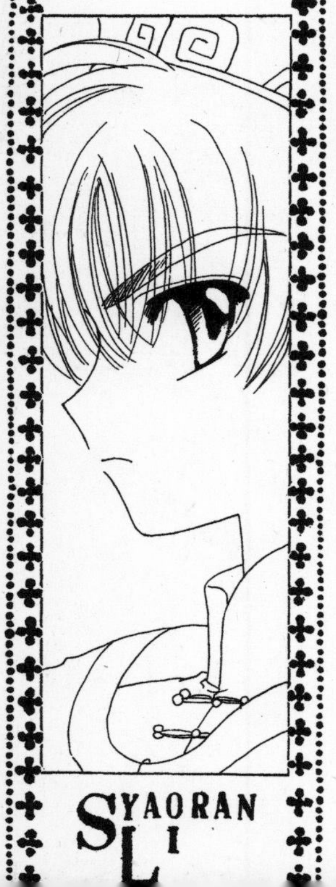

SYAORAN LI

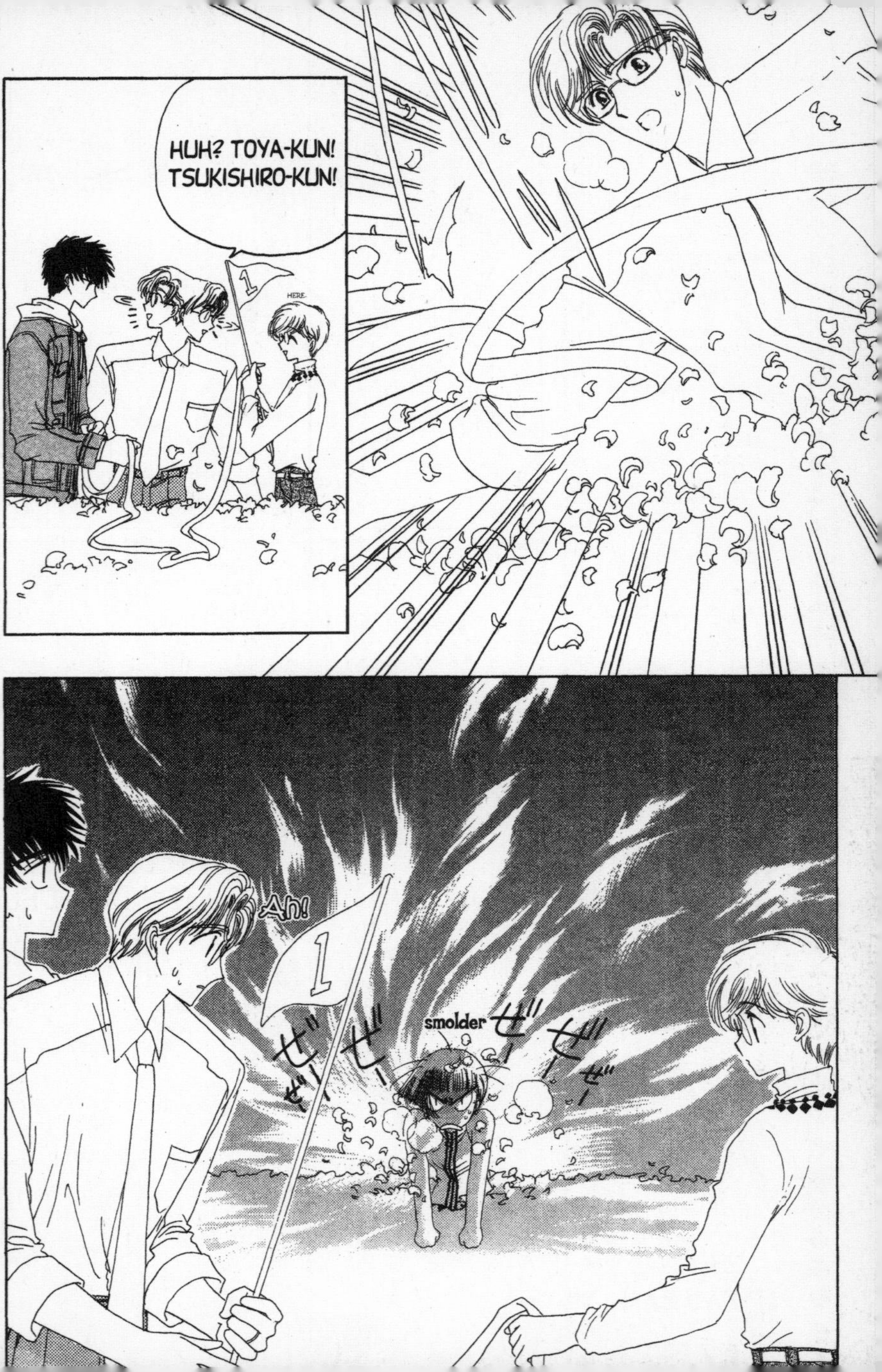
HUH? TOYA-KUN! TSUKISHIRO-KUN!
HERE.
Ah!
smolder

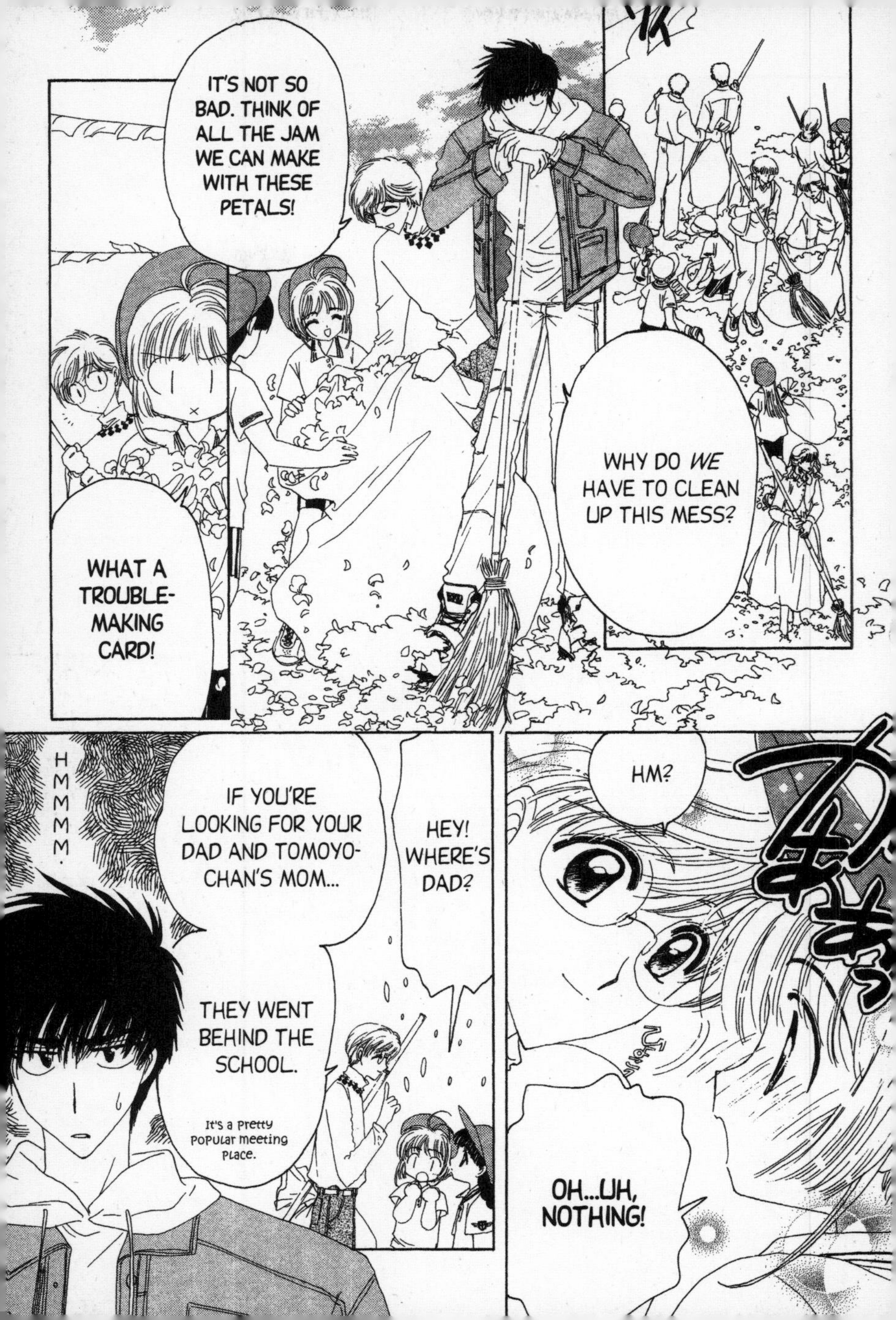
WHY DO *WE* HAVE TO CLEAN UP THIS MESS?
IT'S NOT SO BAD. THINK OF ALL THE JAM WE CAN MAKE WITH THESE PETALS!
WHAT A TROUBLE-MAKING CARD!
HM?
OH...UH, NOTHING!
HEY! WHERE'S DAD?
IF YOU'RE LOOKING FOR YOUR DAD AND TOMOYO-CHAN'S MOM...
THEY WENT BEHIND THE SCHOOL.
It's a pretty popular meeting place.
HMMMM.

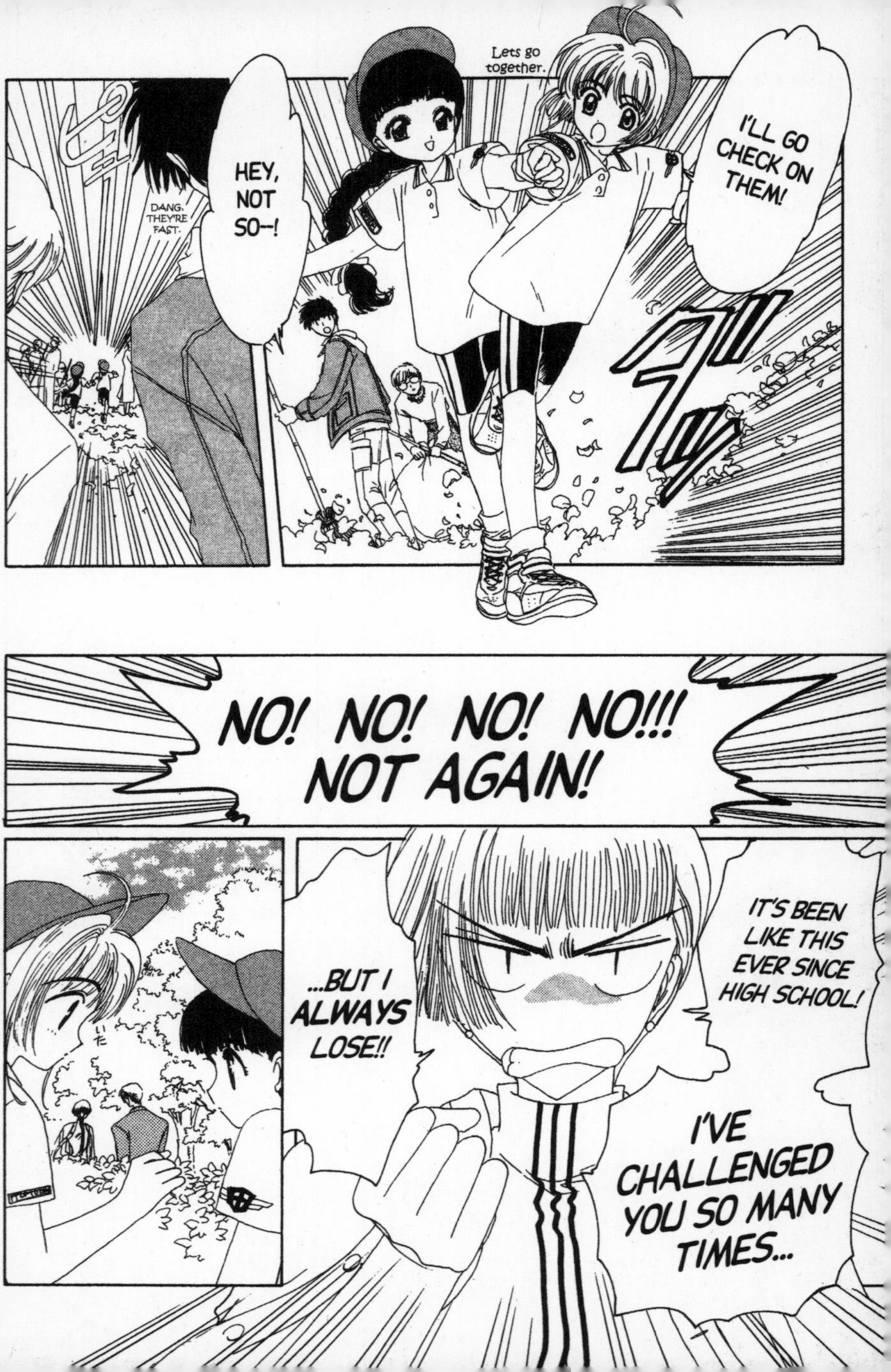
I'LL GO CHECK ON THEM!
Lets go together.
HEY, NOT SO--!
DANG, THEY'RE FAST.
NO! NO! NO! NO!!! NOT AGAIN!
IT'S BEEN LIKE THIS EVER SINCE HIGH SCHOOL!
I'VE CHALLENGED YOU SO MANY TIMES...
...BUT I ALWAYS LOSE!!

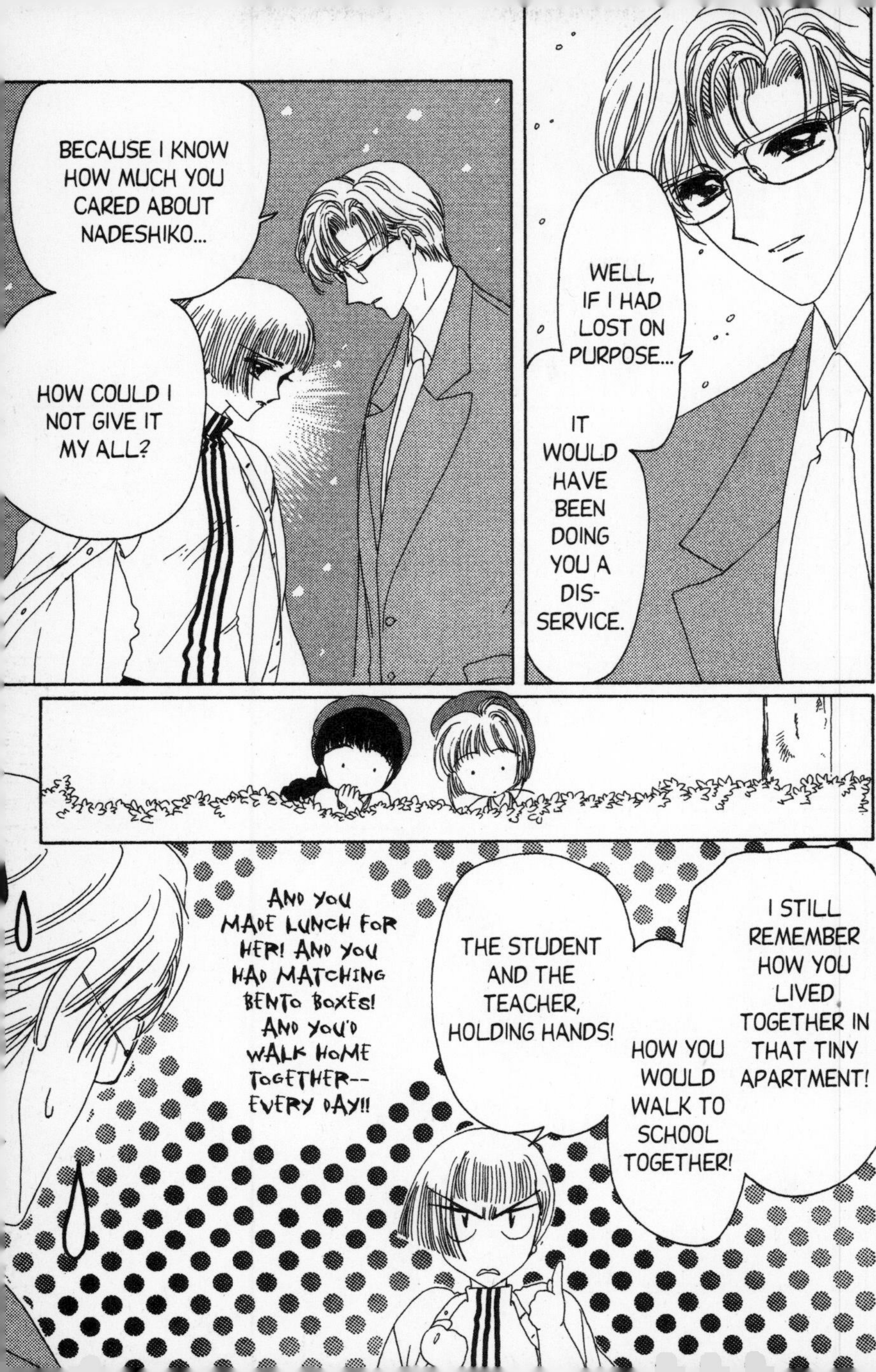
WELL, IF I HAD LOST ON PURPOSE...
IT WOULD HAVE BEEN DOING YOU A DIS-SERVICE.
BECAUSE I KNOW HOW MUCH YOU CARED ABOUT NADESHIKO...
HOW COULD I NOT GIVE IT MY ALL?
I STILL REMEMBER HOW YOU LIVED TOGETHER IN THAT TINY APARTMENT!
HOW YOU WOULD WALK TO SCHOOL TOGETHER!
THE STUDENT AND THE TEACHER, HOLDING HANDS!
AND YOU MADE LUNCH FOR HER! AND YOU HAD MATCHING BENTO BOXES! AND YOU'D WALK HOME TOGETHER--EVERY DAY!!

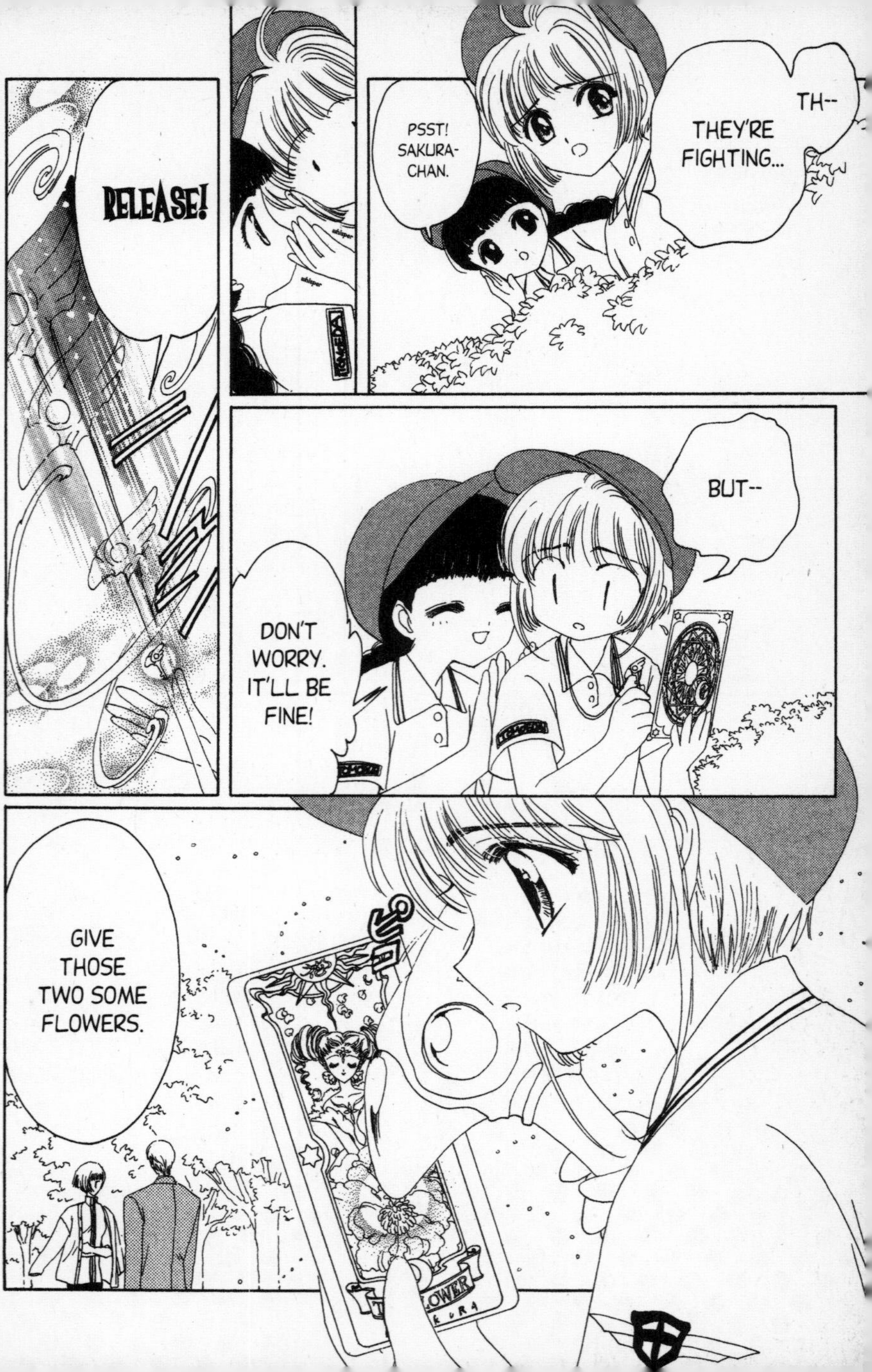
TH-- THEY'RE FIGHTING...
PSST! SAKURA-CHAN.
BUT--
DON'T WORRY. IT'LL BE FINE!
RELEASE!
GIVE THOSE TWO SOME FLOWERS.

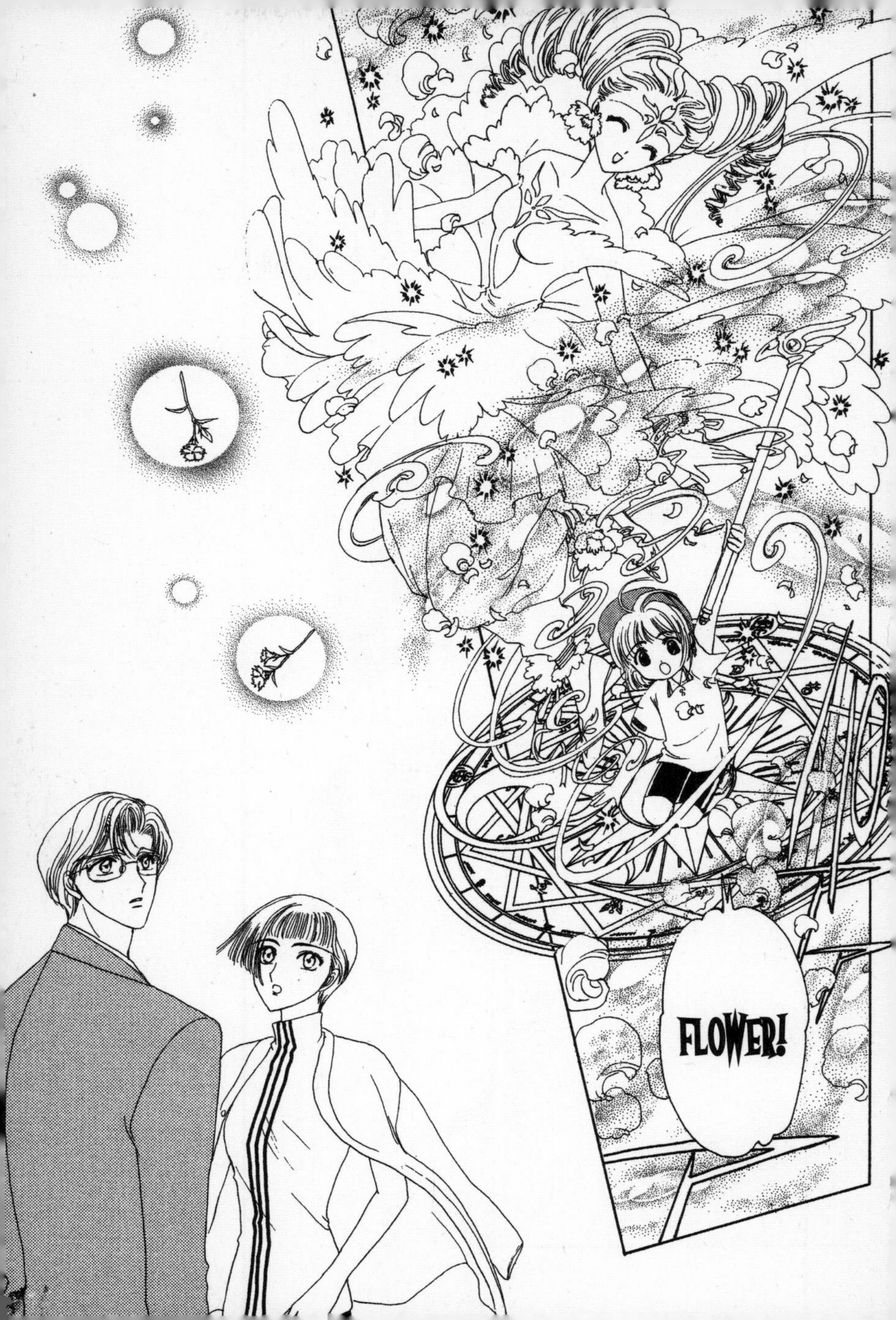
FLOWER!

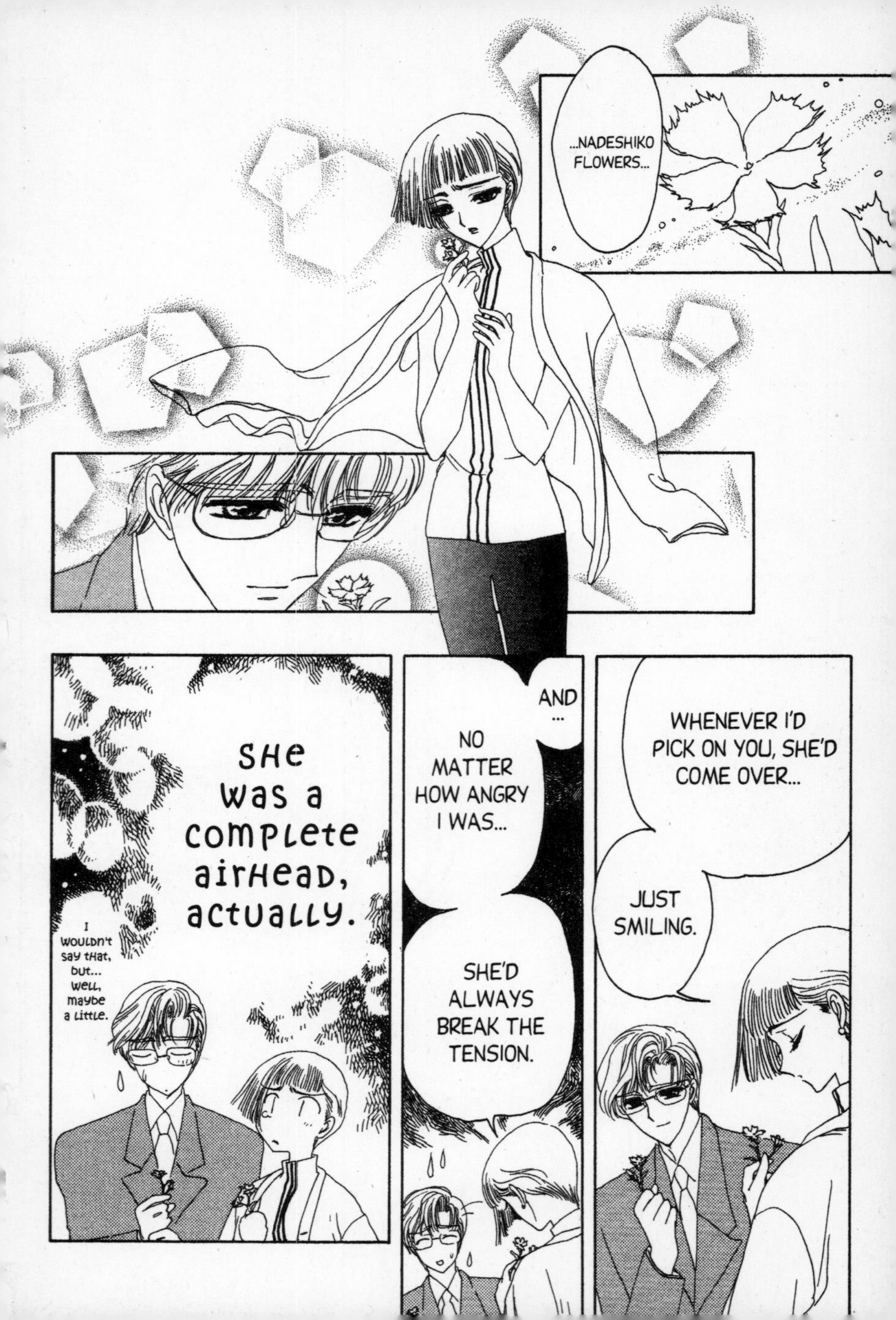
...NADESHIKO FLOWERS...
WHENEVER I'D PICK ON YOU, SHE'D COME OVER...
JUST SMILING.
AND...
NO MATTER HOW ANGRY I WAS...
SHE'D ALWAYS BREAK THE TENSION.
SHE WAS A COMPLETE AIRHEAD, ACTUALLY.
I WOULDN'T SAY THAT, BUT... WELL, MAYBE A LITTLE.

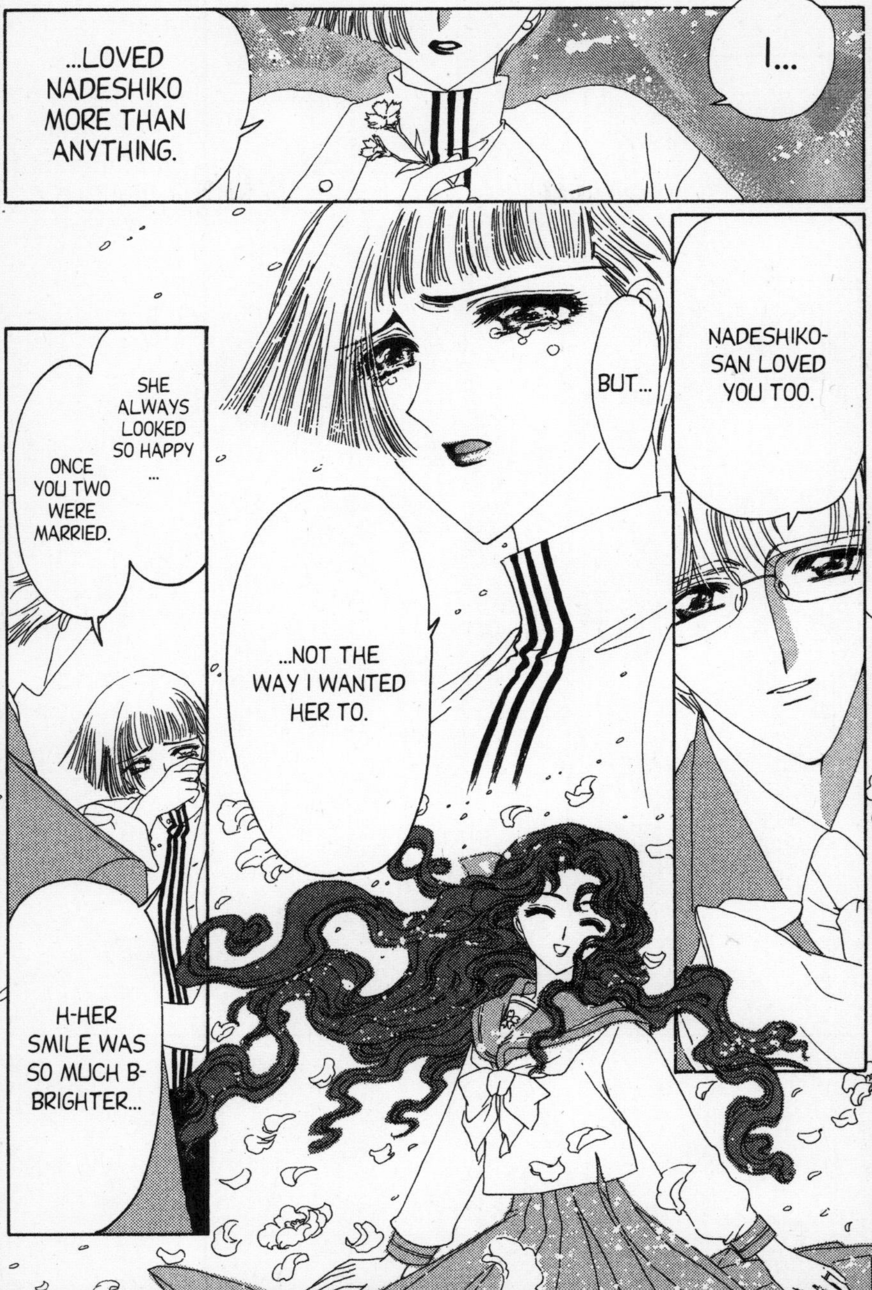
I...
...LOVED NADESHIKO MORE THAN ANYTHING.
NADESHIKO-SAN LOVED YOU TOO.
BUT...
...NOT THE WAY I WANTED HER TO.
SHE ALWAYS LOOKED SO HAPPY ...
ONCE YOU TWO WERE MARRIED.
H-HER SMILE WAS SO MUCH B-BRIGHTER...

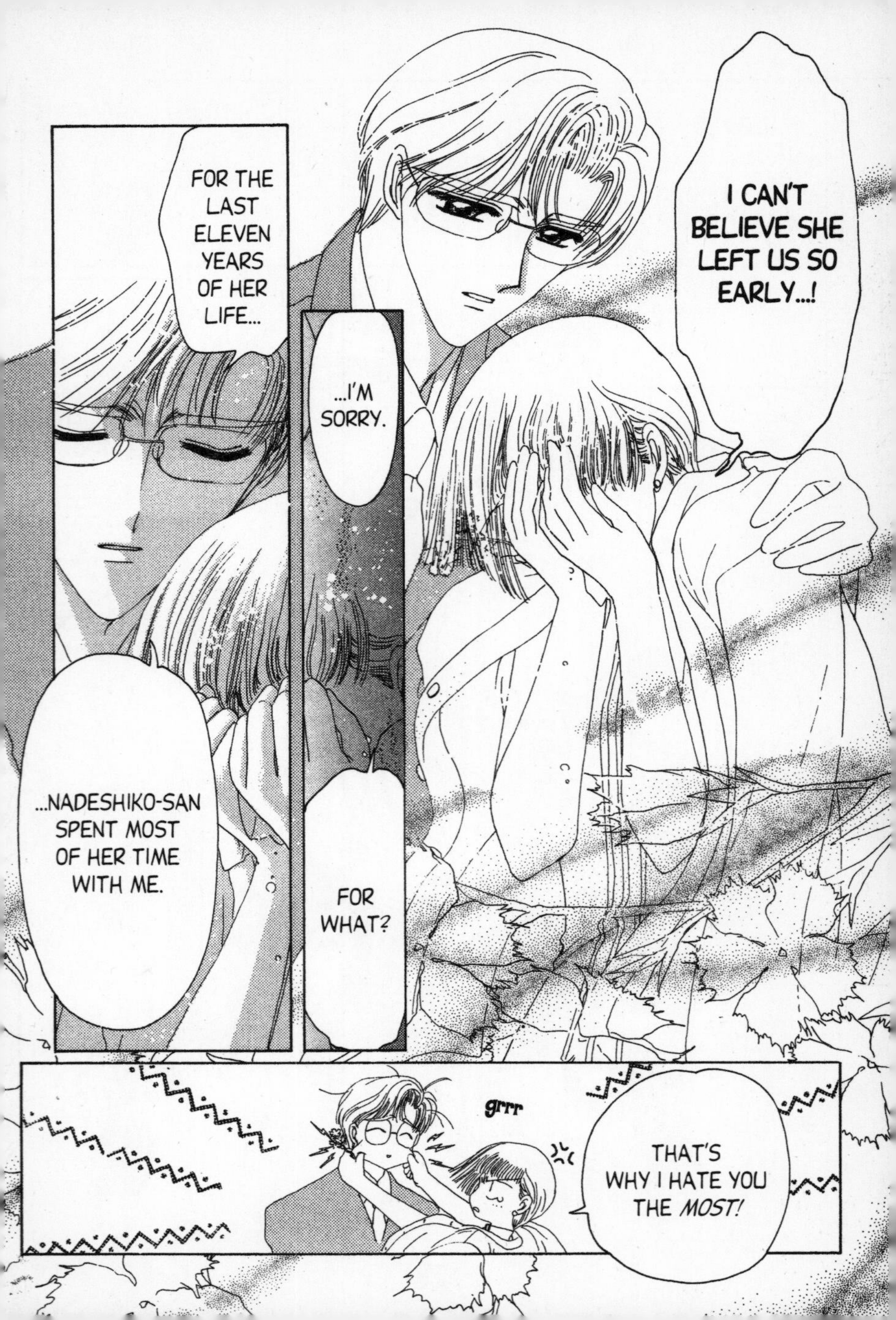
I CAN'T BELIEVE SHE LEFT US SO EARLY...!
...I'M SORRY.
FOR WHAT?
FOR THE LAST ELEVEN YEARS OF HER LIFE...
...NADESHIKO-SAN SPENT MOST OF HER TIME WITH ME.
THAT'S WHY I HATE YOU THE *MOST!*
grrr

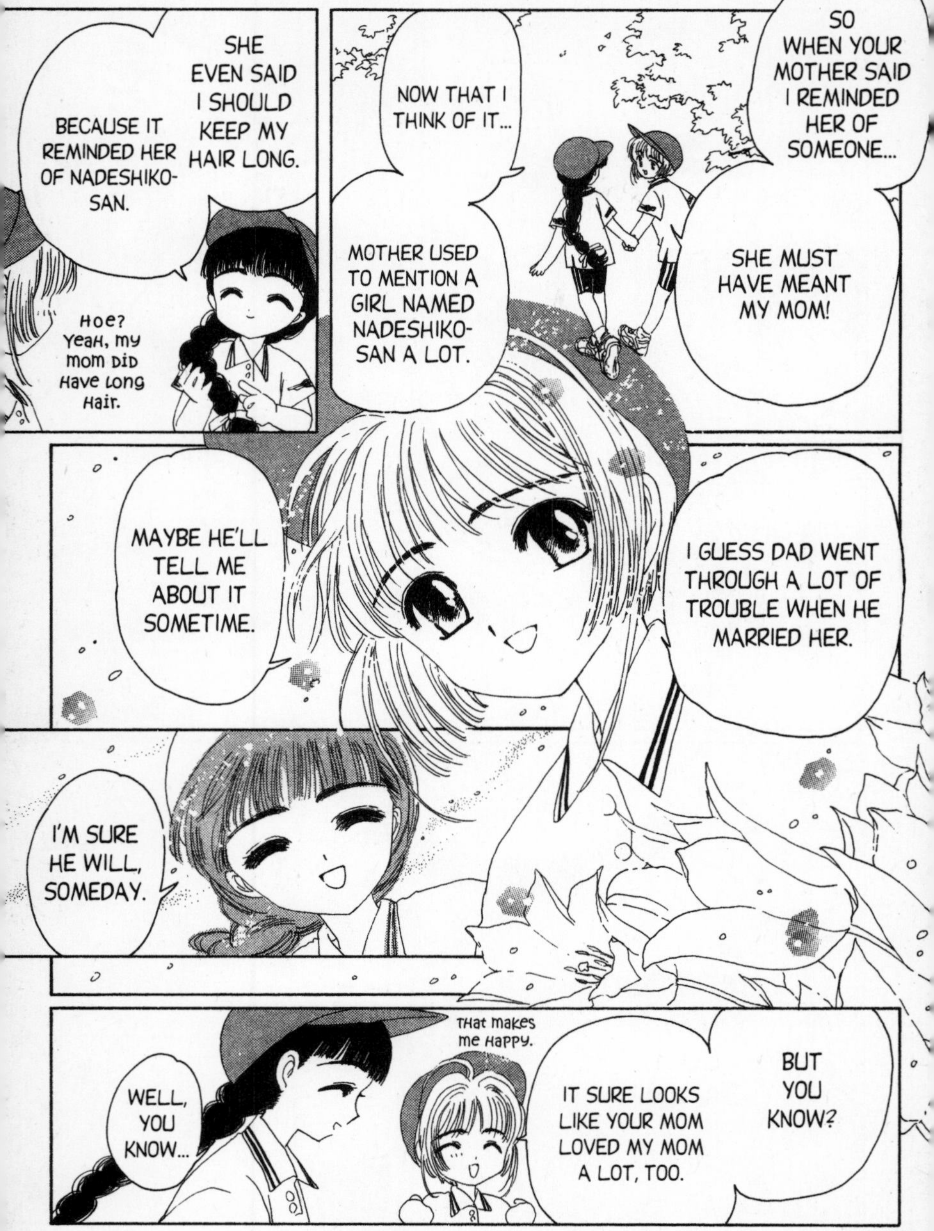
SO WHEN YOUR MOTHER SAID I REMINDED HER OF SOMEONE...
SHE MUST HAVE MEANT MY MOM!
NOW THAT I THINK OF IT...
MOTHER USED TO MENTION A GIRL NAMED NADESHIKO-SAN A LOT.
SHE EVEN SAID I SHOULD KEEP MY HAIR LONG.
BECAUSE IT REMINDED HER OF NADESHIKO-SAN.
Hoe? Yeah, my mom did have long hair.
I GUESS DAD WENT THROUGH A LOT OF TROUBLE WHEN HE MARRIED HER.
MAYBE HE'LL TELL ME ABOUT IT SOMETIME.
I'M SURE HE WILL, SOMEDAY.
BUT YOU KNOW?
IT SURE LOOKS LIKE YOUR MOM LOVED MY MOM A LOT, TOO.
That makes me happy.
WELL, YOU KNOW...

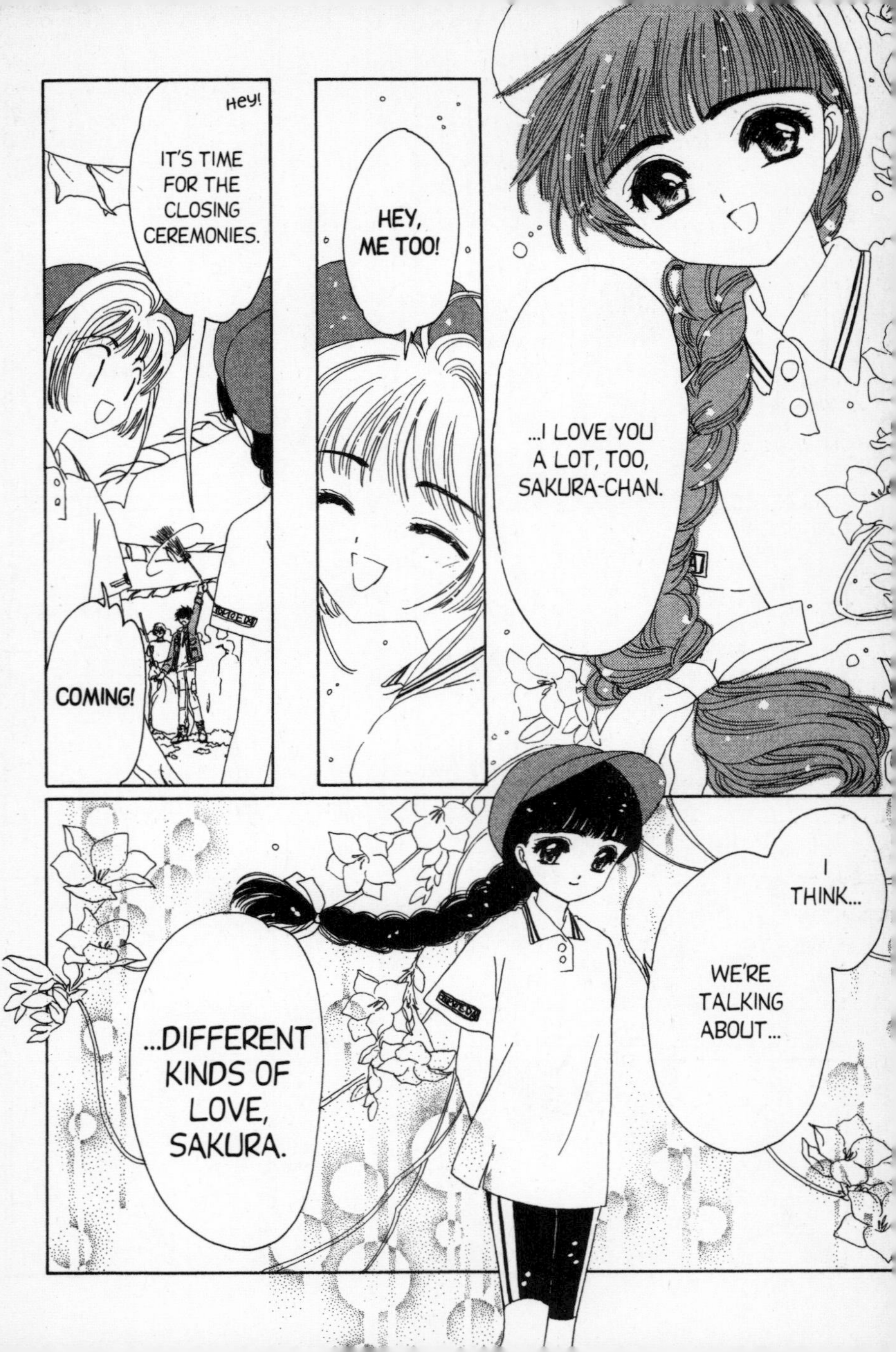
...I LOVE YOU A LOT, TOO, SAKURA-CHAN.
HEY, ME TOO!
Hey!
IT'S TIME FOR THE CLOSING CEREMONIES.
COMING!
I THINK...
WE'RE TALKING ABOUT...
...DIFFERENT KINDS OF LOVE, SAKURA.

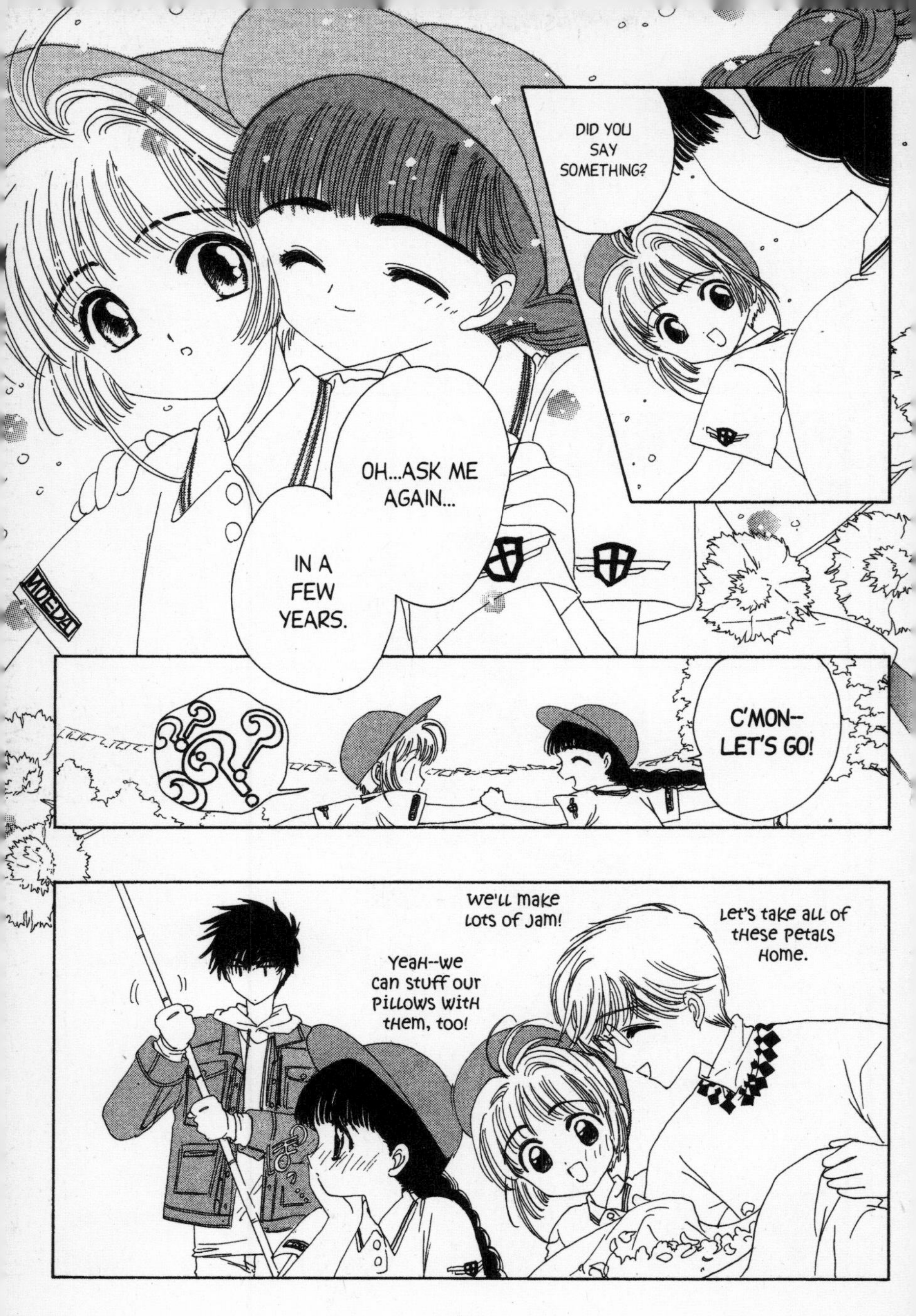
DID YOU SAY SOMETHING?
OH...ASK ME AGAIN...
IN A FEW YEARS.
C'MON--LET'S GO!
Let's take all of these petals home.
We'll make lots of jam!
Yeah--we can stuff our pillows with them, too!

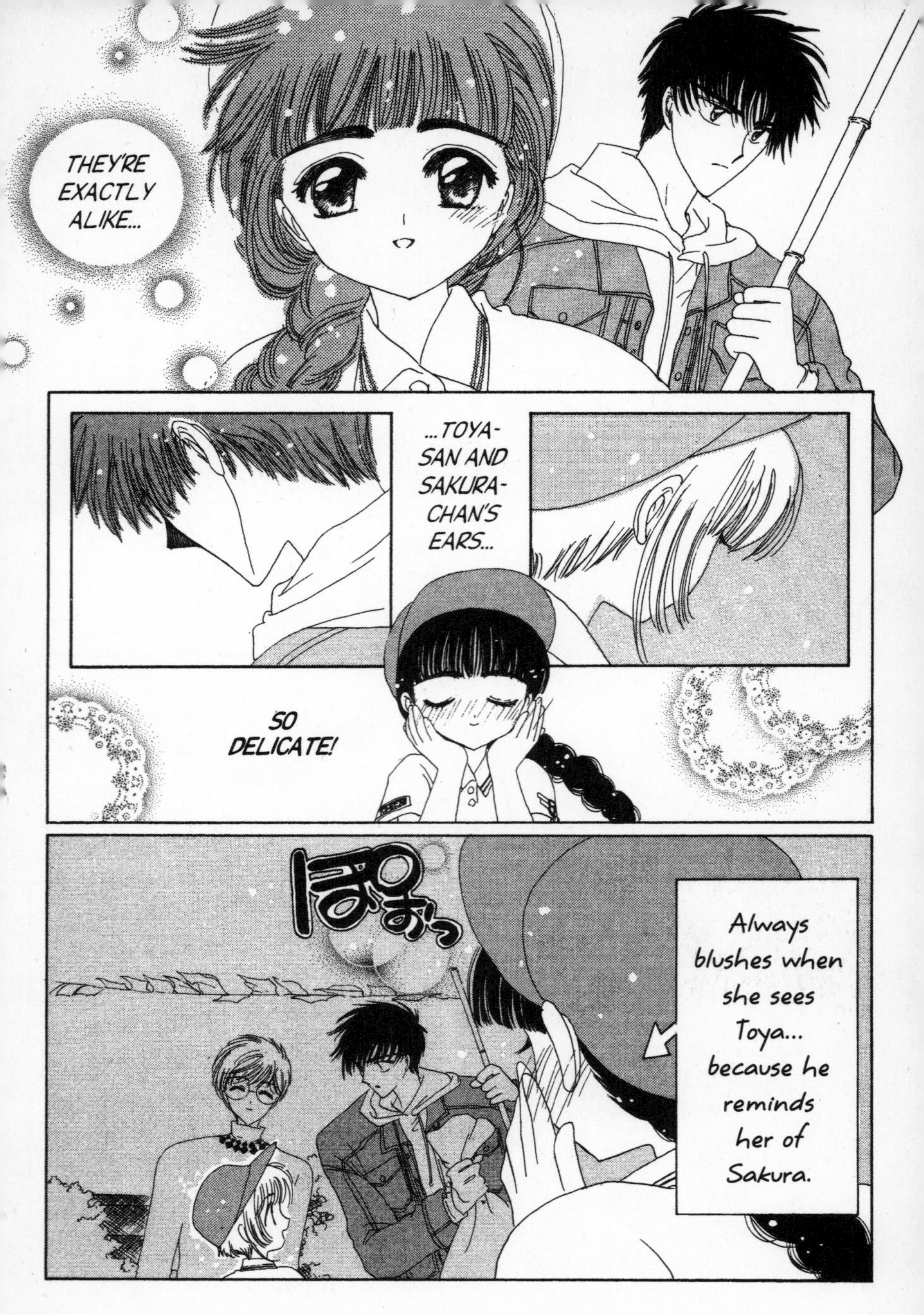
THEY'RE EXACTLY ALIKE...
...TOYA-SAN AND SAKURA-CHAN'S EARS...
SO DELICATE!
Always blushes when she sees Toya... because he reminds her of Sakura.

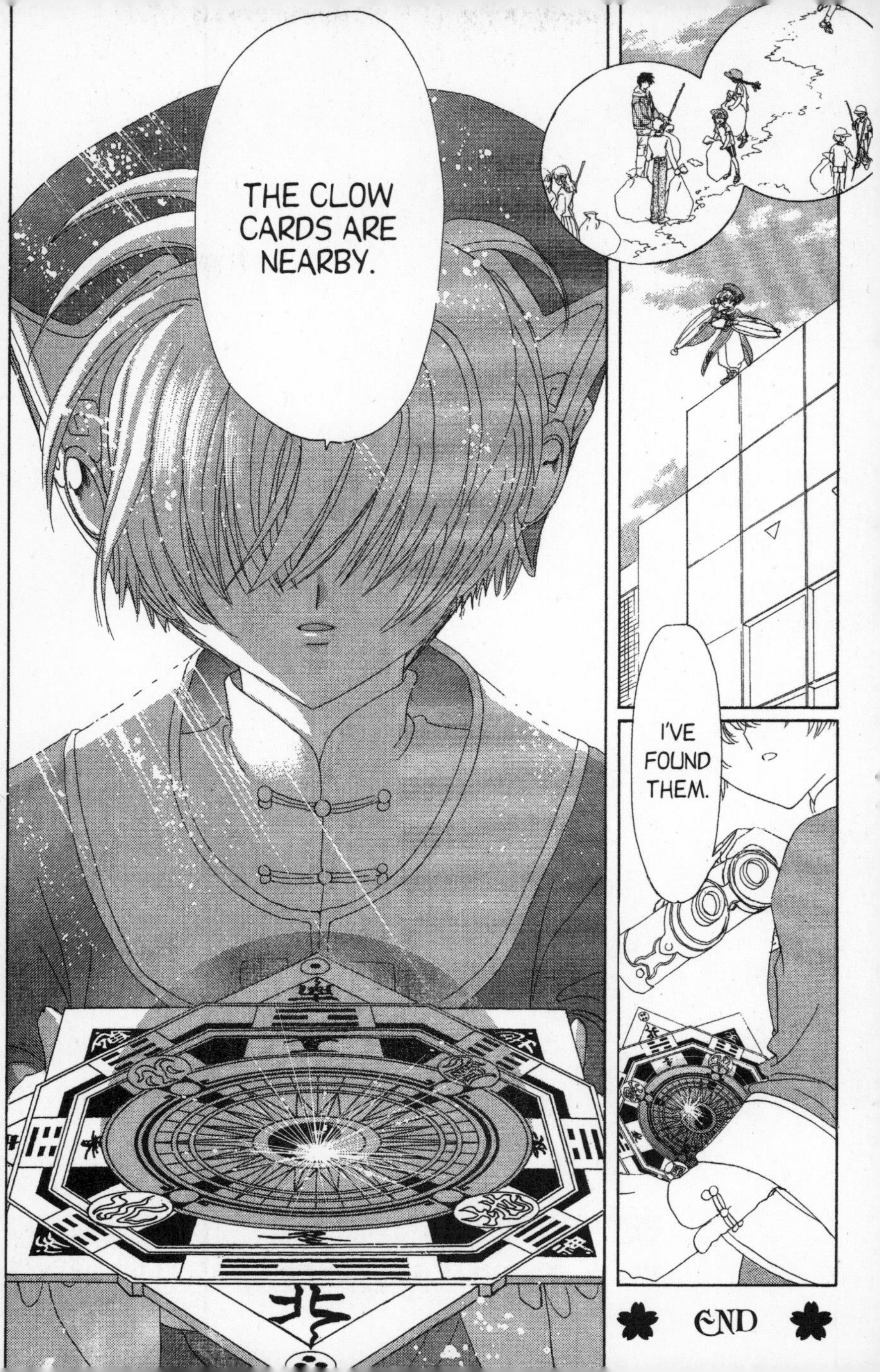
I'VE FOUND THEM.
THE CLOW CARDS ARE NEARBY.
END

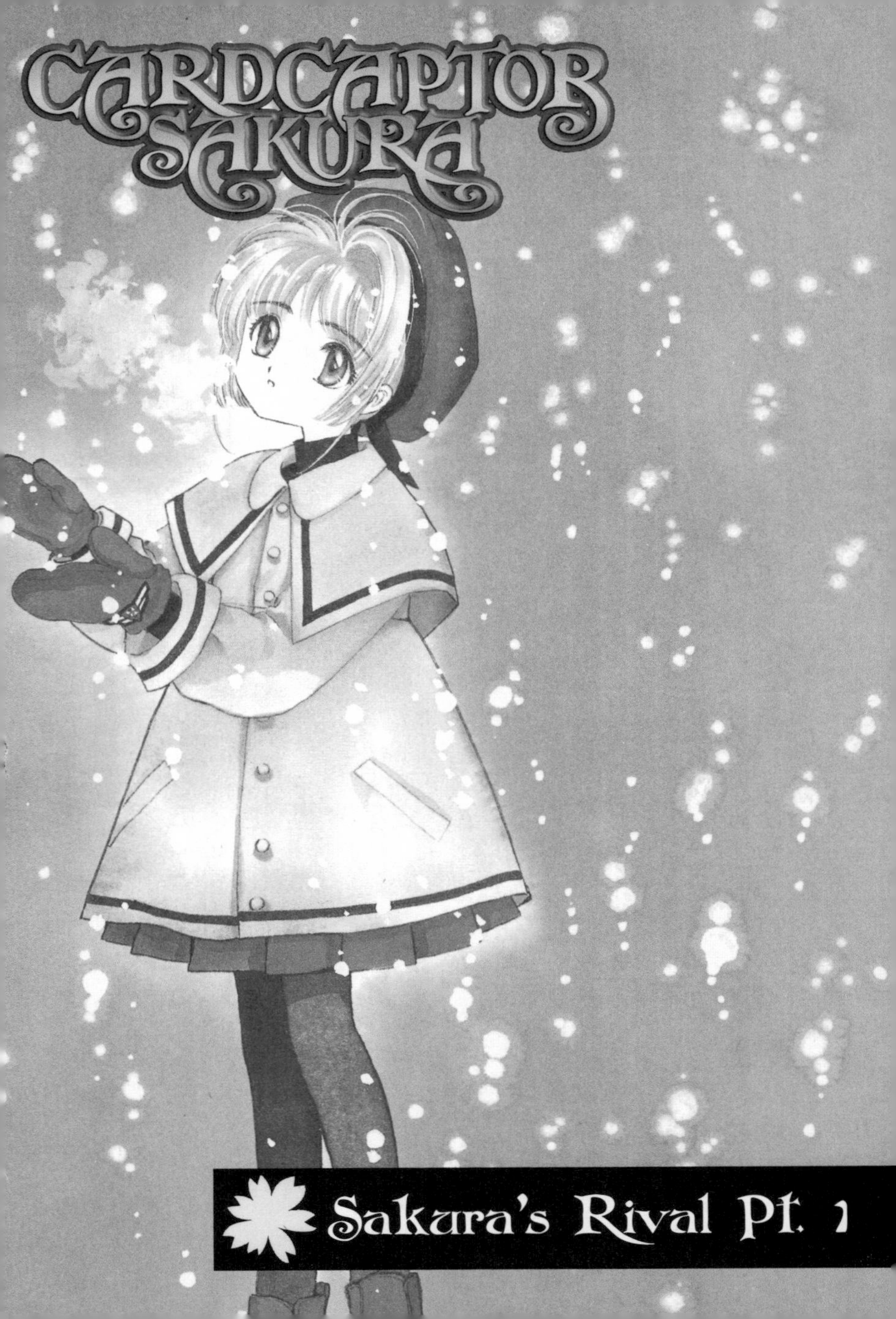
CARDCAPTOR SAKURA
Sakura's Rival Pt. 1

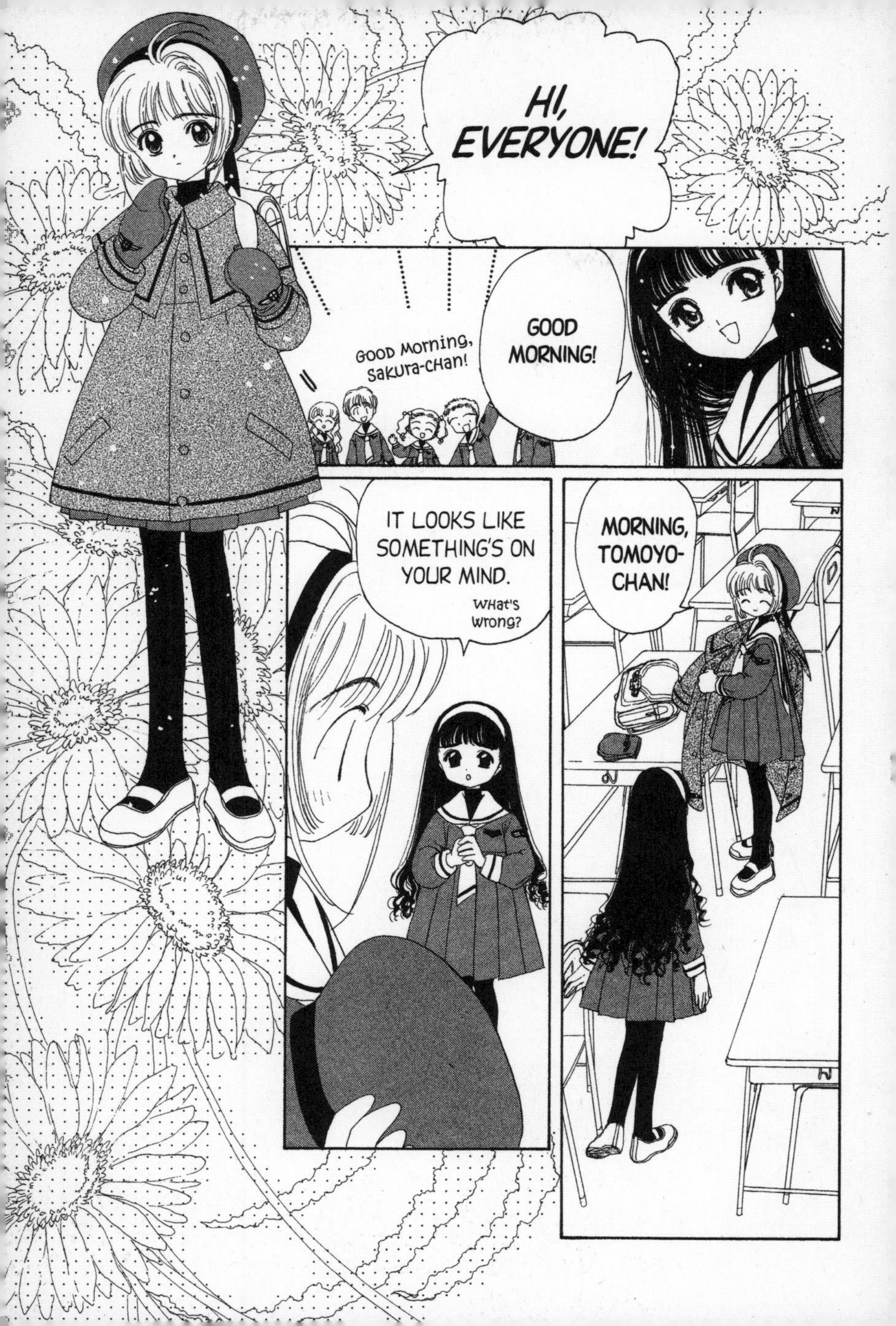
HI, EVERYONE!
GOOD MORNING!
Good Morning, Sakura-chan!
MORNING, TOMOYO-CHAN!
IT LOOKS LIKE SOMETHING'S ON YOUR MIND.
What's wrong?

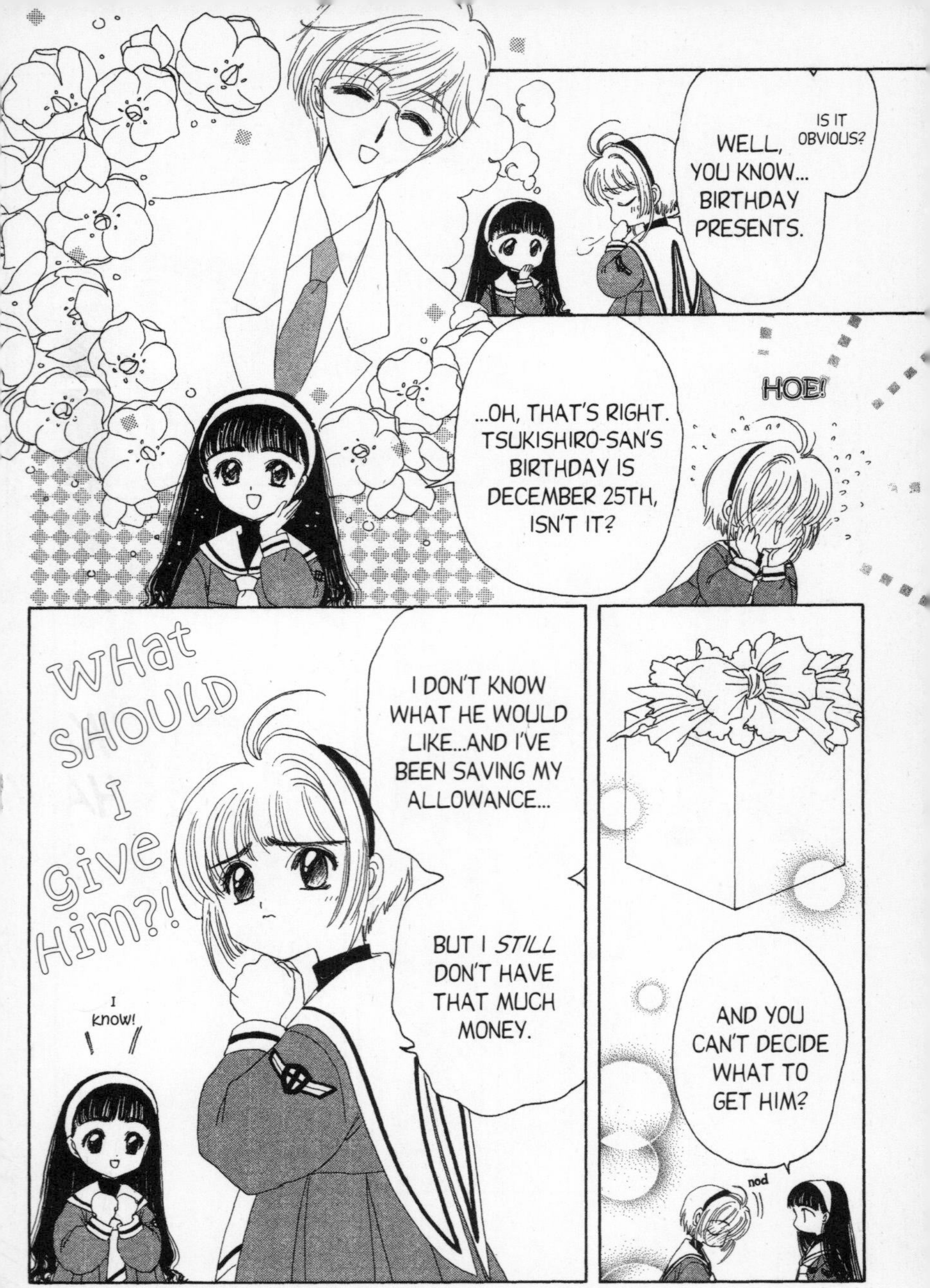
IS IT OBVIOUS?
WELL, YOU KNOW... BIRTHDAY PRESENTS.
HOE!
...OH, THAT'S RIGHT. TSUKISHIRO-SAN'S BIRTHDAY IS DECEMBER 25TH, ISN'T IT?
AND YOU CAN'T DECIDE WHAT TO GET HIM?
nod
I DON'T KNOW WHAT HE WOULD LIKE...AND I'VE BEEN SAVING MY ALLOWANCE...
BUT I *STILL* DON'T HAVE THAT MUCH MONEY.
WHAT SHOULD I GIVE HIM?!
I know!

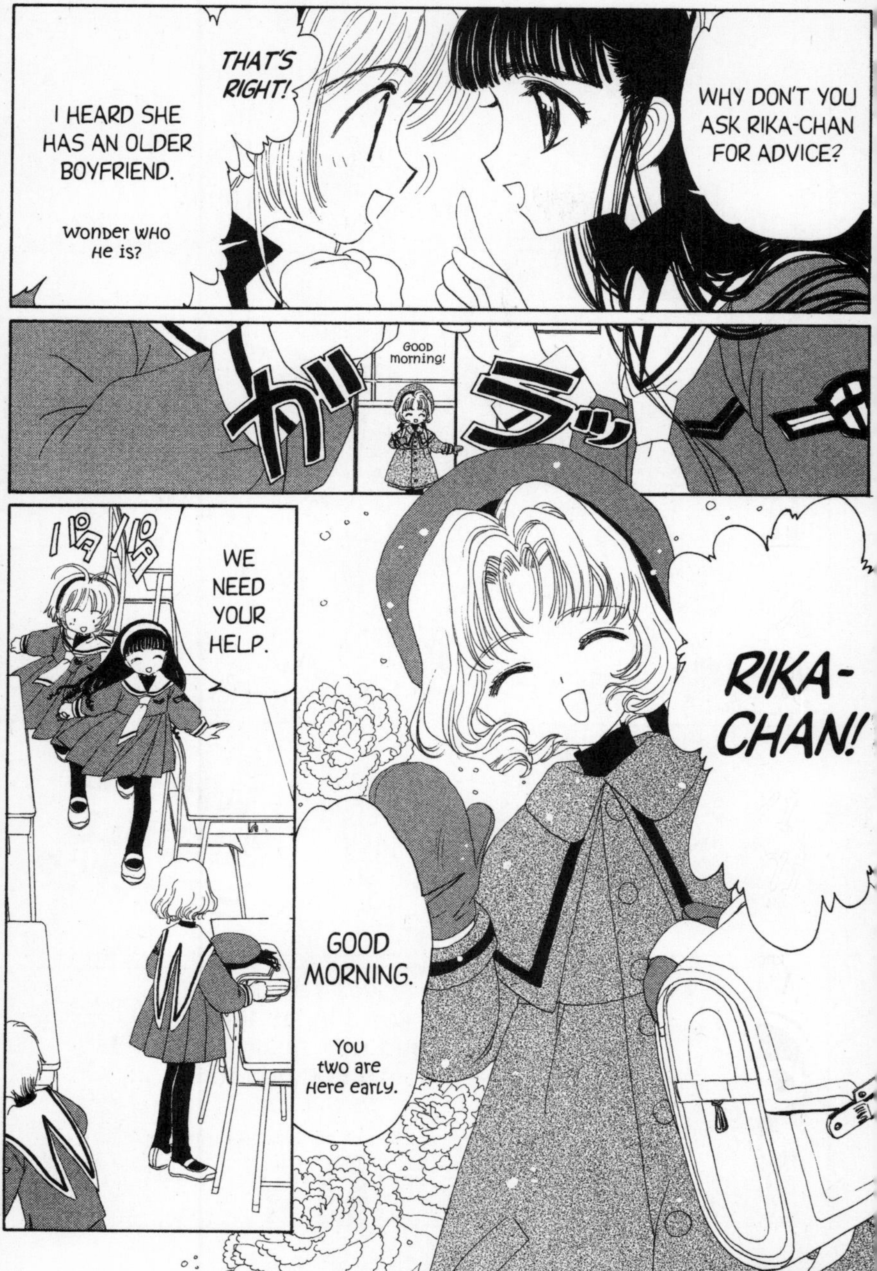

WHY DON'T YOU ASK RIKA-CHAN FOR ADVICE?
THAT'S RIGHT!
I HEARD SHE HAS AN OLDER BOYFRIEND.
Wonder who he is?
ガラッ
Good morning!
RIKA-CHAN!
GOOD MORNING.
You two are here early.
パタパタ
WE NEED YOUR HELP.

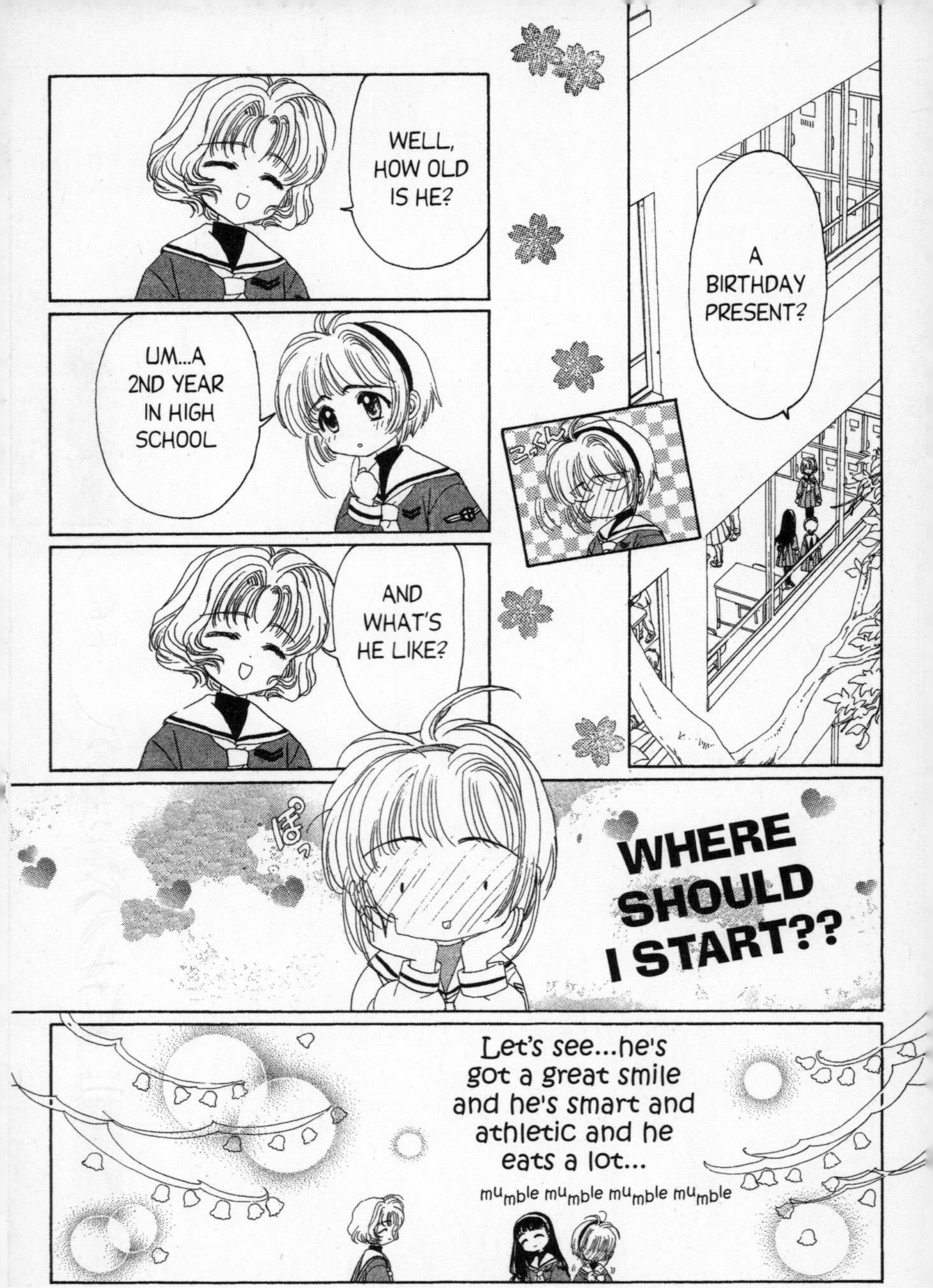
A BIRTHDAY PRESENT?
WELL, HOW OLD IS HE?
UM...A 2ND YEAR IN HIGH SCHOOL
AND WHAT'S HE LIKE?
WHERE SHOULD I START??
Let's see...he's got a great smile and he's smart and athletic and he eats a lot...
mumble mumble mumble mumble

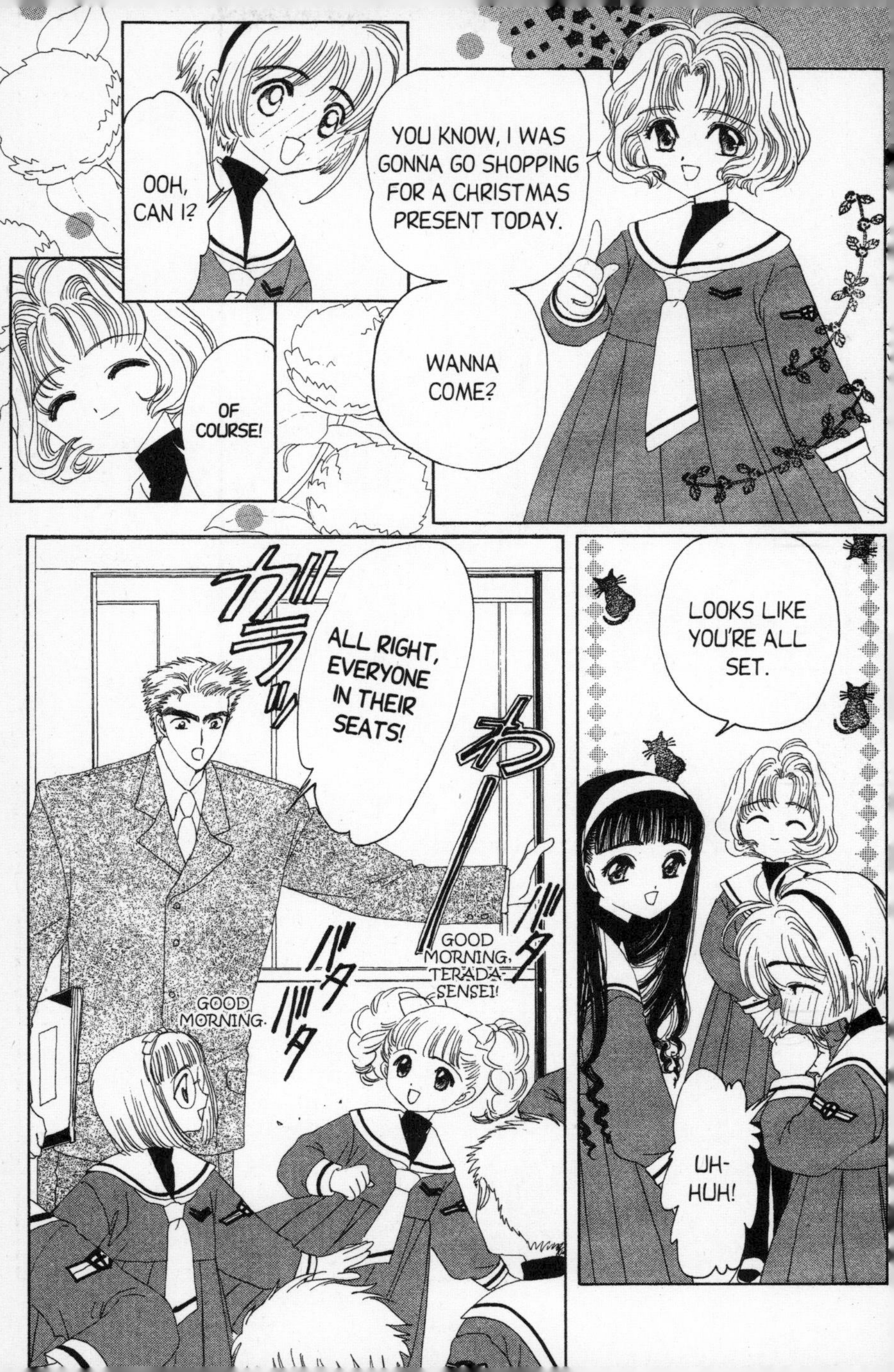
YOU KNOW, I WAS GONNA GO SHOPPING FOR A CHRISTMAS PRESENT TODAY.
WANNA COME?
OOH, CAN I?
OF COURSE!
LOOKS LIKE YOU'RE ALL SET.
UH-HUH!
ガラッ
ALL RIGHT, EVERYONE IN THEIR SEATS!
わー
バタ
GOOD MORNING, TERADA-SENSEI!
バタバタ
GOOD MORNING.

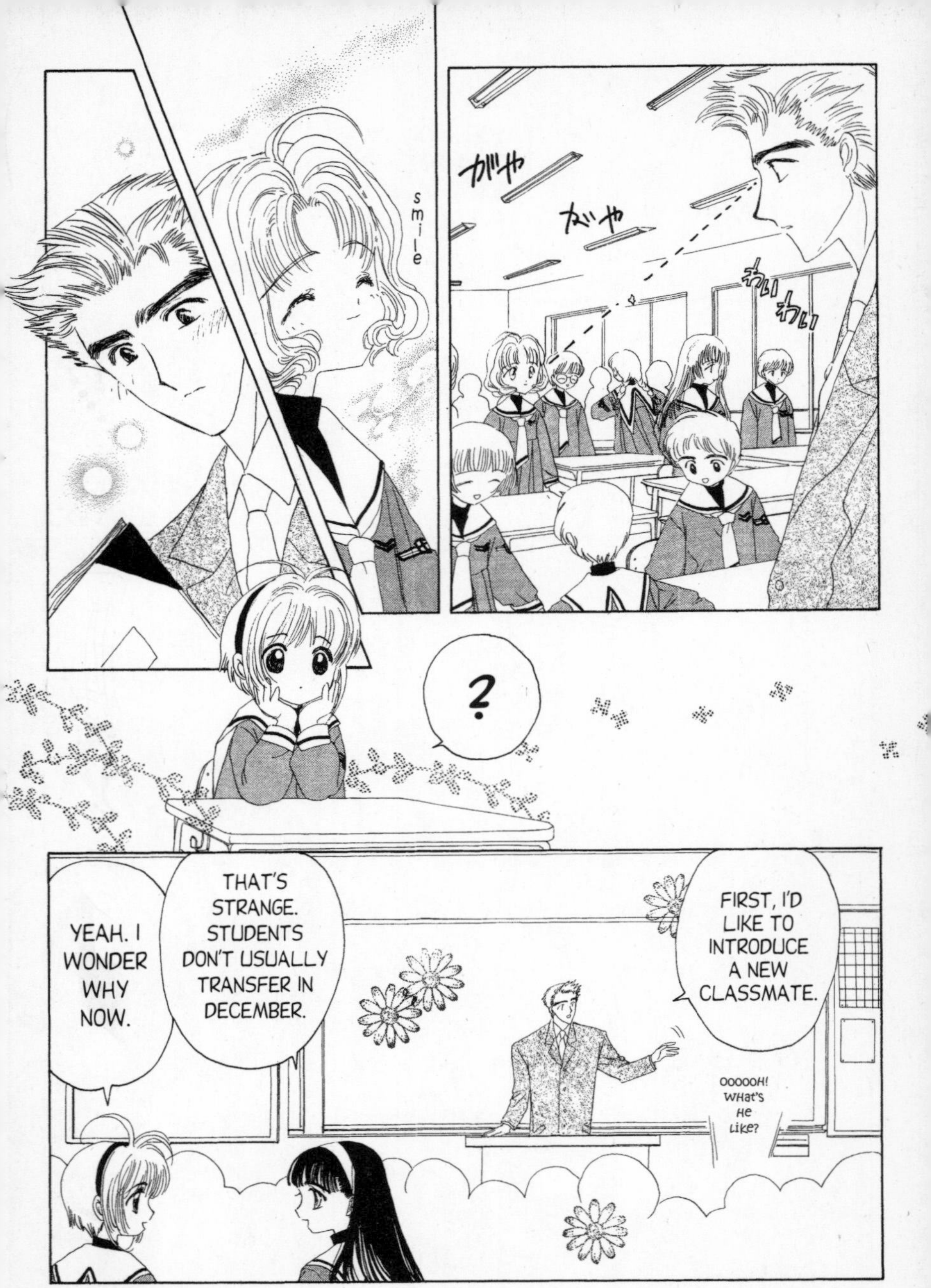

がや
がや
わい わい
smile
?
FIRST, I'D LIKE TO INTRODUCE A NEW CLASSMATE.
OOOOOH! WHAT'S HE LIKE?
THAT'S STRANGE. STUDENTS DON'T USUALLY TRANSFER IN DECEMBER.
YEAH. I WONDER WHY NOW.

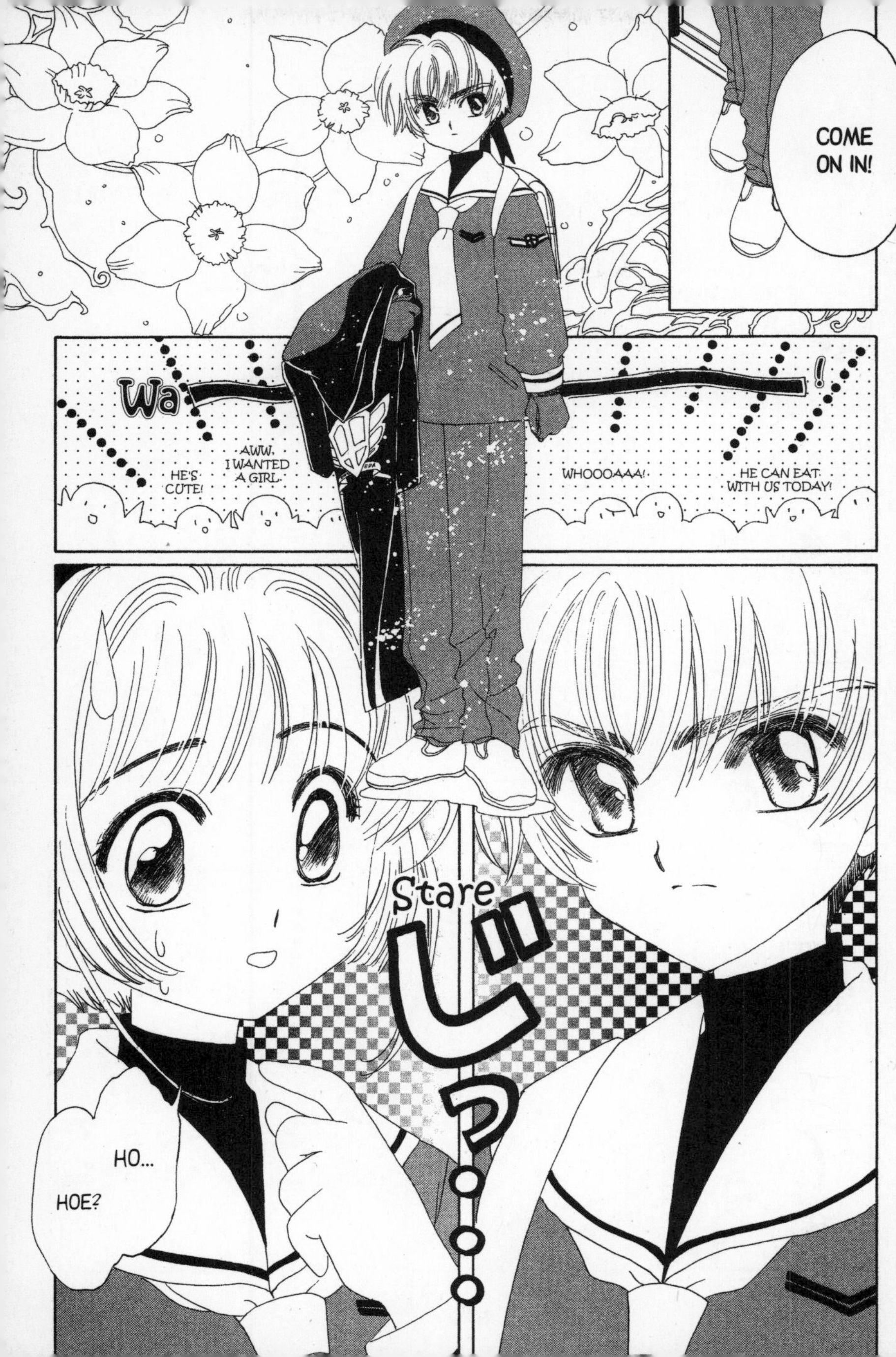
COME ON IN!
Wa———!
HE CAN EAT WITH US TODAY!
WHOOOAAA!
AWW, I WANTED A GIRL.
HE'S CUTE!
Stare
じーっ
HO...
HOE?

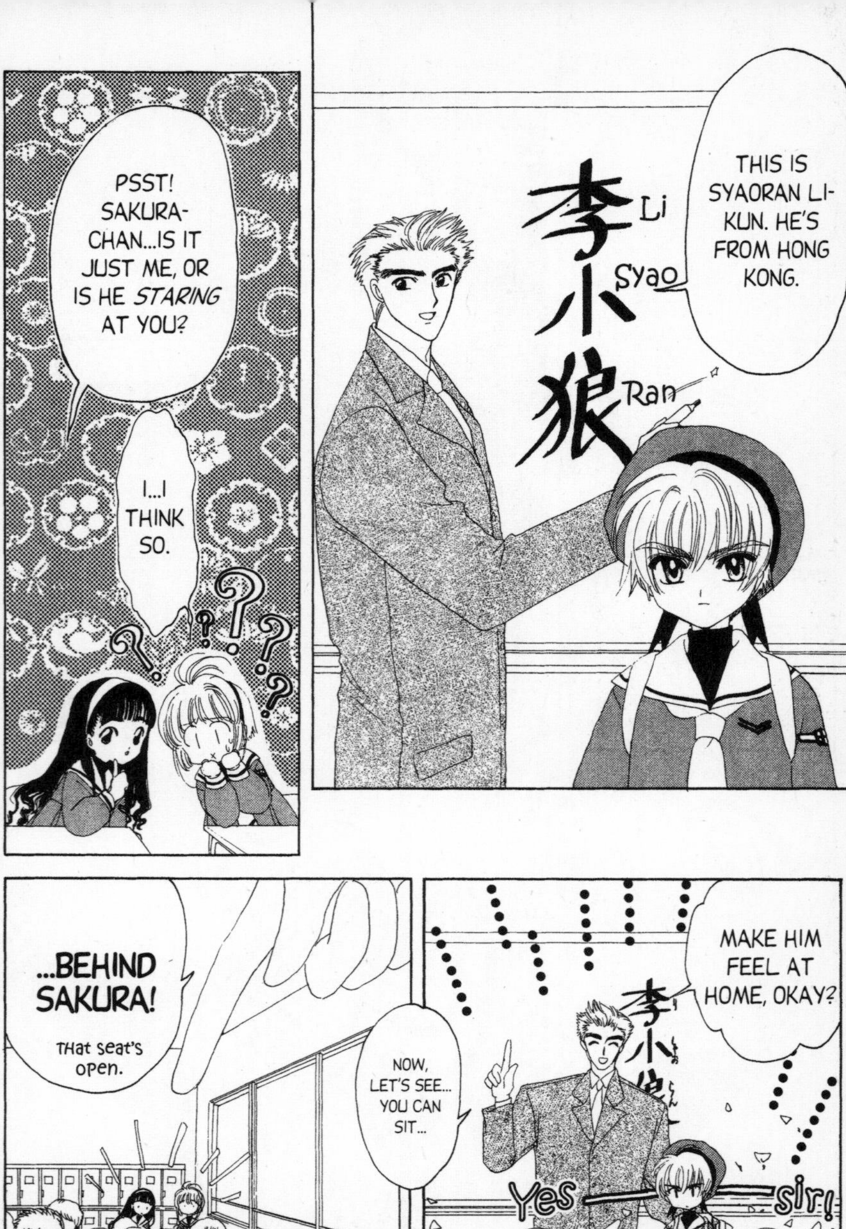
THIS IS SYAORAN LI-KUN. HE'S FROM HONG KONG.
李小狼
Li Syao Ran
PSST! SAKURA-CHAN...IS IT JUST ME, OR IS HE *STARING* AT YOU?
I...I THINK SO.
MAKE HIM FEEL AT HOME, OKAY?
Yes sir!
NOW, LET'S SEE... YOU CAN SIT...
...BEHIND SAKURA!
That seat's open.

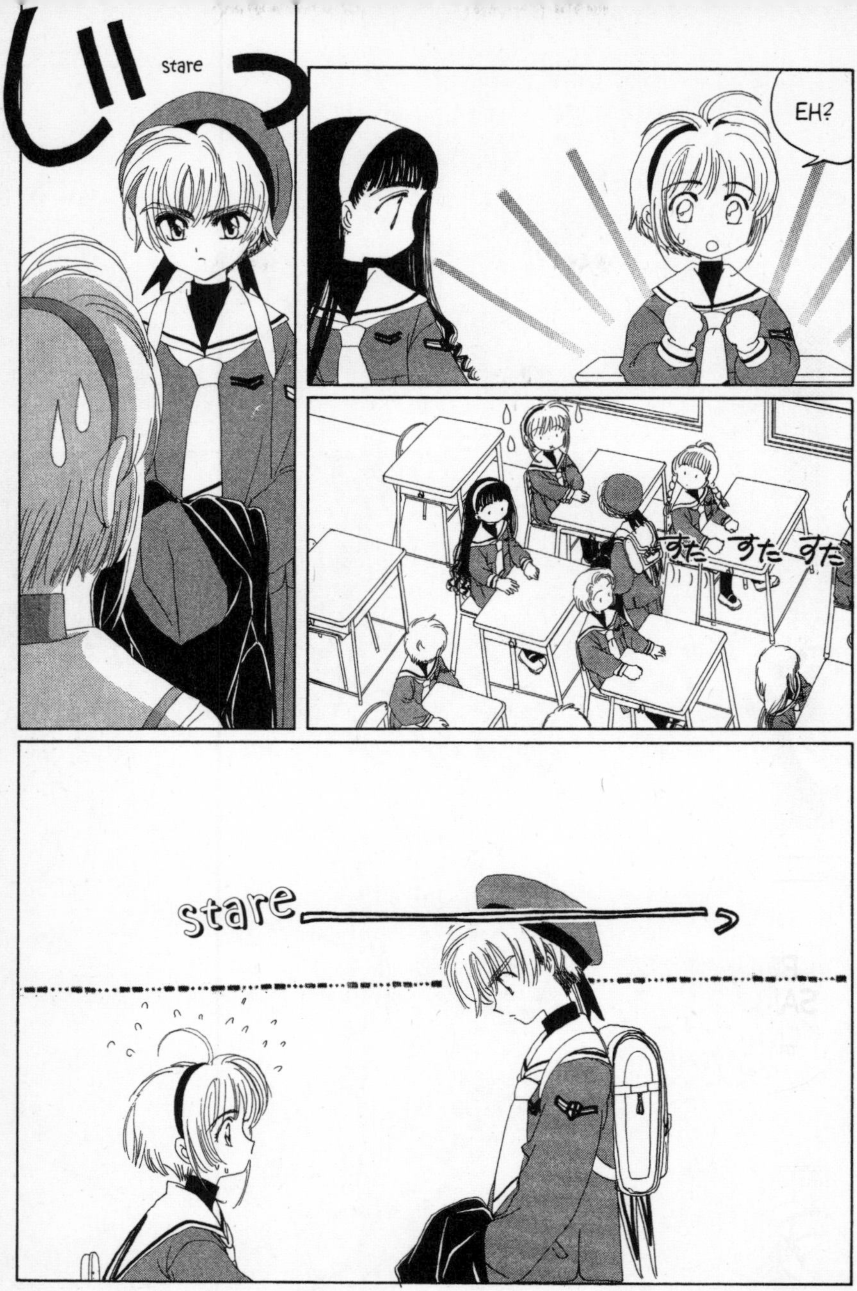
EH?
すた すた すた
じーっ
stare
stare

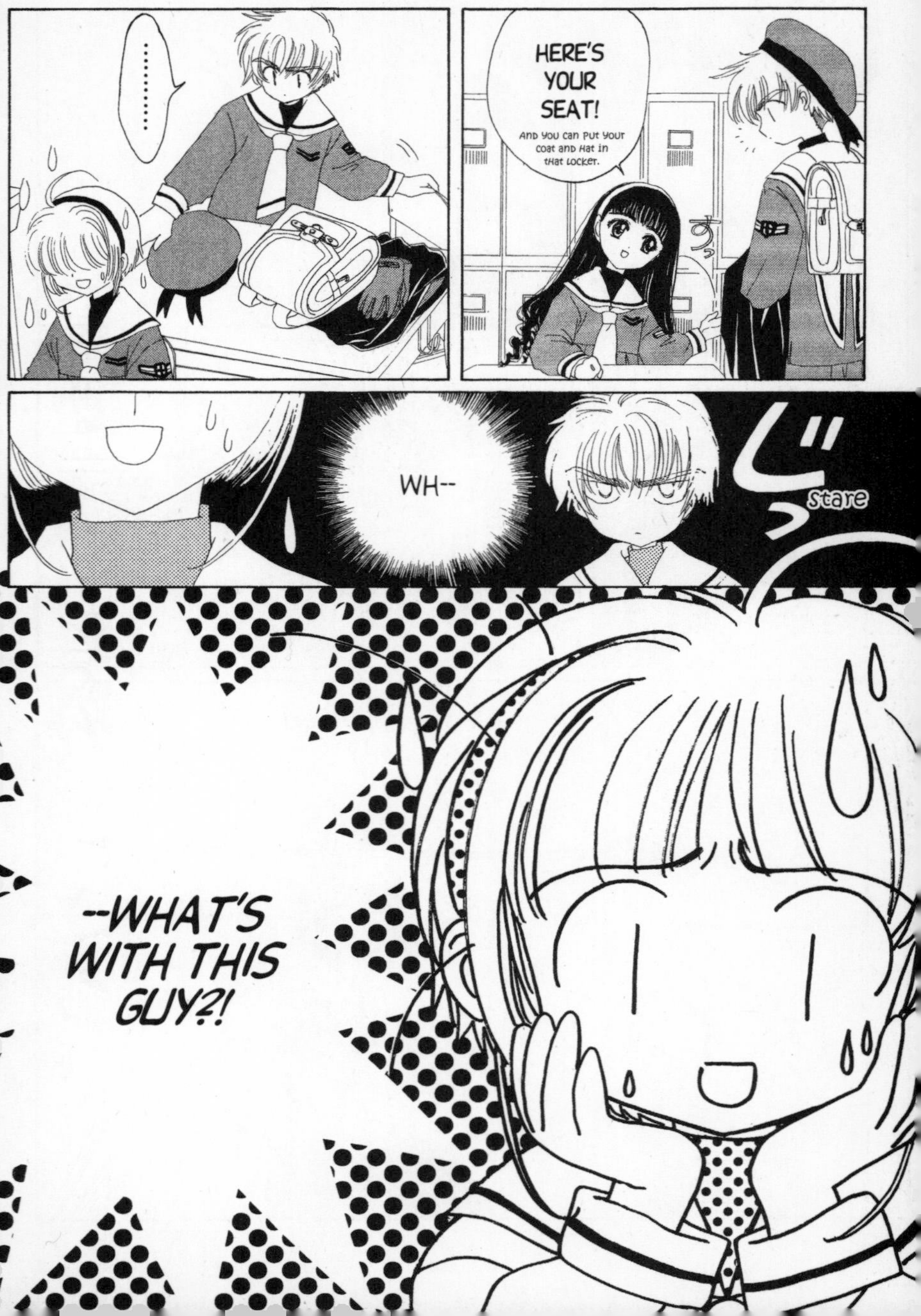
HERE'S YOUR SEAT!
And you can put your coat and hat in that locker.
すっ
......
じっ stare
WH--
--WHAT'S WITH THIS GUY?!

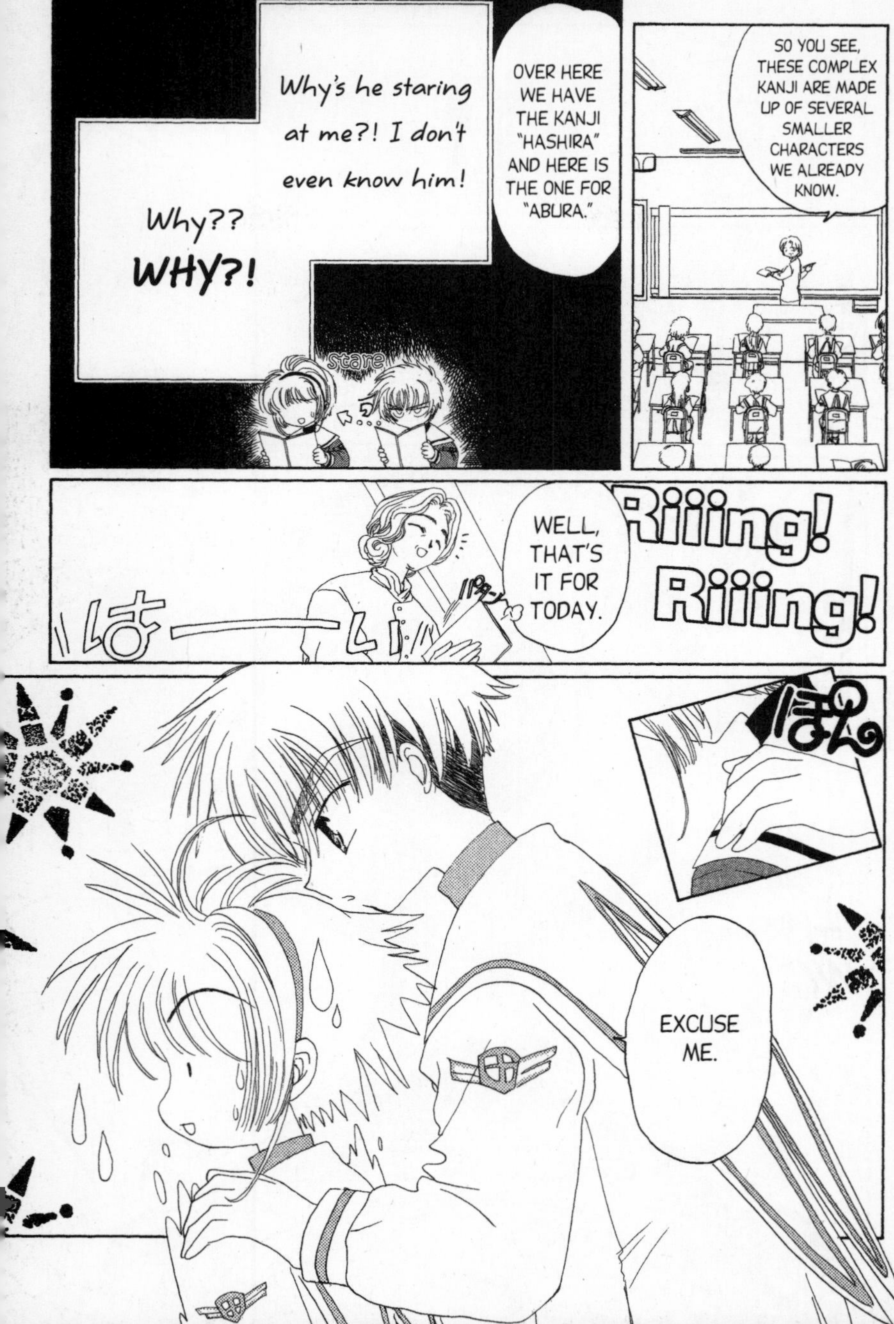
SO YOU SEE, THESE COMPLEX KANJI ARE MADE UP OF SEVERAL SMALLER CHARACTERS WE ALREADY KNOW.
OVER HERE WE HAVE THE KANJI "HASHIRA" AND HERE IS THE ONE FOR "ABURA."
Why's he staring at me?! I don't even know him!
Why?? WHY?!
stare
Riiing! Riiing!
WELL, THAT'S IT FOR TODAY.
はーーい
ぽん
EXCUSE ME.

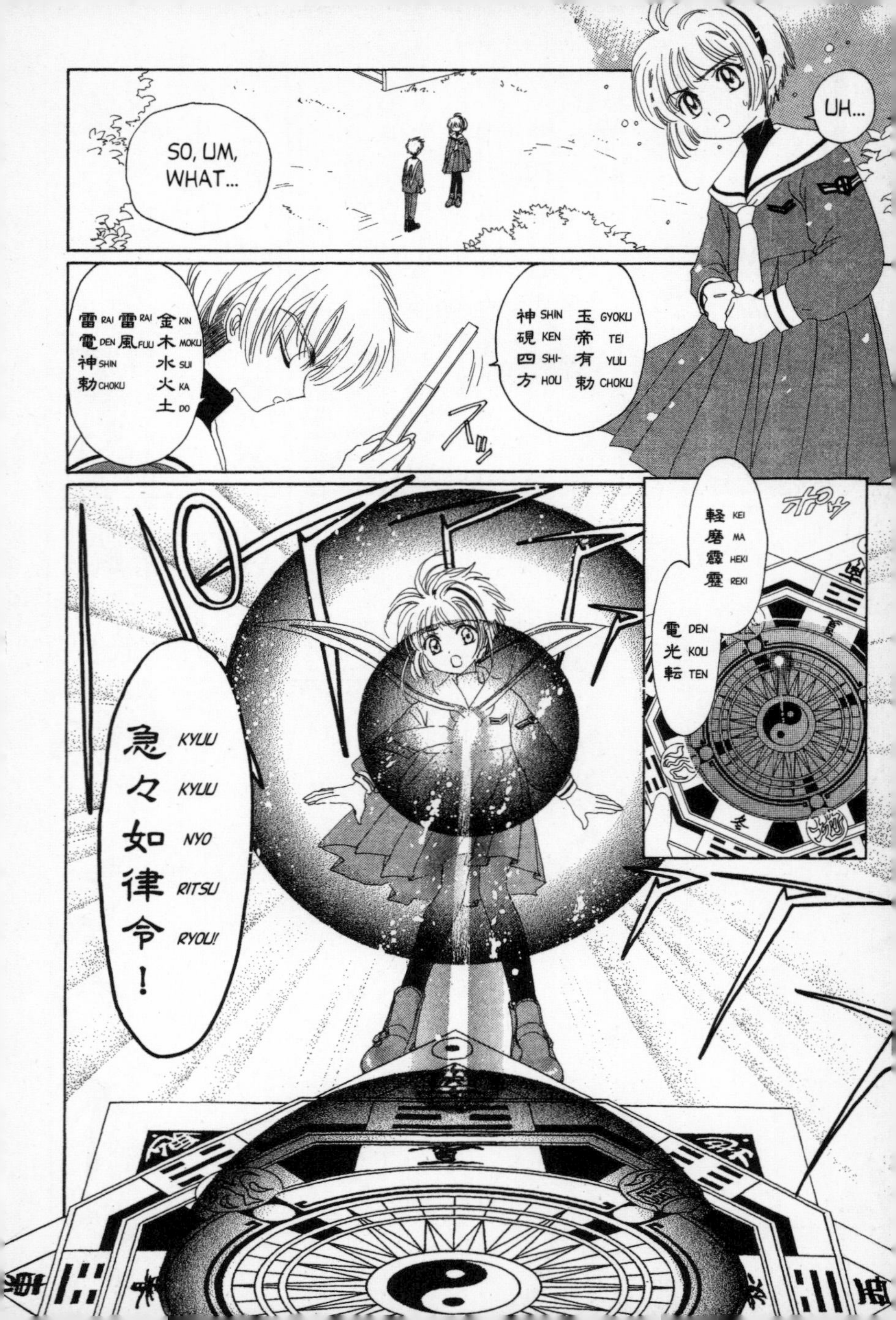
UH...
SO, UM, WHAT...
玉帝有勅 GYOKU TEI YUU CHOKU
神硯四方 SHIN KEN SHI-HOU
金木水火土 KIN MOKU SUI KA DO
雷風 RAI FUU
雷電神勅 RAI DEN SHIN CHOKU
軽磨霹靂 KEI MA HEKI REKI
電光転 DEN KOU TEN
急々如律令! KYUU KYUU NYO RITSU RYOU!

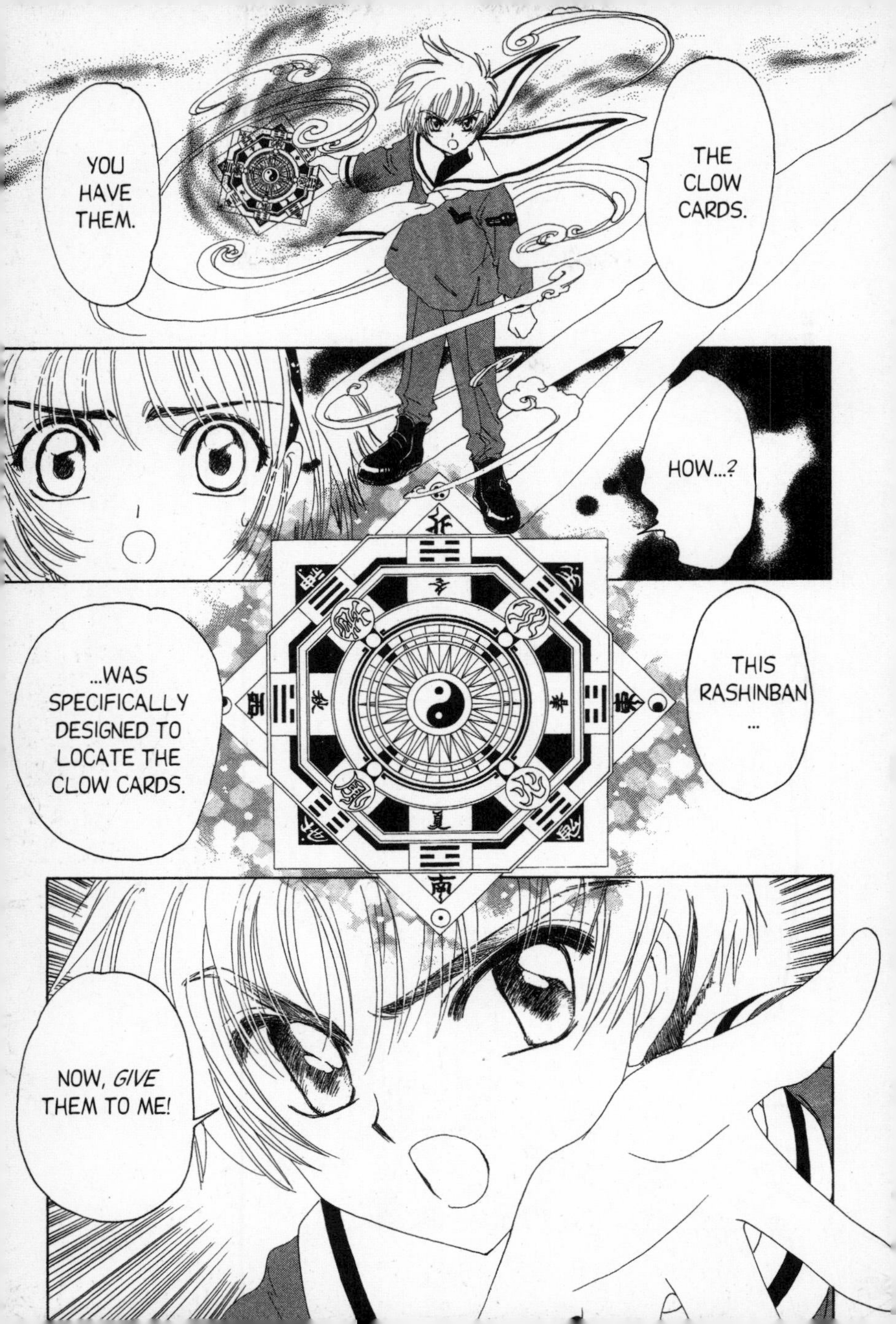
THE CLOW CARDS.
YOU HAVE THEM.
HOW...?
THIS RASHINBAN ...
...WAS SPECIFICALLY DESIGNED TO LOCATE THE CLOW CARDS.
NOW, *GIVE* THEM TO ME!

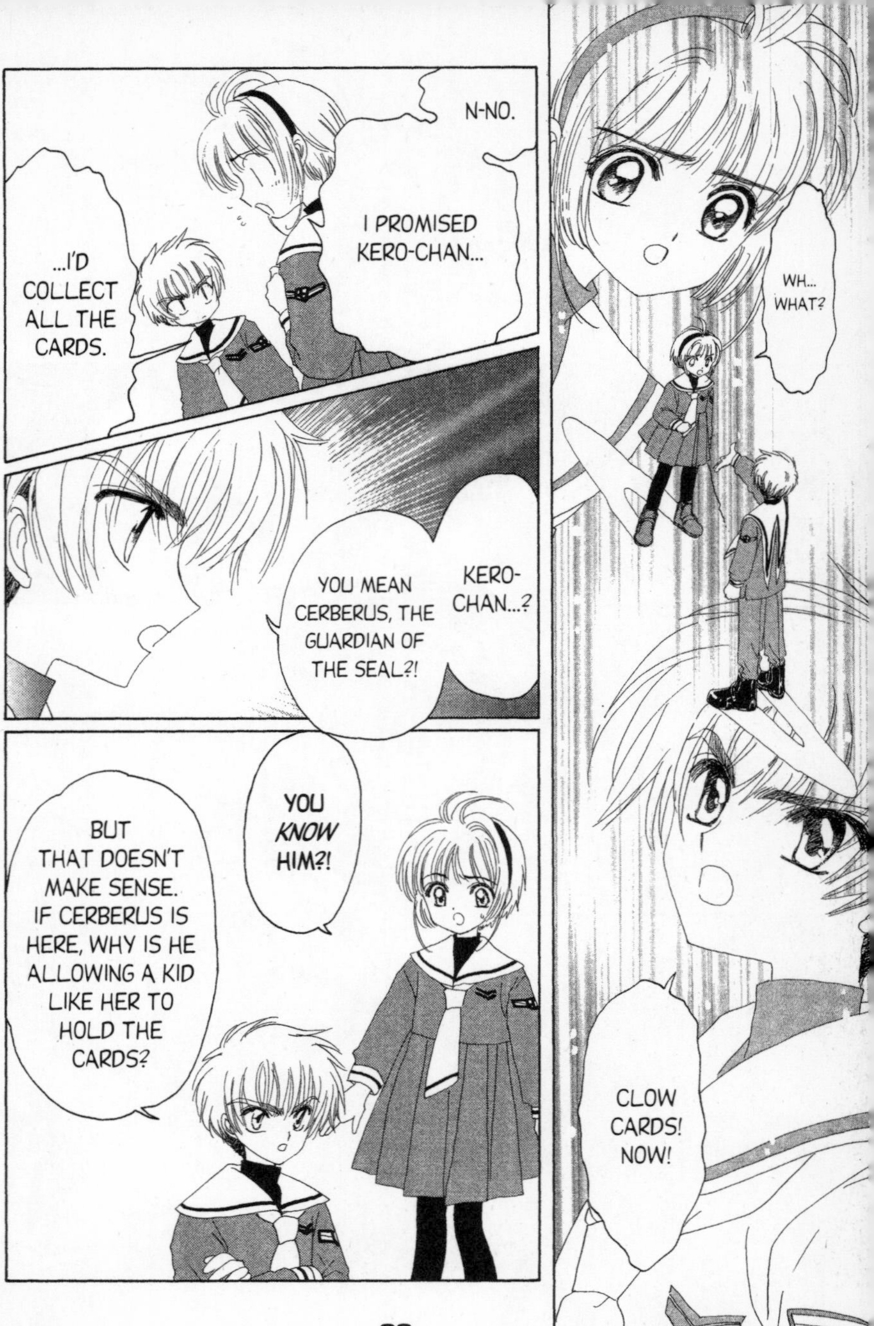
WH... WHAT?
CLOW CARDS! NOW!
N-NO.
I PROMISED KERO-CHAN...
...I'D COLLECT ALL THE CARDS.
KERO-CHAN...?
YOU MEAN CERBERUS, THE GUARDIAN OF THE SEAL?!
YOU *KNOW* HIM?!
BUT THAT DOESN'T MAKE SENSE. IF CERBERUS IS HERE, WHY IS HE ALLOWING A KID LIKE HER TO HOLD THE CARDS?

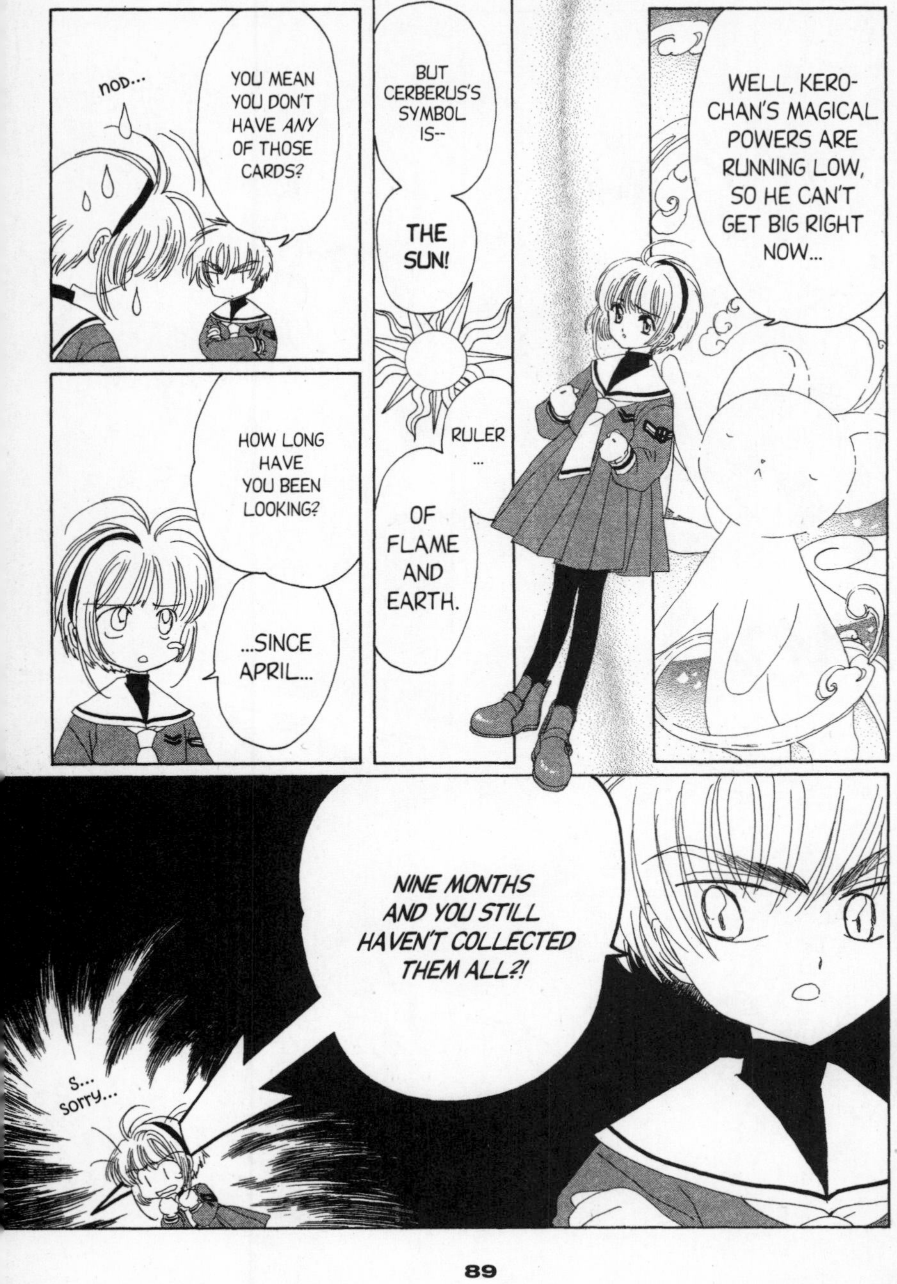
WELL, KERO-CHAN'S MAGICAL POWERS ARE RUNNING LOW, SO HE CAN'T GET BIG RIGHT NOW...
BUT CERBERUS'S SYMBOL IS--
THE SUN!
RULER ...
OF FLAME AND EARTH.
YOU MEAN YOU DON'T HAVE *ANY* OF THOSE CARDS?
nod...
HOW LONG HAVE YOU BEEN LOOKING?
...SINCE APRIL...
NINE MONTHS AND YOU STILL HAVEN'T COLLECTED THEM ALL?!
S... sorry...

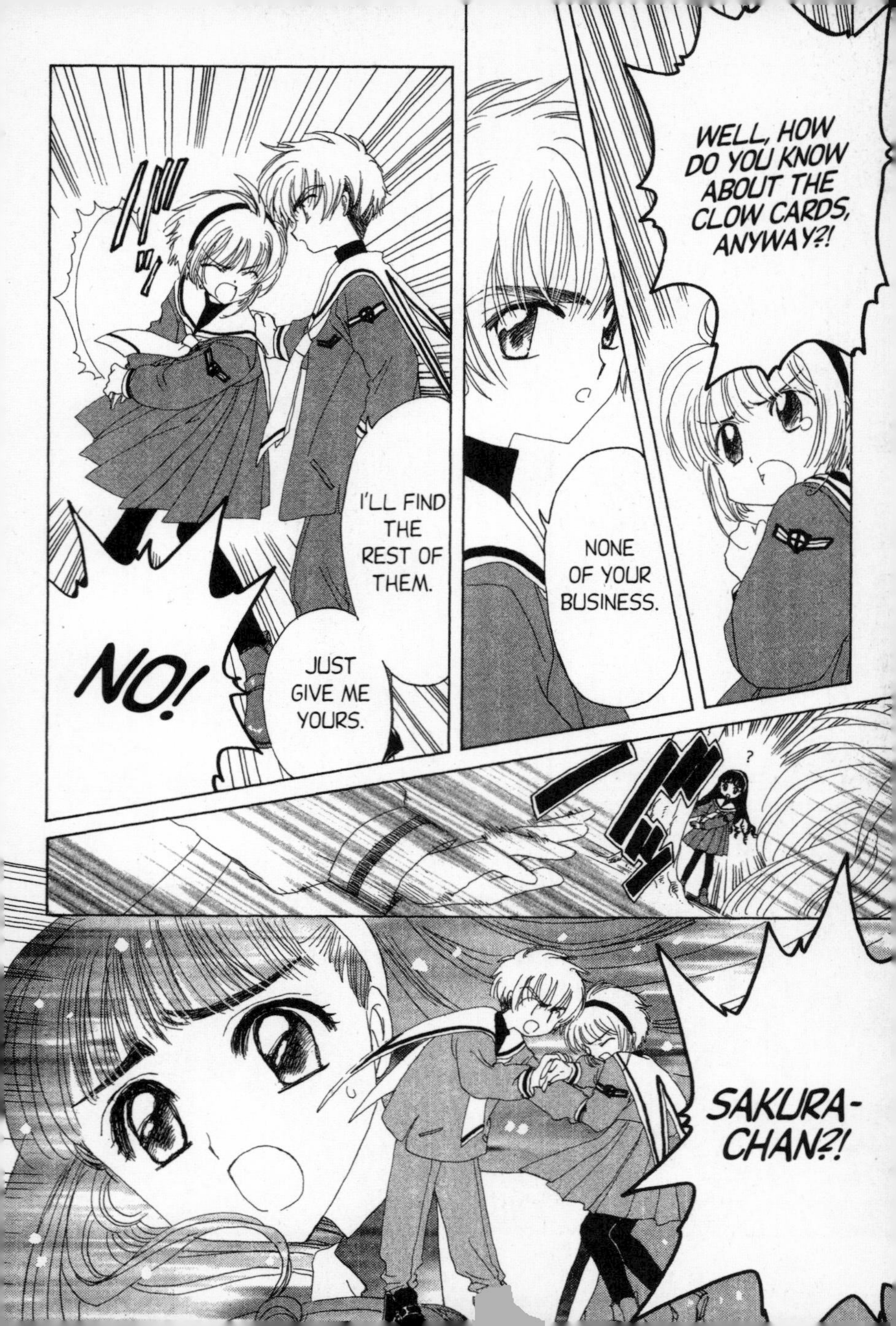
WELL, HOW DO YOU KNOW ABOUT THE CLOW CARDS, ANYWAY?!
NONE OF YOUR BUSINESS.
I'LL FIND THE REST OF THEM.
JUST GIVE ME YOURS.
NO!
?
SAKURA-CHAN?!

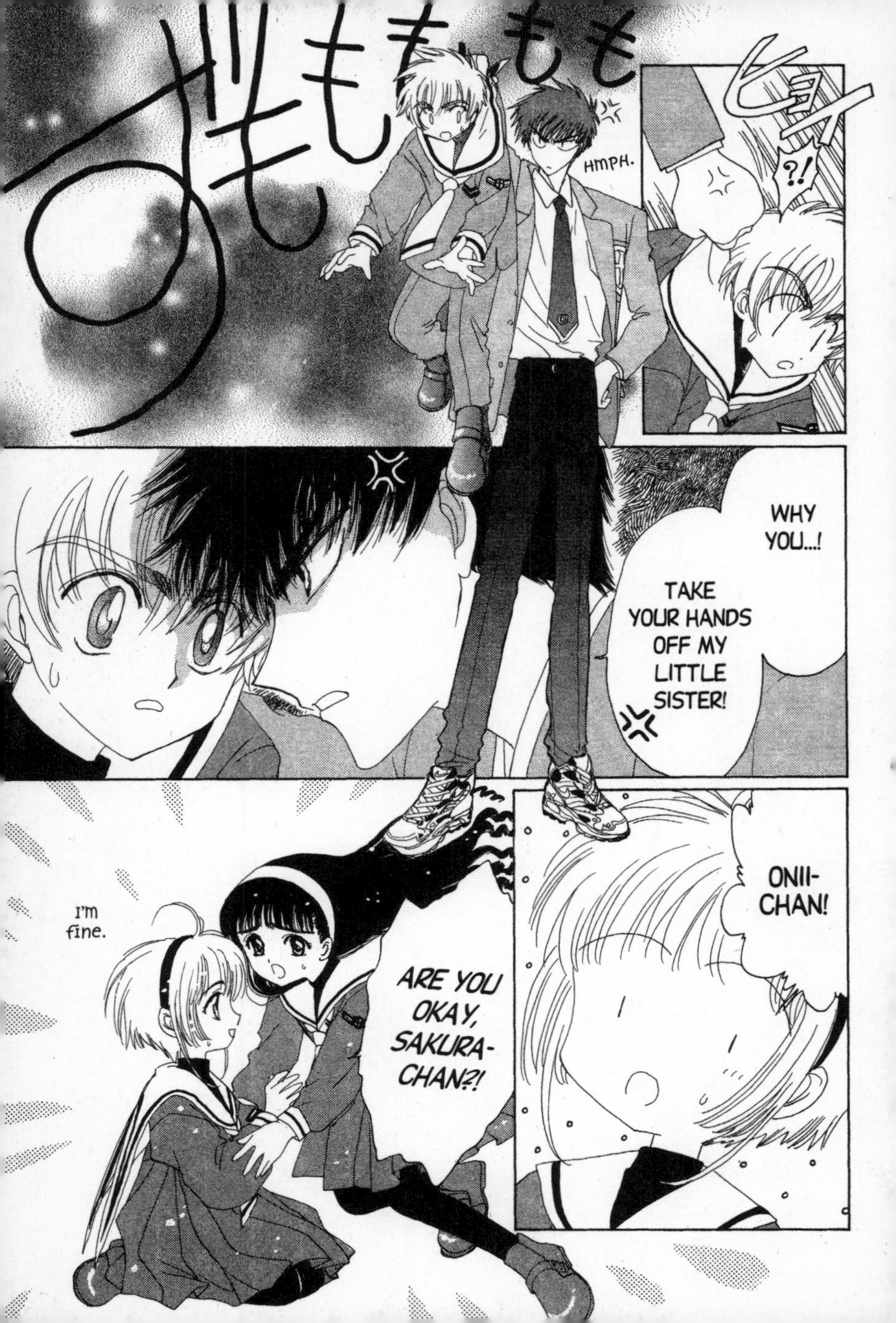
ヒョイ
?!
HMPH.
WHY YOU...!
TAKE YOUR HANDS OFF MY LITTLE SISTER!
ONII-CHAN!
ARE YOU OKAY, SAKURA-CHAN?!
I'm fine.

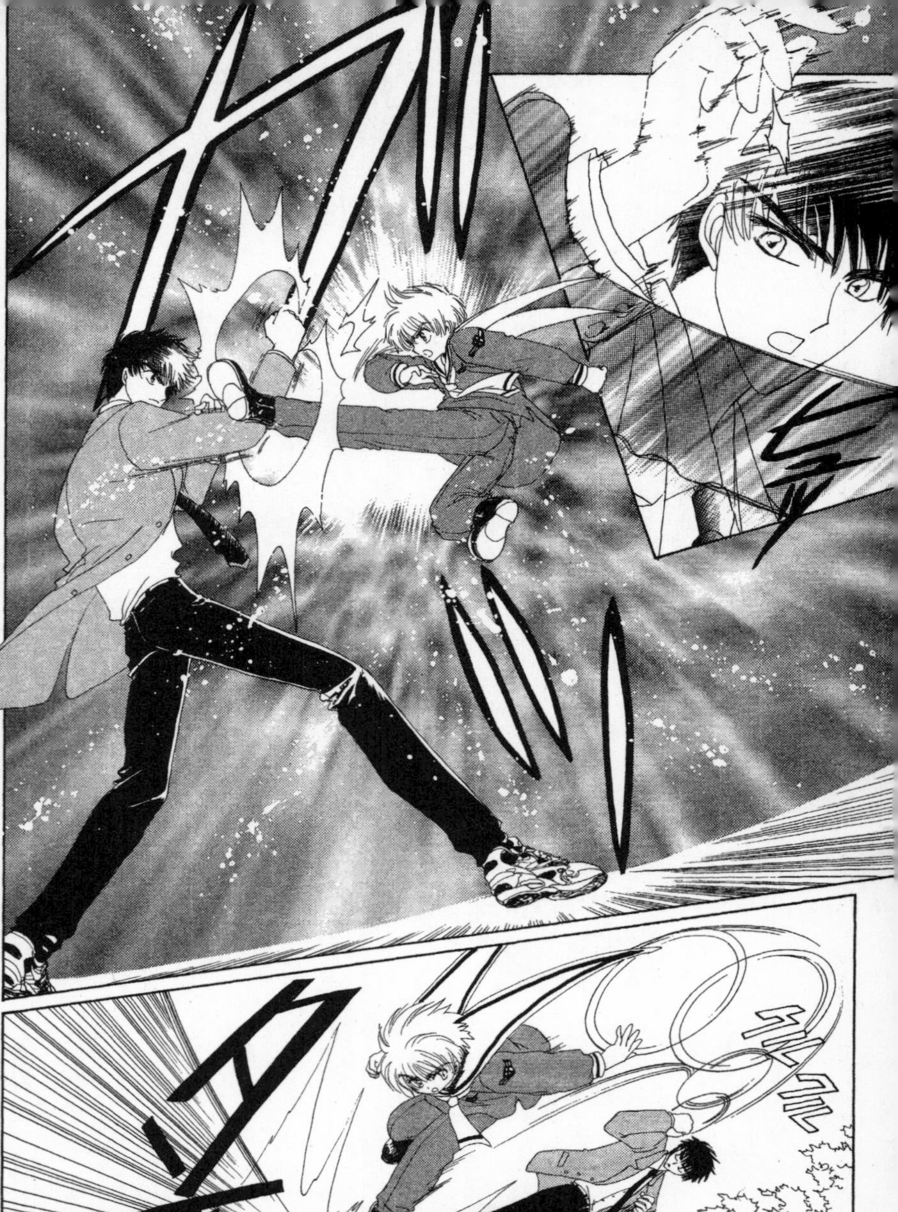

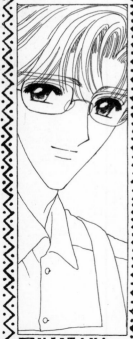

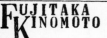

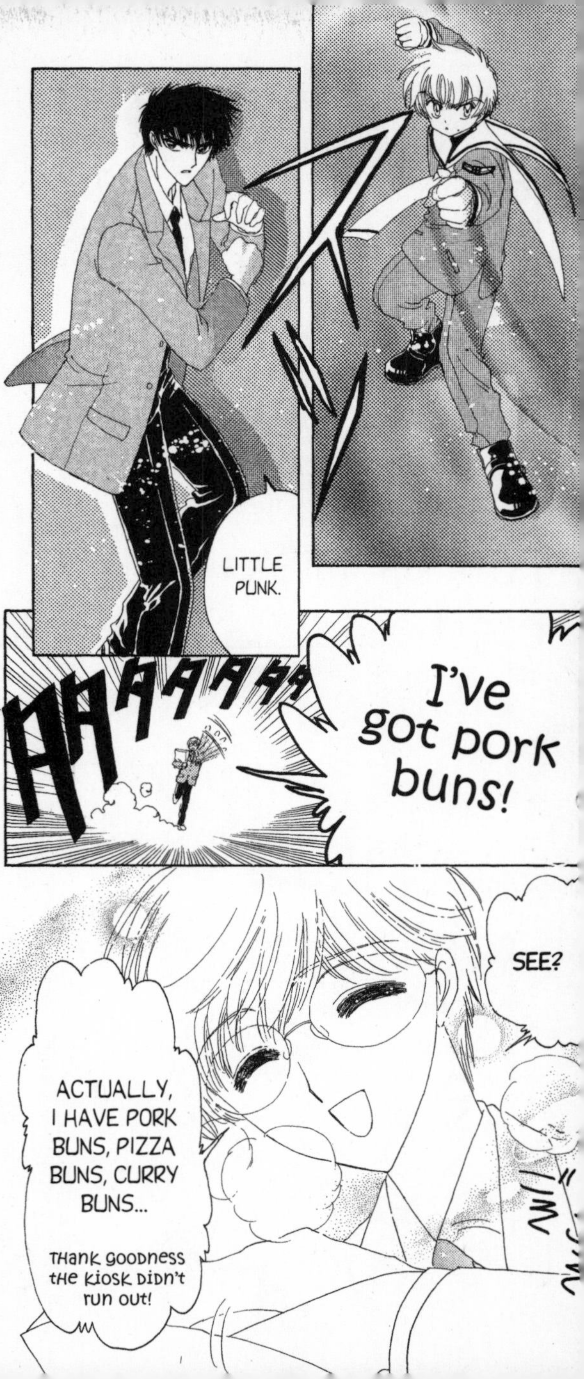
LITTLE PUNK.
AAAAAAA
I've got pork buns!
SEE?
ACTUALLY, I HAVE PORK BUNS, PIZZA BUNS, CURRY BUNS...
Thank goodness the kiosk didn't run out!

7

Fujitaka Kinomoto

Birthdate:
January 3
Occupation:
University professor
Favorite Foods:
Sweets, noodles
Least Favorite Food: **None**
Favorite Pastime:
Video games
Favorite Colors:
White, ivory, brown
Favorite Flowers:
Nadeshiko, peach blossom, cherry blossom
Favorite Recipe:
Sweets
Special Skill: **Remembering people's faces and names**
Hobby:
Cooking
Wish List:
Nothing

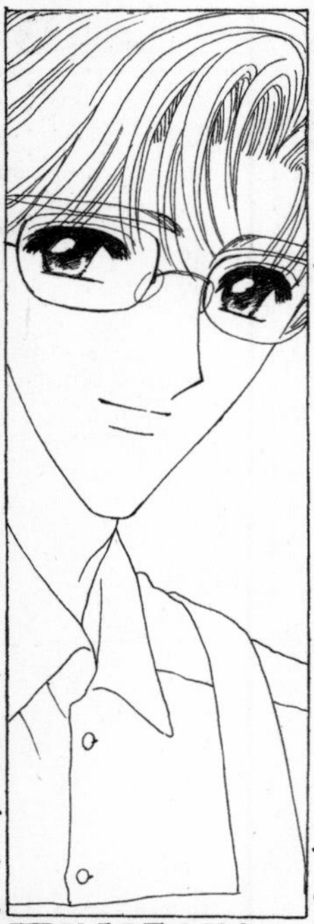

FUJITAKA KINOMOTO

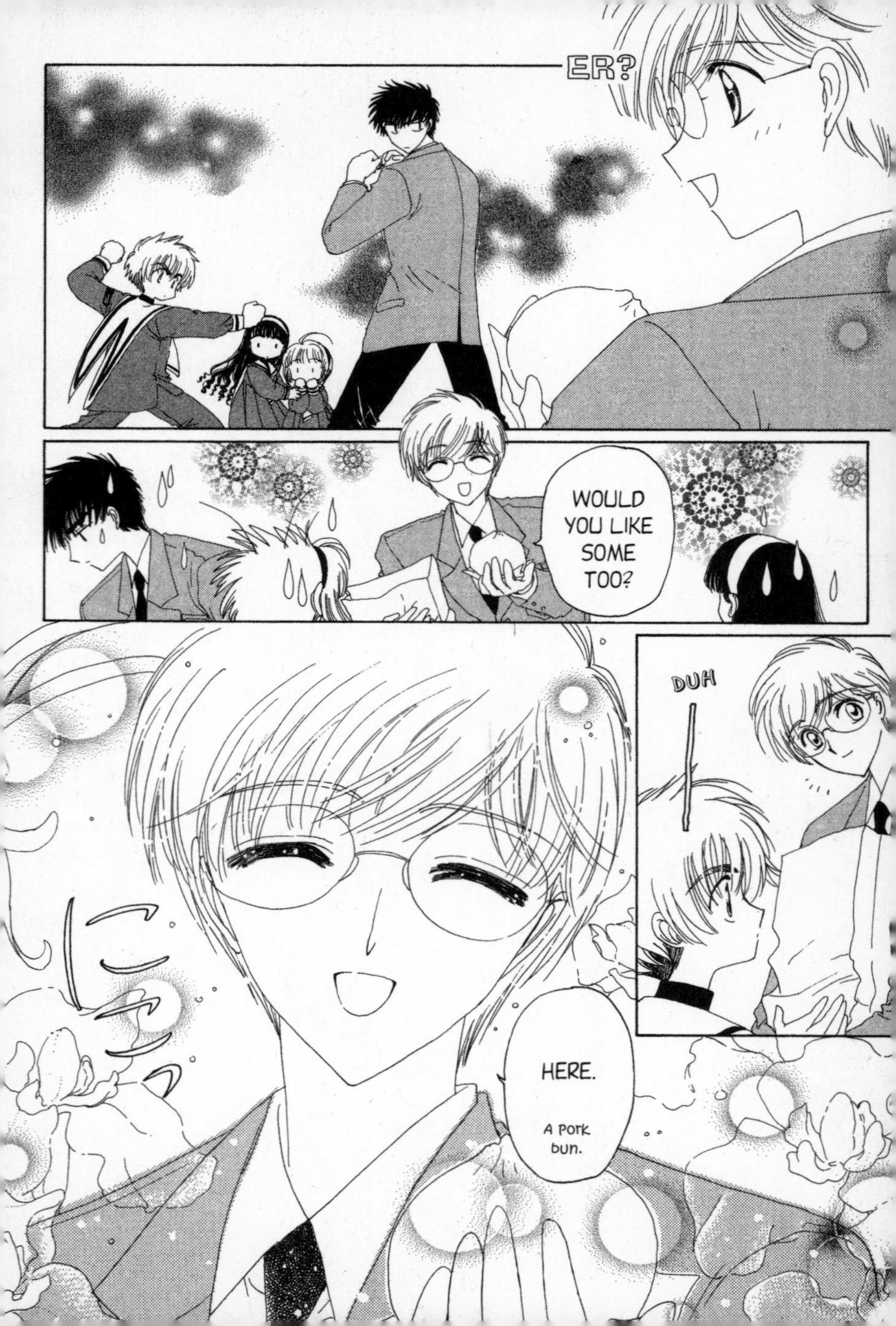
ER?
WOULD YOU LIKE SOME TOO?
DUH
HERE.
A pork bun.

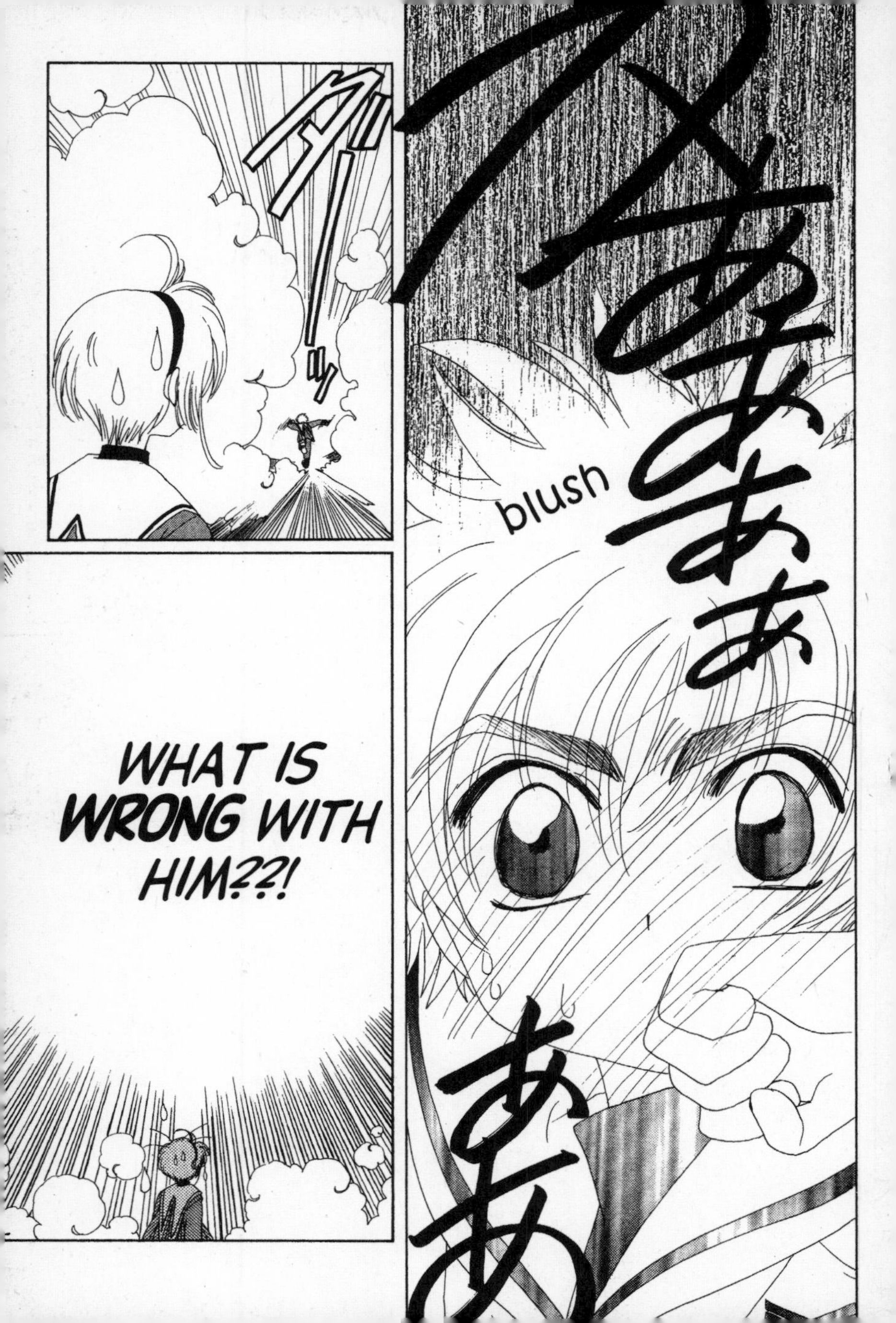
blush
WHAT IS WRONG WITH HIM??!

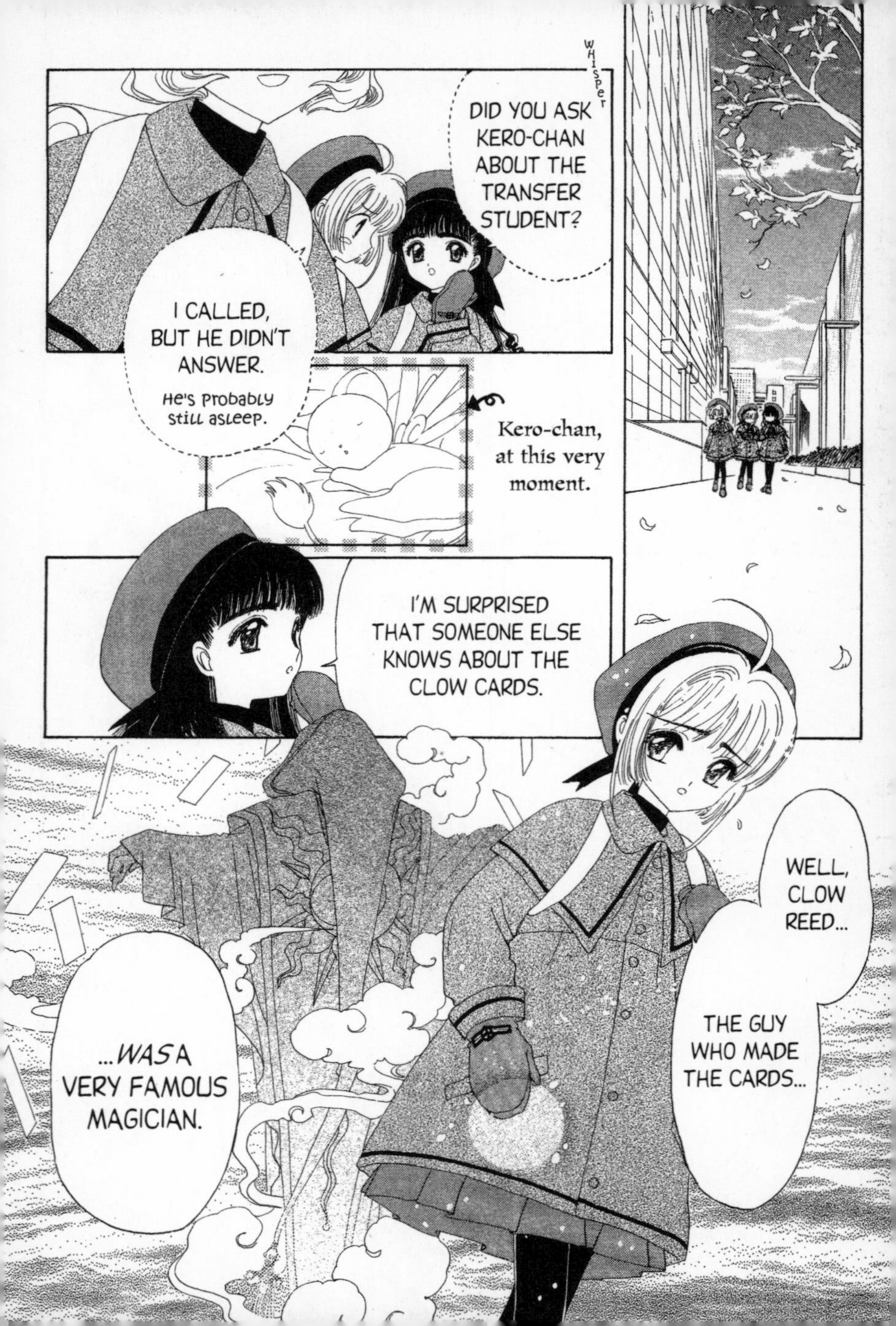
WHISPER
DID YOU ASK KERO-CHAN ABOUT THE TRANSFER STUDENT?
I CALLED, BUT HE DIDN'T ANSWER.
He's probably still asleep.
Kero-chan, at this very moment.
I'M SURPRISED THAT SOMEONE ELSE KNOWS ABOUT THE CLOW CARDS.
WELL, CLOW REED...
THE GUY WHO MADE THE CARDS...
...WAS A VERY FAMOUS MAGICIAN.

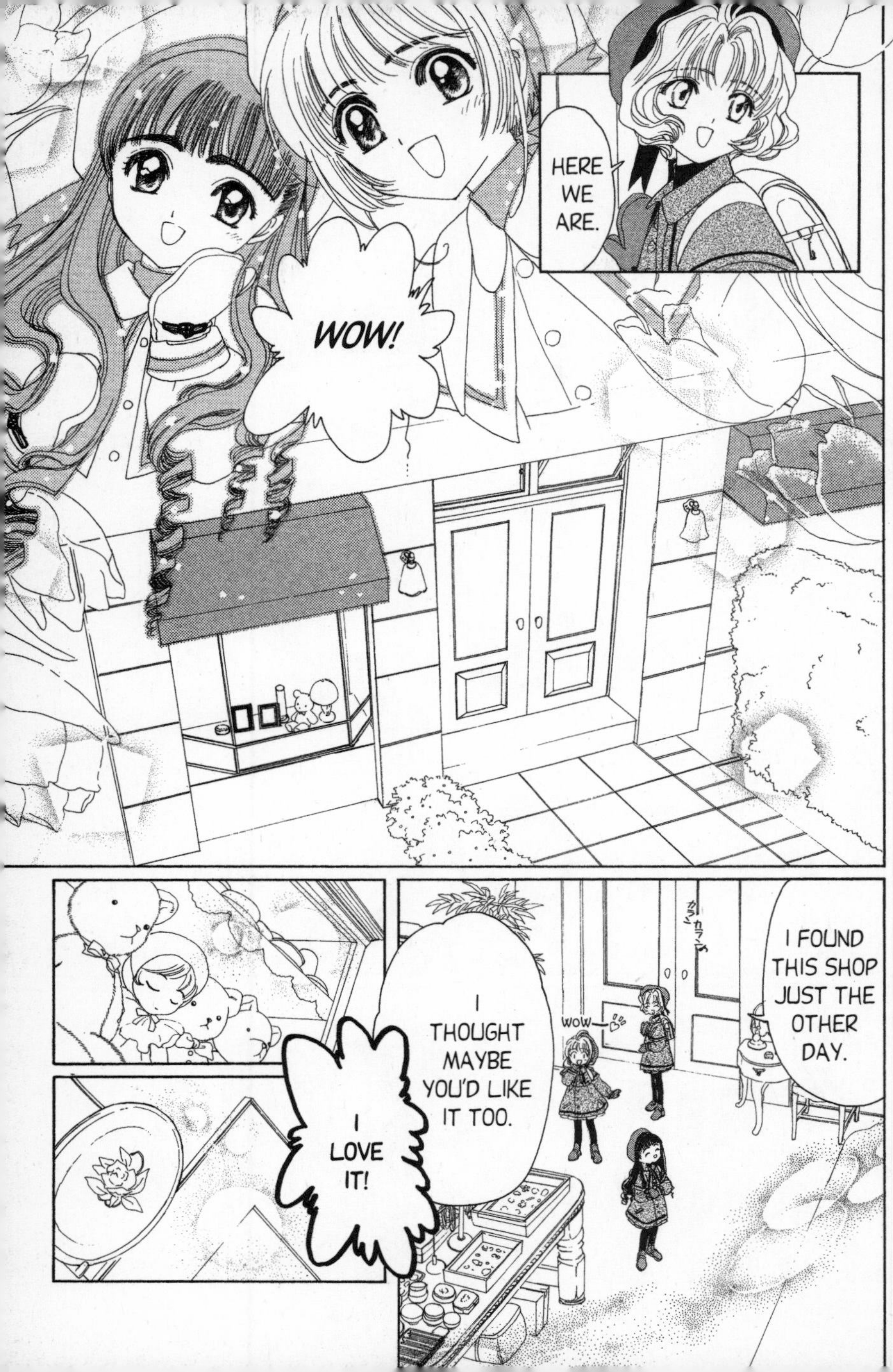
HERE WE ARE.
WOW!
I FOUND THIS SHOP JUST THE OTHER DAY.
I THOUGHT MAYBE YOU'D LIKE IT TOO.
WOW—
I LOVE IT!

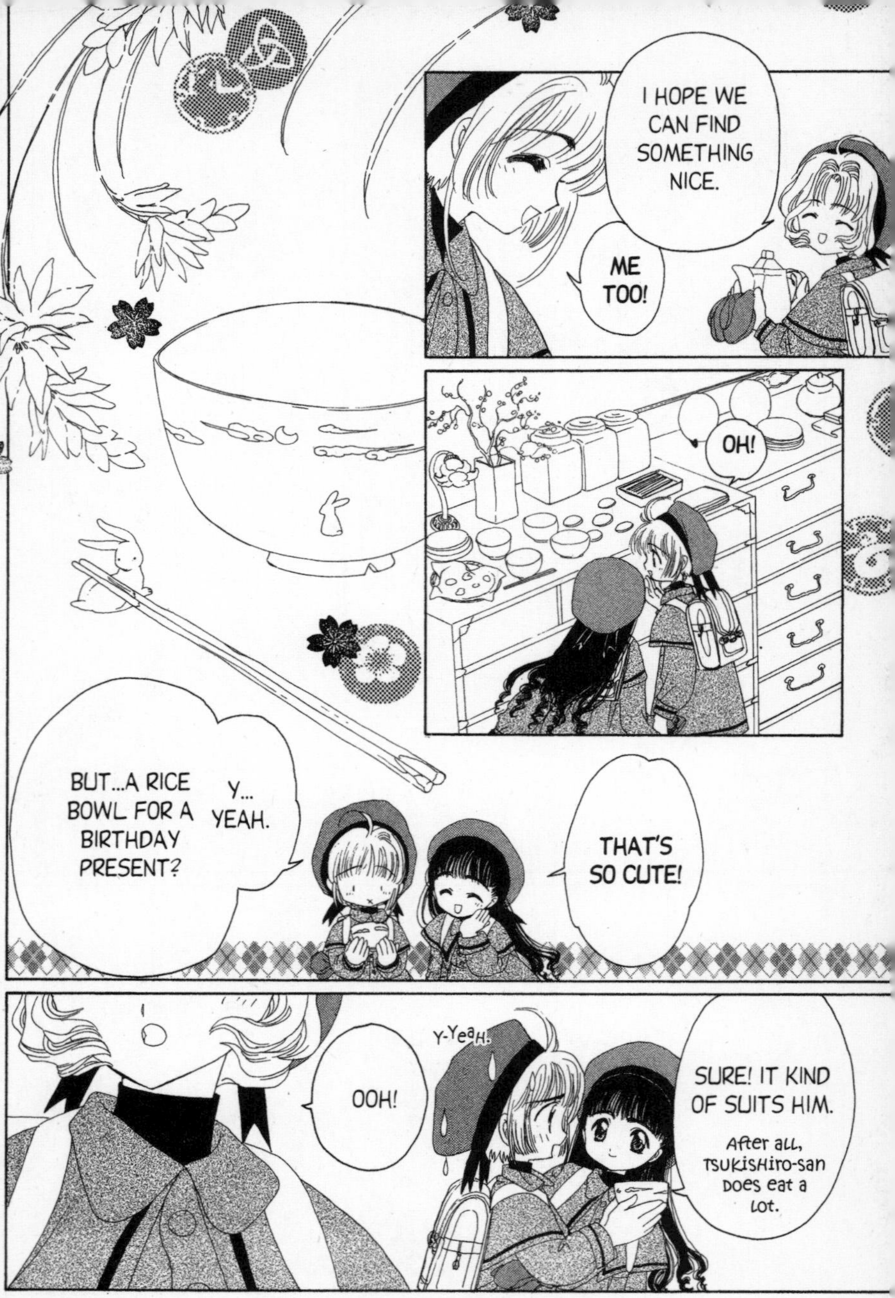
I HOPE WE CAN FIND SOMETHING NICE.
ME TOO!
OH!
THAT'S SO CUTE!
Y... YEAH.
BUT...A RICE BOWL FOR A BIRTHDAY PRESENT?
SURE! IT KIND OF SUITS HIM.
After all, TSUKISHIRO-san Does eat a lot.
Y-YeaH.
OOH!

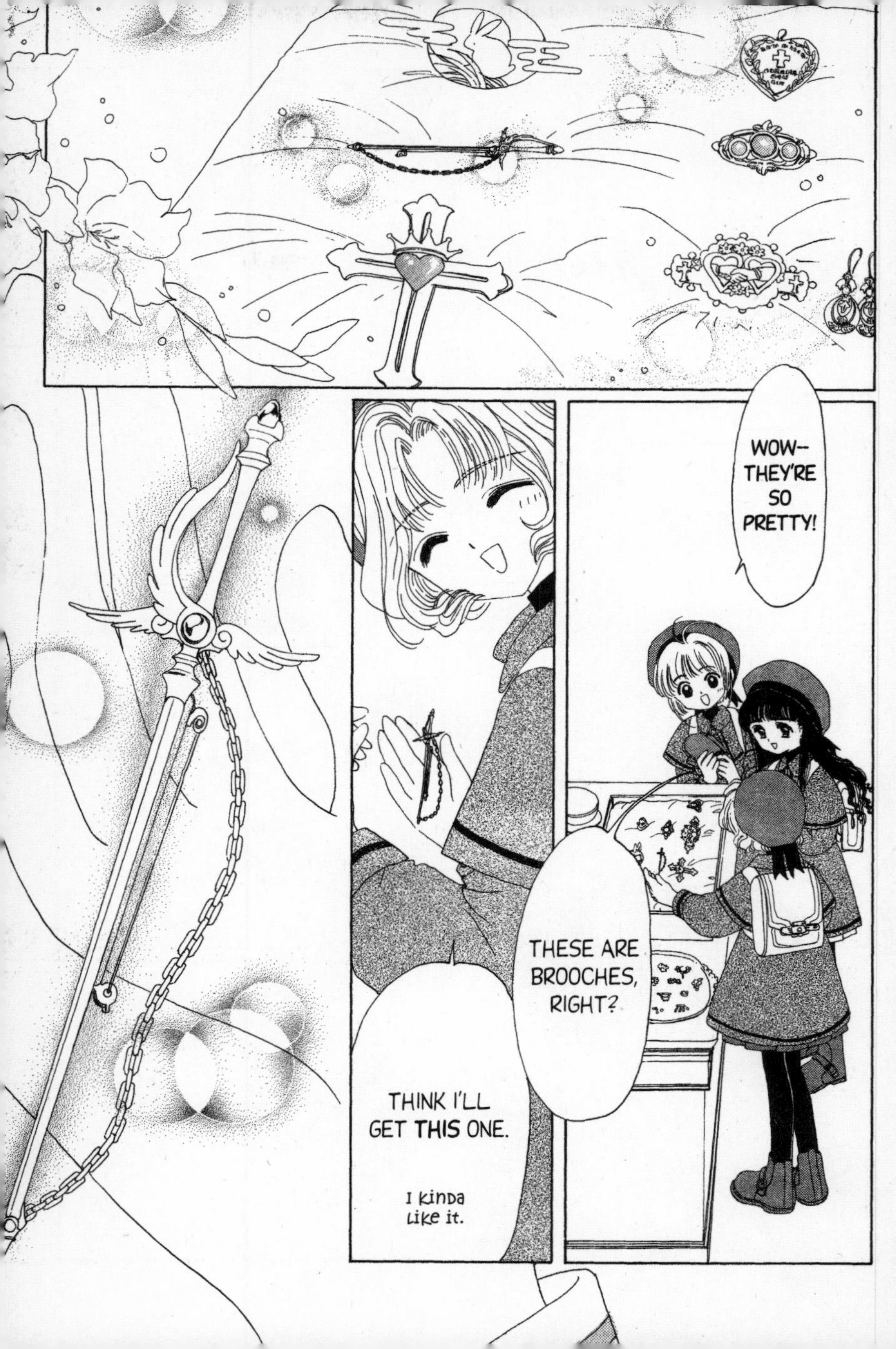
WOW— THEY'RE SO PRETTY!
THESE ARE BROOCHES, RIGHT?
THINK I'LL GET THIS ONE.
I kinda like it.

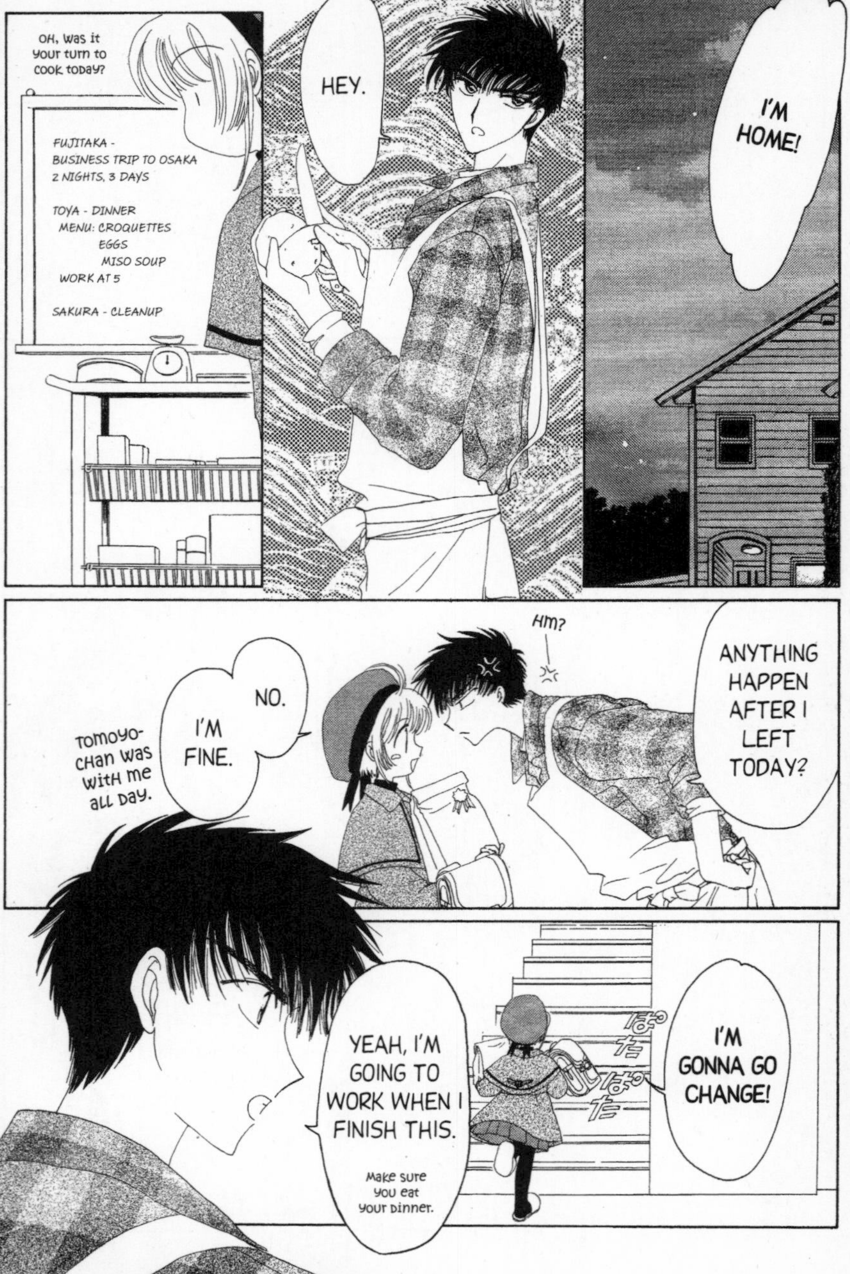
I'M HOME!
HEY.
OH, Was it your turn to cook today?
FUJITAKA - BUSINESS TRIP TO OSAKA 2 NIGHTS, 3 DAYS
TOYA - DINNER MENU: CROQUETTES EGGS MISO SOUP WORK AT 5
SAKURA - CLEANUP
ANYTHING HAPPEN AFTER I LEFT TODAY?
HM?
NO.
I'M FINE.
Tomoyo-chan was with me all day.
I'M GONNA GO CHANGE!
ぱたぱた
YEAH, I'M GOING TO WORK WHEN I FINISH THIS.
Make sure you eat your dinner.

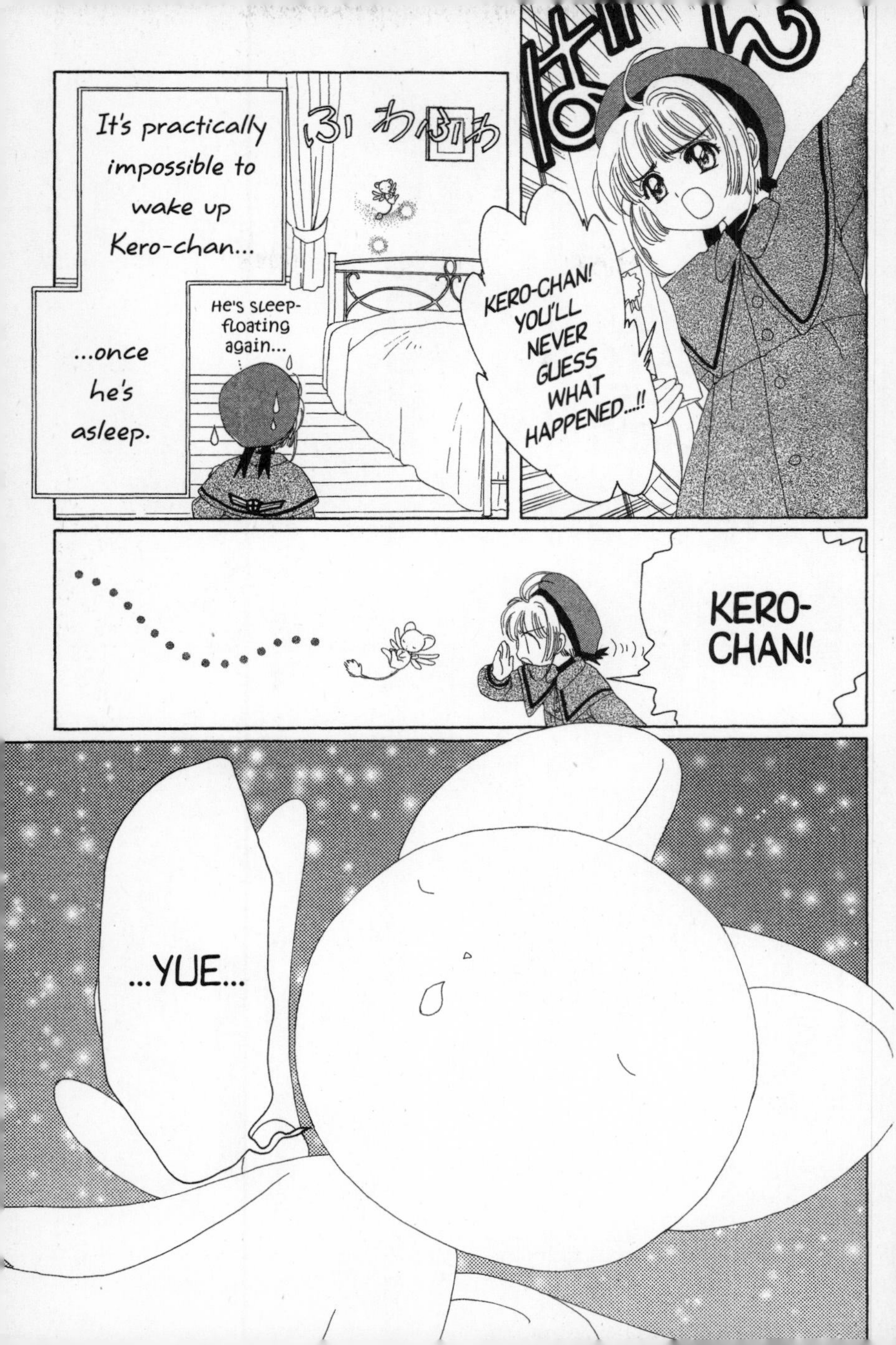
KERO-CHAN! YOU'LL NEVER GUESS WHAT HAPPENED...!!
ふわふわ
It's practically impossible to wake up Kero-chan...
He's sleep-floating again...
...once he's asleep.
KERO-CHAN!
...YUE...

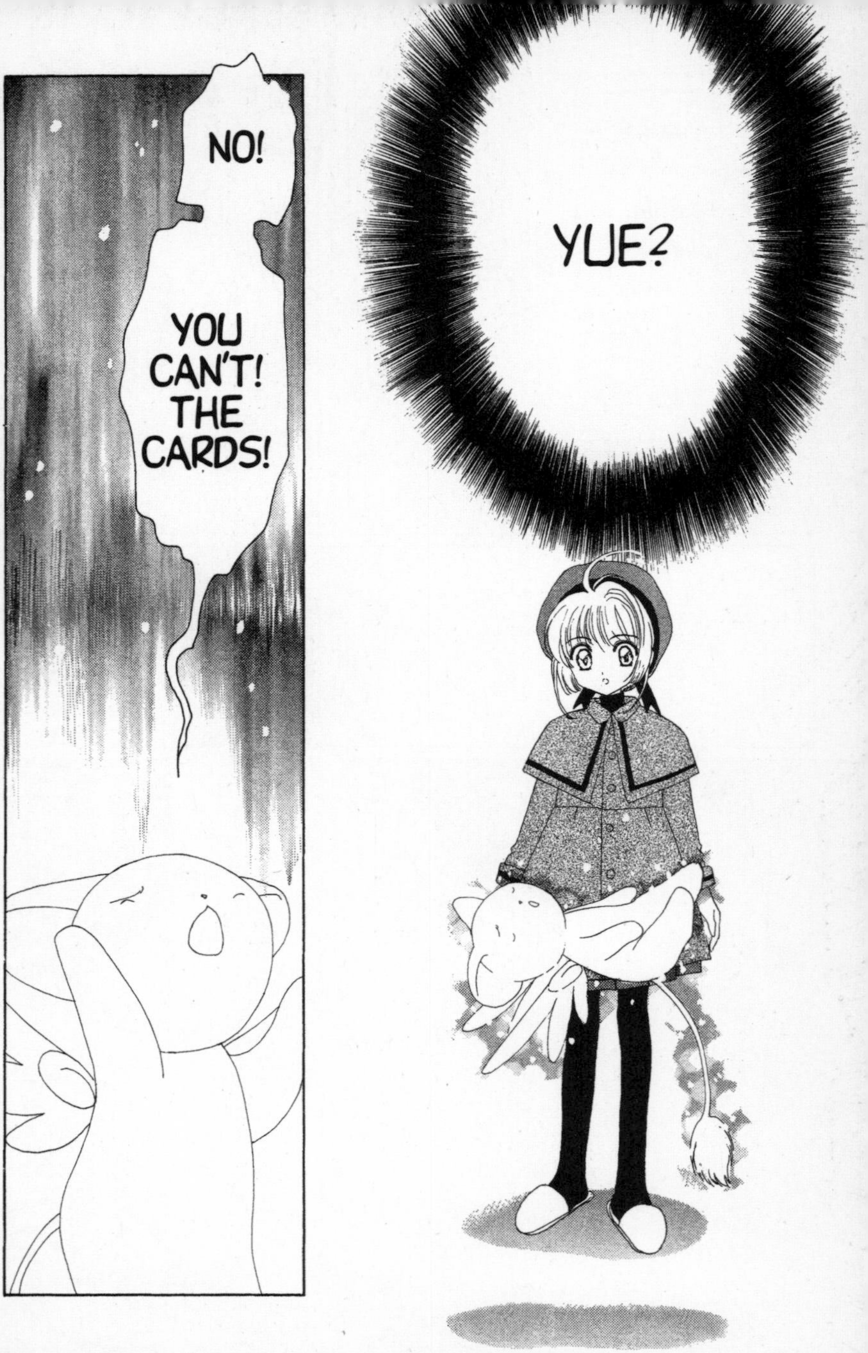
YUE?
NO!
YOU CAN'T! THE CARDS!

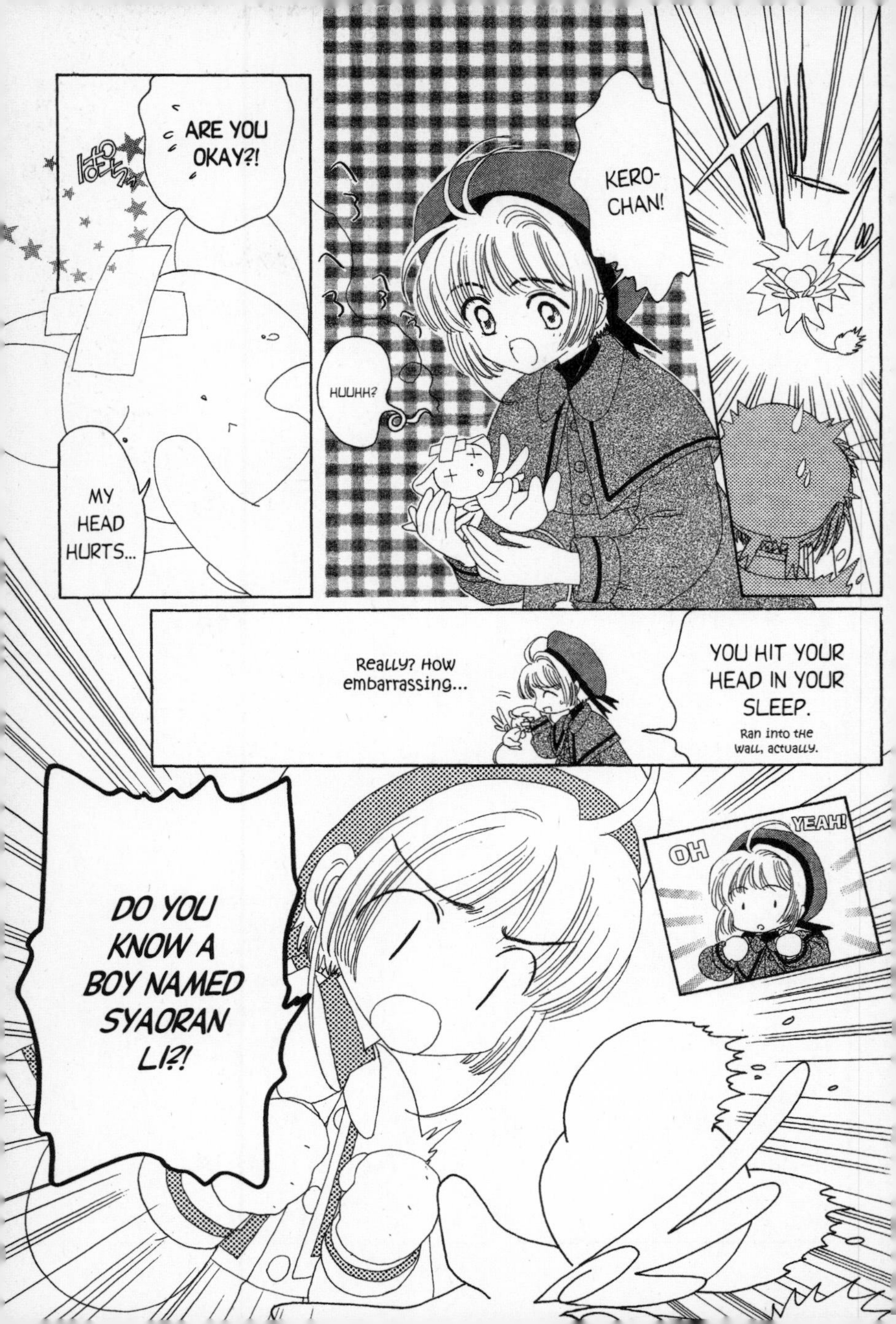
KERO-CHAN!
HUUHH?
ARE YOU OKAY?!
MY HEAD HURTS...
YOU HIT YOUR HEAD IN YOUR SLEEP.
Ran into the wall, actually.
Really? How embarrassing...
OH
YEAH!
DO YOU KNOW A BOY NAMED SYAORAN LI?!

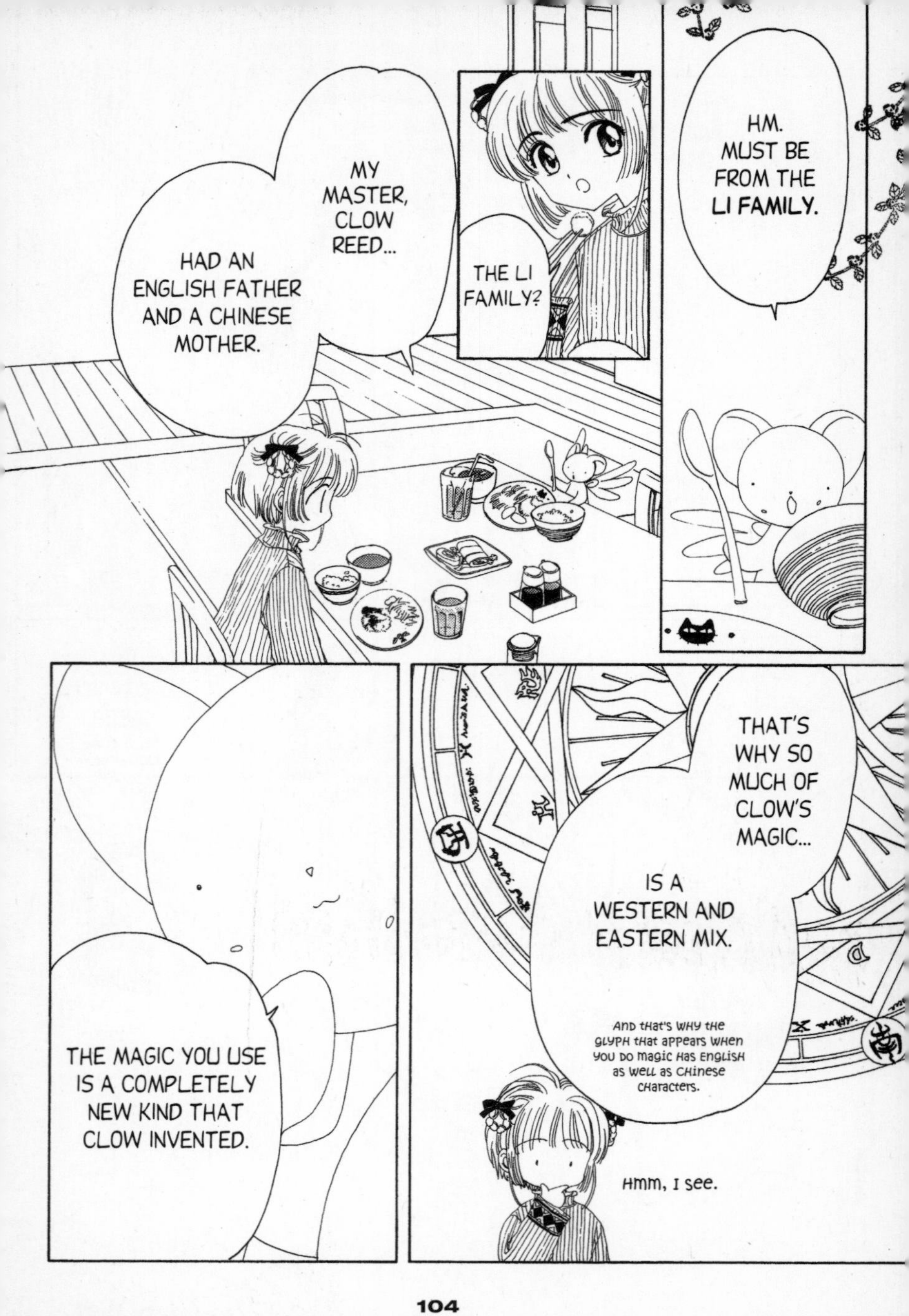
HM. MUST BE FROM THE LI FAMILY.
THE LI FAMILY?
MY MASTER, CLOW REED...
HAD AN ENGLISH FATHER AND A CHINESE MOTHER.
THAT'S WHY SO MUCH OF CLOW'S MAGIC...
IS A WESTERN AND EASTERN MIX.
And that's why the glyph that appears when you do magic has English as well as Chinese characters.
Hmm, I see.
THE MAGIC YOU USE IS A COMPLETELY NEW KIND THAT CLOW INVENTED.

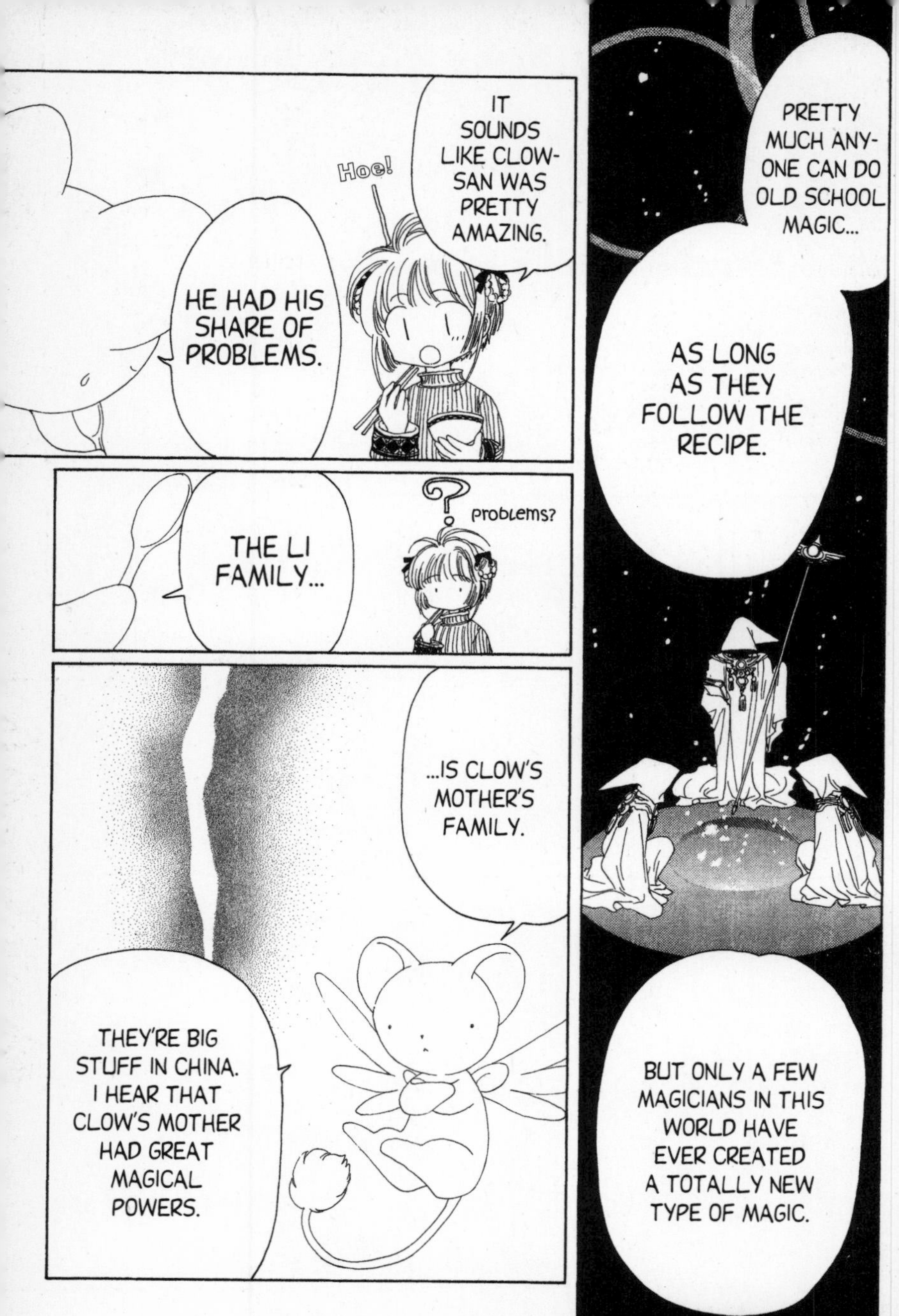
PRETTY MUCH ANYONE CAN DO OLD SCHOOL MAGIC...
AS LONG AS THEY FOLLOW THE RECIPE.
BUT ONLY A FEW MAGICIANS IN THIS WORLD HAVE EVER CREATED A TOTALLY NEW TYPE OF MAGIC.
IT SOUNDS LIKE CLOW-SAN WAS PRETTY AMAZING.
Hoe!
HE HAD HIS SHARE OF PROBLEMS.
problems?
THE LI FAMILY...
...IS CLOW'S MOTHER'S FAMILY.
THEY'RE BIG STUFF IN CHINA. I HEAR THAT CLOW'S MOTHER HAD GREAT MAGICAL POWERS.

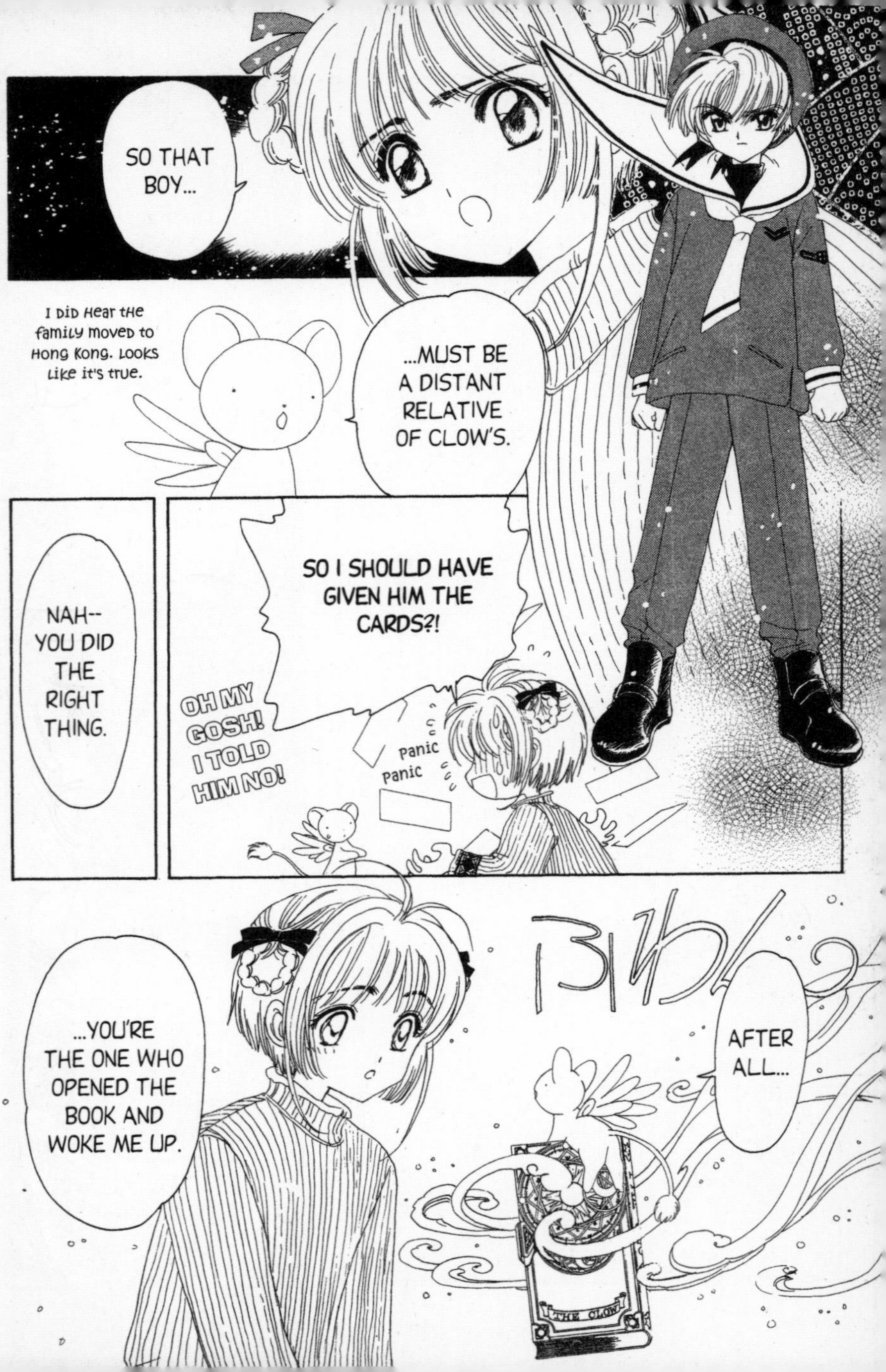

SO THAT BOY...
...MUST BE A DISTANT RELATIVE OF CLOW'S.
I did hear the family moved to Hong Kong. Looks like it's true.
SO I SHOULD HAVE GIVEN HIM THE CARDS?!
OH MY GOSH! I TOLD HIM NO!
Panic Panic
NAH-- YOU DID THE RIGHT THING.
AFTER ALL...
...YOU'RE THE ONE WHO OPENED THE BOOK AND WOKE ME UP.
THE CLOW

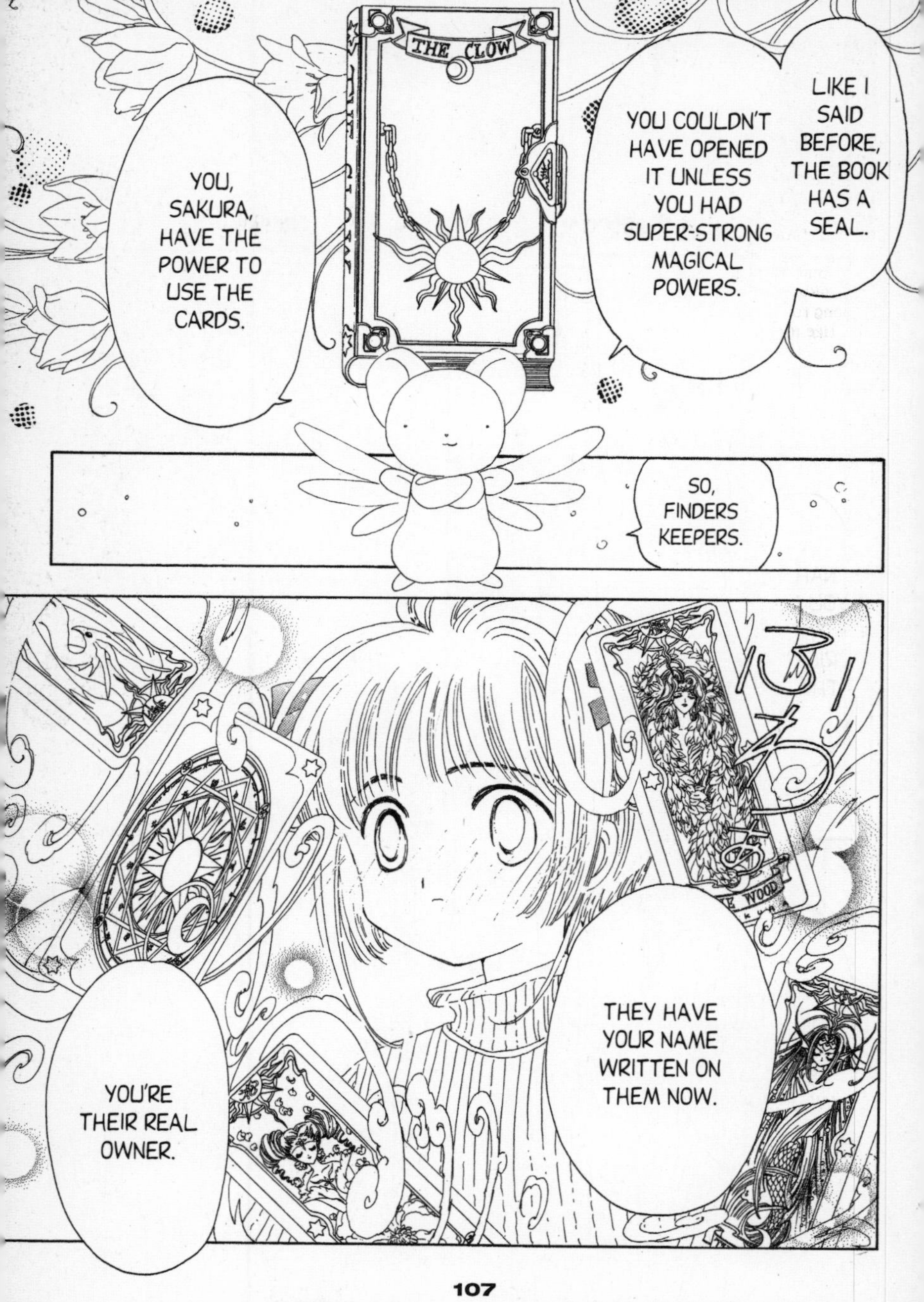
THE CLOW
LIKE I SAID BEFORE, THE BOOK HAS A SEAL.
YOU COULDN'T HAVE OPENED IT UNLESS YOU HAD SUPER-STRONG MAGICAL POWERS.
YOU, SAKURA, HAVE THE POWER TO USE THE CARDS.
SO, FINDERS KEEPERS.
THEY HAVE YOUR NAME WRITTEN ON THEM NOW.
YOU'RE THEIR REAL OWNER.

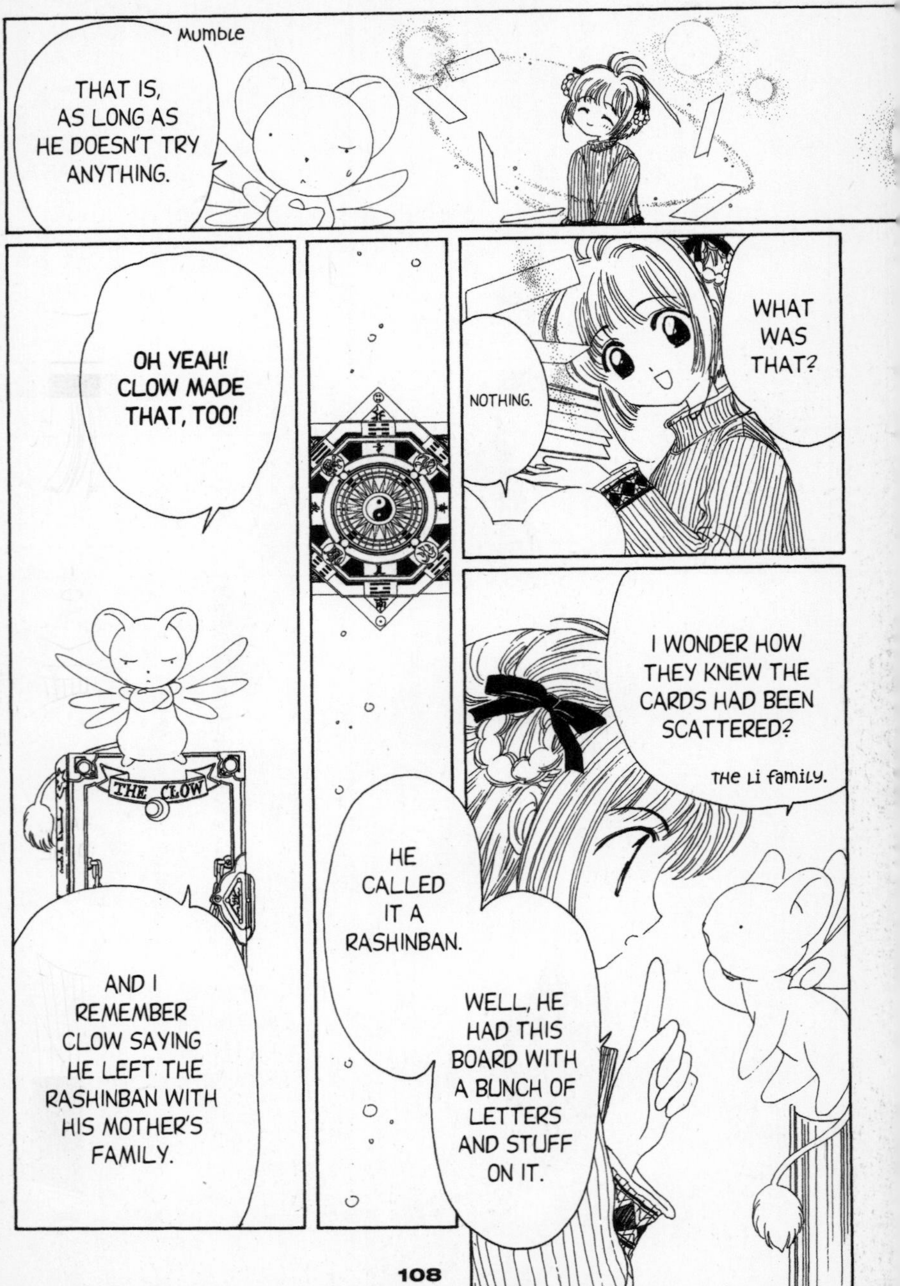
Mumble
THAT IS, AS LONG AS HE DOESN'T TRY ANYTHING.
WHAT WAS THAT?
NOTHING.
I WONDER HOW THEY KNEW THE CARDS HAD BEEN SCATTERED?
THE Li family.
WELL, HE HAD THIS BOARD WITH A BUNCH OF LETTERS AND STUFF ON IT.
HE CALLED IT A RASHINBAN.
OH YEAH! CLOW MADE THAT, TOO!
THE CLOW
AND I REMEMBER CLOW SAYING HE LEFT THE RASHINBAN WITH HIS MOTHER'S FAMILY.

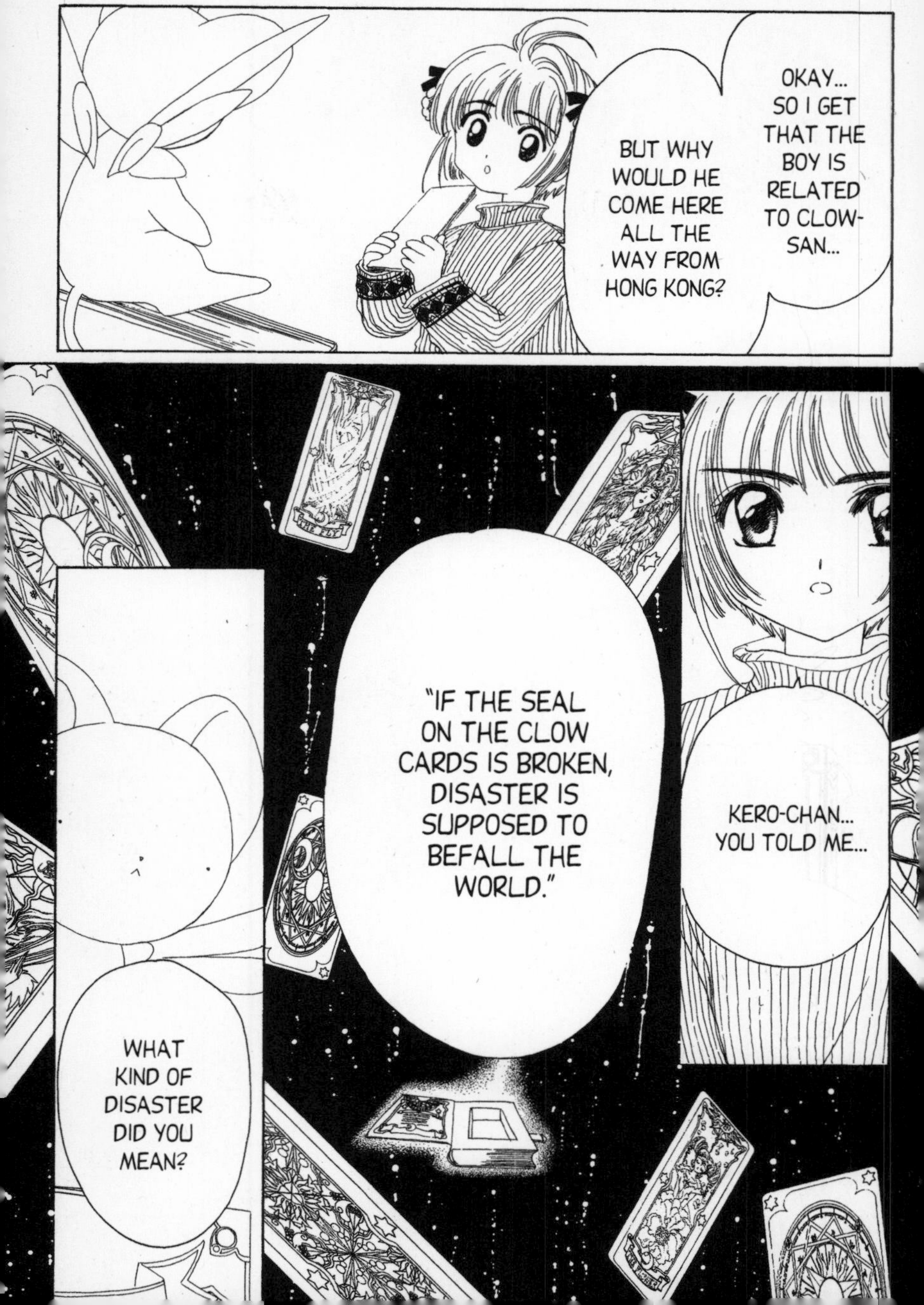
OKAY... SO I GET THAT THE BOY IS RELATED TO CLOW-SAN...
BUT WHY WOULD HE COME HERE ALL THE WAY FROM HONG KONG?
KERO-CHAN... YOU TOLD ME...
"IF THE SEAL ON THE CLOW CARDS IS BROKEN, DISASTER IS SUPPOSED TO BEFALL THE WORLD."
WHAT KIND OF DISASTER DID YOU MEAN?

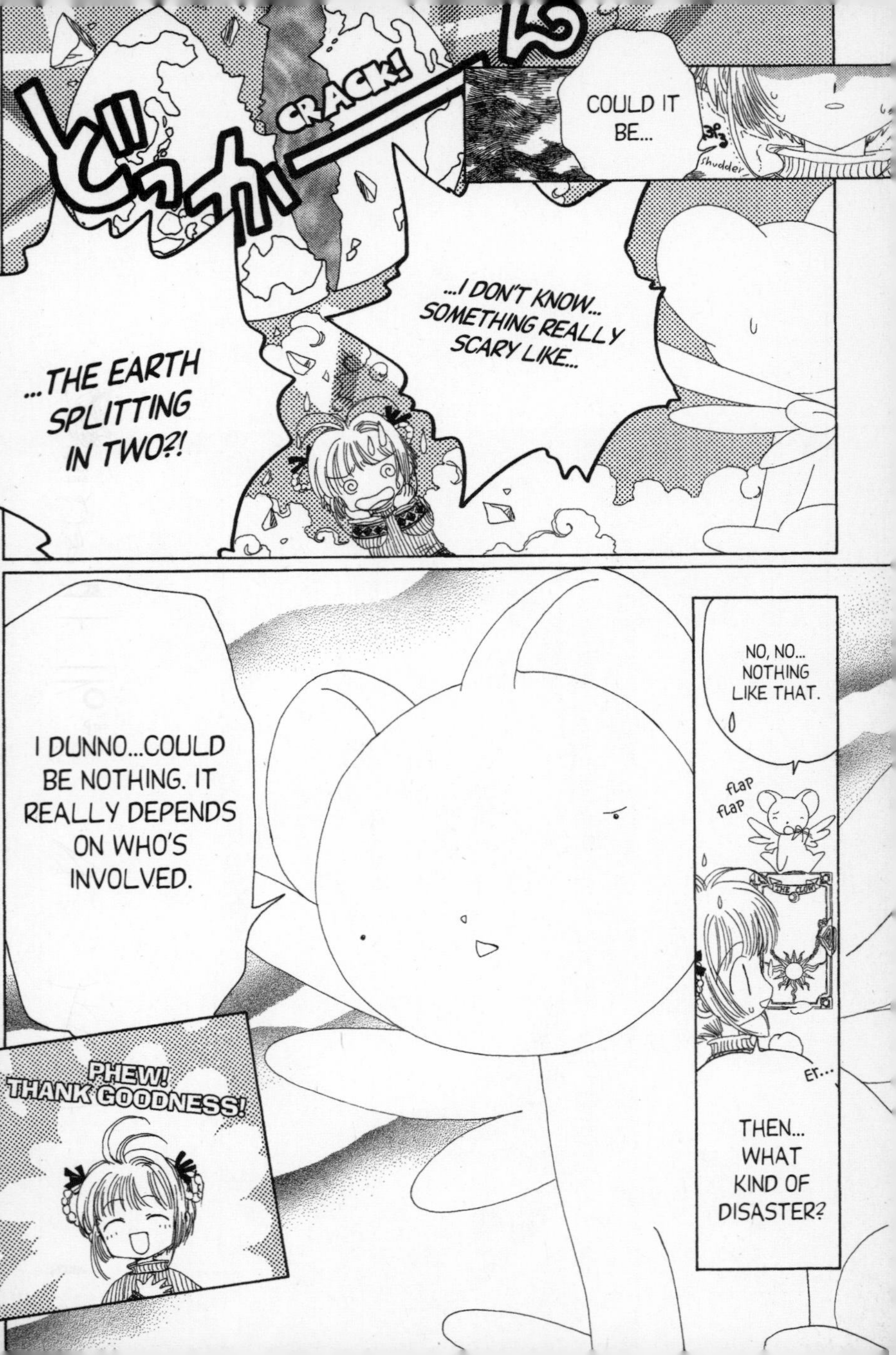
COULD IT BE...
shudder
...I DON'T KNOW... SOMETHING REALLY SCARY LIKE...
...THE EARTH SPLITTING IN TWO?!
CRACK!
NO, NO... NOTHING LIKE THAT.
flap flap
er...
THEN... WHAT KIND OF DISASTER?
I DUNNO...COULD BE NOTHING. IT REALLY DEPENDS ON WHO'S INVOLVED.
PHEW! THANK GOODNESS!

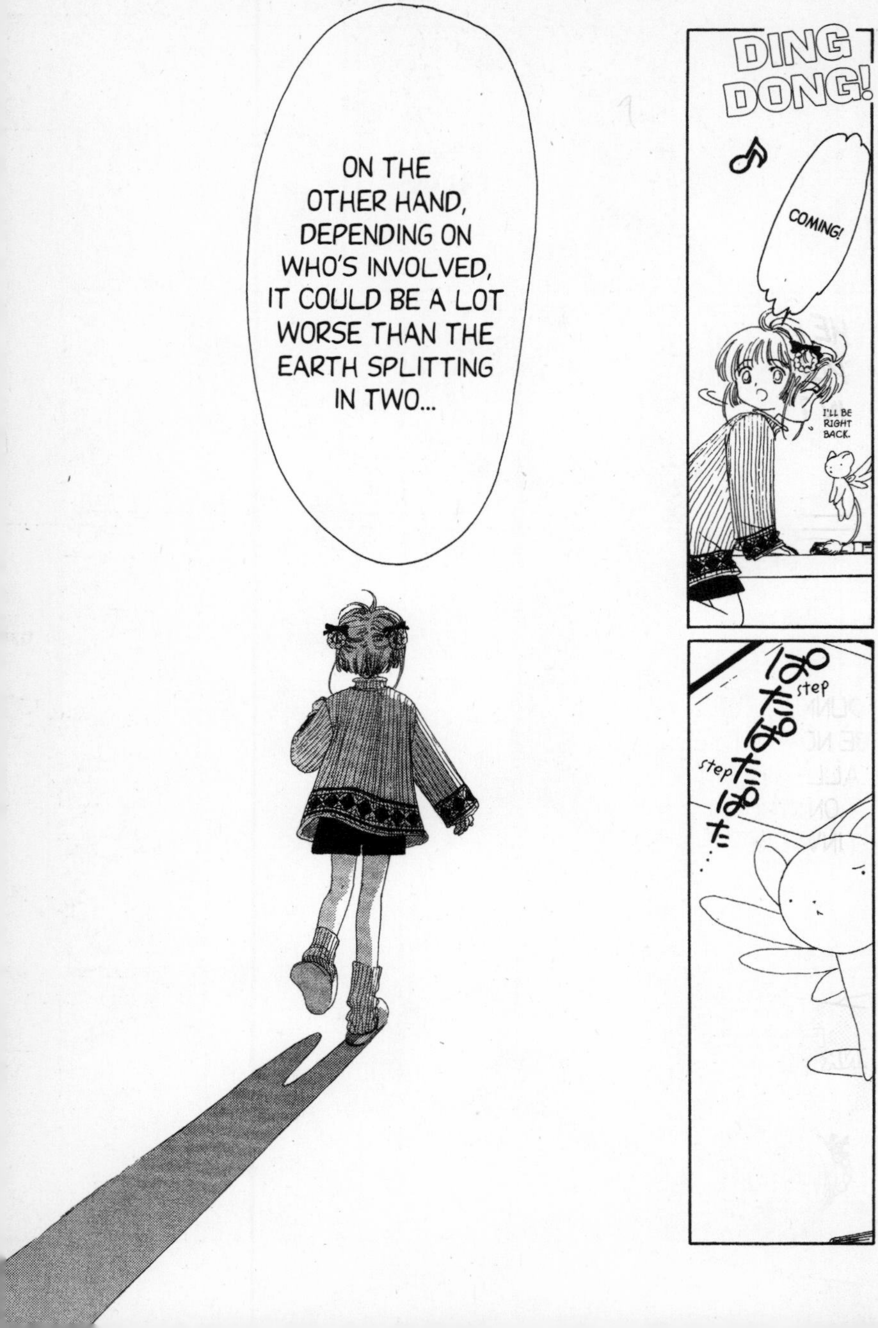
DING DONG!
COMING!
I'LL BE RIGHT BACK.
ぱたぱたぱたぱた…
step
step
ON THE OTHER HAND, DEPENDING ON WHO'S INVOLVED, IT COULD BE A LOT WORSE THAN THE EARTH SPLITTING IN TWO...

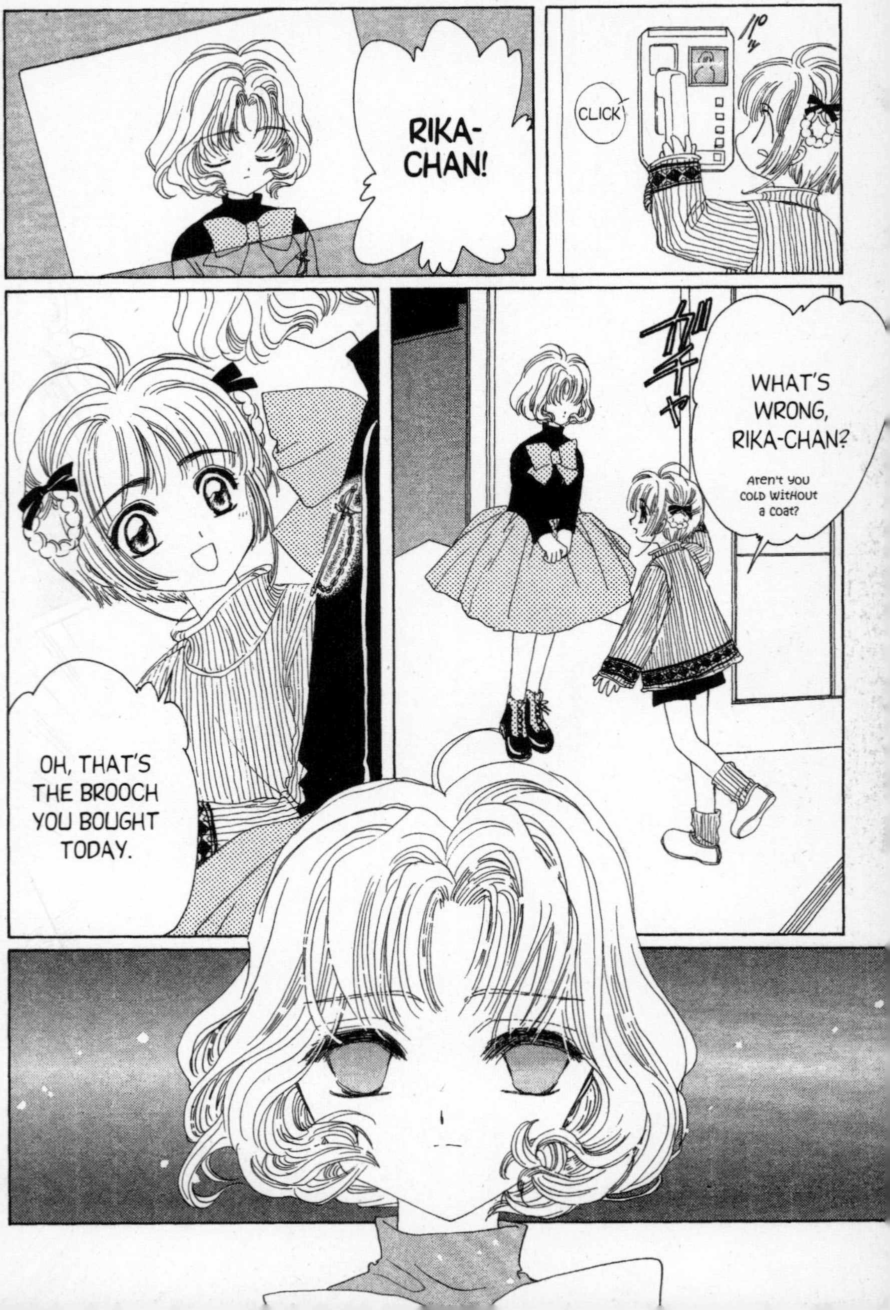
パッ
CLICK
RIKA-CHAN!
ガチャ
WHAT'S WRONG, RIKA-CHAN?
Aren't you cold without a coat?
OH, THAT'S THE BROOCH YOU BOUGHT TODAY.

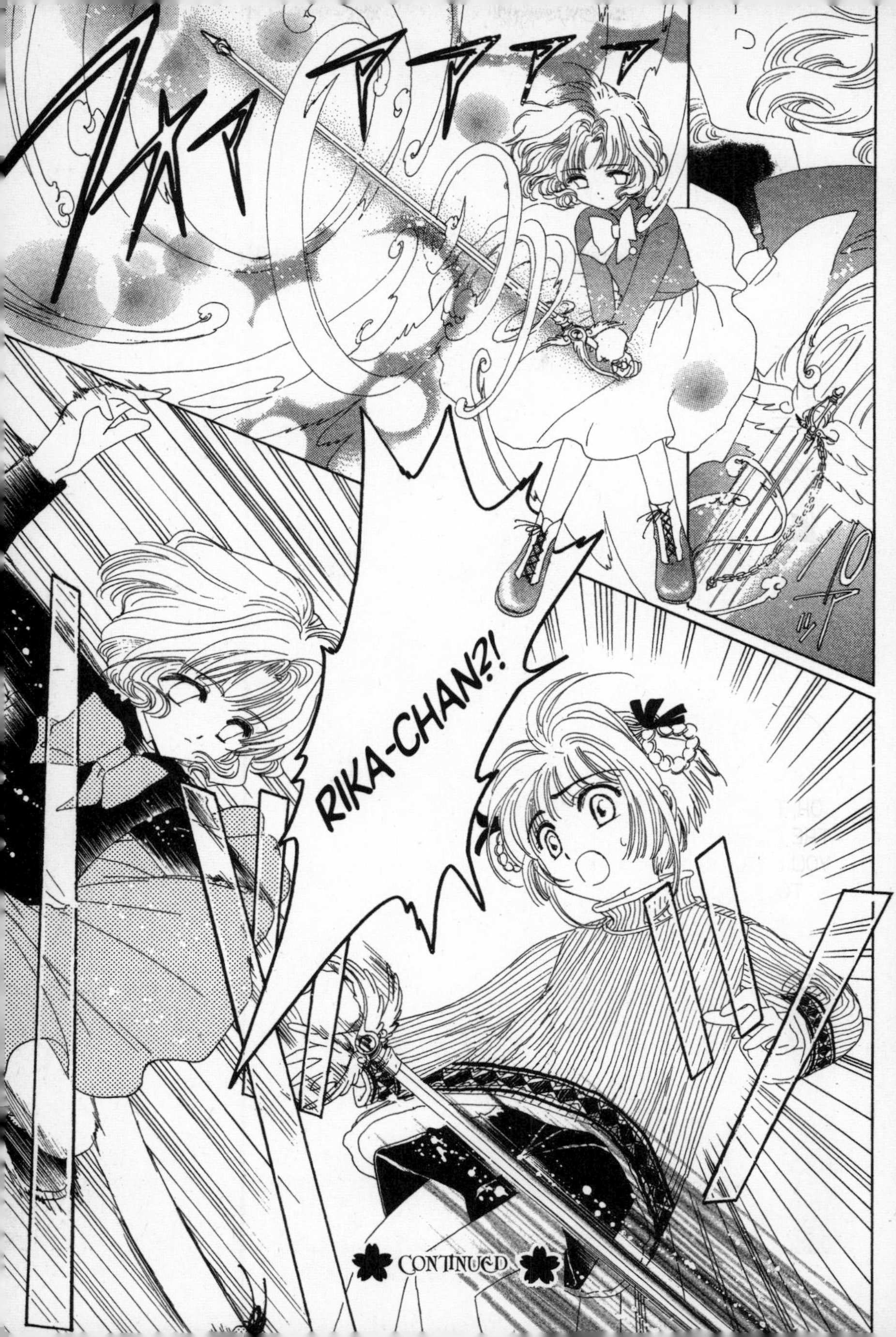
RIKA-CHAN?!
CONTINUED

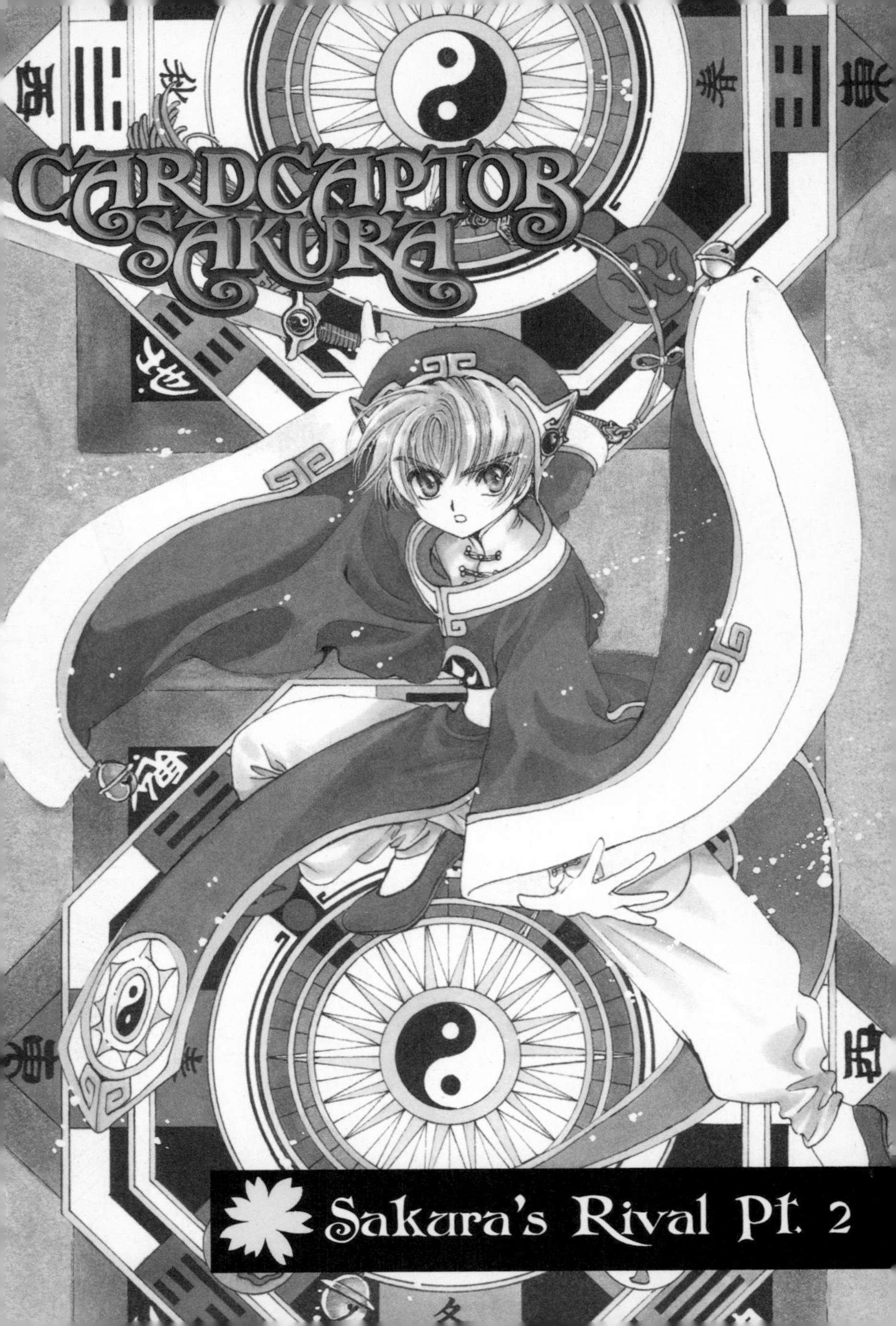
CARDCAPTOR SAKURA
Sakura's Rival Pt. 2

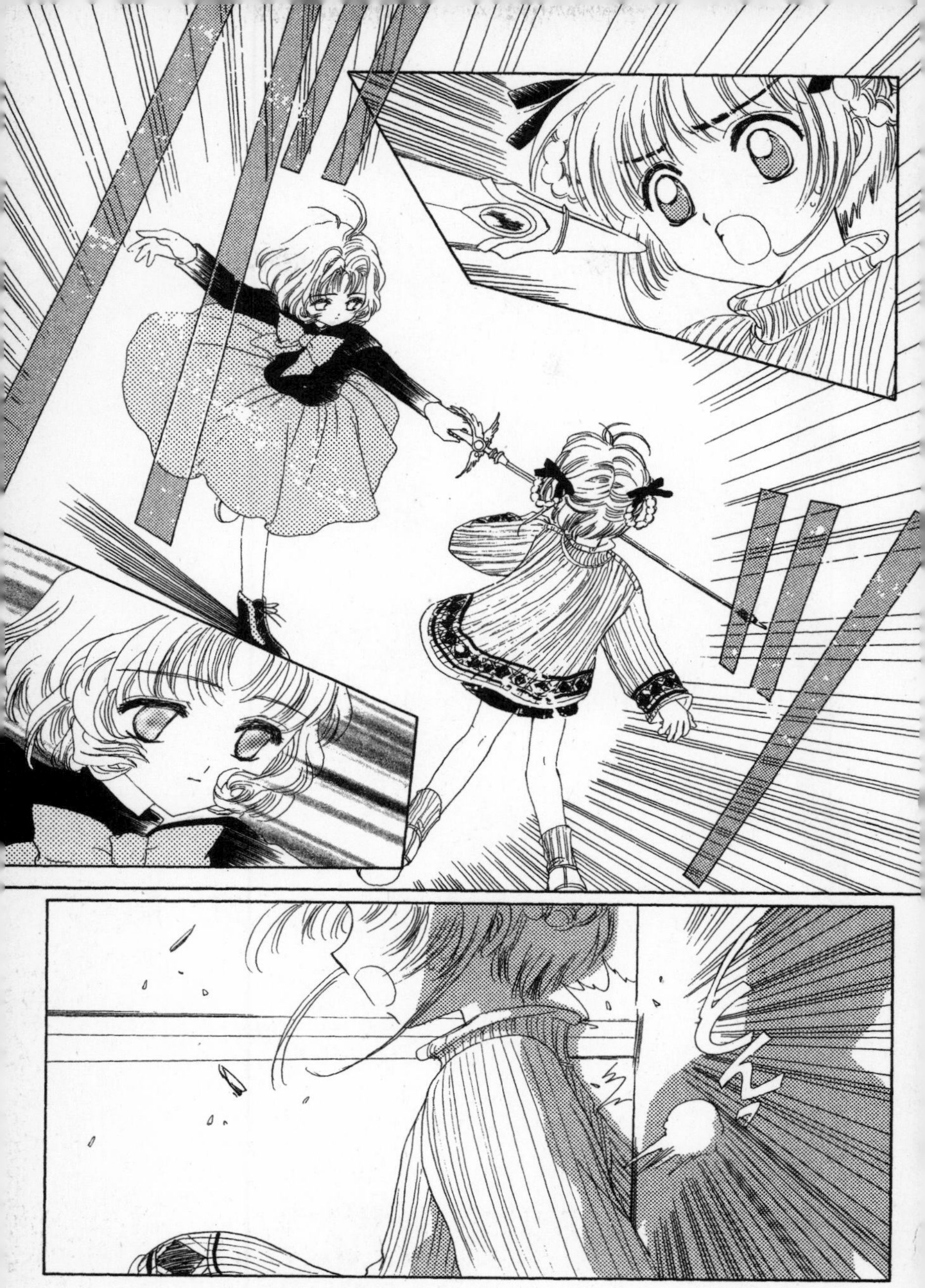

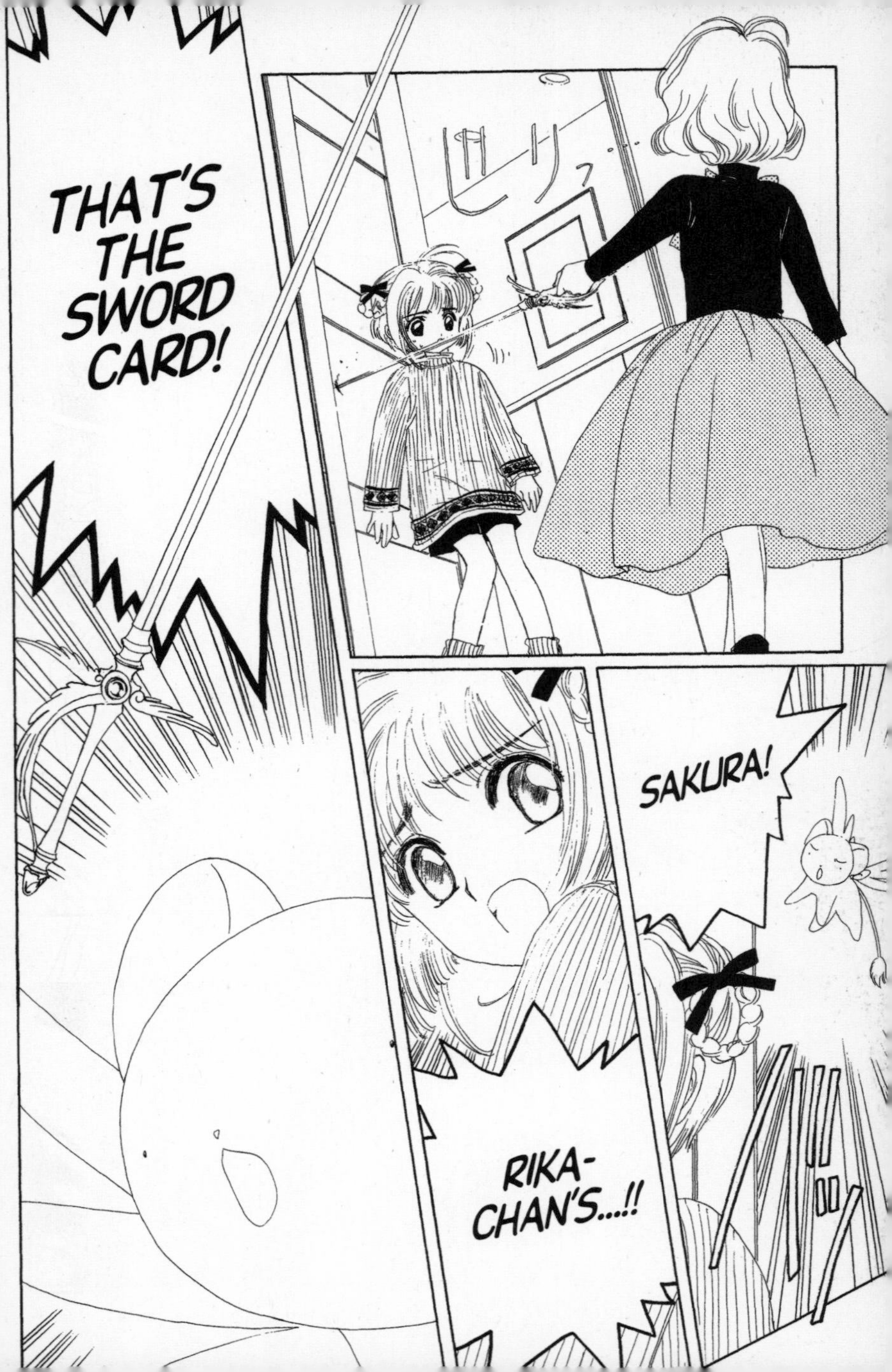
SAKURA!
RIKA-CHAN'S...!!
THAT'S THE SWORD CARD!

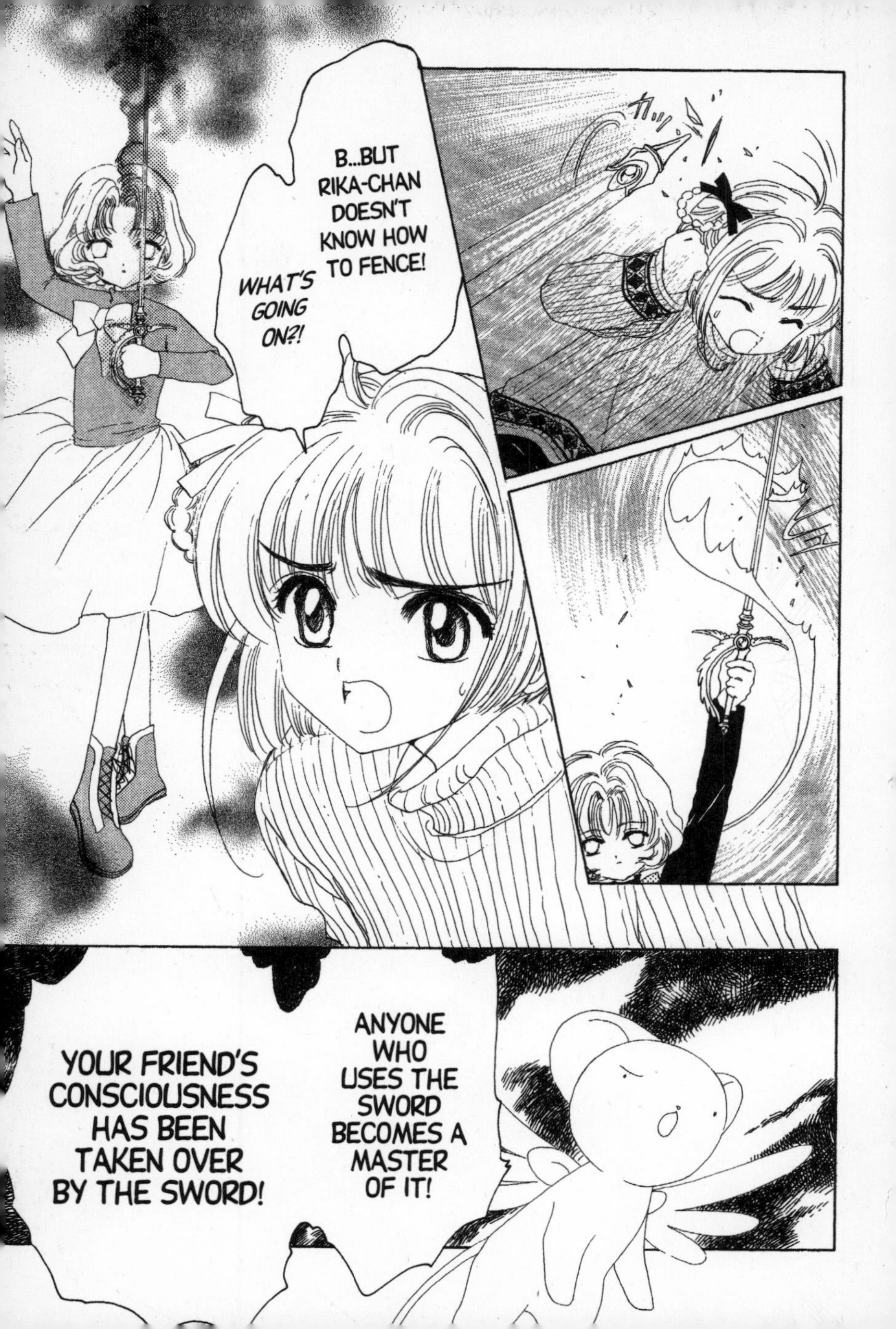
B...BUT RIKA-CHAN DOESN'T KNOW HOW TO FENCE!
WHAT'S GOING ON?!
ANYONE WHO USES THE SWORD BECOMES A MASTER OF IT!
YOUR FRIEND'S CONSCIOUSNESS HAS BEEN TAKEN OVER BY THE SWORD!

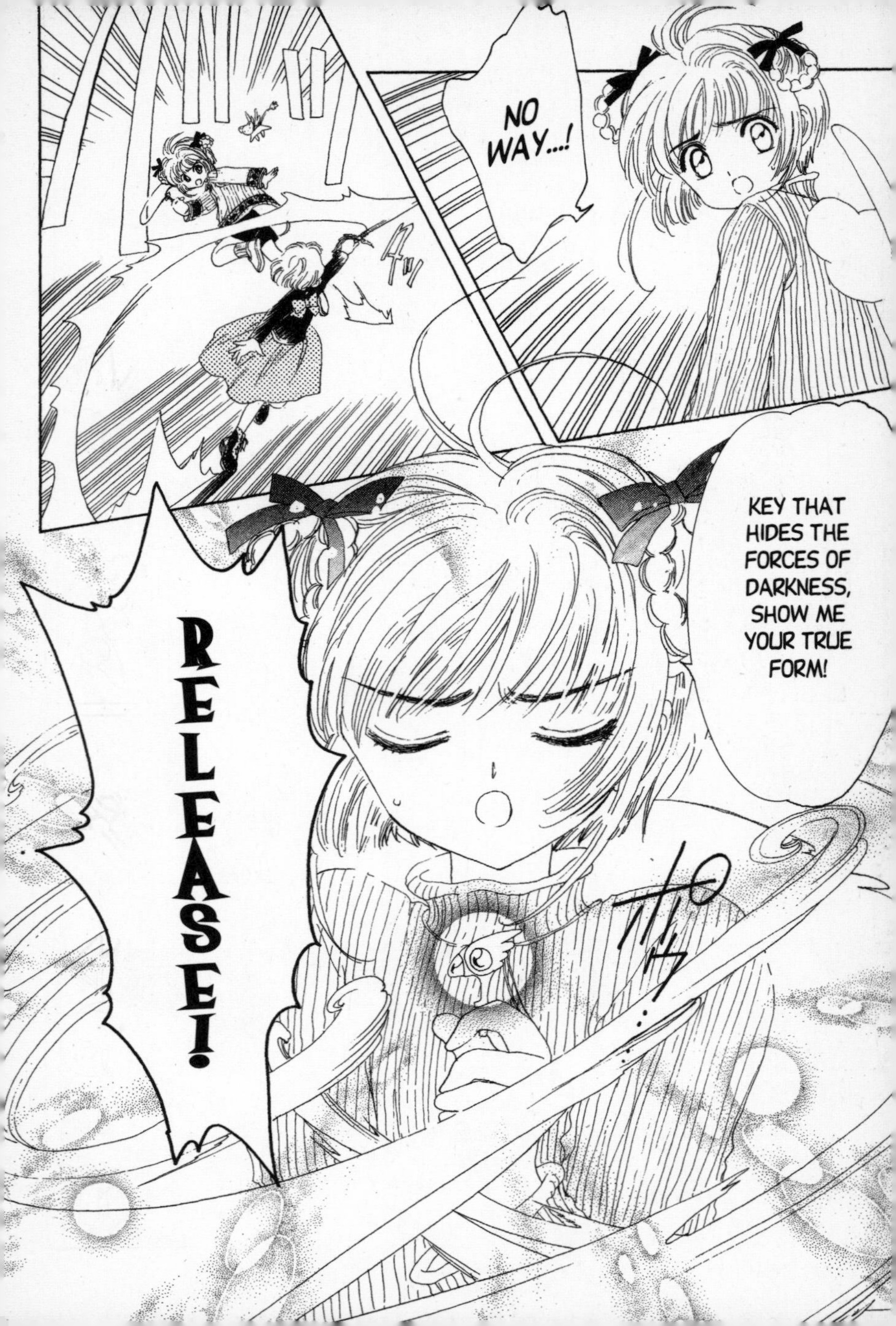
NO WAY...!
KEY THAT HIDES THE FORCES OF DARKNESS, SHOW ME YOUR TRUE FORM!
RELEASE!

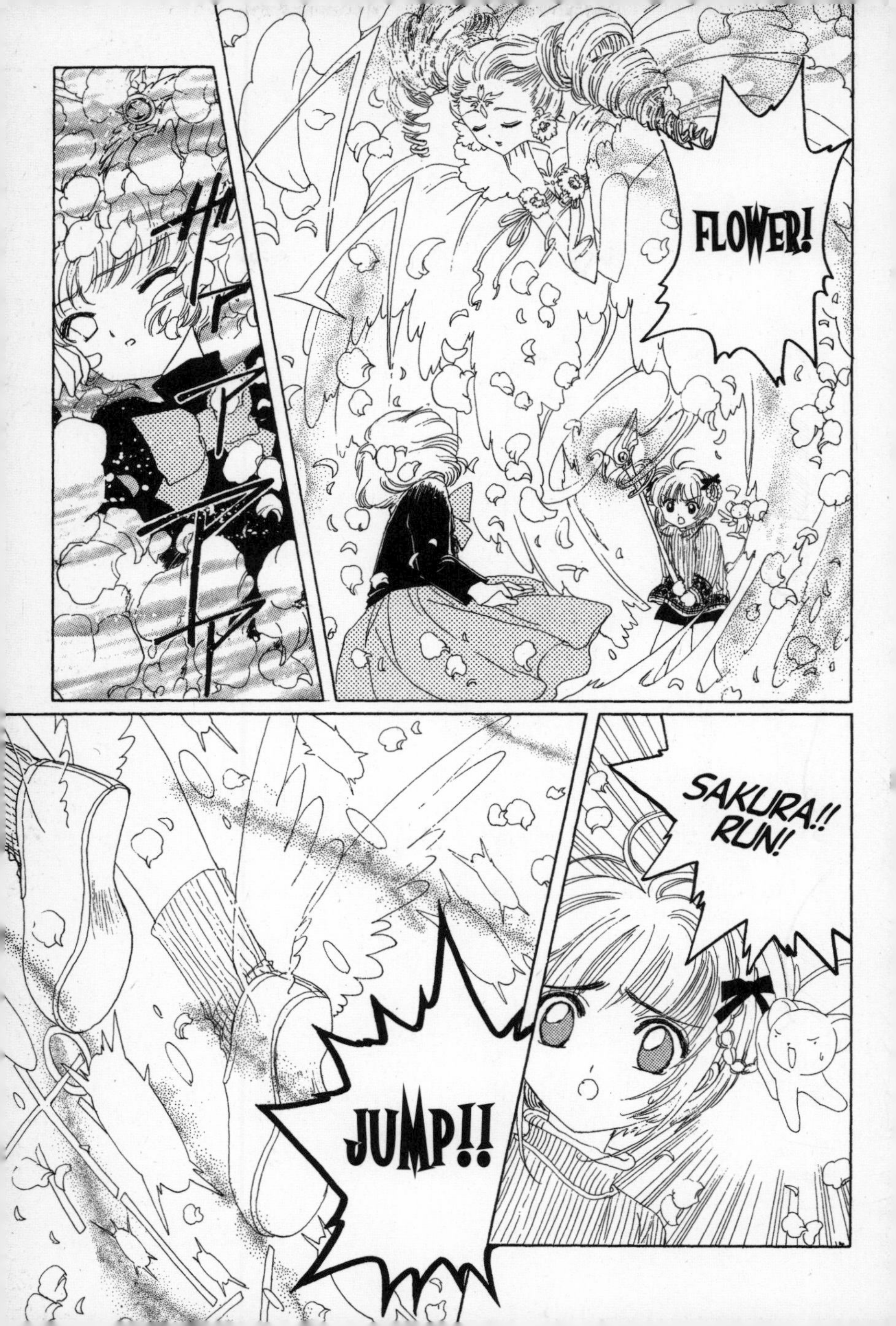
FLOWER!
SAKURA!! RUN!
JUMP!!

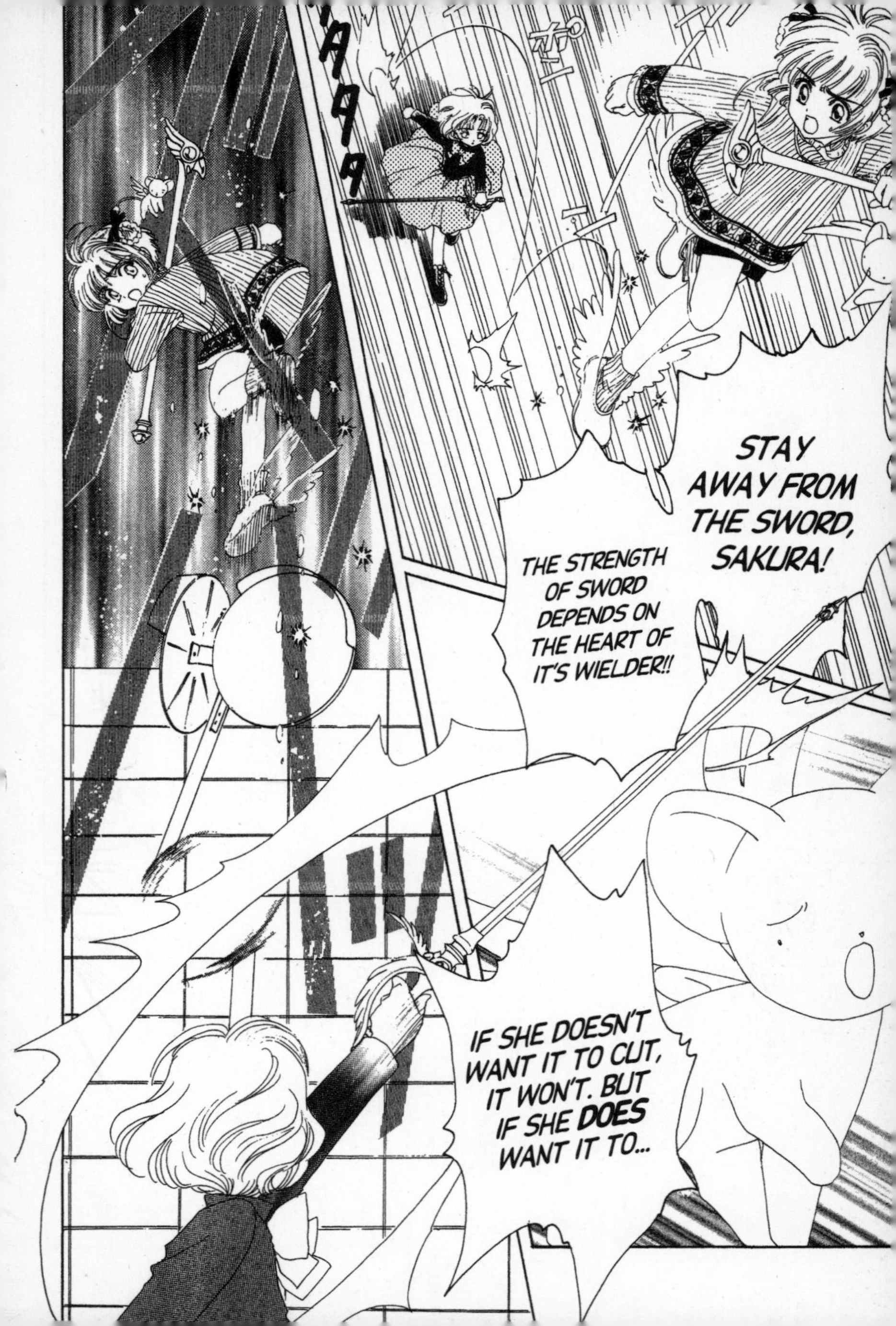
STAY AWAY FROM THE SWORD, SAKURA!
THE STRENGTH OF SWORD DEPENDS ON THE HEART OF IT'S WIELDER!!
IF SHE DOESN'T WANT IT TO CUT, IT WON'T. BUT IF SHE **DOES** WANT IT TO...

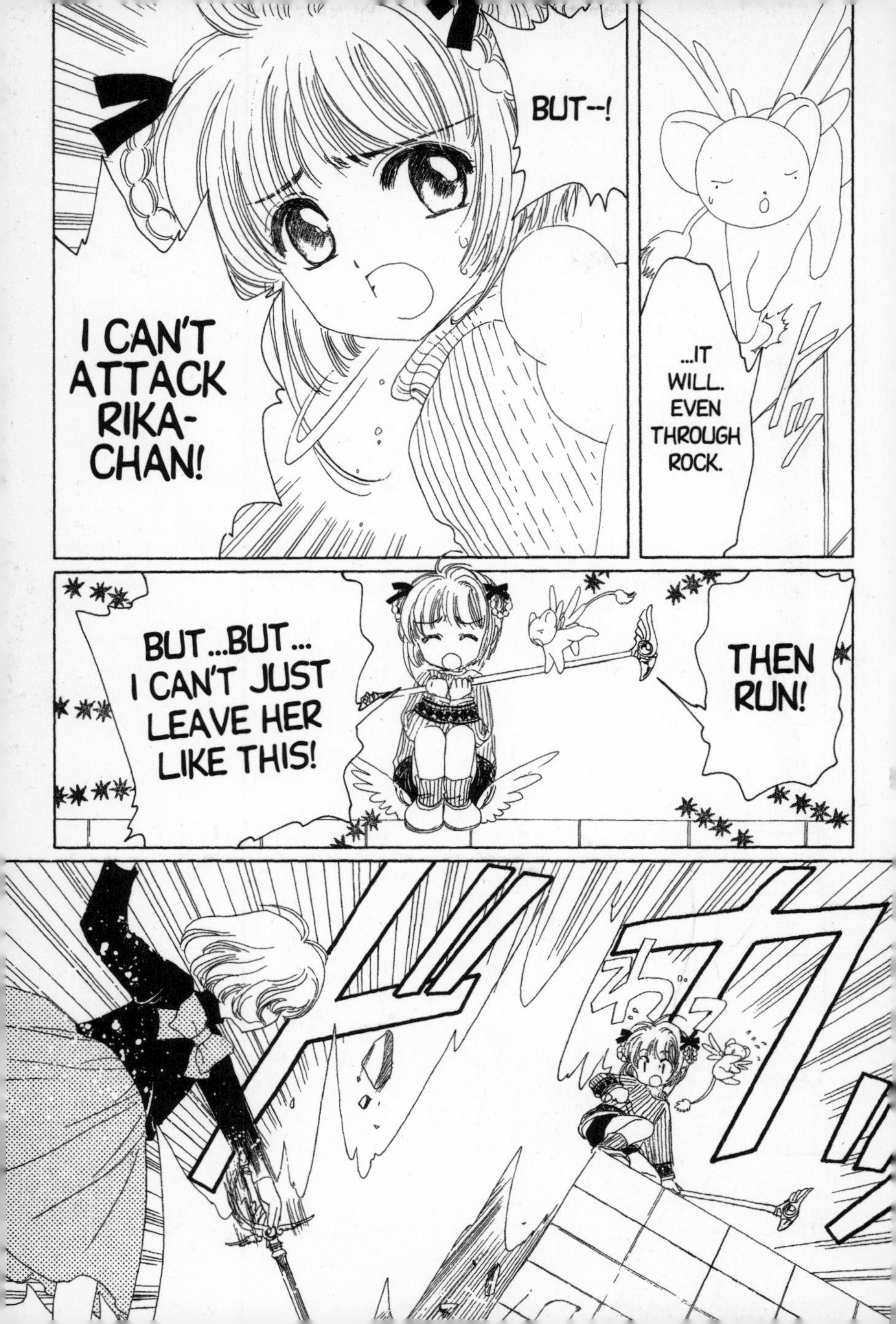
...IT WILL. EVEN THROUGH ROCK.
BUT--!
I CAN'T ATTACK RIKA-CHAN!
THEN RUN!
BUT...BUT... I CAN'T JUST LEAVE HER LIKE THIS!

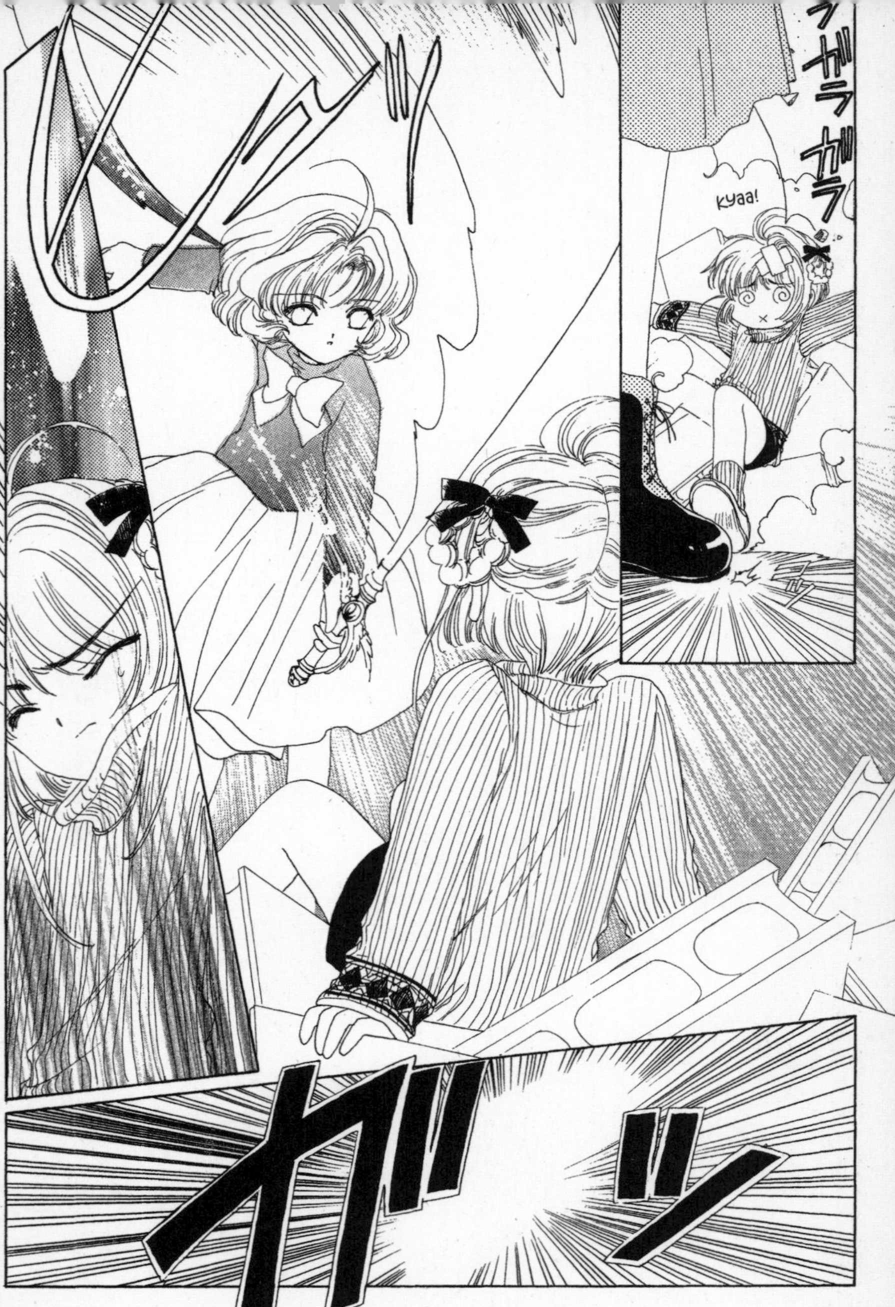
Kyaa!

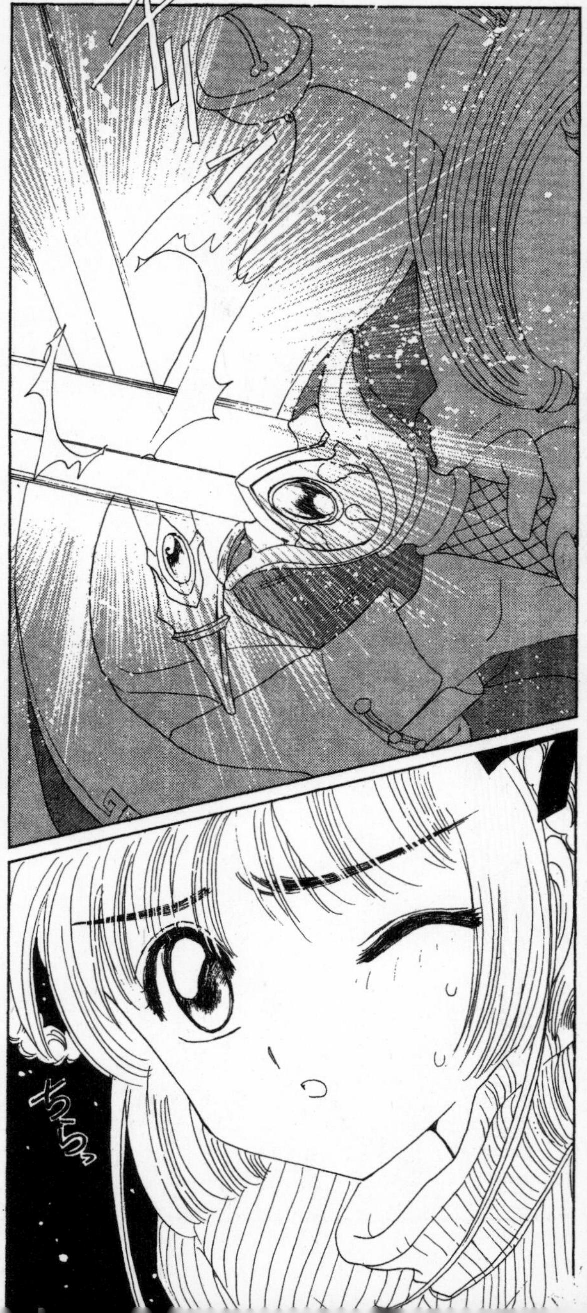

8

Nadeshiko Kinomoto

Birthdate:
May 20
Occupation:
Model
Favorite Foods:
Sweets, red tea
Least Favorite Thing:
Warm sunlight
Favorite Color:
White
Favorite Flower:
Wisteria, peach blossom, cherry blossom
Favorite Recipe:
Can't cook
Thing she's not good at:
Remembering people's faces and names
Hobby:
Sleeping
Special Skill:
Can fall asleep anywhere

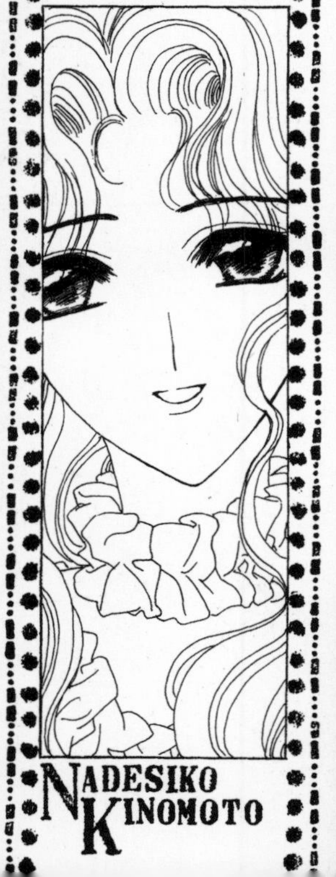

NADESIKO KINOMOTO

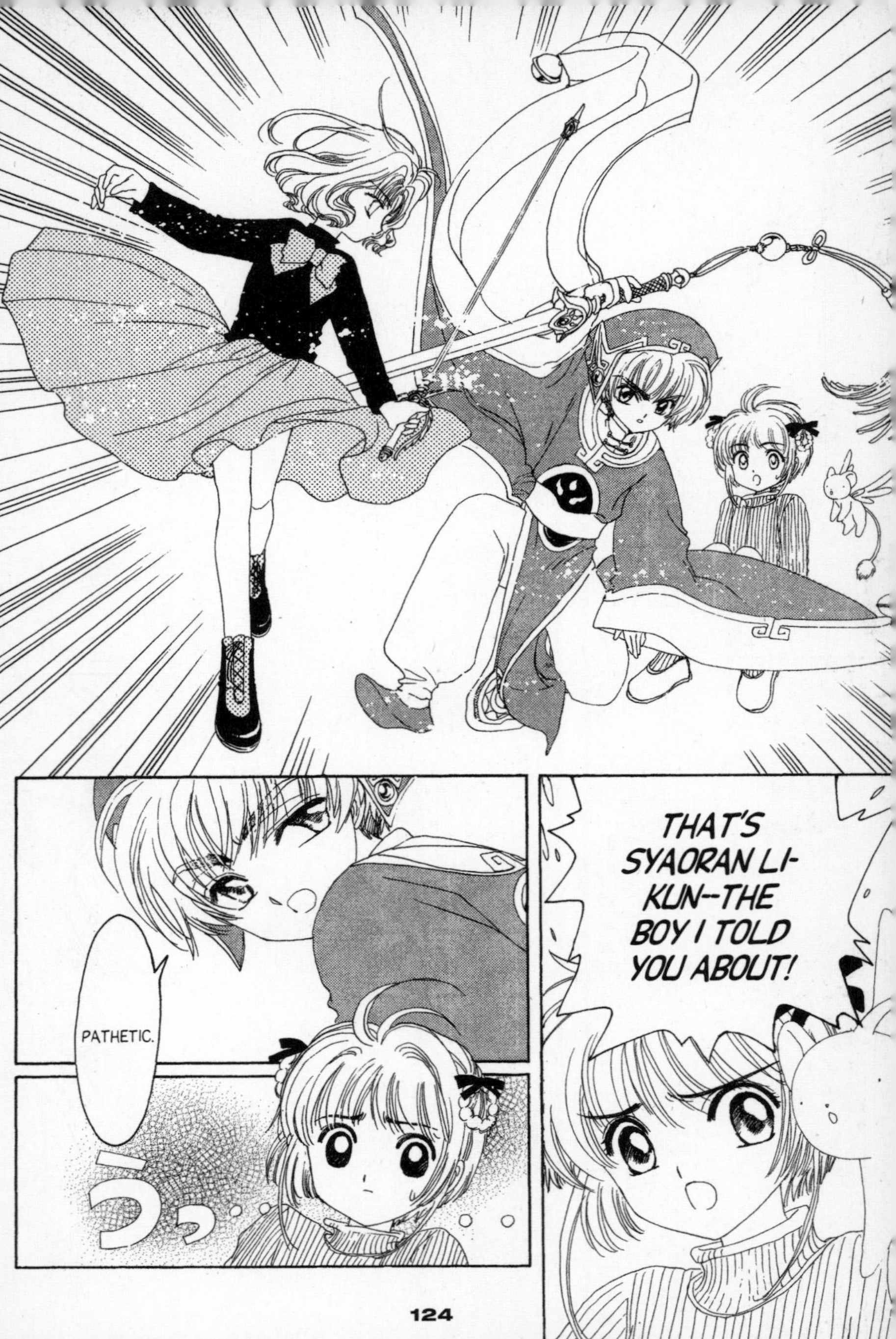
THAT'S SYAORAN LI-KUN--THE BOY I TOLD YOU ABOUT!
PATHETIC.
うっ

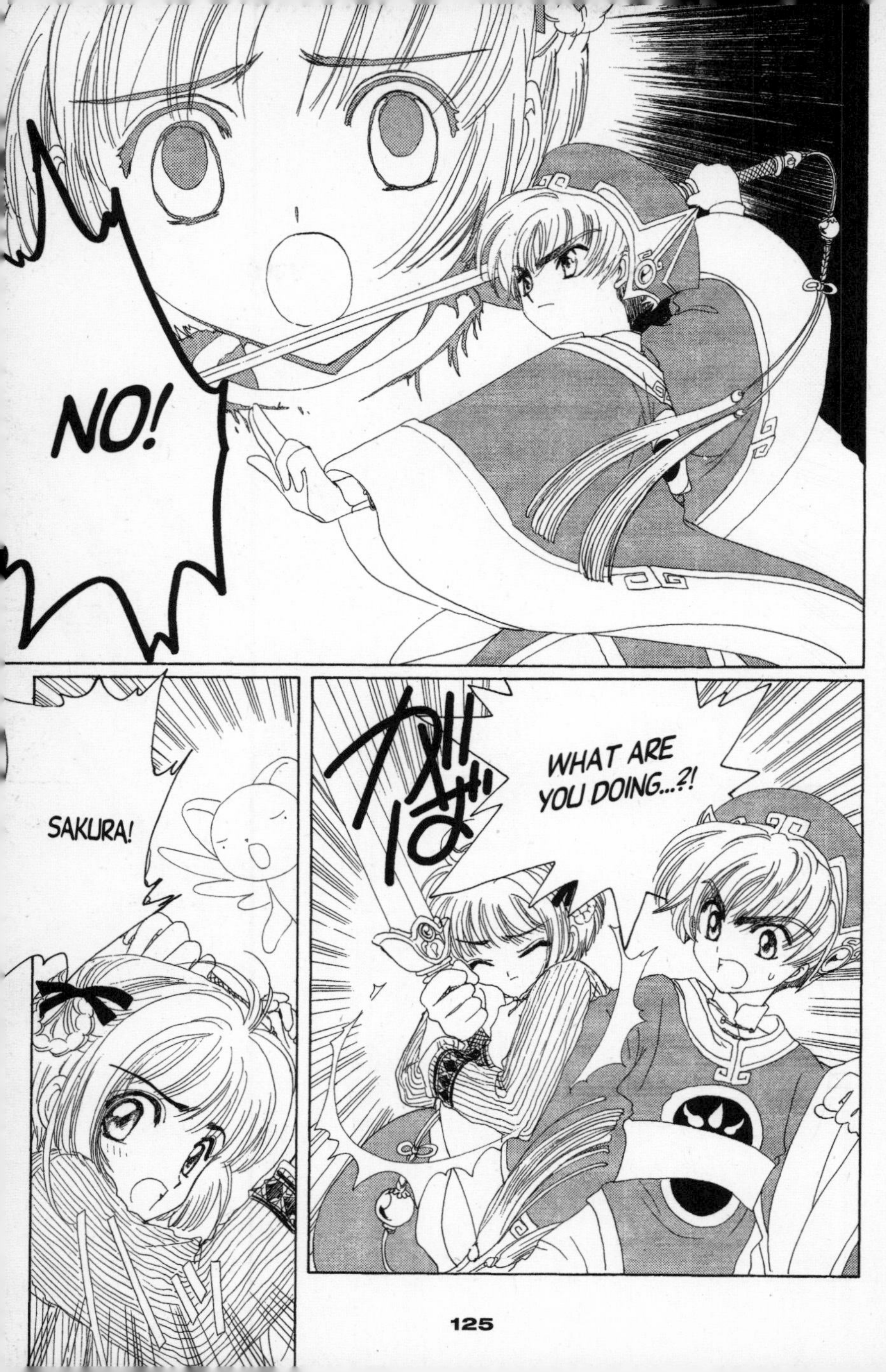
NO!
WHAT ARE YOU DOING...?!
SAKURA!

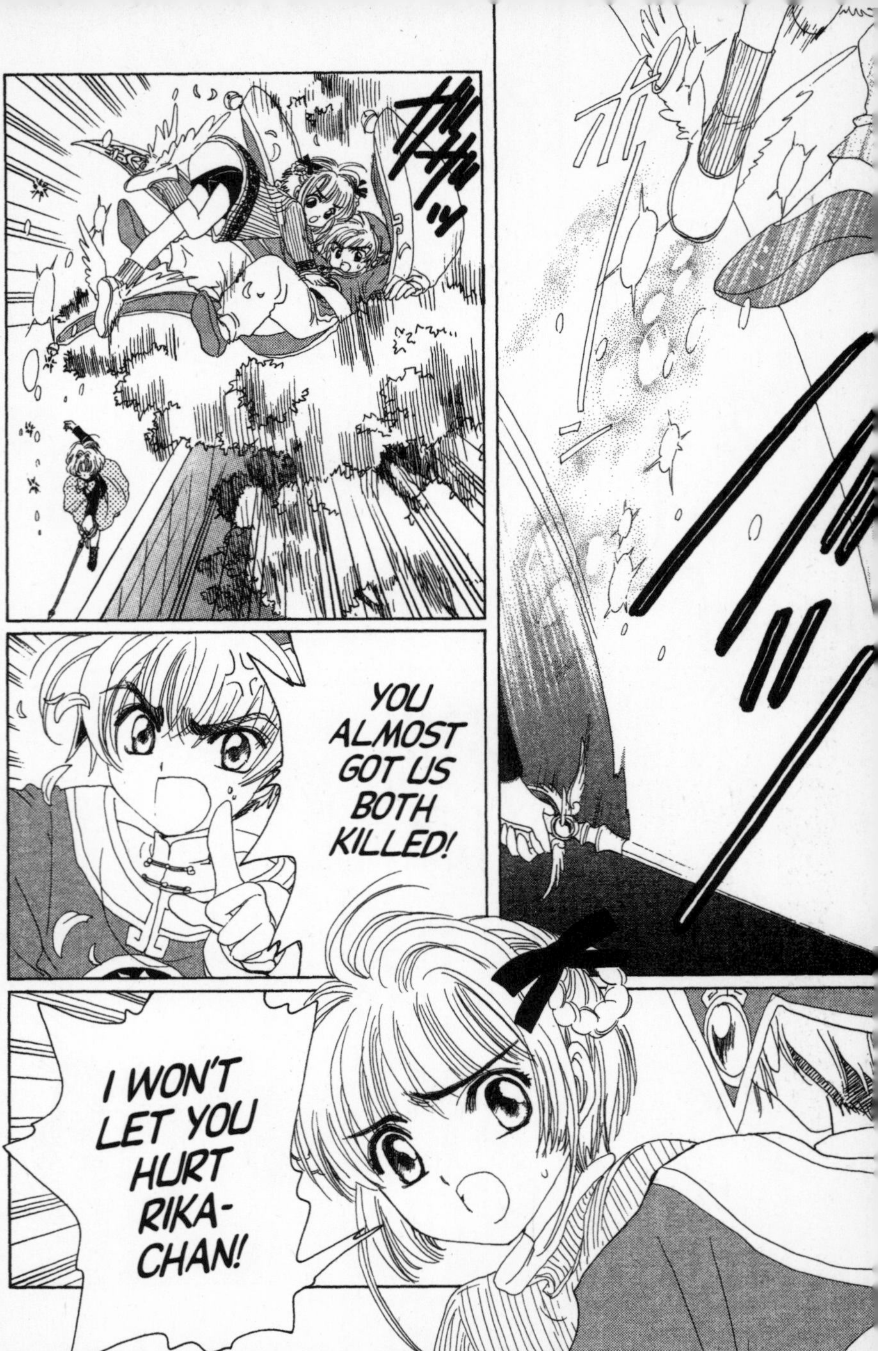
YOU ALMOST GOT US BOTH KILLED!
I WON'T LET YOU HURT RIKA-CHAN!

Lakeville Library
508-947-9028

Date due: 7/16/2019,23:59
Title: Cardcaptor Sakura.
Master of the Clow
Item ID: 33577009161104
Author: CLAMP (Mangaka
group)

Date due: 7/16/2019,23:59
Title: How music works
Item ID: 33577007079894
Author: Byrne, David, 1952-

Total price of checked out
items: $41.99

Lakeville Library
508-947-9028

Date due: 7/6/2019,23:59
Title: Cardcaptor Sakura.
Master of the Clow
Item ID: 33577000916104
Author: CLAMP (Mangaka
group)

Date due: 7/6/2019,23:59
Title: How music works
Item ID: 33577001079894
Author: Byrne, David, 1952-

Total price of checked out
items: $41.99

.
.
.

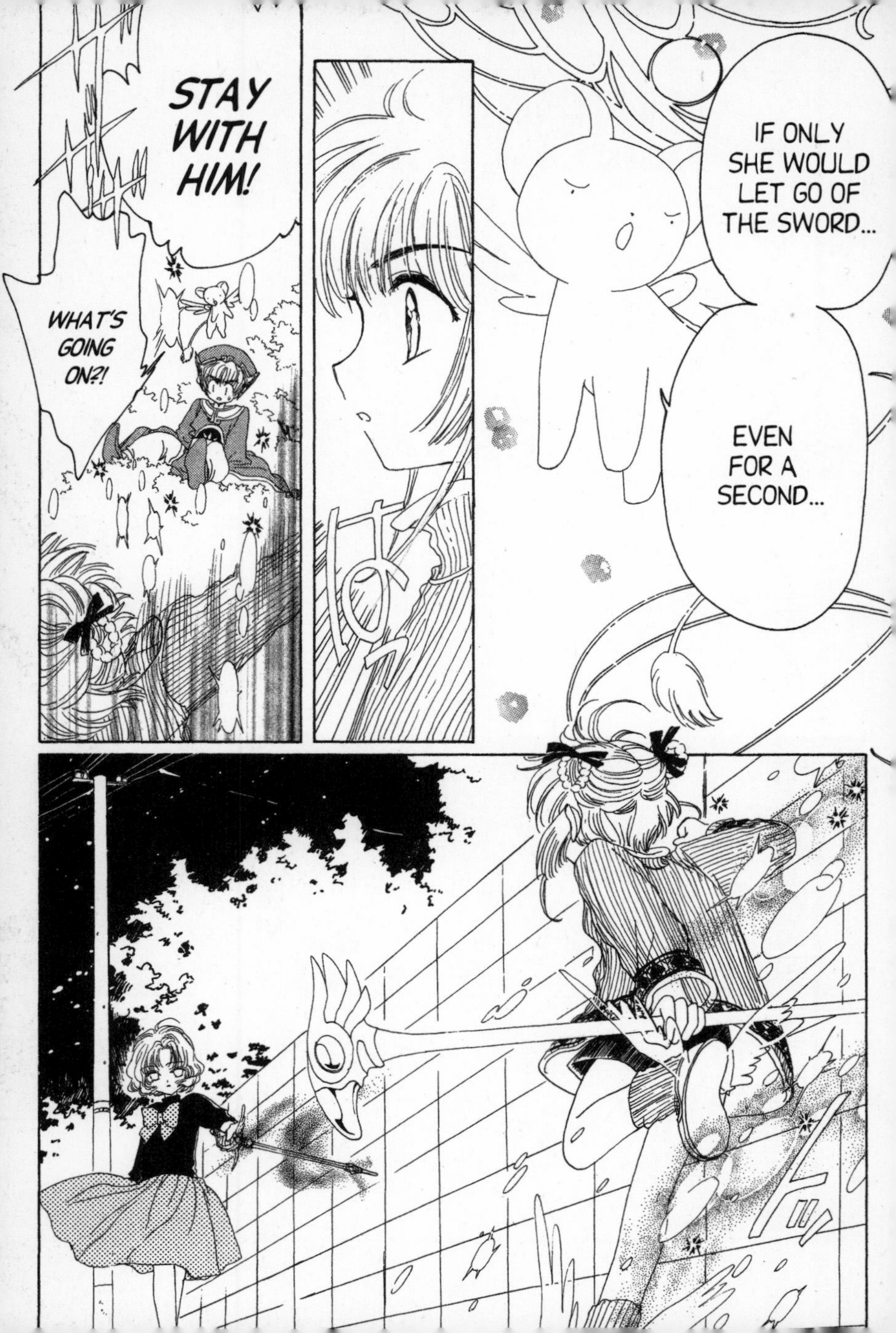
IF ONLY SHE WOULD LET GO OF THE SWORD...
EVEN FOR A SECOND...
はっ
STAY WITH HIM!
WHAT'S GOING ON?!

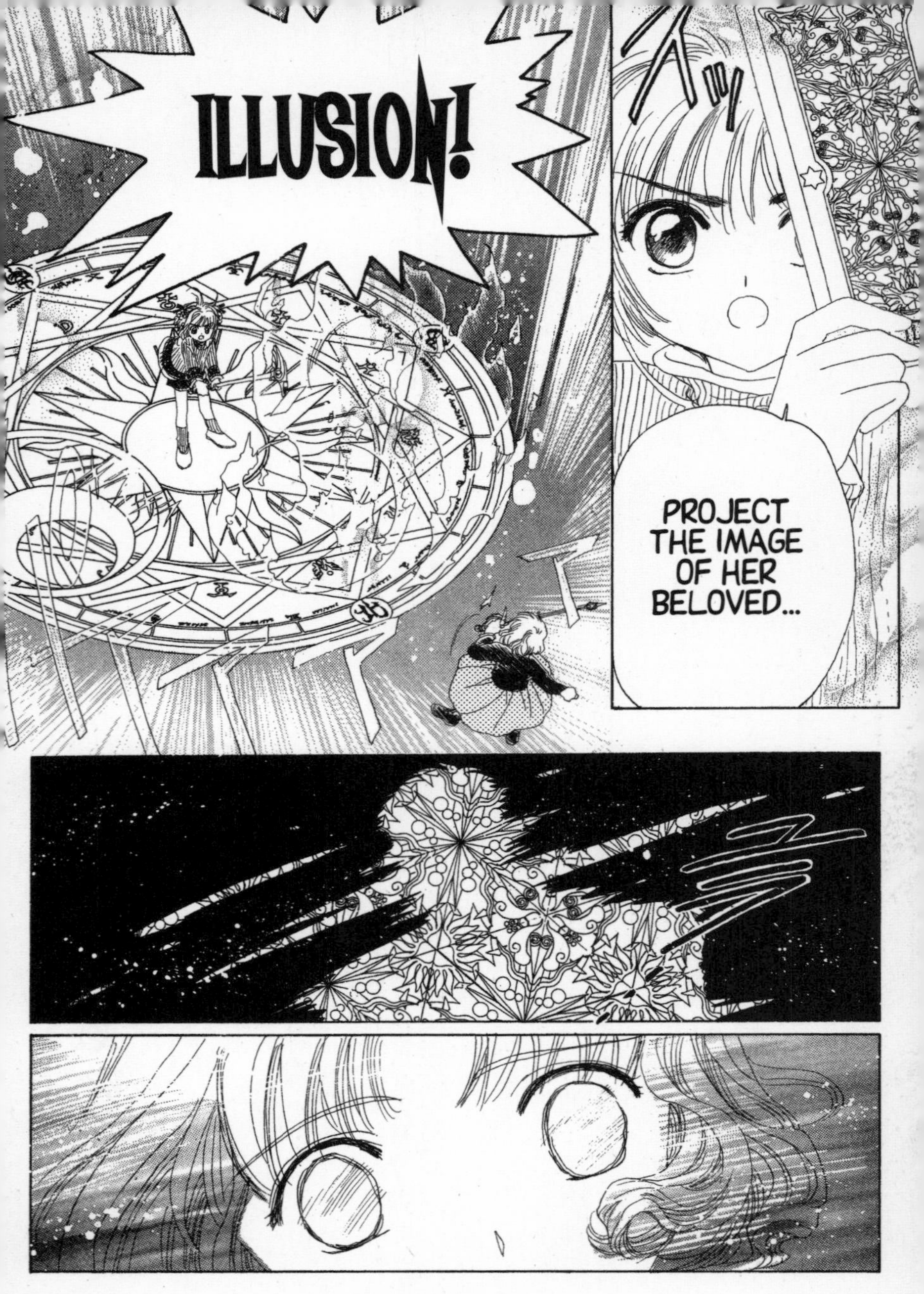
ILLUSION!
PROJECT THE IMAGE OF HER BELOVED...

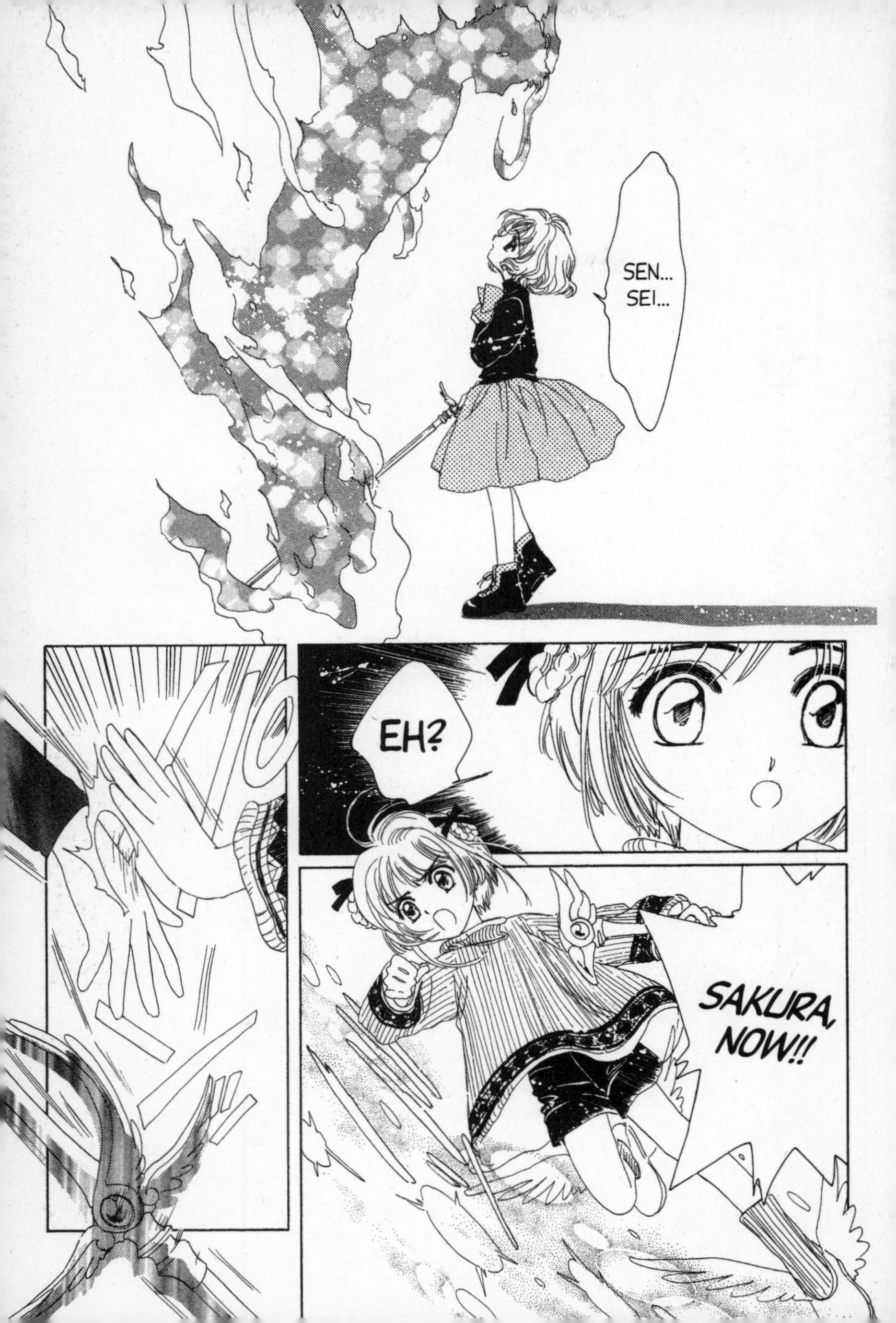
SEN... SEI...
EH?
SAKURA, NOW!!

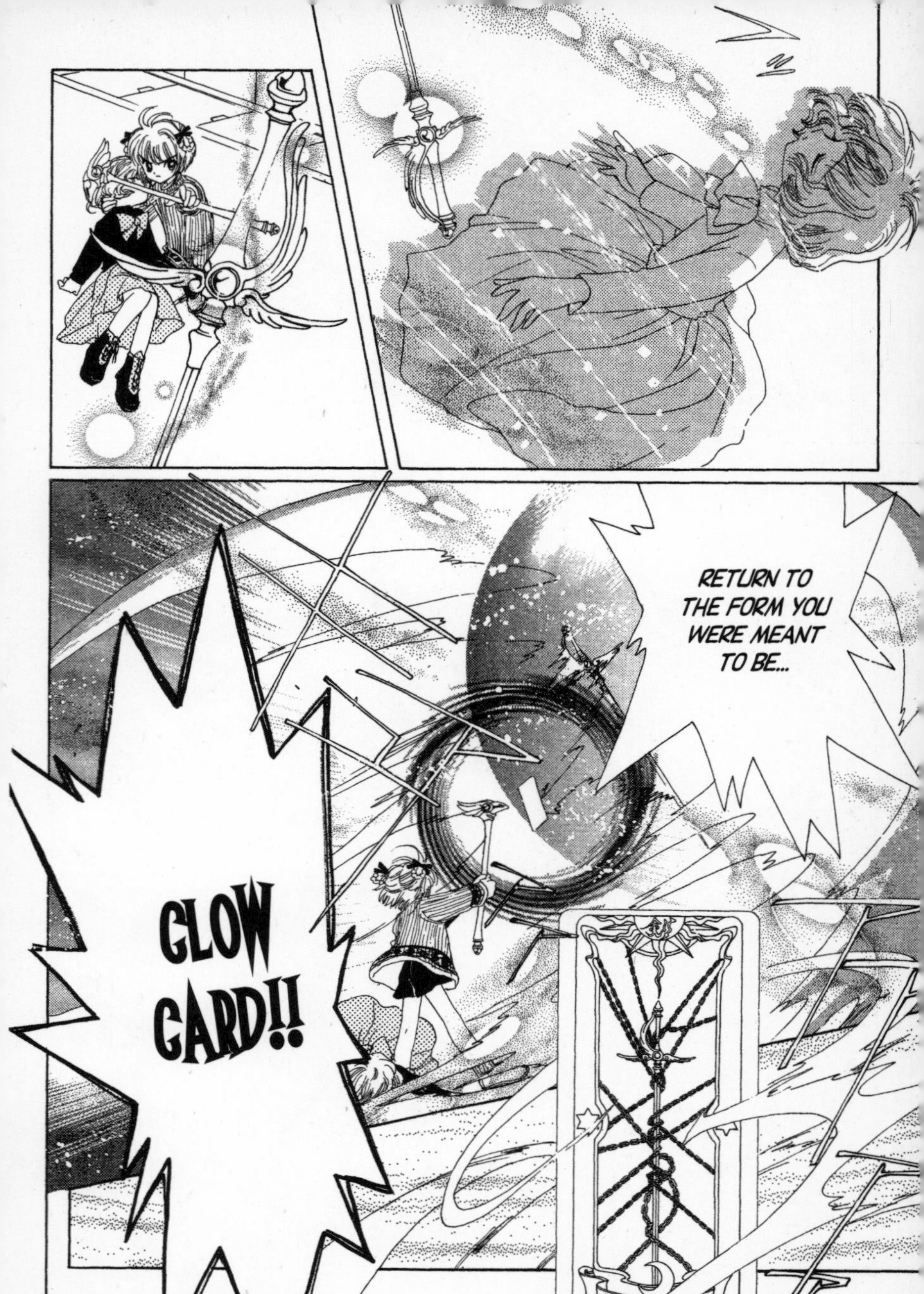
RETURN TO THE FORM YOU WERE MEANT TO BE...
GLOW CARD!!

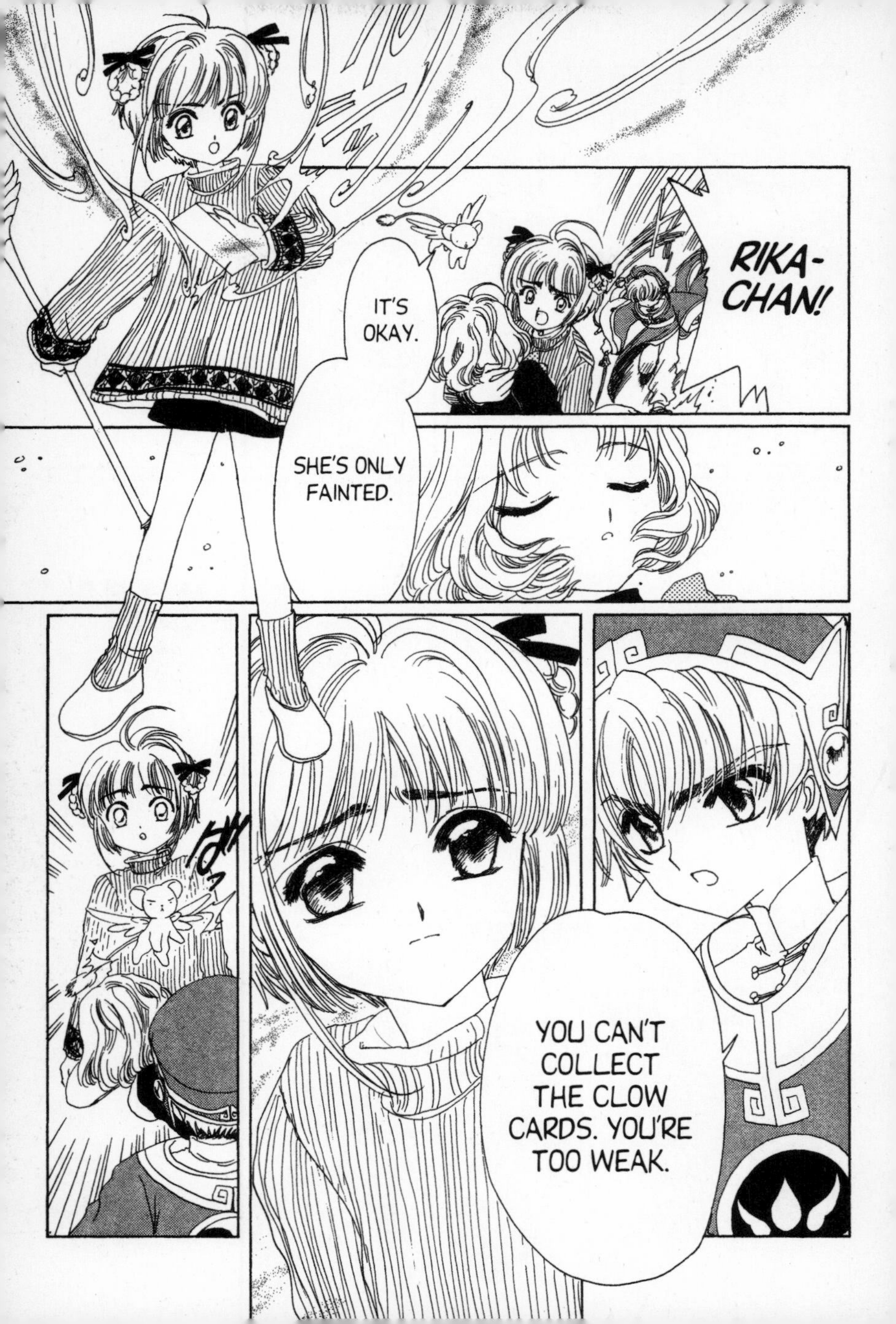
RIKA-CHAN!
IT'S OKAY.
SHE'S ONLY FAINTED.
YOU CAN'T COLLECT THE CLOW CARDS. YOU'RE TOO WEAK.

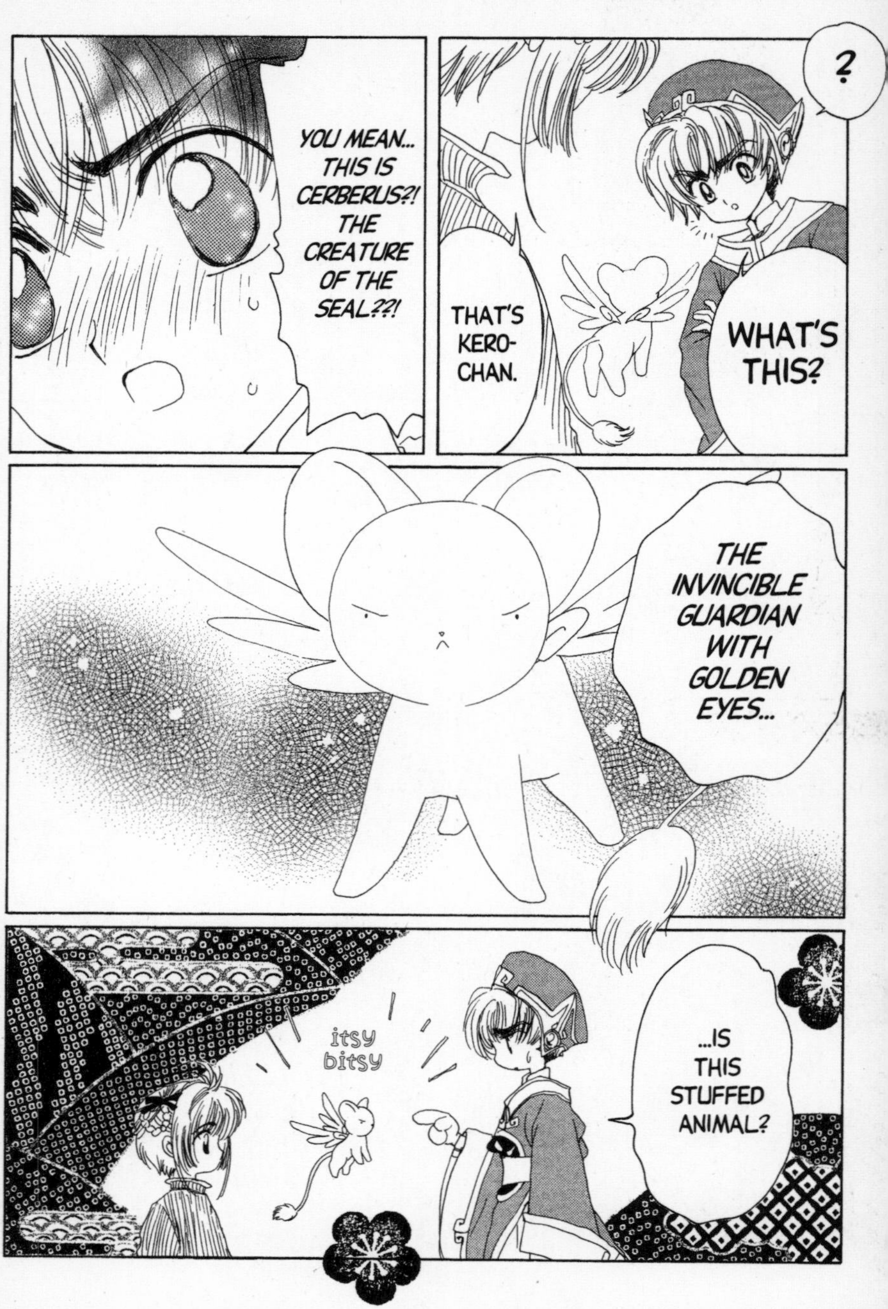
?
WHAT'S THIS?
THAT'S KERO-CHAN.
YOU MEAN... THIS IS CERBERUS?! THE CREATURE OF THE SEAL??!
THE INVINCIBLE GUARDIAN WITH GOLDEN EYES...
...IS THIS STUFFED ANIMAL?
itsy bitsy

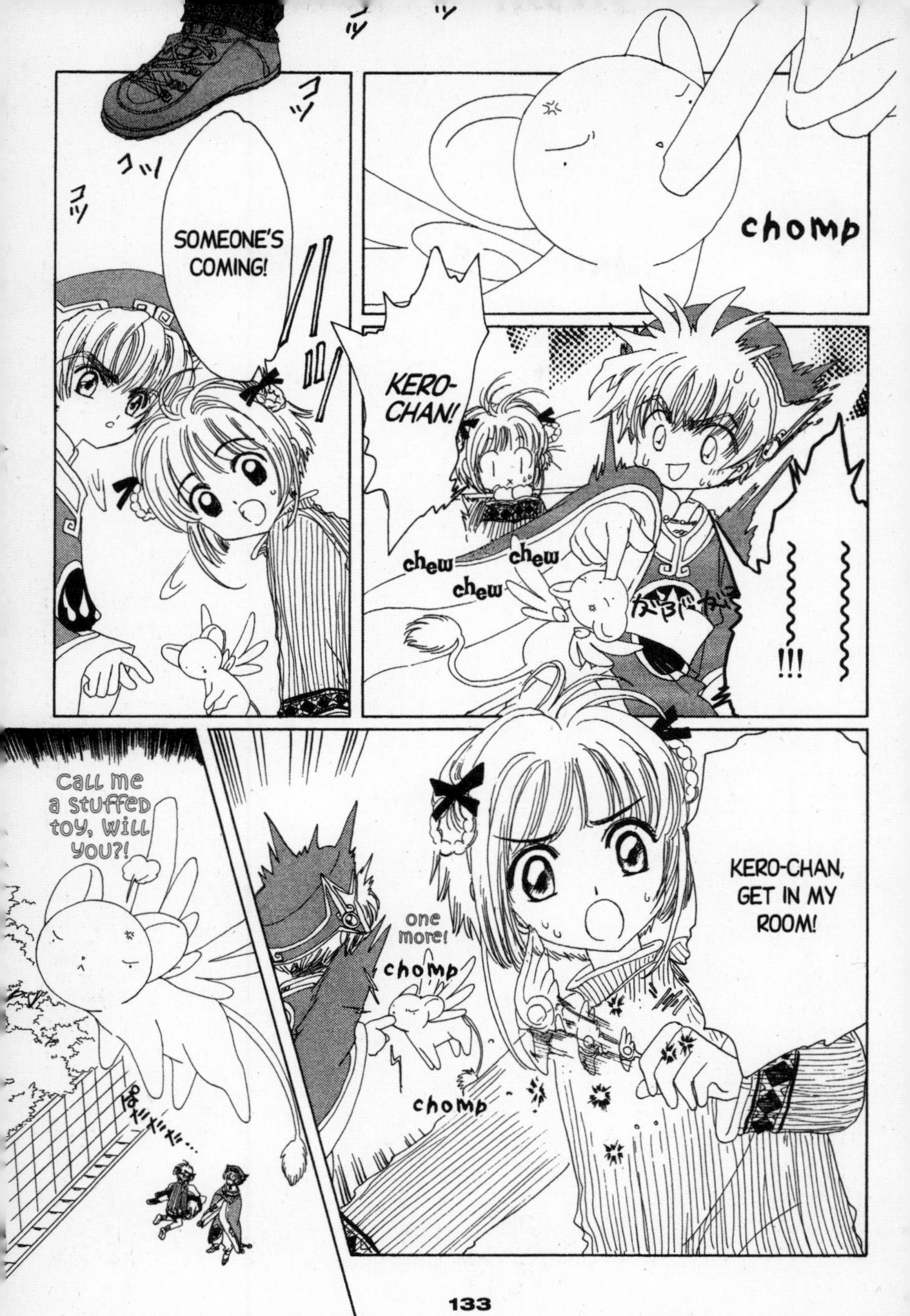
chomp
KERO-CHAN!
chew
chew
chew
!!!
SOMEONE'S COMING!
KERO-CHAN, GET IN MY ROOM!
one more!
chomp
chomp
Call me a stuffed toy, will you?!

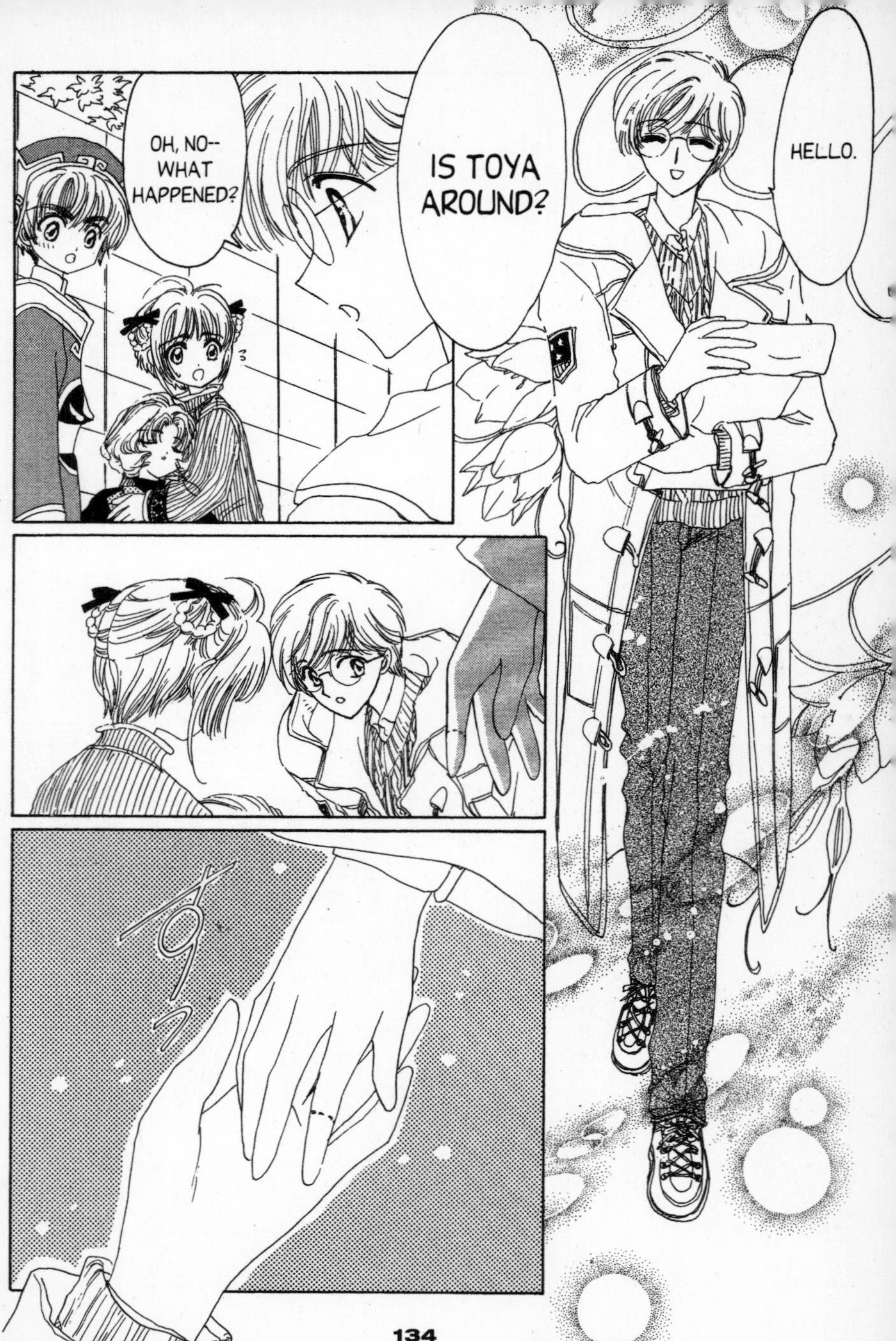
HELLO.
IS TOYA AROUND?
OH, NO-- WHAT HAPPENED?

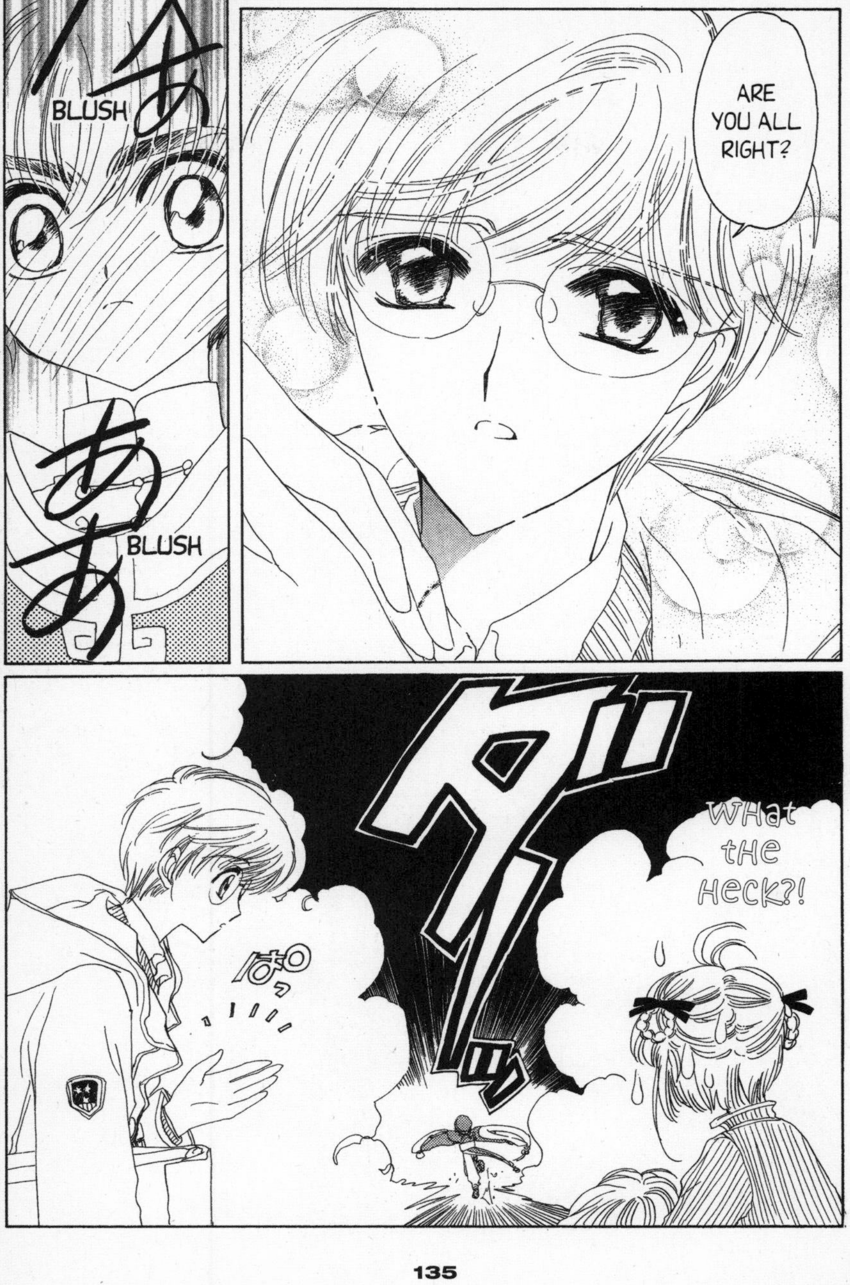
ARE YOU ALL RIGHT?
BLUSH
BLUSH
WHAT THE HECK?!

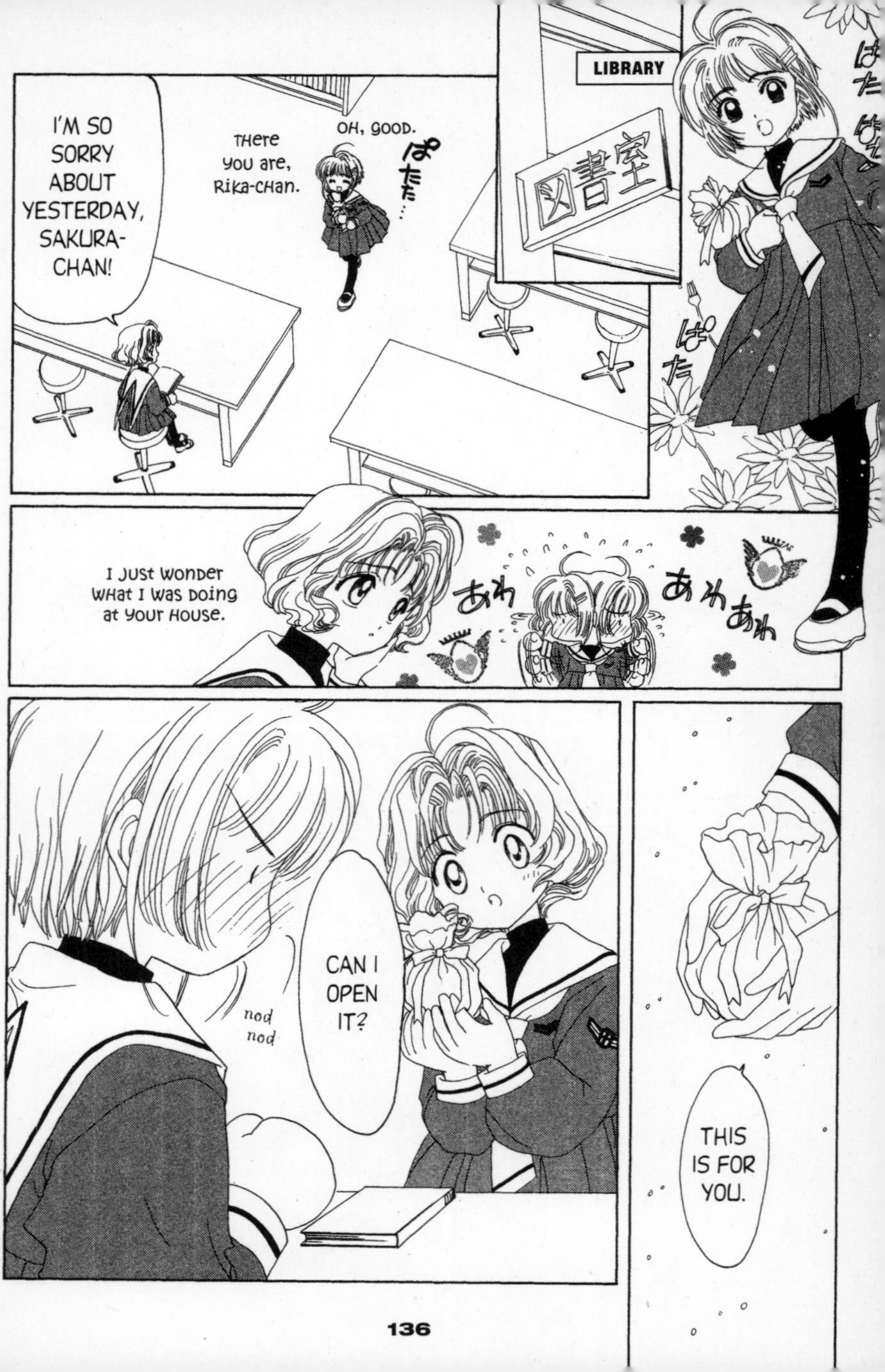
はたぱた
ぱた
LIBRARY
図書室
OH, GOOD.
There you are, Rika-chan.
ぱたた…
I'M SO SORRY ABOUT YESTERDAY, SAKURA-CHAN!
あわあわあわ
I just wonder what I was doing at your house.
THIS IS FOR YOU.
CAN I OPEN IT?
nod nod

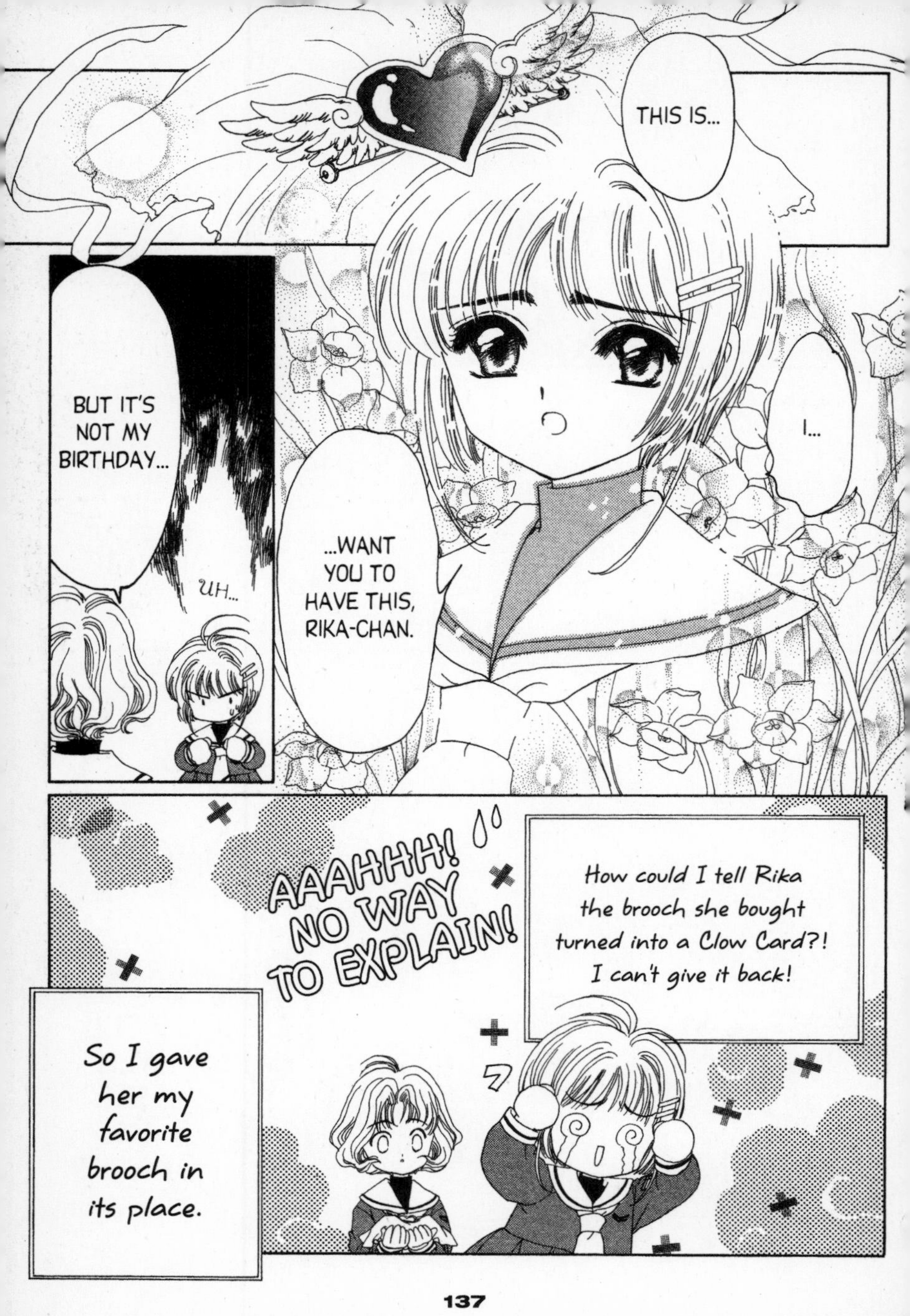
THIS IS...
I...
...WANT YOU TO HAVE THIS, RIKA-CHAN.
BUT IT'S NOT MY BIRTHDAY...
UH...
How could I tell Rika the brooch she bought turned into a Clow Card?! I can't give it back!
AAAHHH! NO WAY TO EXPLAIN!
So I gave her my favorite brooch in its place.

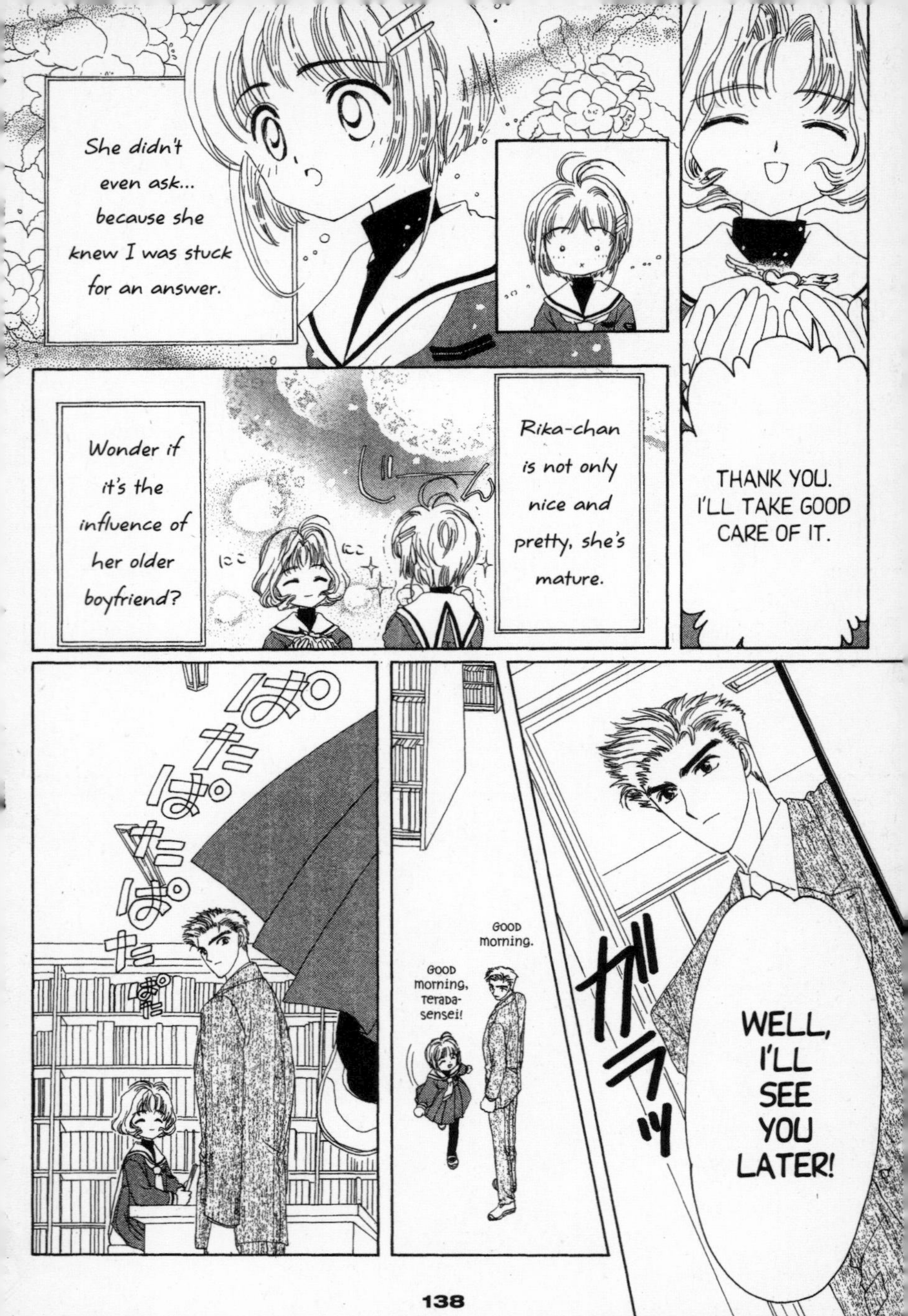
THANK YOU. I'LL TAKE GOOD CARE OF IT.
She didn't even ask... because she knew I was stuck for an answer.
Rika-chan is not only nice and pretty, she's mature.
にこ
にこ
Wonder if it's the influence of her older boyfriend?
ガラッ
WELL, I'LL SEE YOU LATER!
GOOD morning.
GOOD morning, TERADA-SENSEI!
ぱたぱたぱたぱた

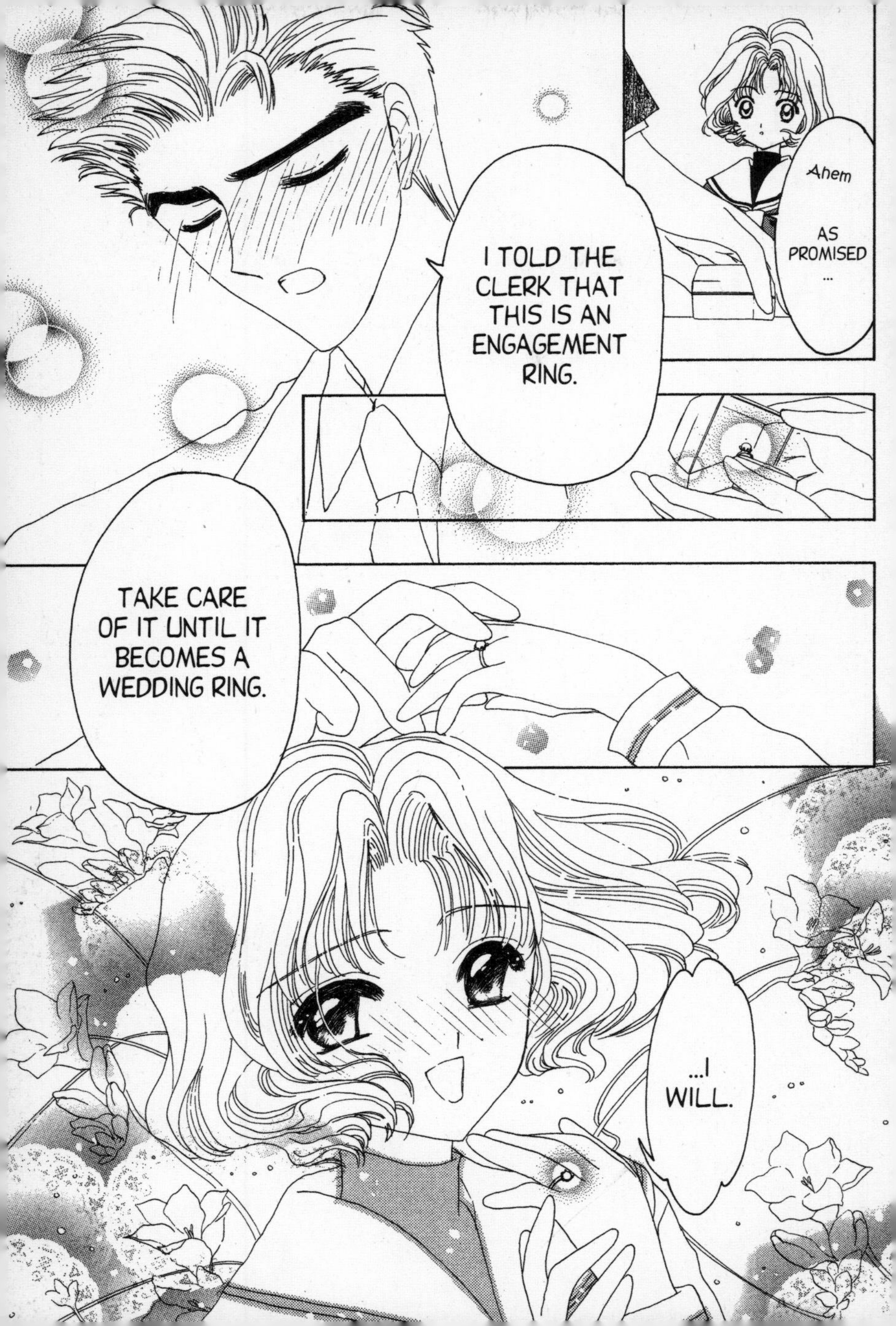
Ahem
AS PROMISED ...
I TOLD THE CLERK THAT THIS IS AN ENGAGEMENT RING.
TAKE CARE OF IT UNTIL IT BECOMES A WEDDING RING.
...I WILL.

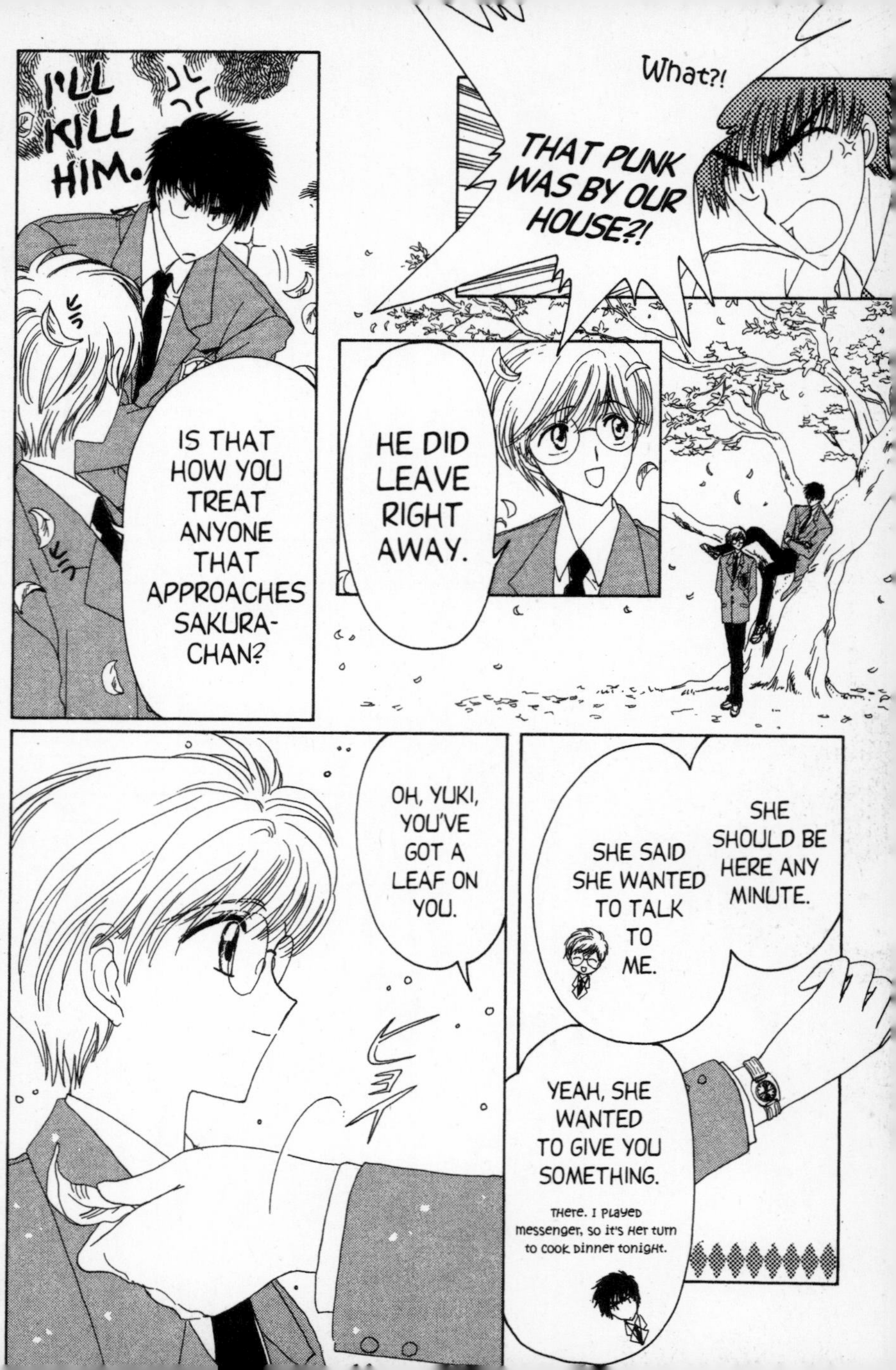
What?!
THAT PUNK WAS BY OUR HOUSE?!
HE DID LEAVE RIGHT AWAY.
I'LL KILL HIM.
IS THAT HOW YOU TREAT ANYONE THAT APPROACHES SAKURA-CHAN?
SHE SAID SHE WANTED TO TALK TO ME.
SHE SHOULD BE HERE ANY MINUTE.
YEAH, SHE WANTED TO GIVE YOU SOMETHING.
There. I played messenger, so it's her turn to cook dinner tonight.
OH, YUKI, YOU'VE GOT A LEAF ON YOU.

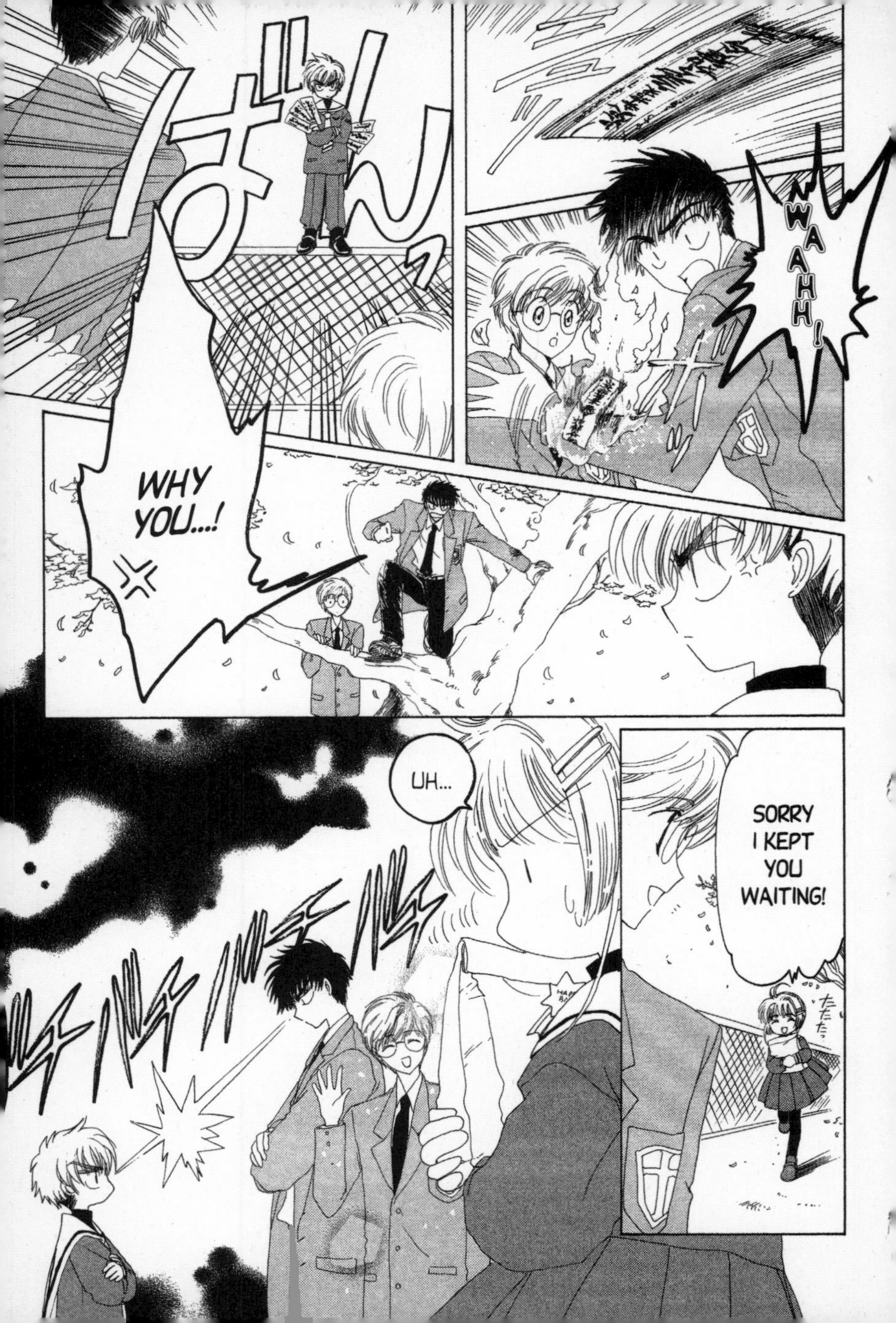
WAAHH!
ばんっ
WHY YOU...!
SORRY I KEPT YOU WAITING!
たたた
UH...
バチバチバチ

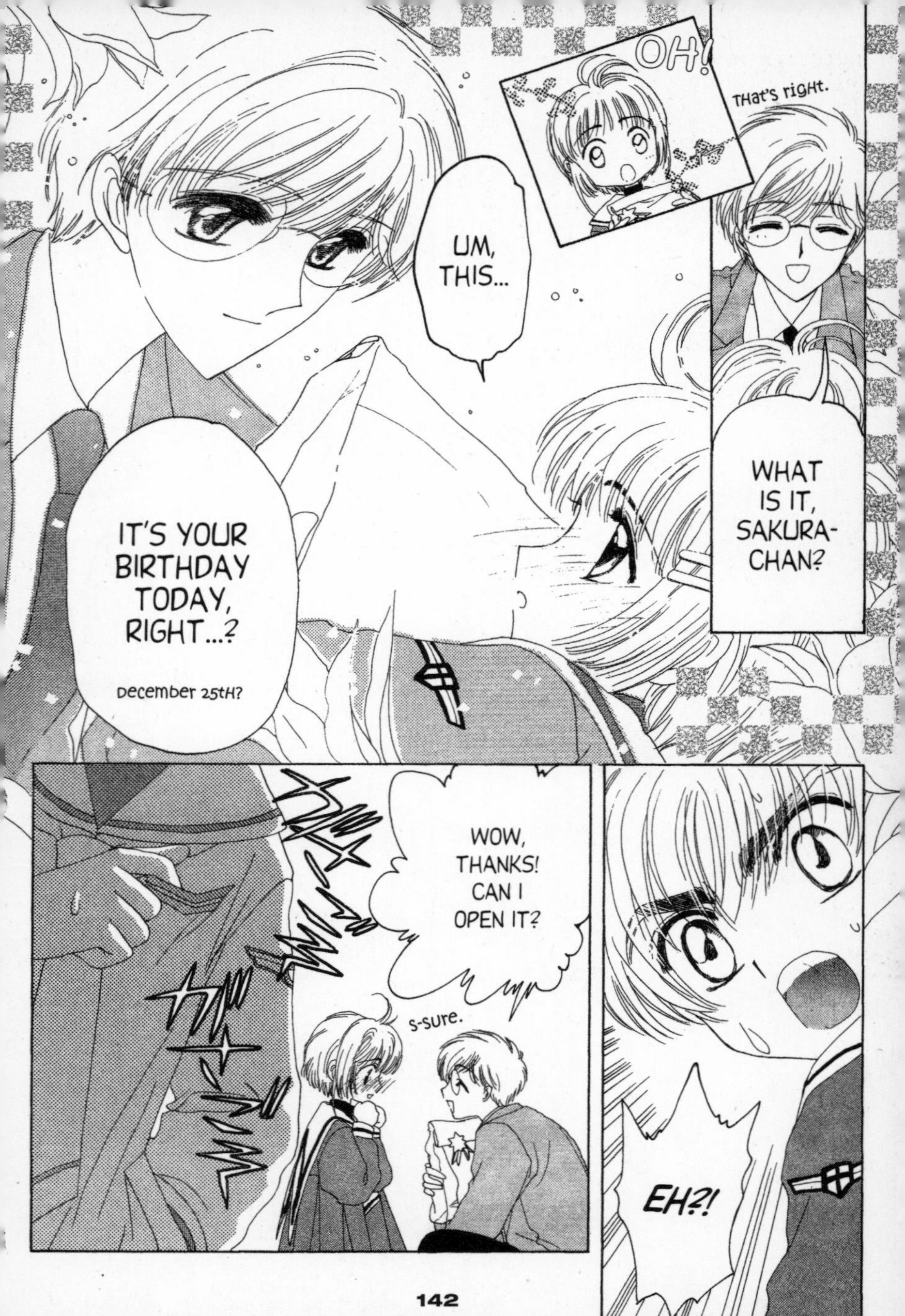
WHAT IS IT, SAKURA-CHAN?
UM, THIS...
IT'S YOUR BIRTHDAY TODAY, RIGHT...?
December 25th?
OH!
That's right.
EH?!
WOW, THANKS! CAN I OPEN IT?
S-sure.

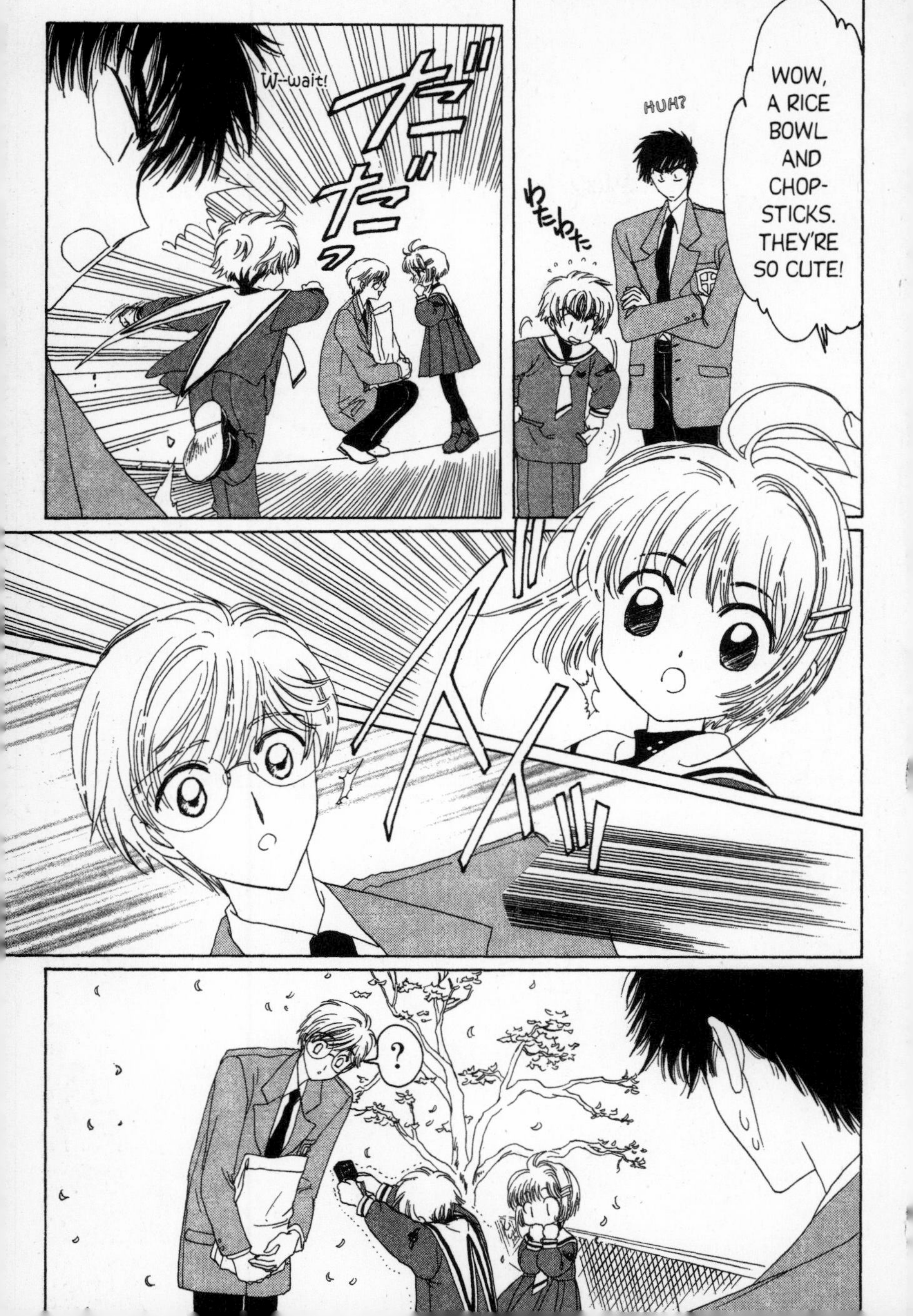
WOW, A RICE BOWL AND CHOP-STICKS. THEY'RE SO CUTE!
HUH?
わたわた
W--wait!
だだだーっ
?

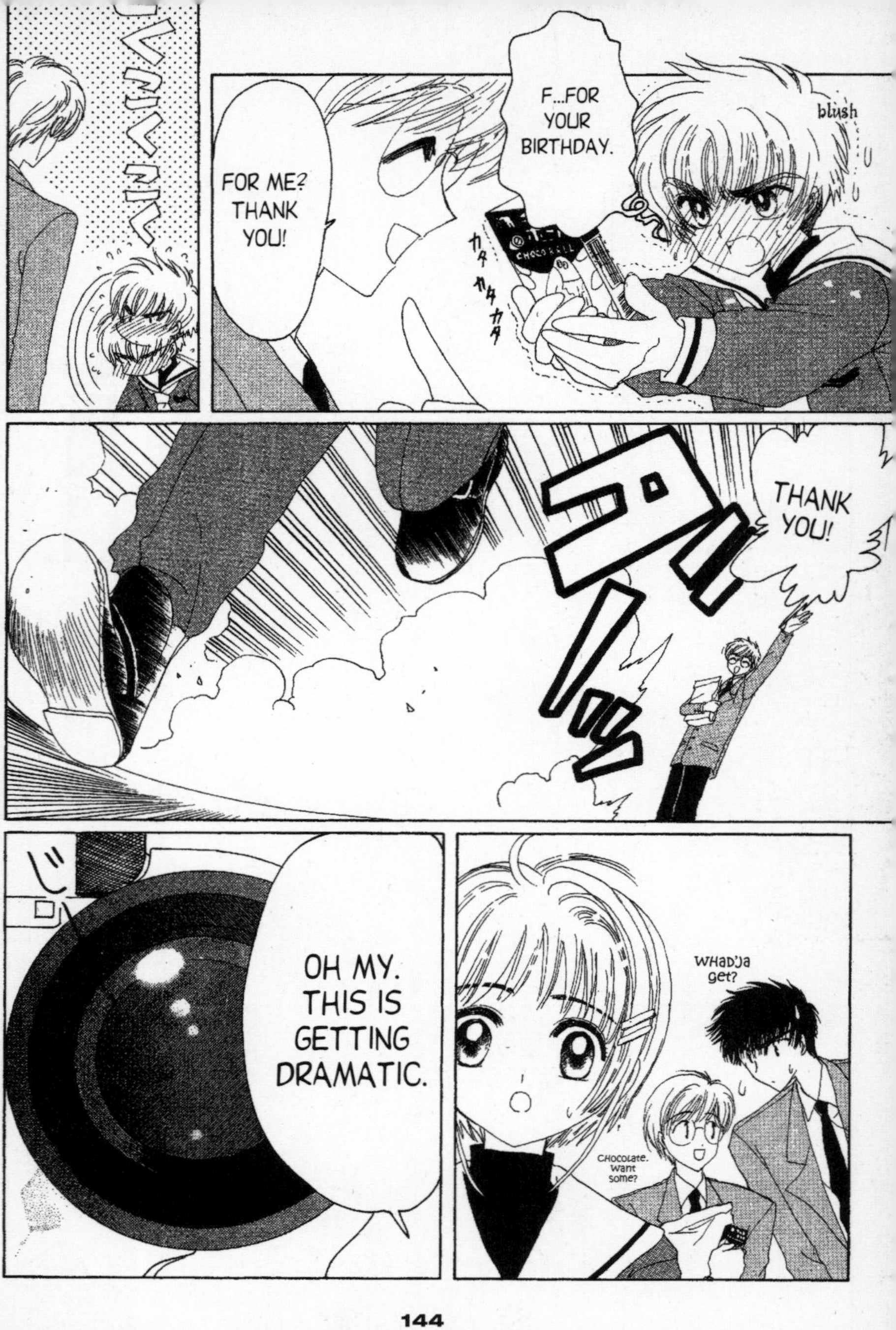
blush
F...FOR YOUR BIRTHDAY.
FOR ME? THANK YOU!
THANK YOU!
WHAD'JA get?
Chocolate. Want some?
OH MY. THIS IS GETTING DRAMATIC.

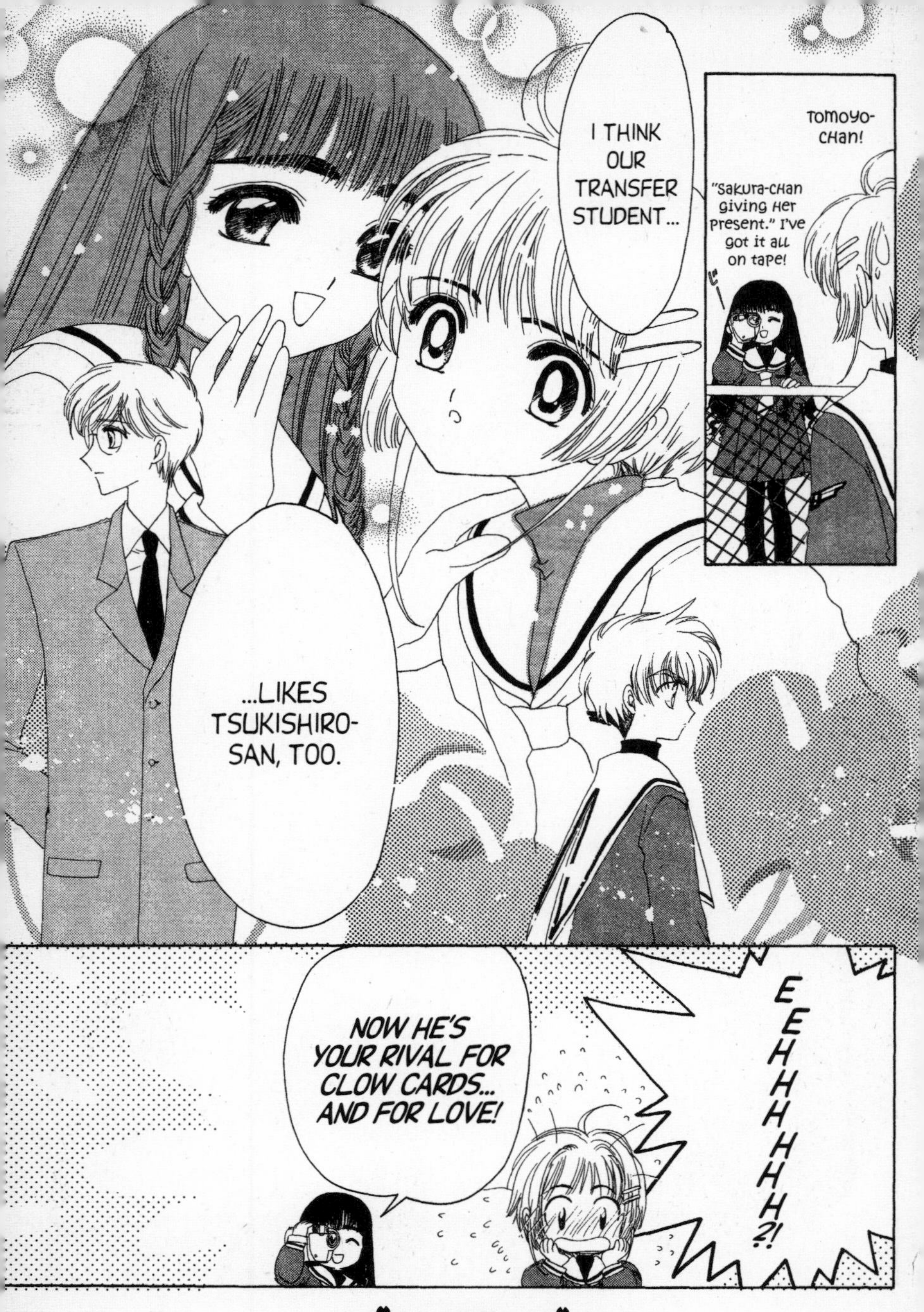
Tomoyo-chan!
"Sakura-chan giving her present." I've got it all on tape!
I THINK OUR TRANSFER STUDENT...
...LIKES TSUKISHIRO-SAN, TOO.
EEHHHHHH?!
NOW HE'S YOUR RIVAL FOR CLOW CARDS... AND FOR LOVE!

END

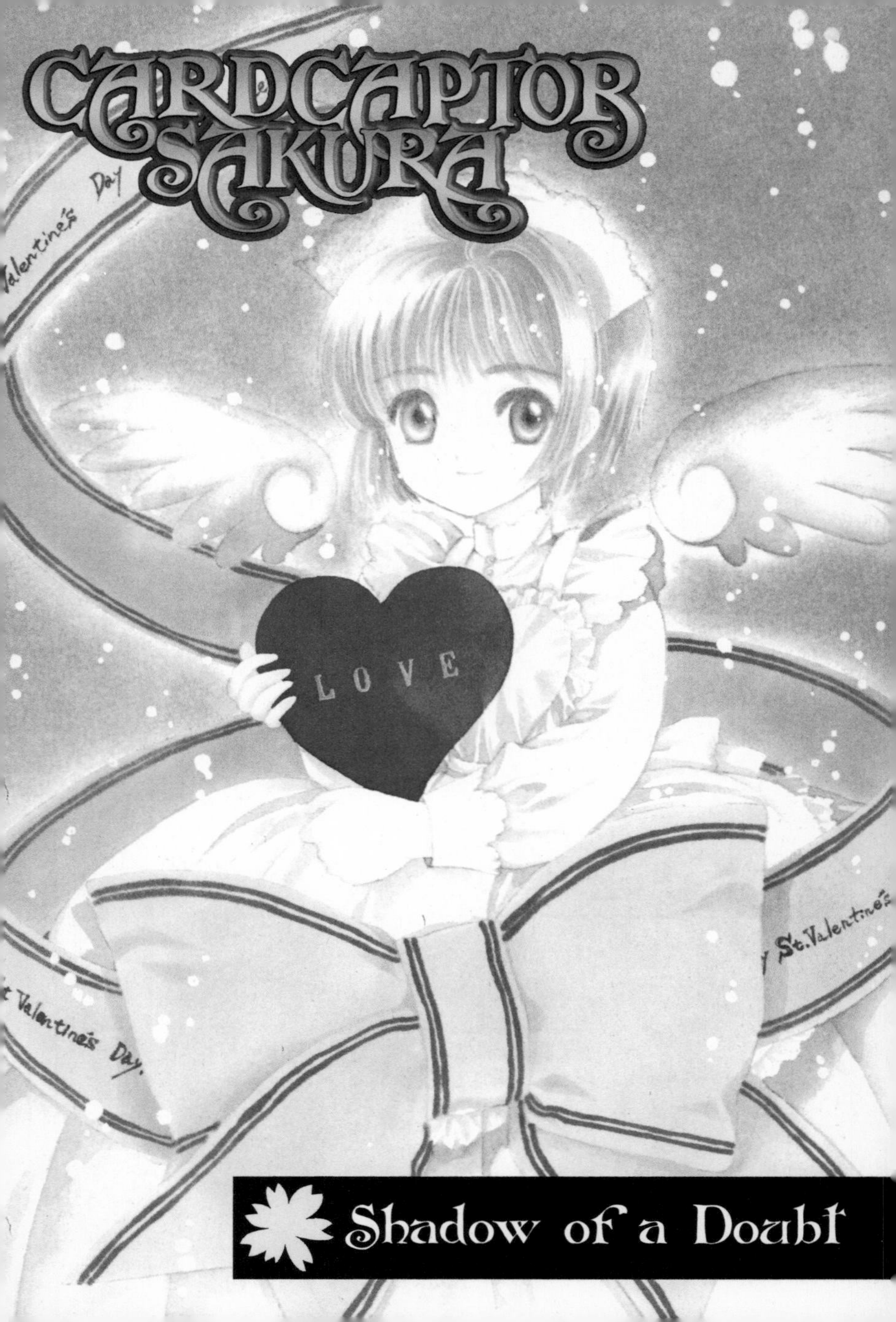
CARDCAPTOR SAKURA
Valentine's Day
LOVE
St. Valentine's
Valentine's Day.
Shadow of a Doubt

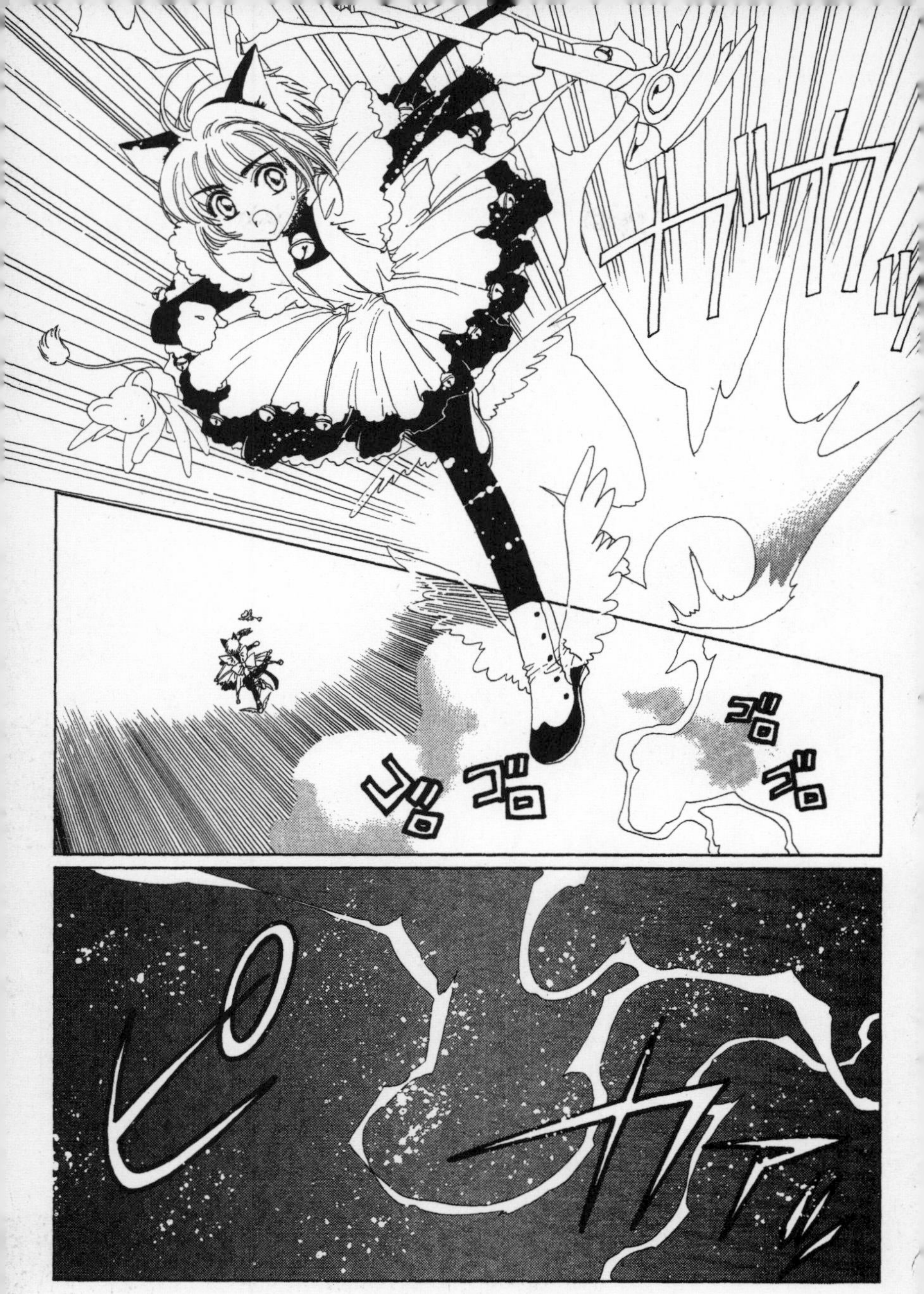
ガカッ
ゴロゴロ
ゴロゴロ
ピカァッ

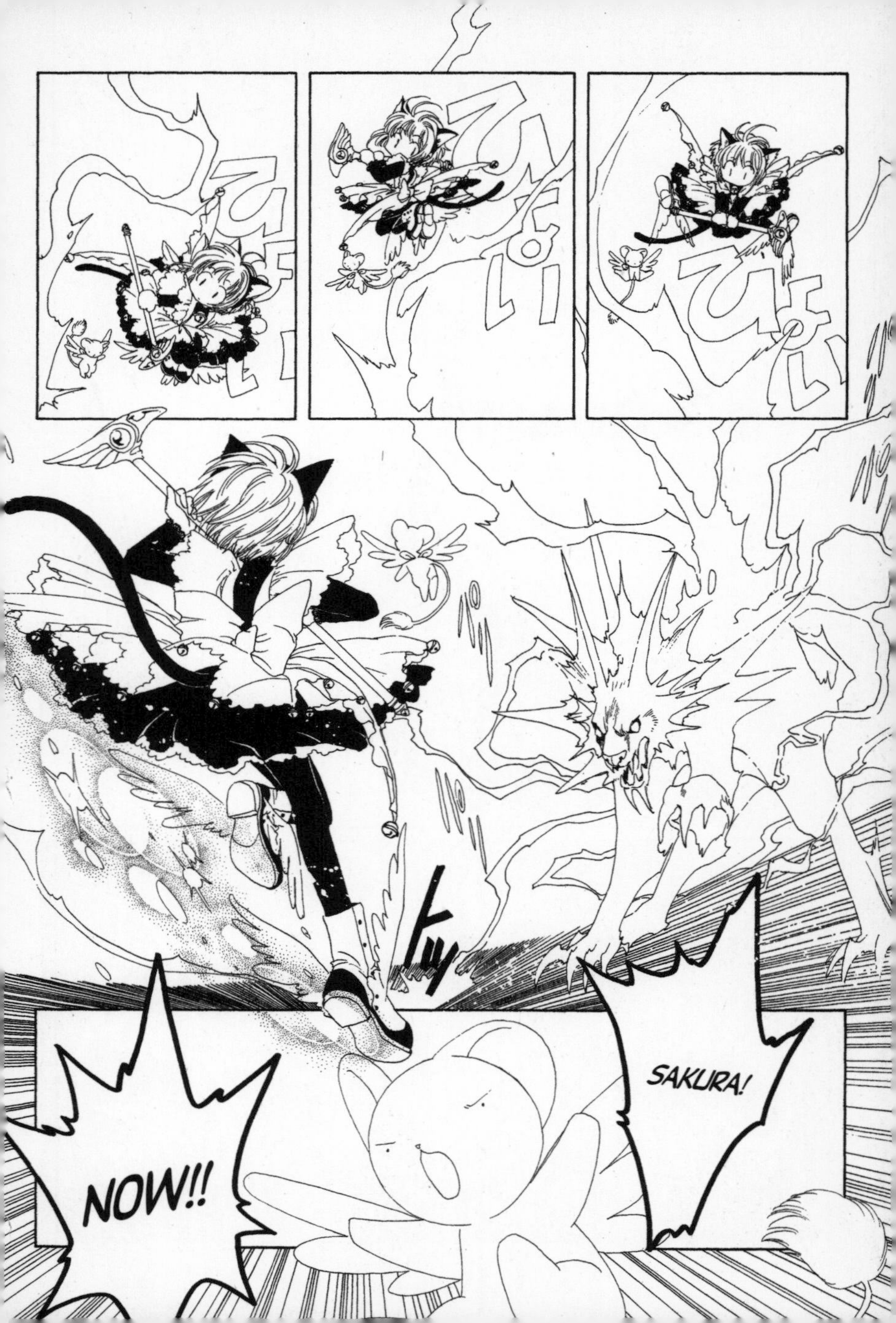
SAKURA!
NOW!!

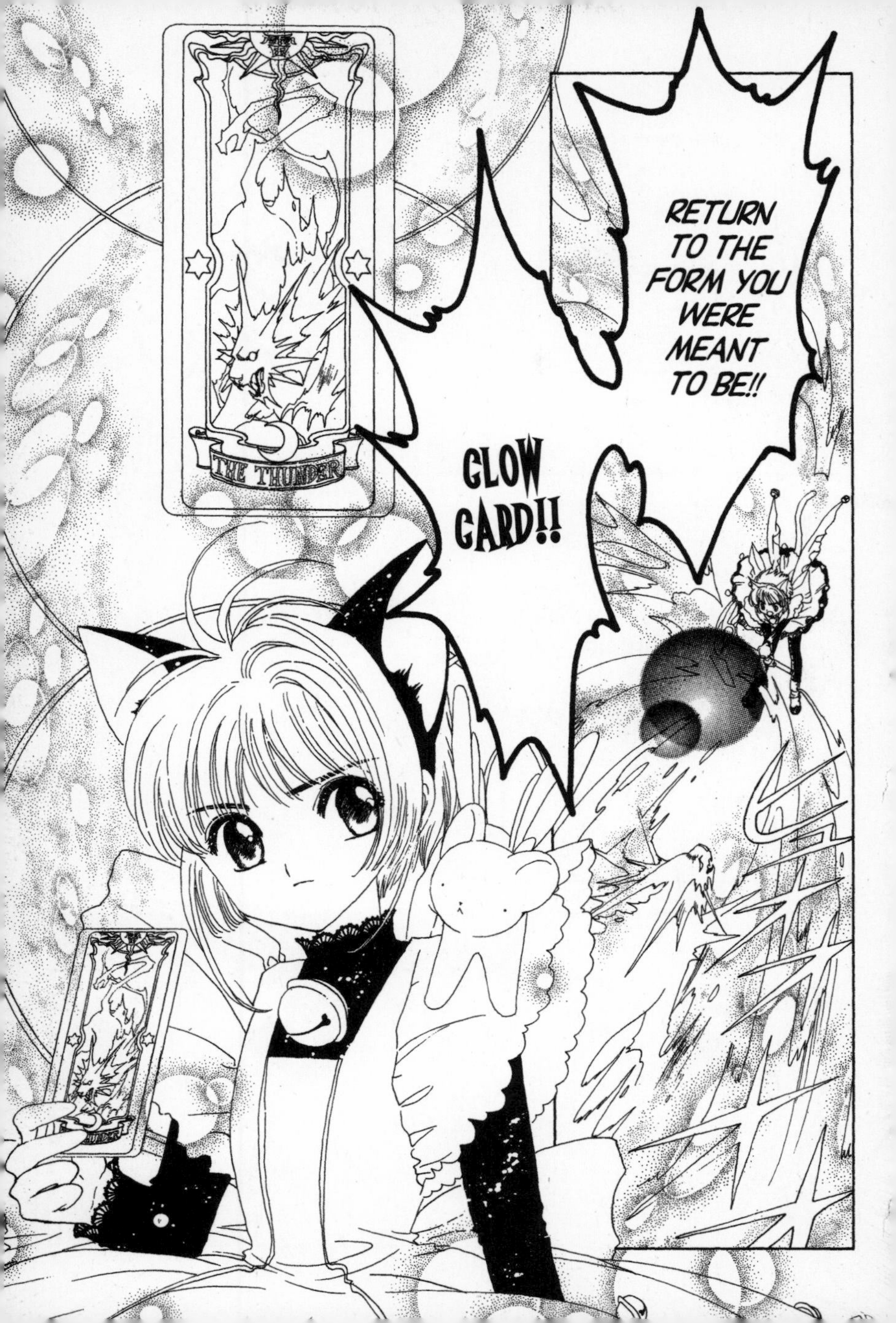
THE THUNDER
RETURN TO THE FORM YOU WERE MEANT TO BE!!
GLOW CARD!!
THUNDER

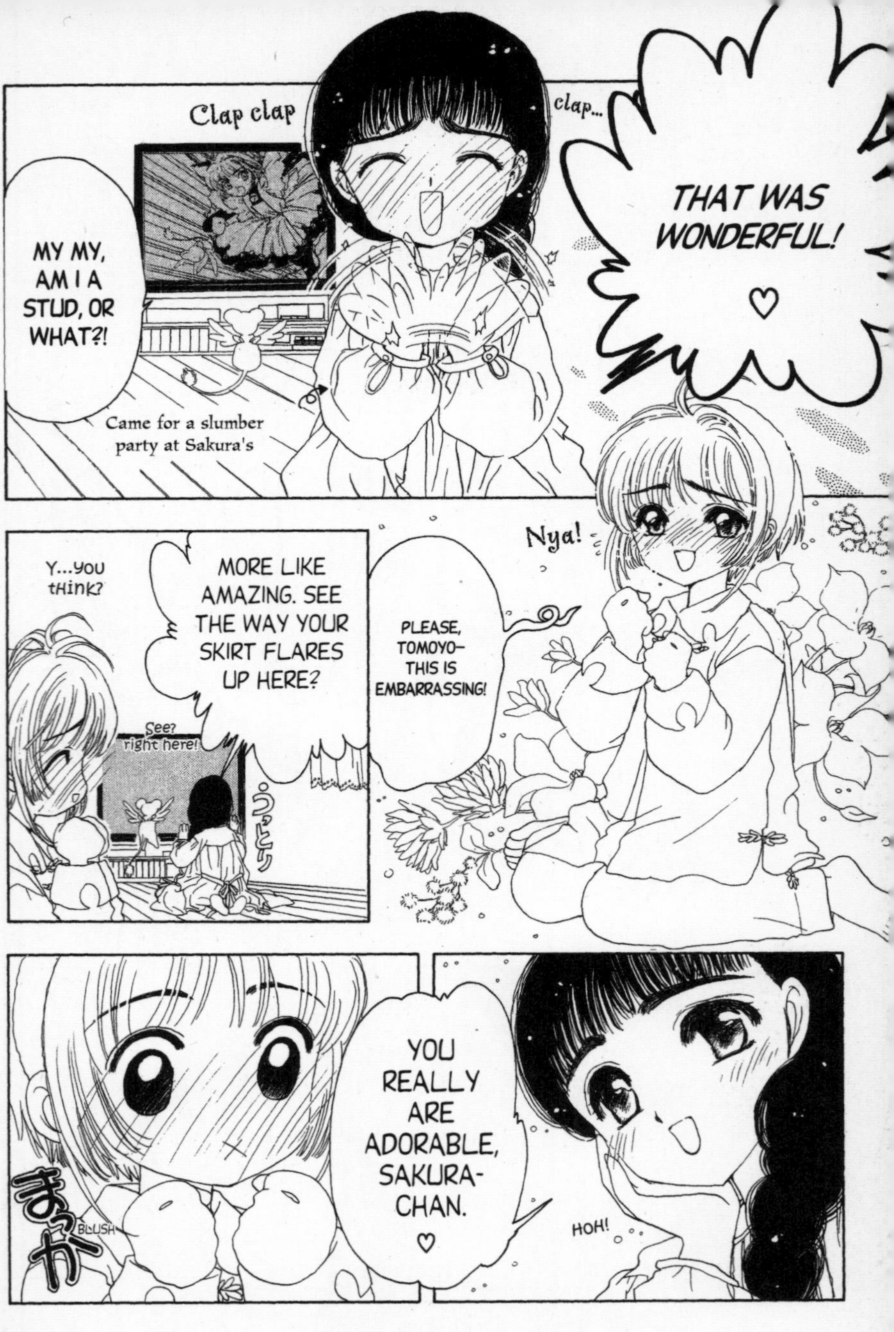
THAT WAS WONDERFUL! ♥
clap...
Clap clap
MY MY, AM I A STUD, OR WHAT?!
Came for a slumber party at Sakura's
Nya!
PLEASE, TOMOYO— THIS IS EMBARRASSING!
MORE LIKE AMAZING. SEE THE WAY YOUR SKIRT FLARES UP HERE?
Y...YOU THINK?
See? right here!
うっとり
YOU REALLY ARE ADORABLE, SAKURA-CHAN. ♥
HOH!
まっか
BLUSH

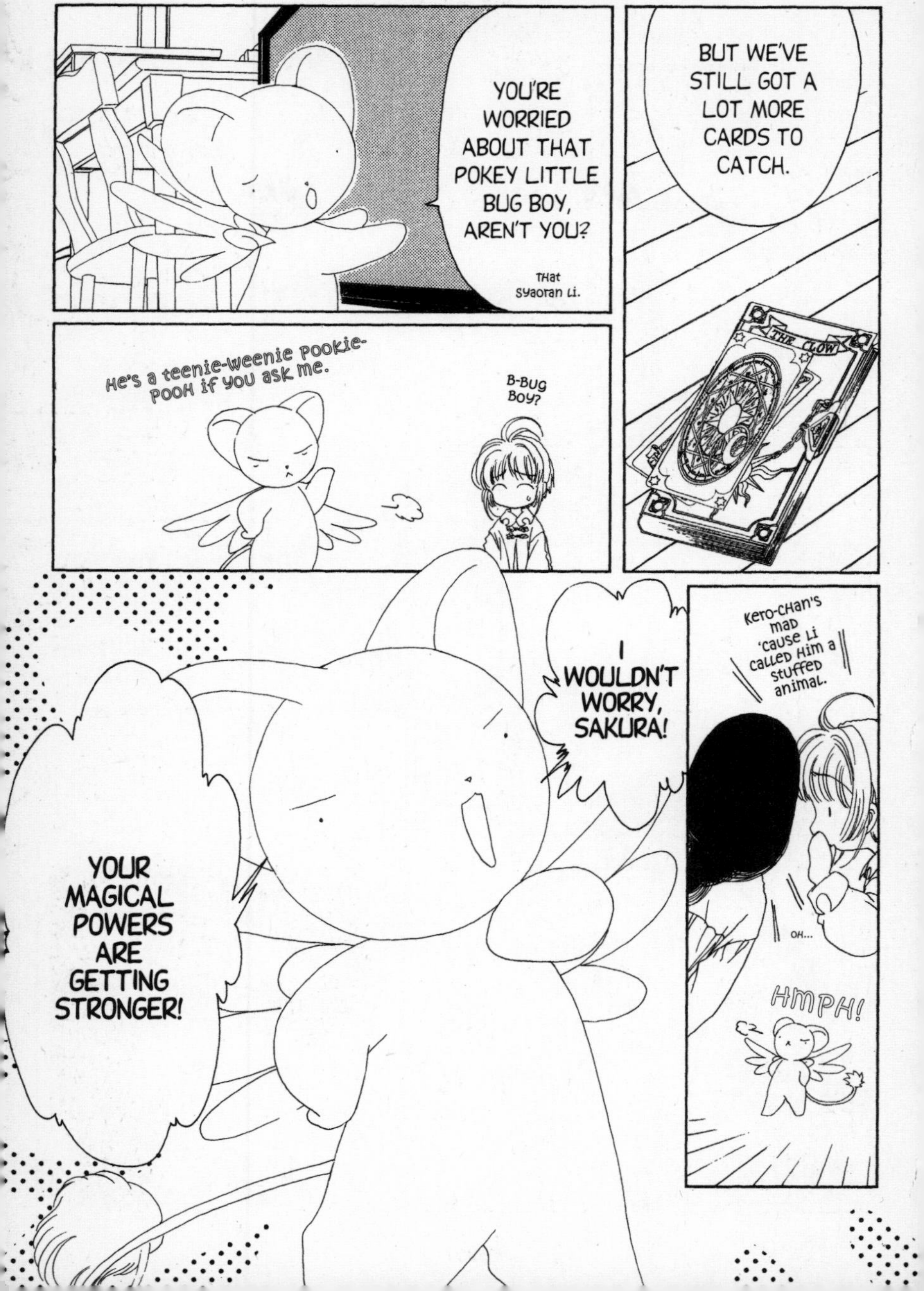
BUT WE'VE STILL GOT A LOT MORE CARDS TO CATCH.
YOU'RE WORRIED ABOUT THAT POKEY LITTLE BUG BOY, AREN'T YOU?
That Syaoran Li.
THE CLOW
B-BUG BOY?
He's a teenie-weenie pookie-pooh if you ask me.
Kero-chan's mad 'cause Li called him a stuffed animal.
OH...
HMPH!
I WOULDN'T WORRY, SAKURA!
YOUR MAGICAL POWERS ARE GETTING STRONGER!

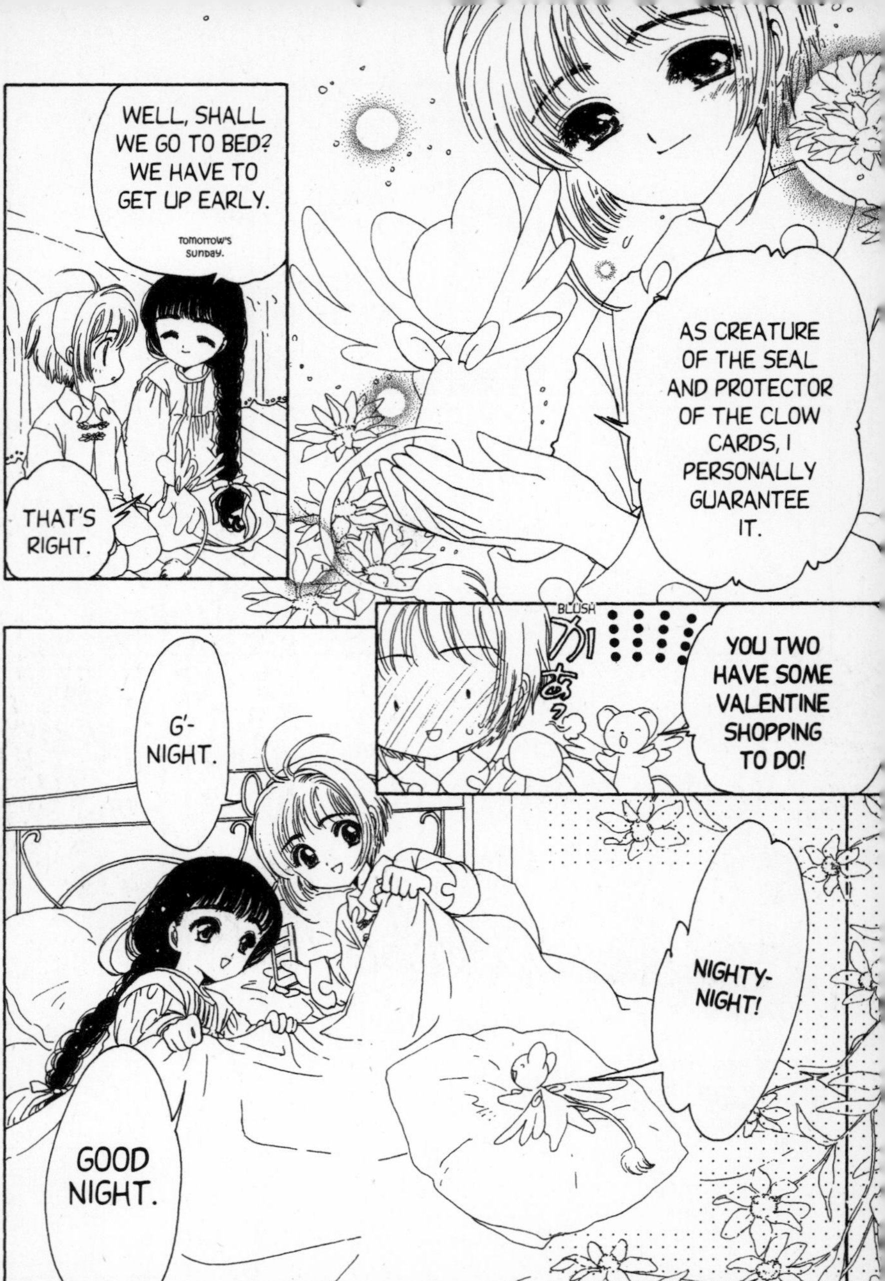
AS CREATURE OF THE SEAL AND PROTECTOR OF THE CLOW CARDS, I PERSONALLY GUARANTEE IT.
BLUSH
YOU TWO HAVE SOME VALENTINE SHOPPING TO DO!
WELL, SHALL WE GO TO BED? WE HAVE TO GET UP EARLY.
TOMORROW'S SUNDAY.
THAT'S RIGHT.
NIGHTY-NIGHT!
G'-NIGHT.
GOOD NIGHT.

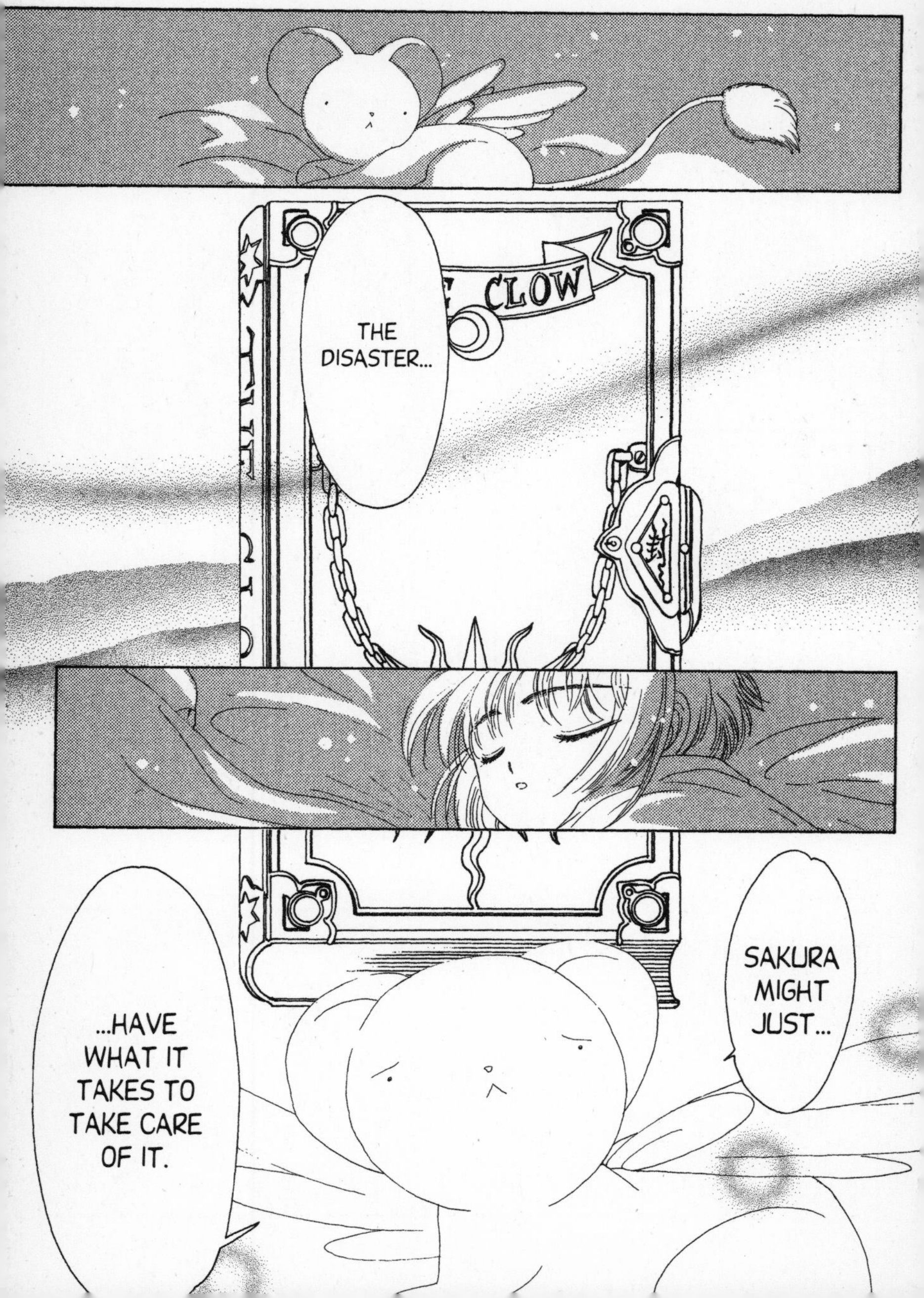
CLOW
THE DISASTER...
SAKURA MIGHT JUST...
...HAVE WHAT IT TAKES TO TAKE CARE OF IT.

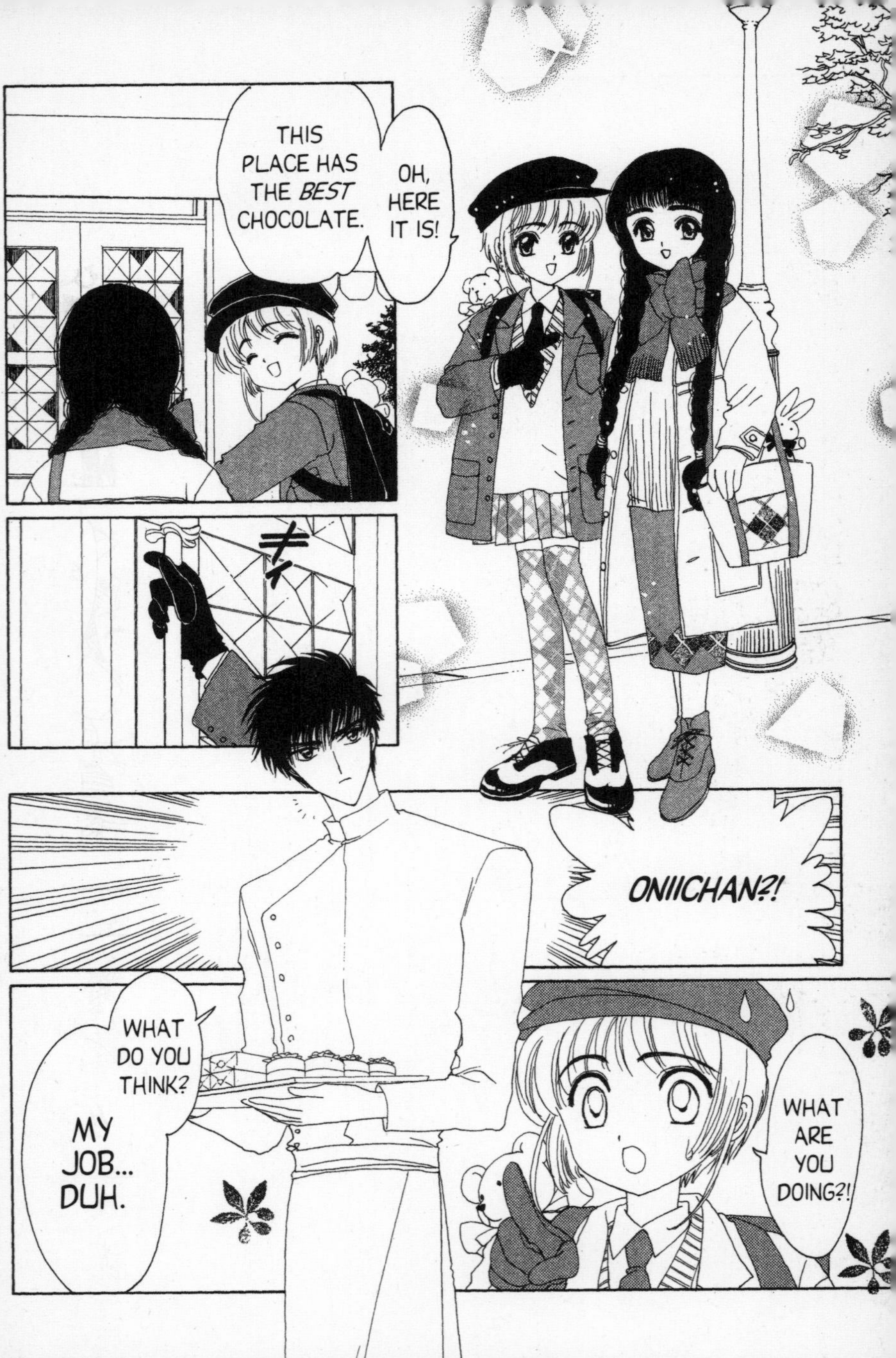
OH, HERE IT IS!
THIS PLACE HAS THE *BEST* CHOCOLATE.
ONIICHAN?!
WHAT ARE YOU DOING?!
WHAT DO YOU THINK?
MY JOB... DUH.

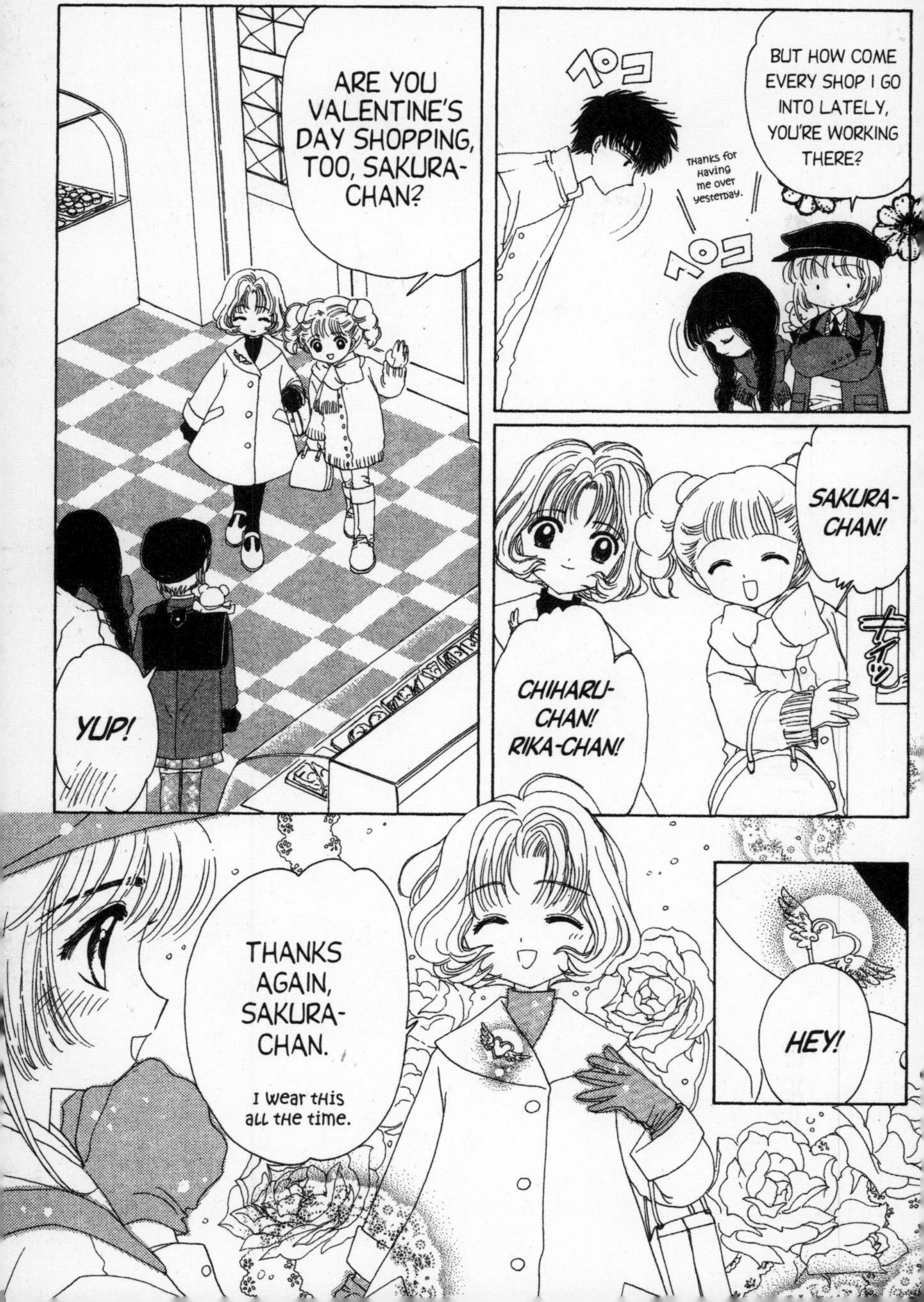
BUT HOW COME EVERY SHOP I GO INTO LATELY, YOU'RE WORKING THERE?
ペコ
Thanks for Having me over yesterday.
ペコ
SAKURA-CHAN!
CHIHARU-CHAN! RIKA-CHAN!
ARE YOU VALENTINE'S DAY SHOPPING, TOO, SAKURA-CHAN?
YUP!
HEY!
THANKS AGAIN, SAKURA-CHAN.
I wear this all the time.

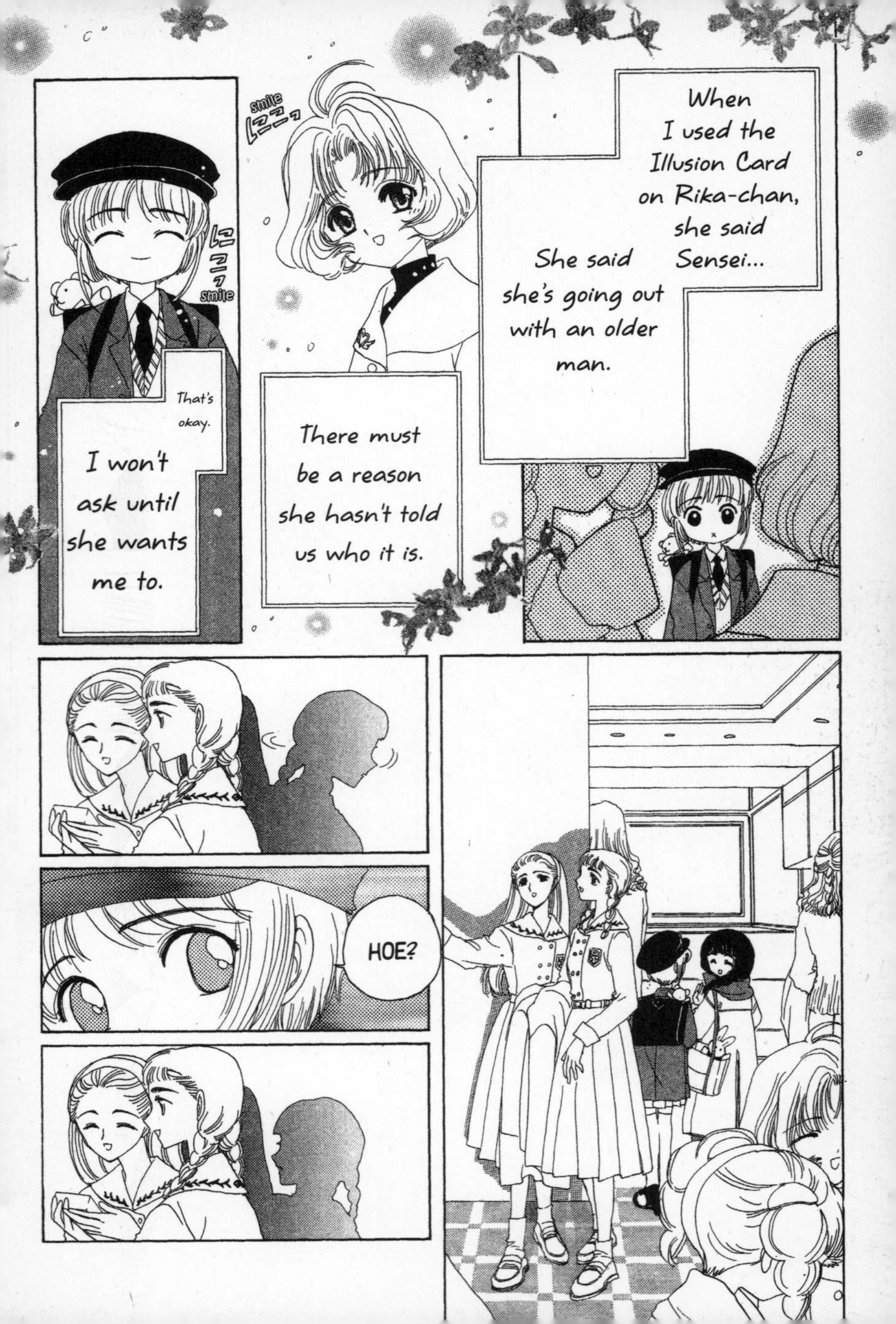
When I used the Illusion Card on Rika-chan, she said Sensei...
She said she's going out with an older man.
smile
There must be a reason she hasn't told us who it is.
smile
That's okay.
I won't ask until she wants me to.
HOE?

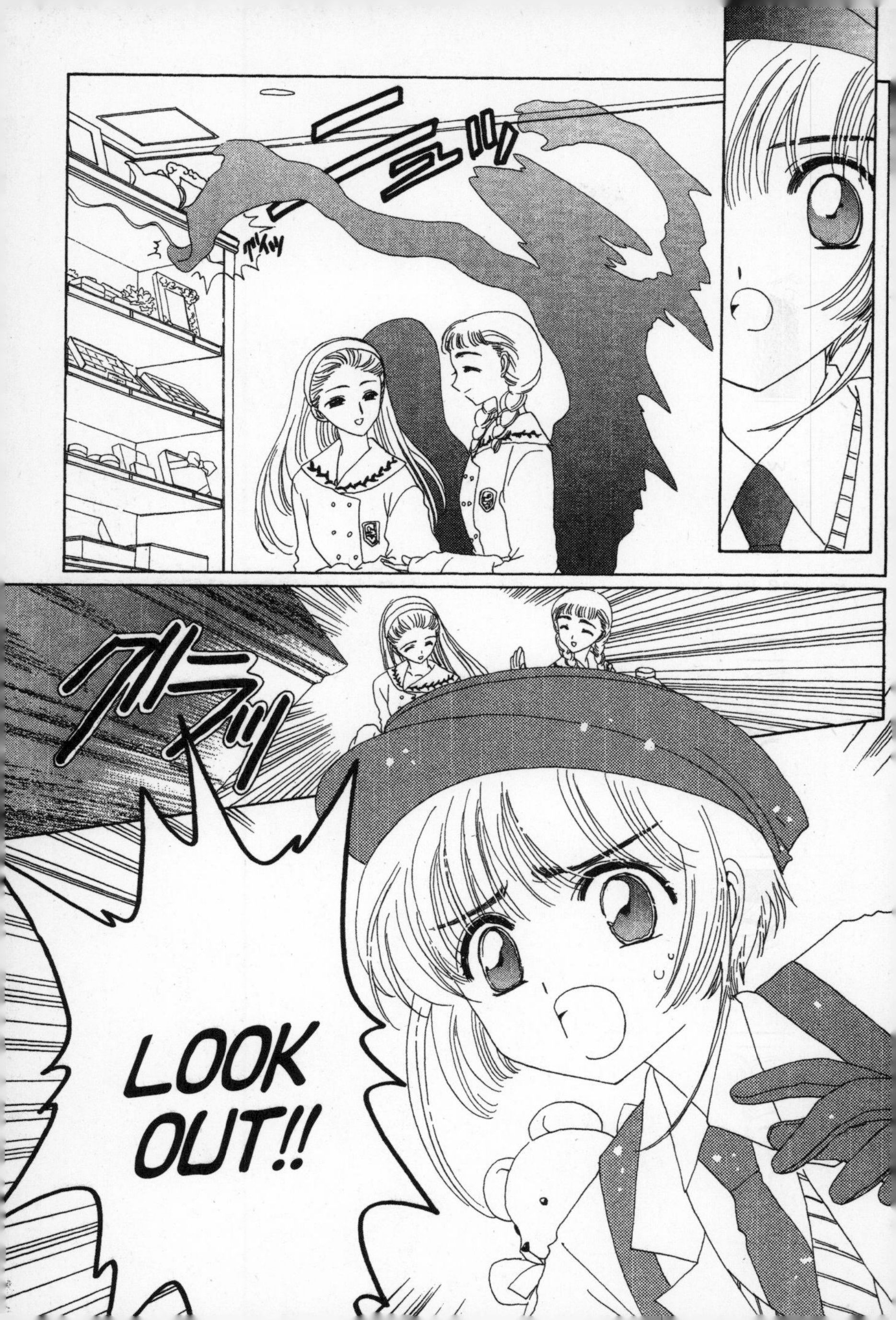
ニュッ
グラッ
LOOK OUT!!

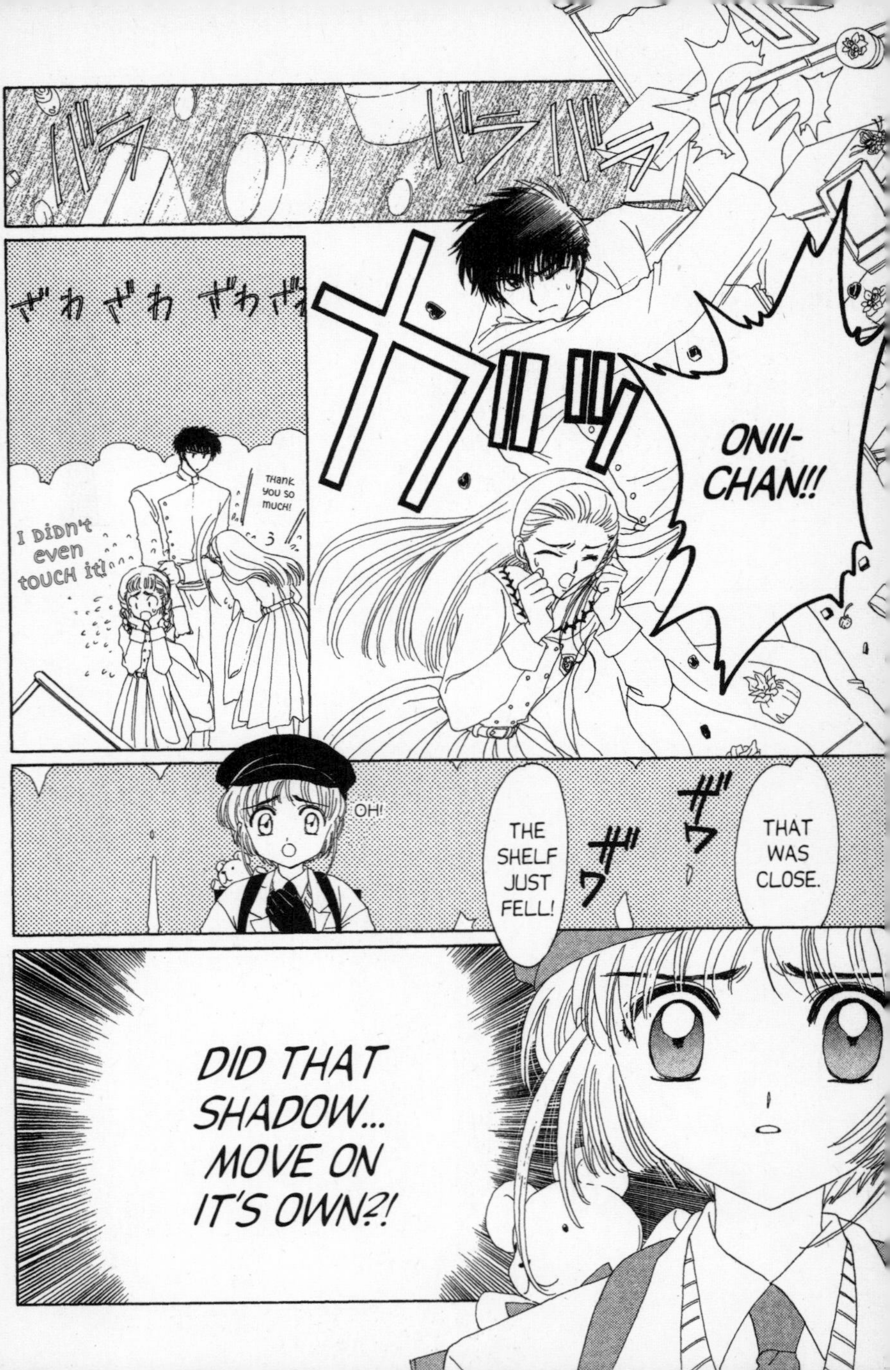
バラ バラバラ
ガッ
ONII-CHAN!!
ざわざわ ざわざわ
Thank you so much!
I didn't even touch it!
THAT WAS CLOSE.
ザワ ザワ
THE SHELF JUST FELL!
OH!
DID THAT SHADOW... MOVE ON IT'S OWN?!

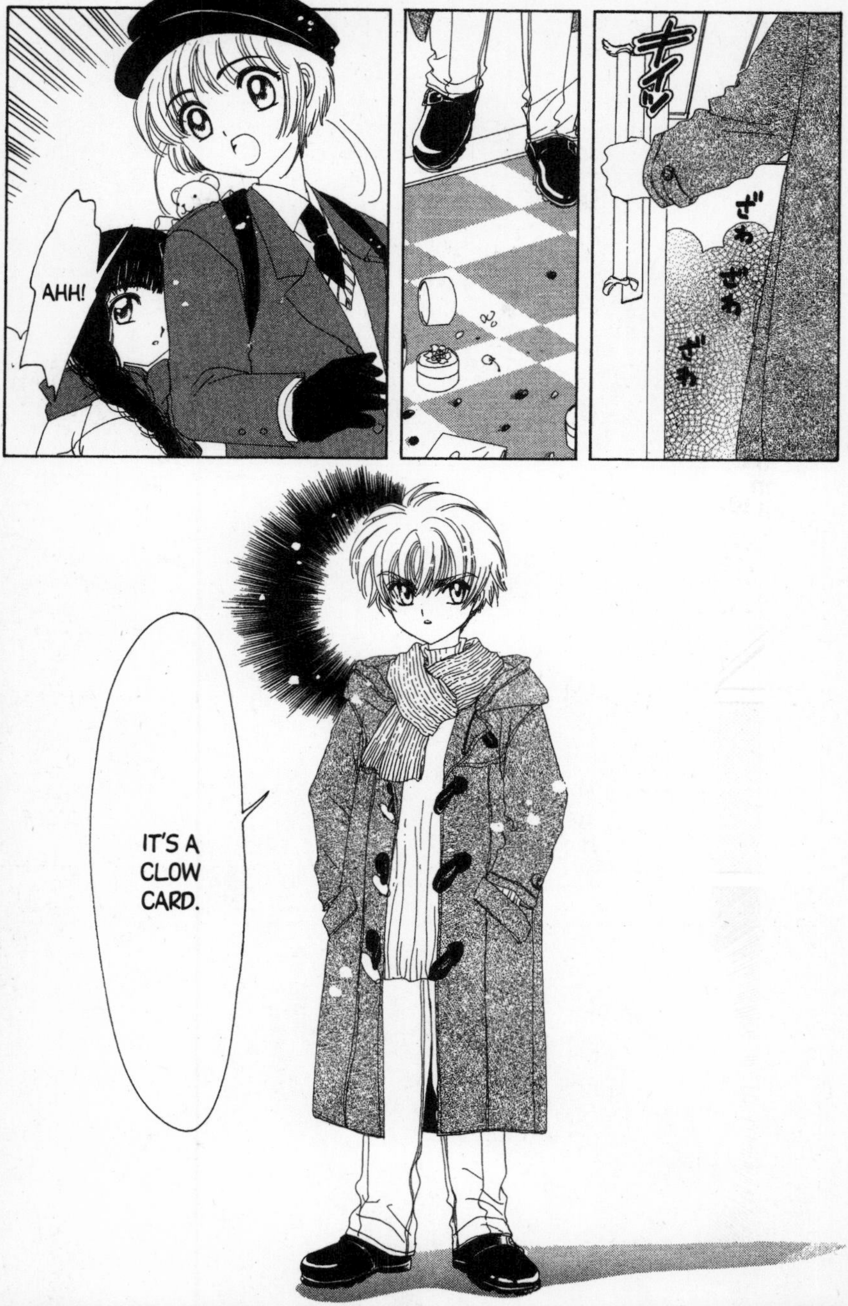
キイッ
ざわざわざわ
AHH!
IT'S A CLOW CARD.

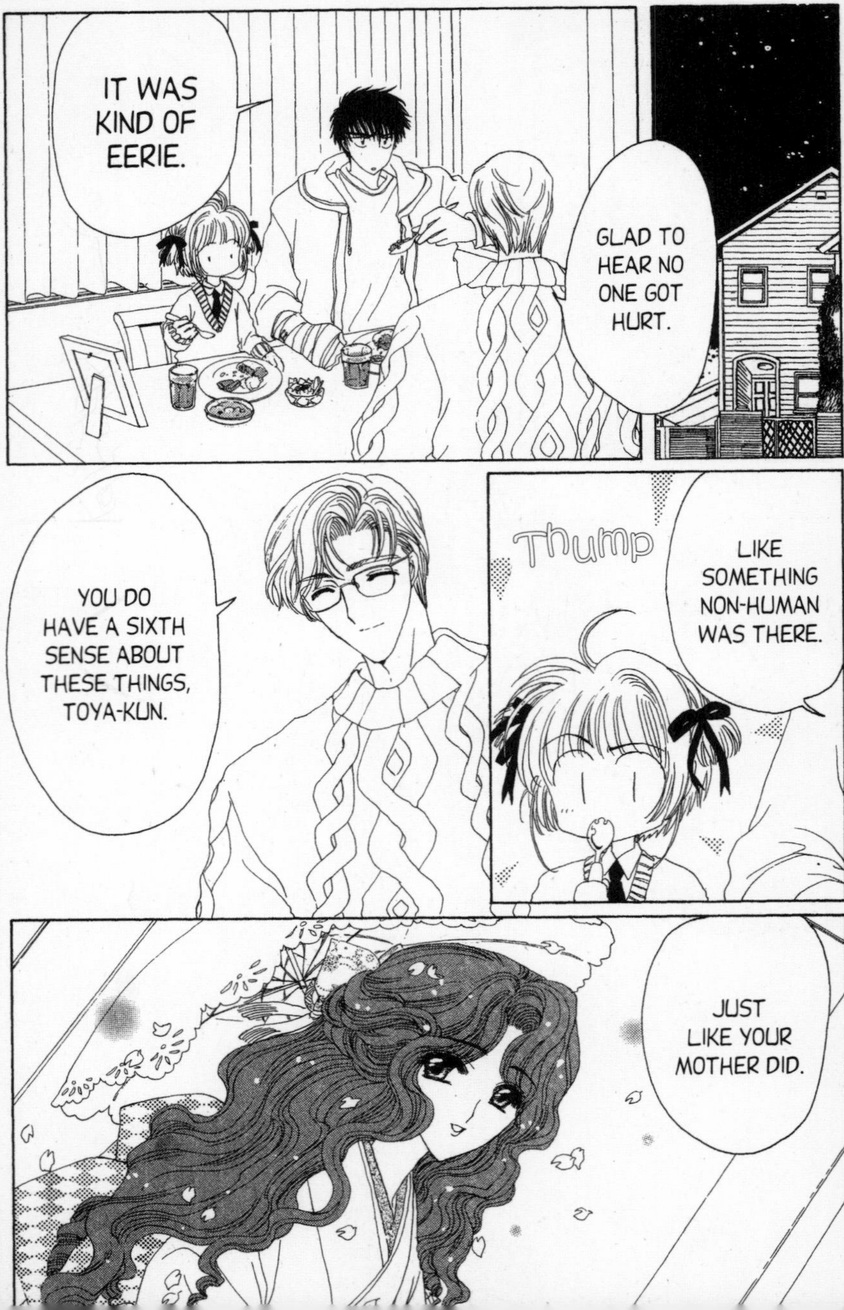
GLAD TO HEAR NO ONE GOT HURT.
IT WAS KIND OF EERIE.
Thump
LIKE SOMETHING NON-HUMAN WAS THERE.
YOU DO HAVE A SIXTH SENSE ABOUT THESE THINGS, TOYA-KUN.
JUST LIKE YOUR MOTHER DID.

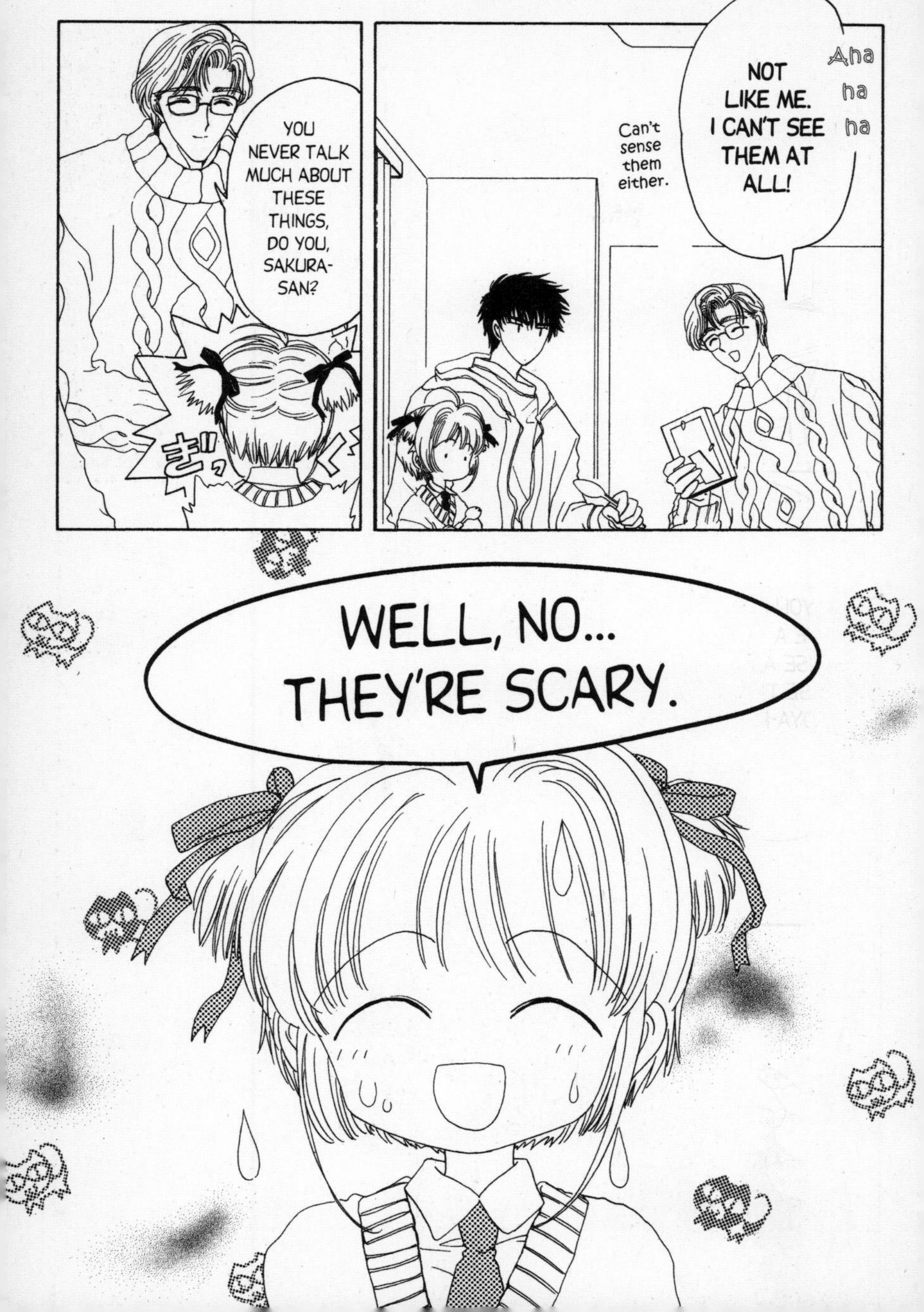
Aha ha ha
NOT LIKE ME. I CAN'T SEE THEM AT ALL!
Can't sense them either.
YOU NEVER TALK MUCH ABOUT THESE THINGS, DO YOU, SAKURA-SAN?
く
ぎっ
WELL, NO... THEY'RE SCARY.

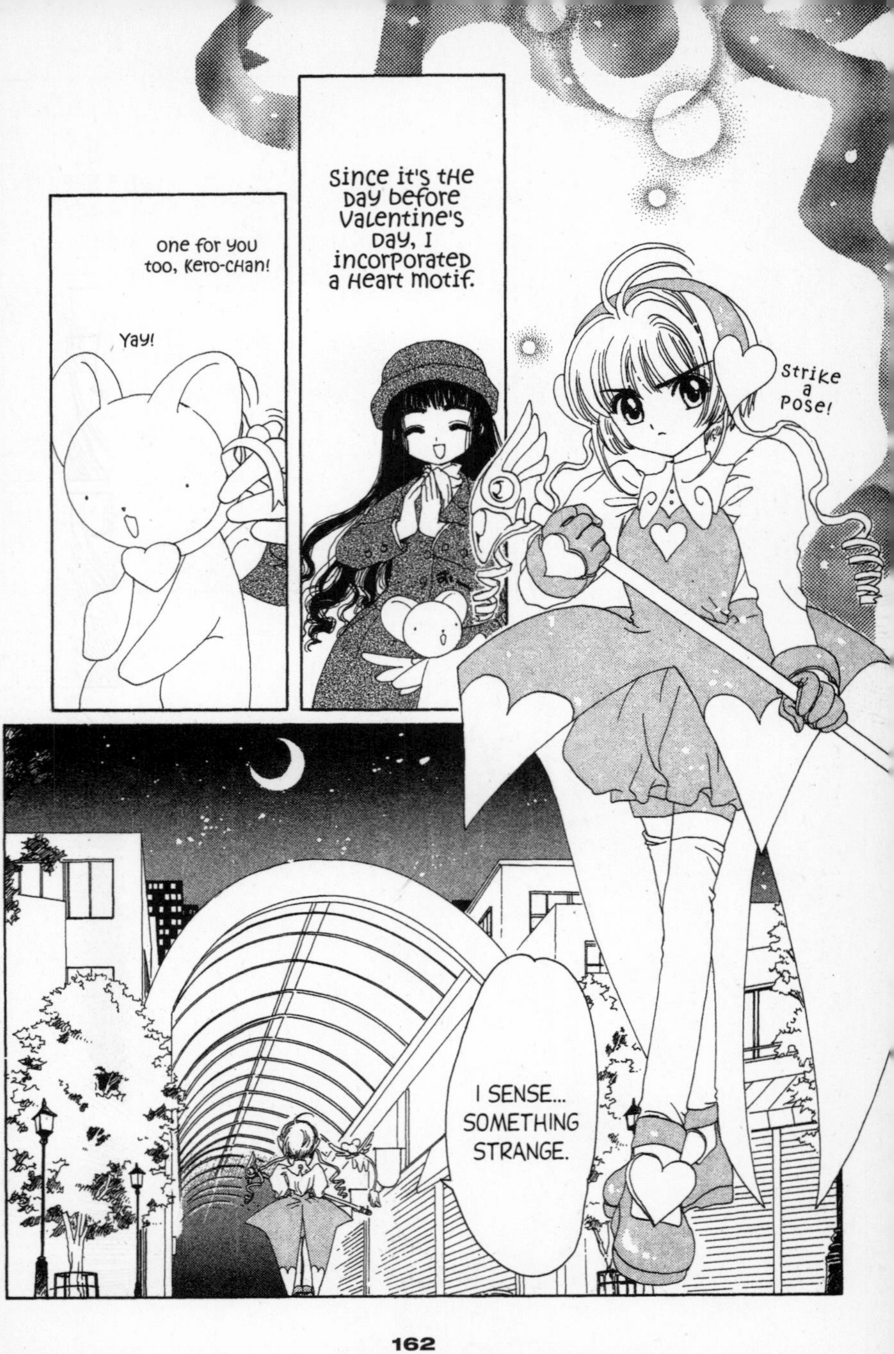
Strike a pose!
Since it's the day before Valentine's day, I incorporated a heart motif.
one for you too, Kero-chan!
Yay!
I SENSE... SOMETHING STRANGE.

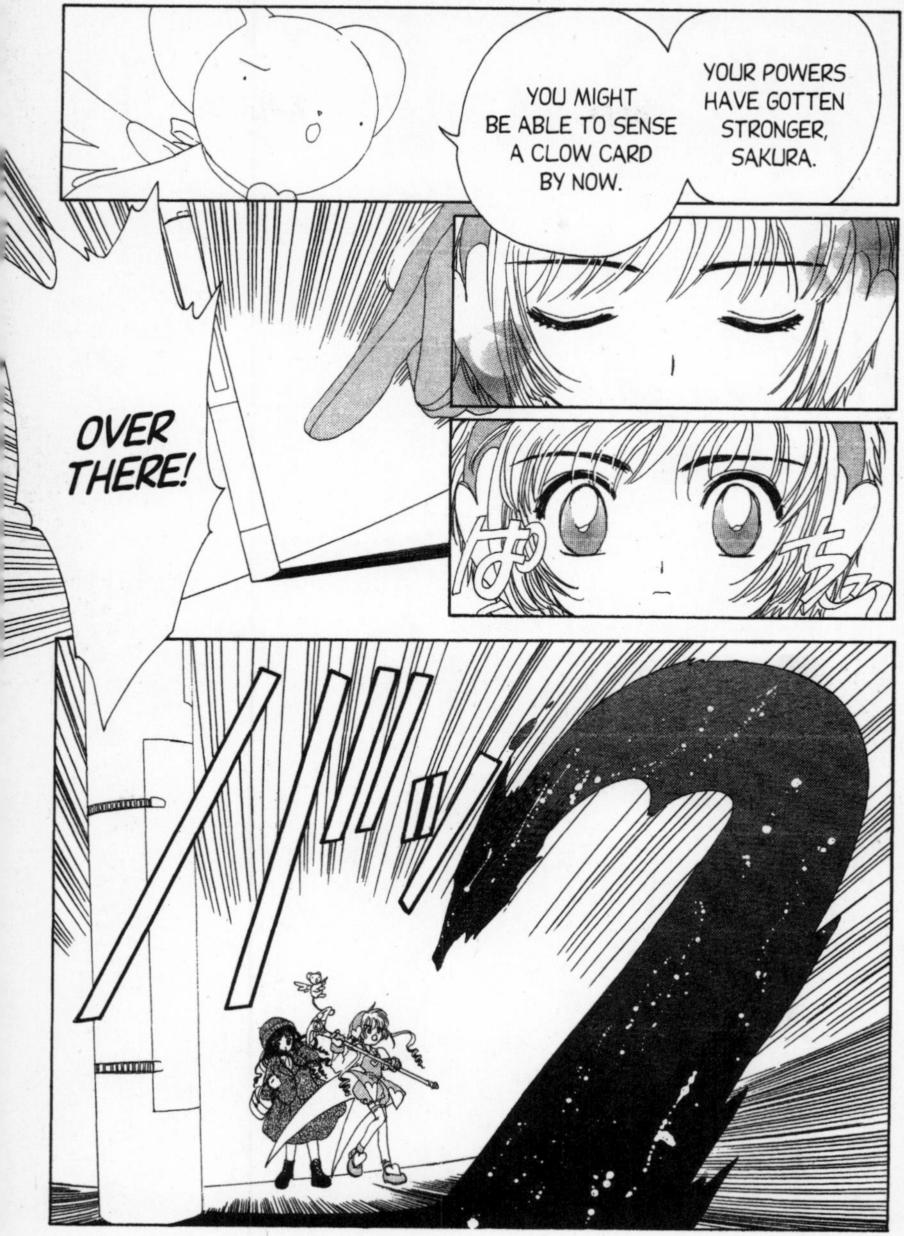
YOUR POWERS HAVE GOTTEN STRONGER, SAKURA.
YOU MIGHT BE ABLE TO SENSE A CLOW CARD BY NOW.
OVER THERE!

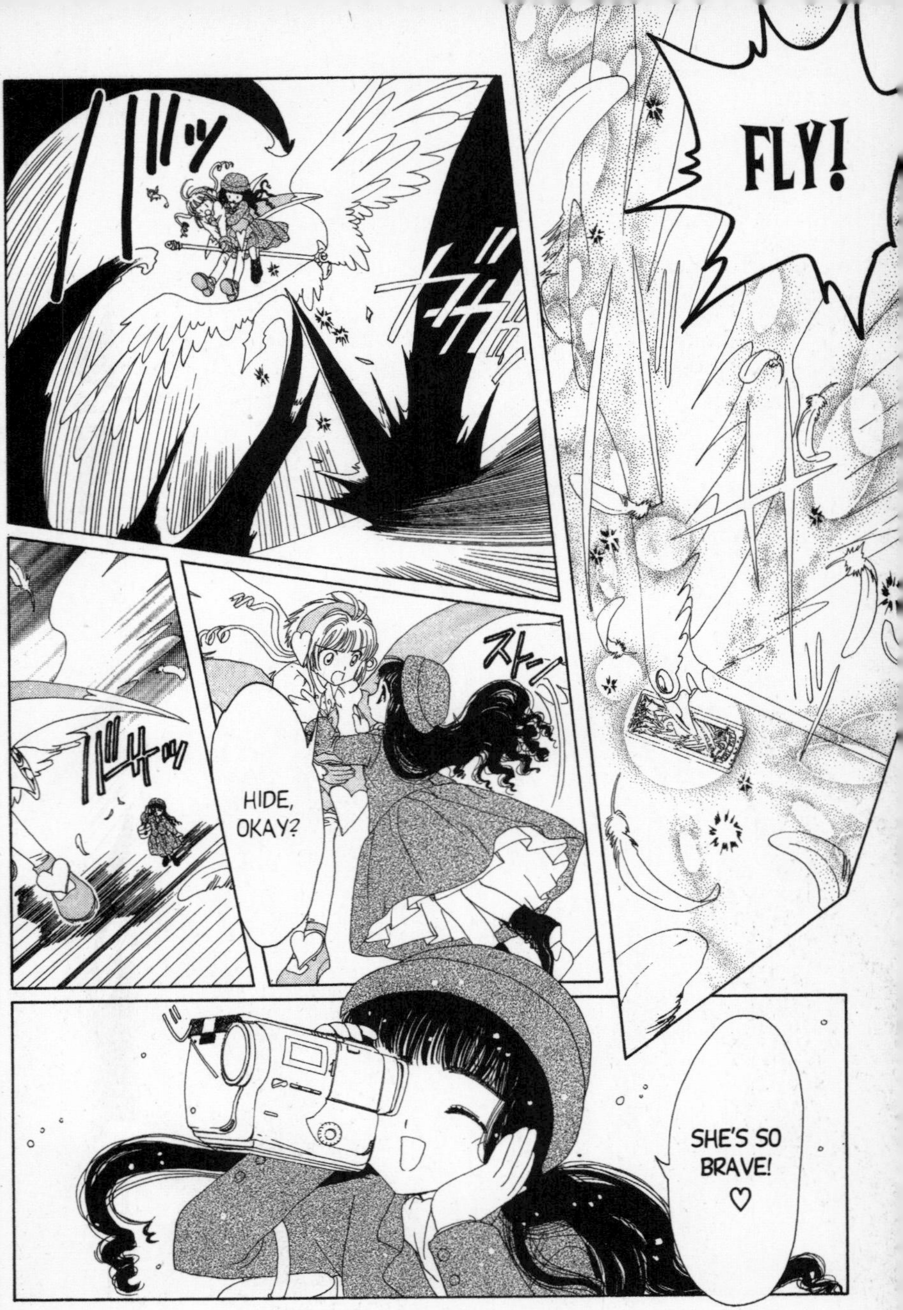
FLY!
HIDE, OKAY?
SHE'S SO BRAVE! ♡

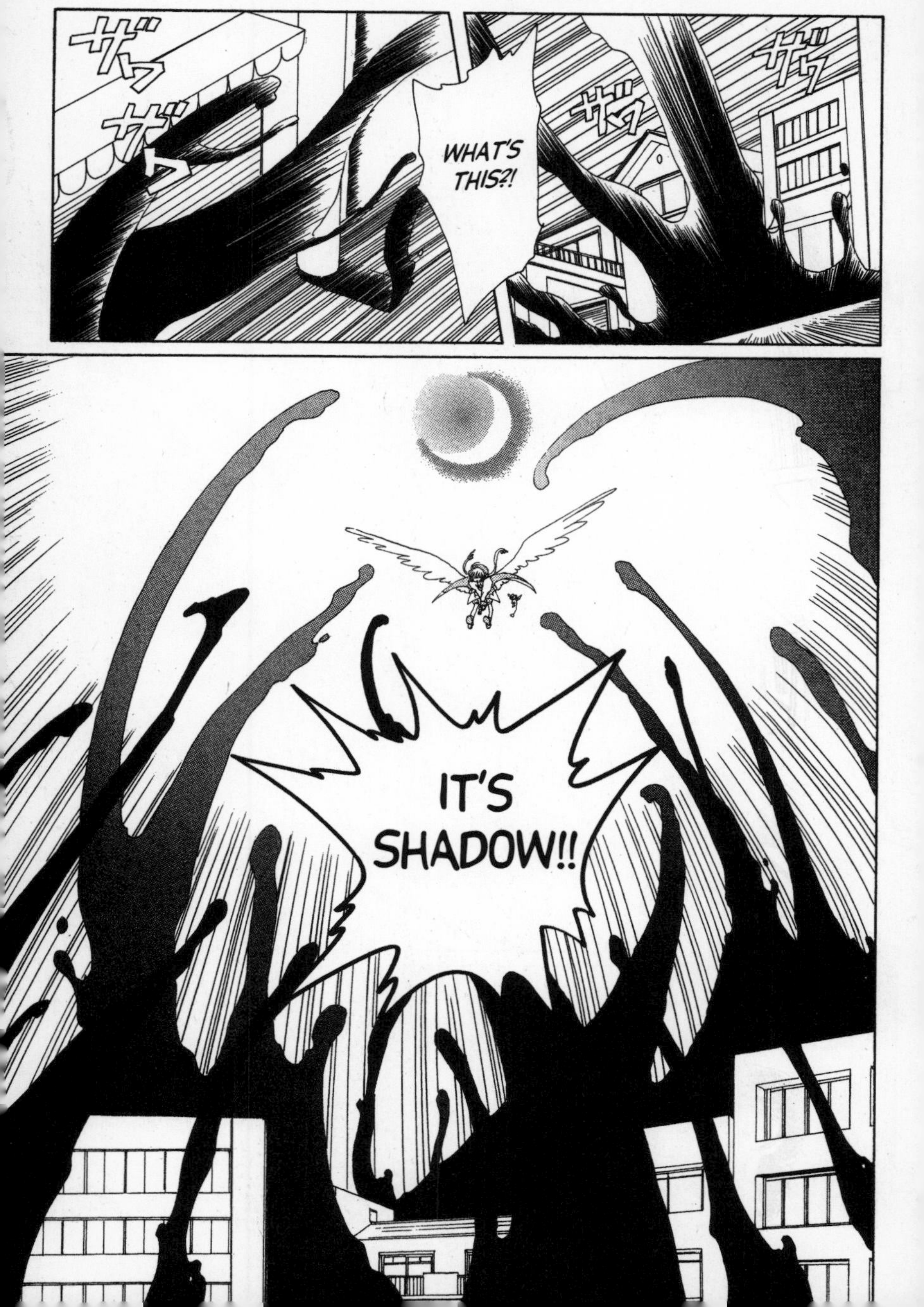
ザヴ
ザヴ
WHAT'S THIS?!
ザヴ
ザヴ
IT'S SHADOW!!

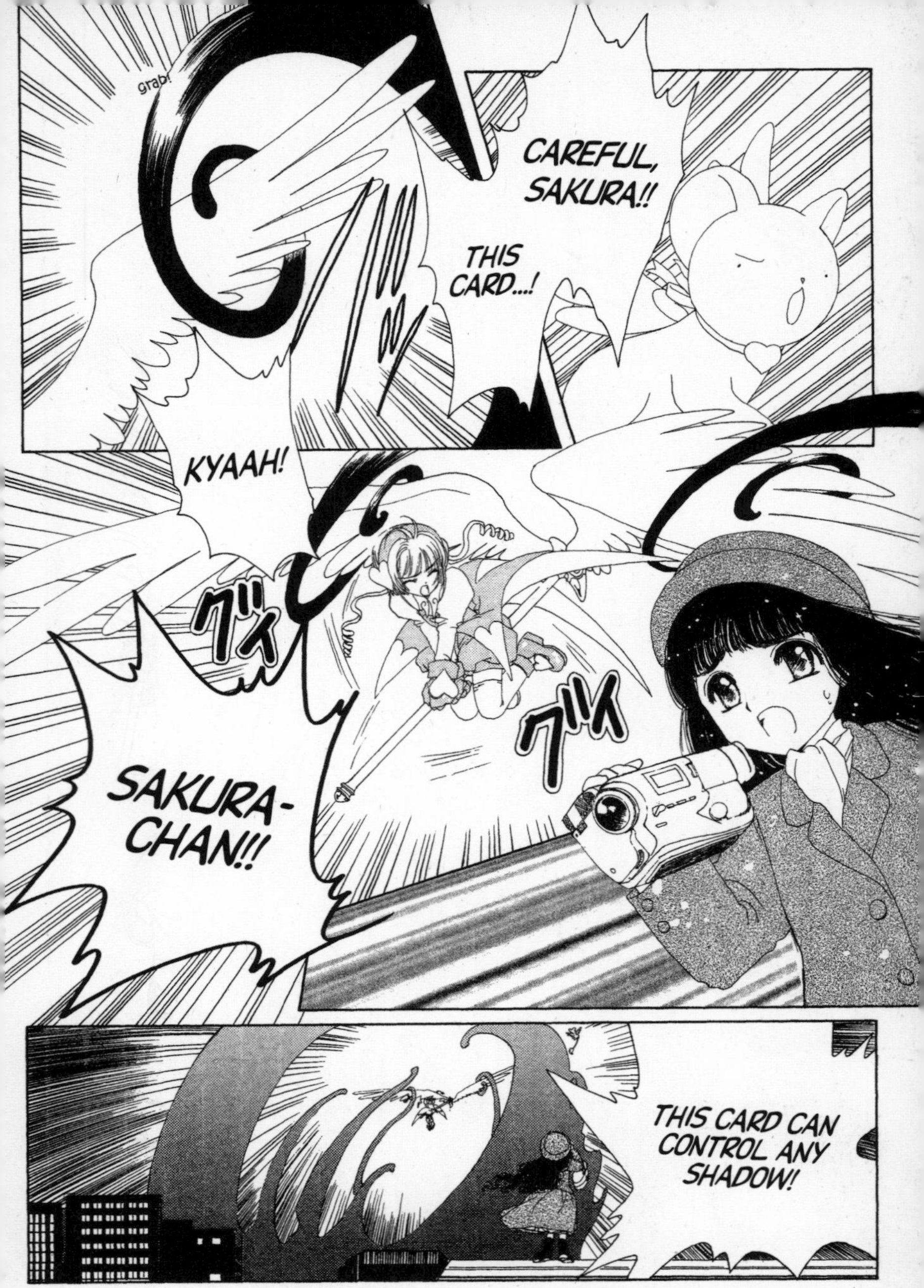
CAREFUL, SAKURA!!
THIS CARD...!
grab!
KYAAH!
グイ
グイ
SAKURA-CHAN!!
THIS CARD CAN CONTROL ANY SHADOW!

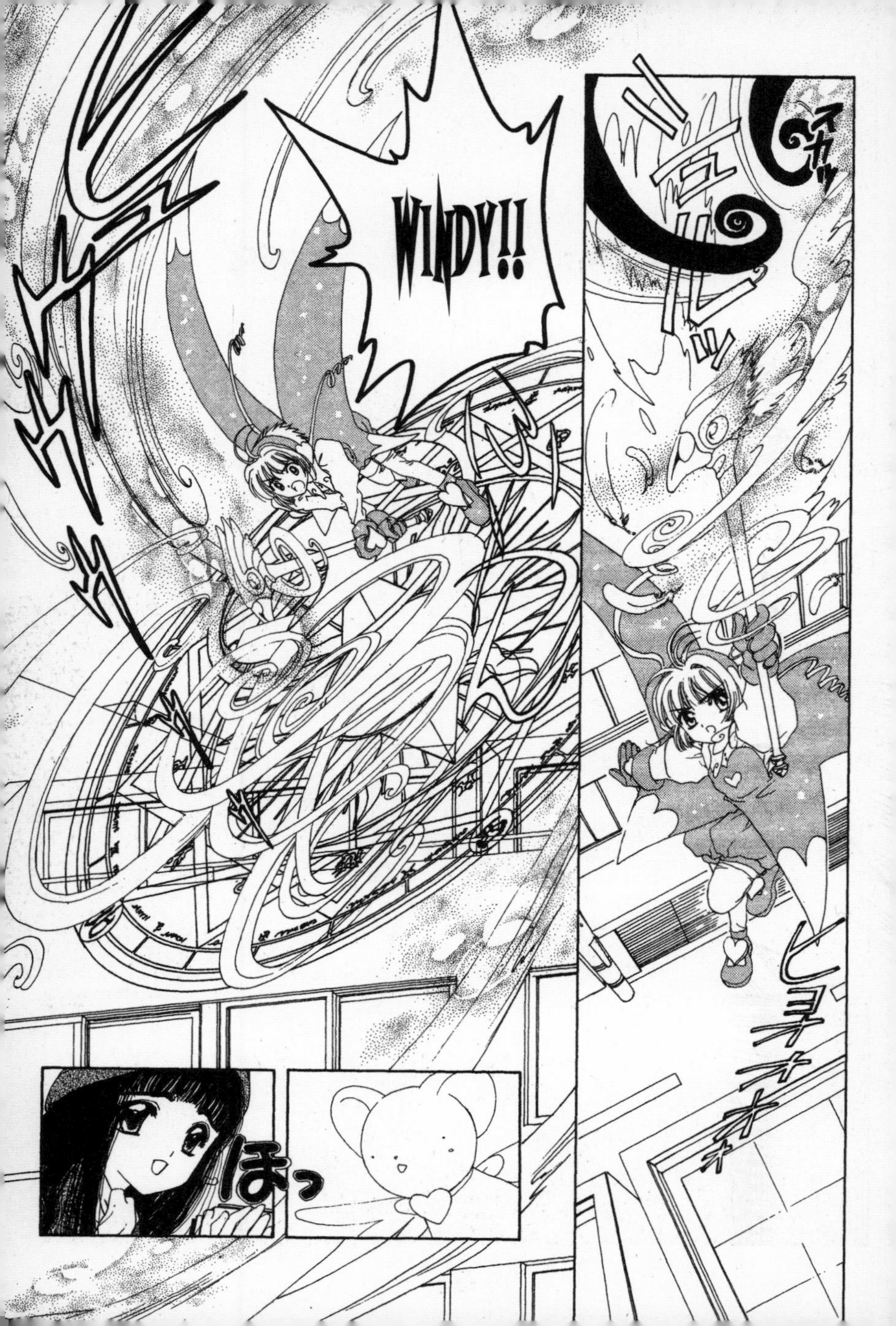
スカッ
WINDY!!
ヒョオオォ
ほっ

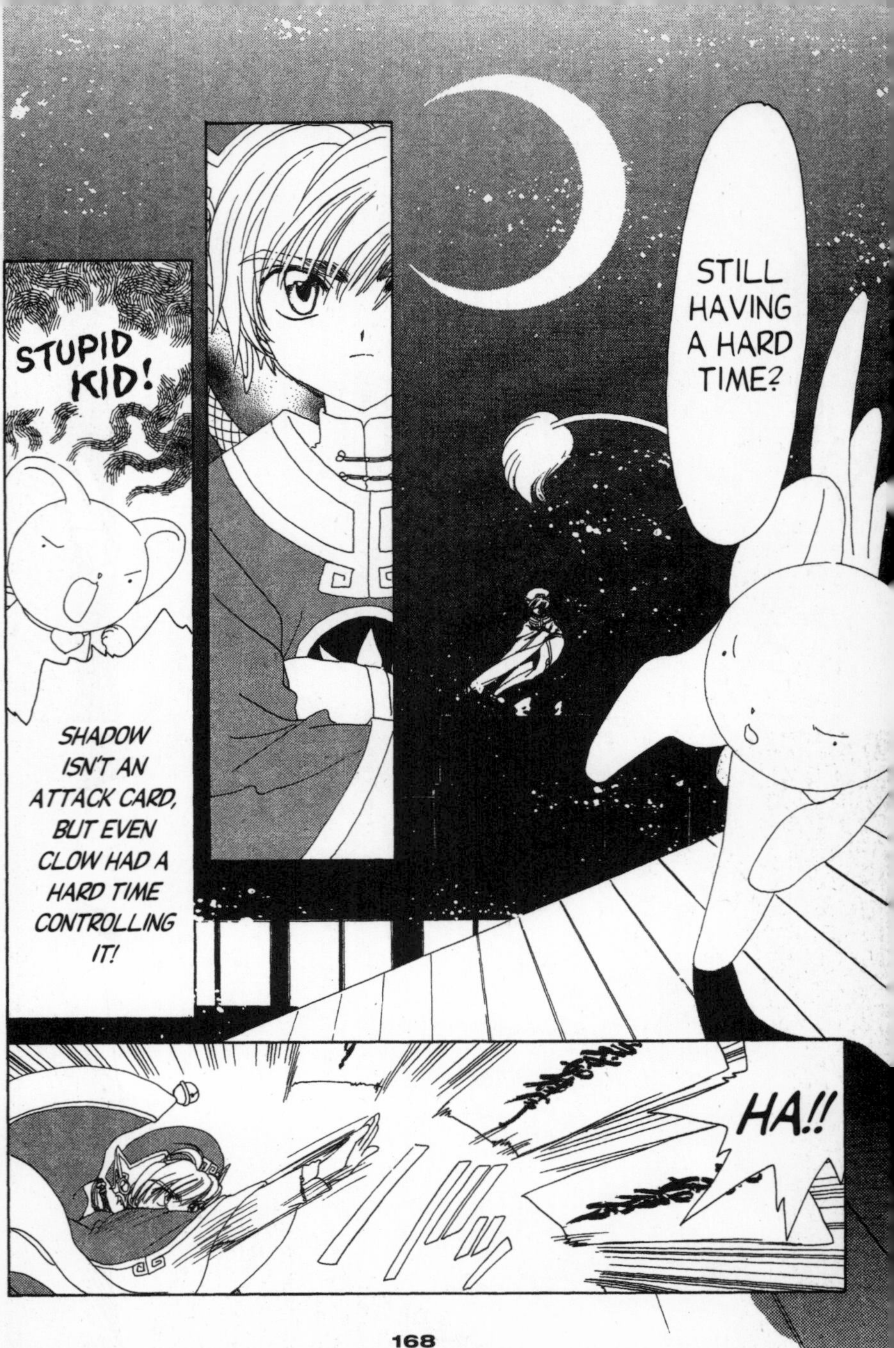
STILL HAVING A HARD TIME?
STUPID KID!
SHADOW ISN'T AN ATTACK CARD, BUT EVEN CLOW HAD A HARD TIME CONTROLLING IT!
HA!!

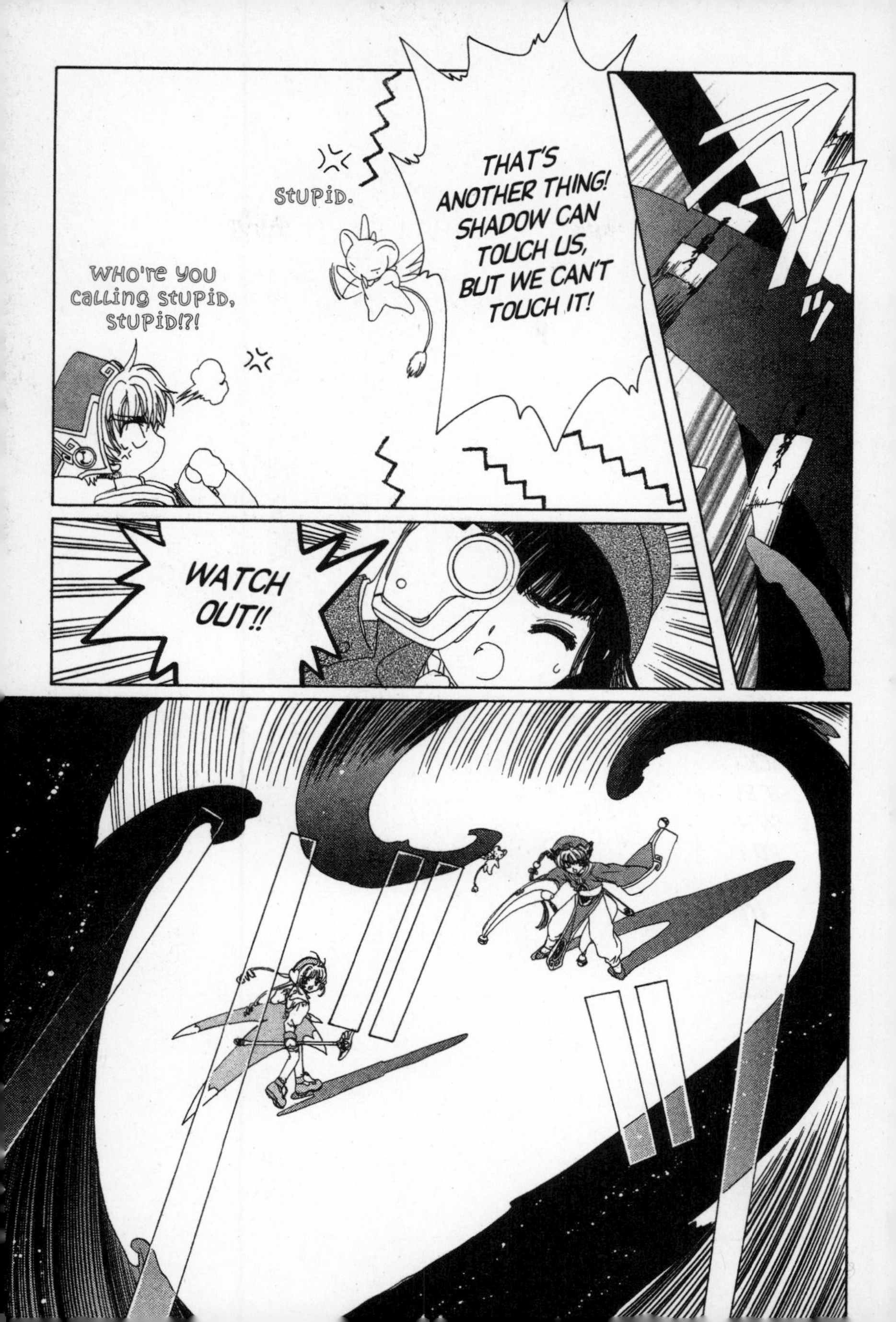
THAT'S ANOTHER THING! SHADOW CAN TOUCH US, BUT WE CAN'T TOUCH IT!
Stupid.
Who're you calling stupid, stupid!?!
WATCH OUT!!

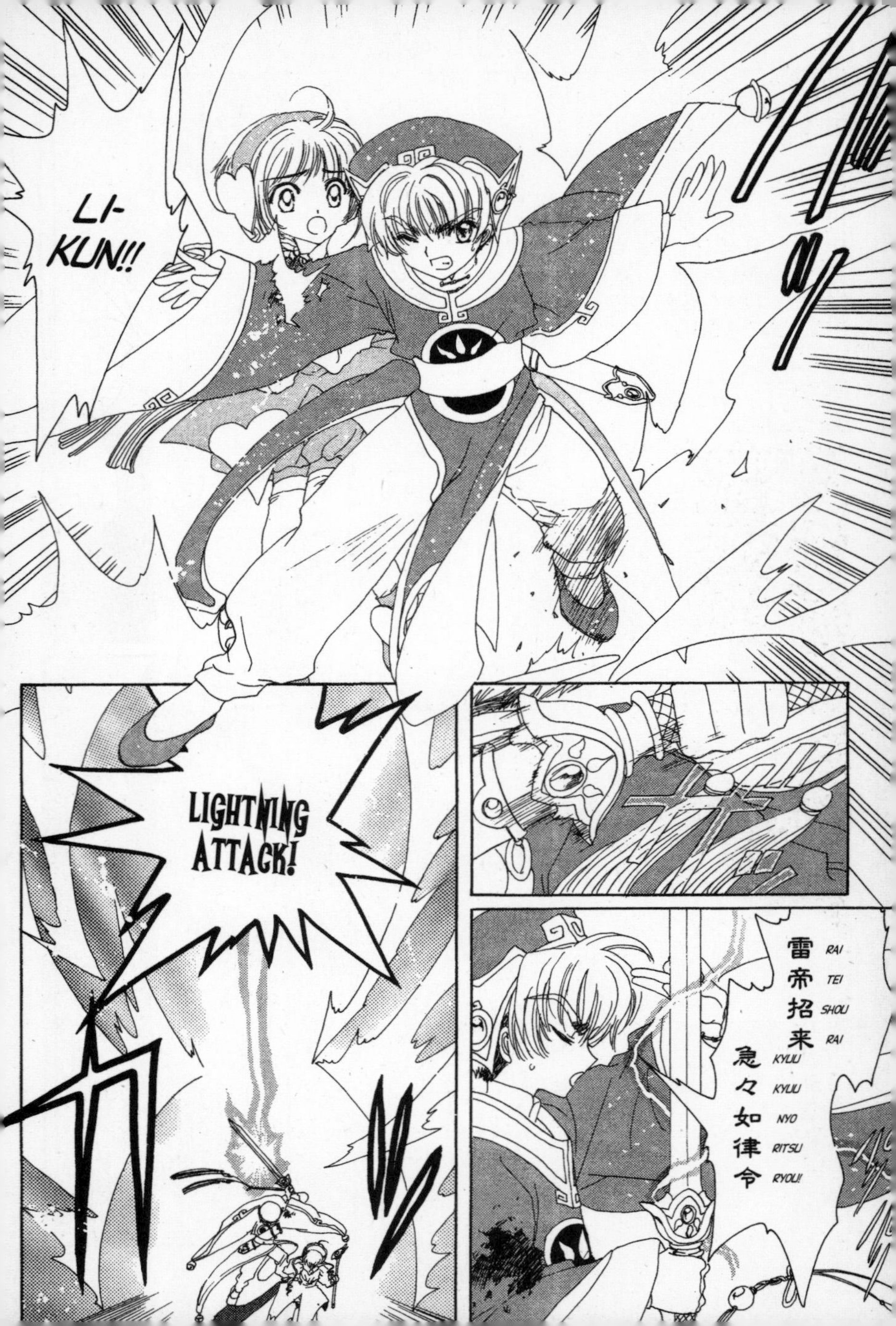
LI-KUN!!
雷帝招来
RAI TEI SHOU RAI
急々如律令
KYUU KYUU NYO RITSU RYOU!
LIGHTNING ATTACK!

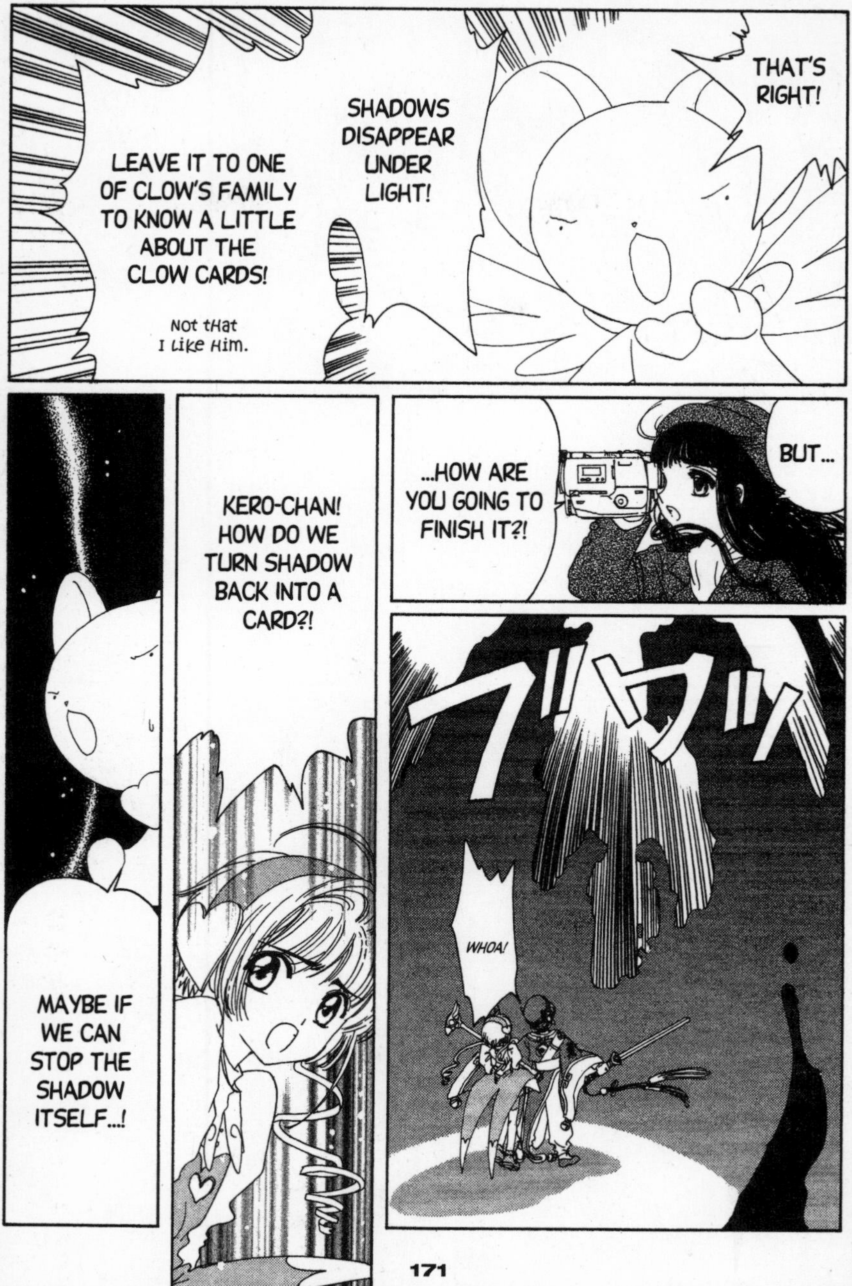
THAT'S RIGHT!
SHADOWS DISAPPEAR UNDER LIGHT!
LEAVE IT TO ONE OF CLOW'S FAMILY TO KNOW A LITTLE ABOUT THE CLOW CARDS!
Not that I like him.
BUT...
...HOW ARE YOU GOING TO FINISH IT?!
WHOA!
KERO-CHAN! HOW DO WE TURN SHADOW BACK INTO A CARD?!
MAYBE IF WE CAN STOP THE SHADOW ITSELF...!

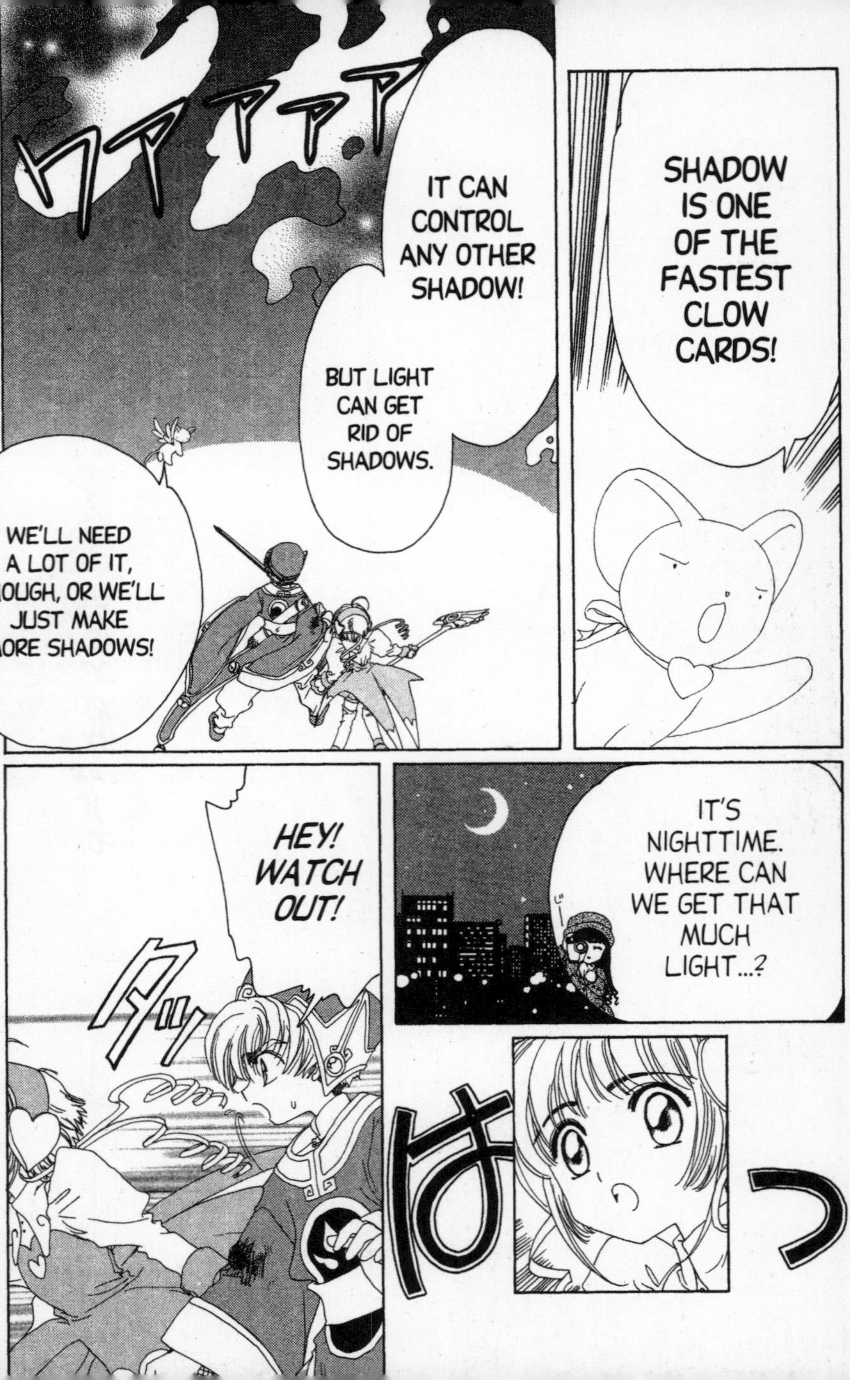
SHADOW IS ONE OF THE FASTEST CLOW CARDS!
ワァァァ
IT CAN CONTROL ANY OTHER SHADOW!
BUT LIGHT CAN GET RID OF SHADOWS.
WE'LL NEED A LOT OF IT, THOUGH, OR WE'LL JUST MAKE MORE SHADOWS!
IT'S NIGHTTIME. WHERE CAN WE GET THAT MUCH LIGHT...?
じー
はっ
HEY! WATCH OUT!
タッ

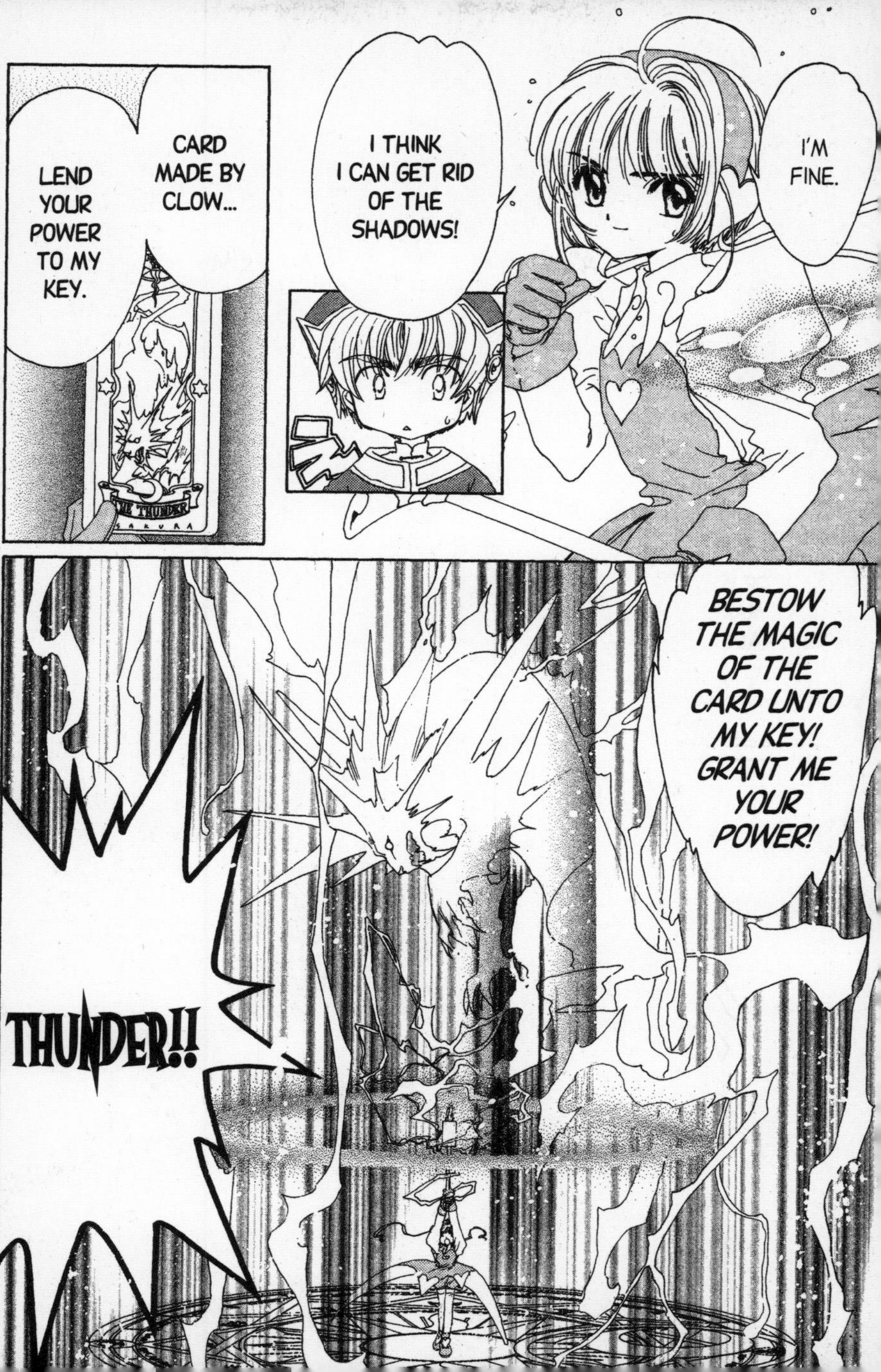
I'M FINE.
I THINK I CAN GET RID OF THE SHADOWS!
CARD MADE BY CLOW...
LEND YOUR POWER TO MY KEY.
THE THUNDER
SAKURA
BESTOW THE MAGIC OF THE CARD UNTO MY KEY! GRANT ME YOUR POWER!
THUNDER!!

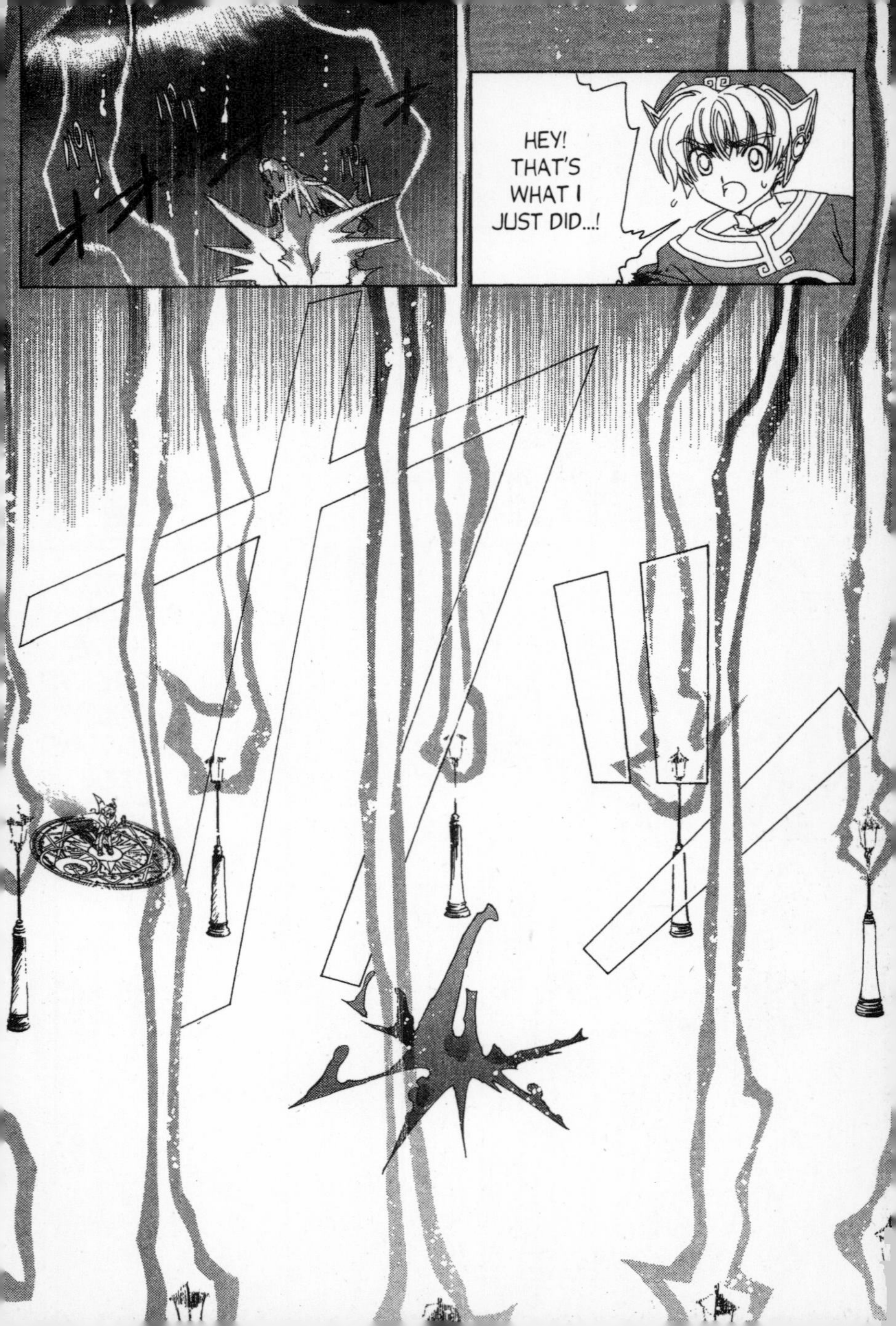
HEY! THAT'S WHAT I JUST DID...!

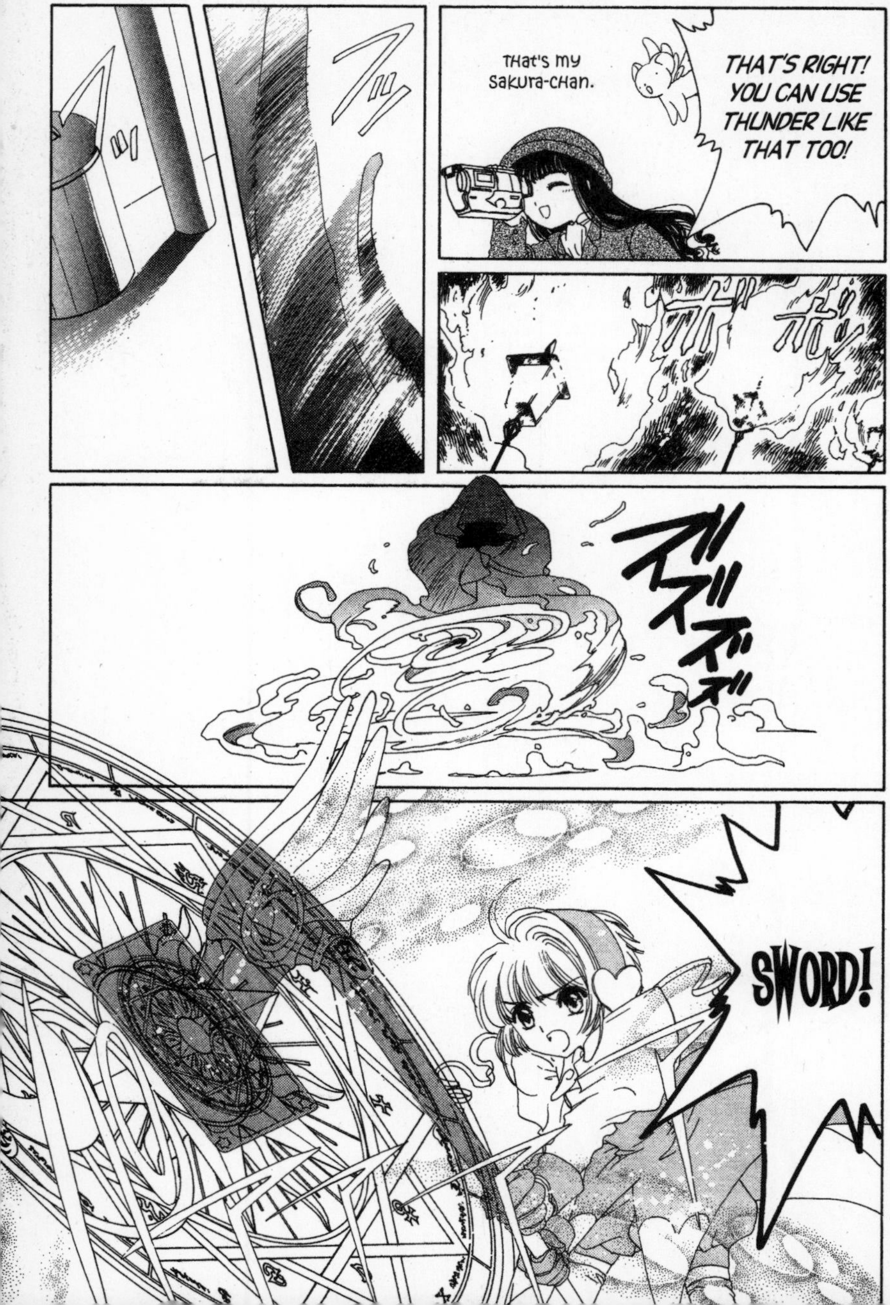
THAT'S RIGHT! YOU CAN USE THUNDER LIKE THAT TOO!
That's my Sakura-chan.
SWORD!

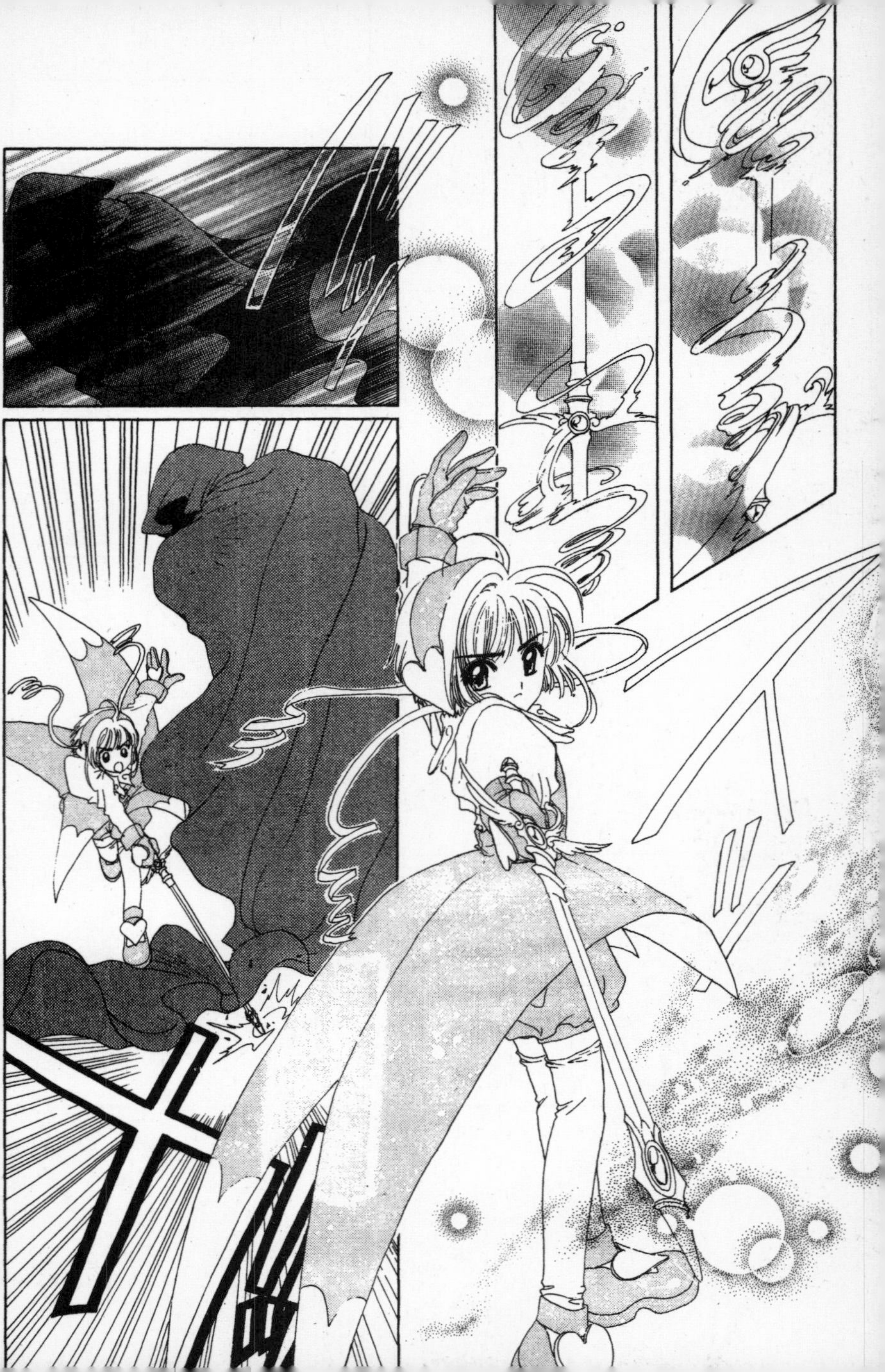

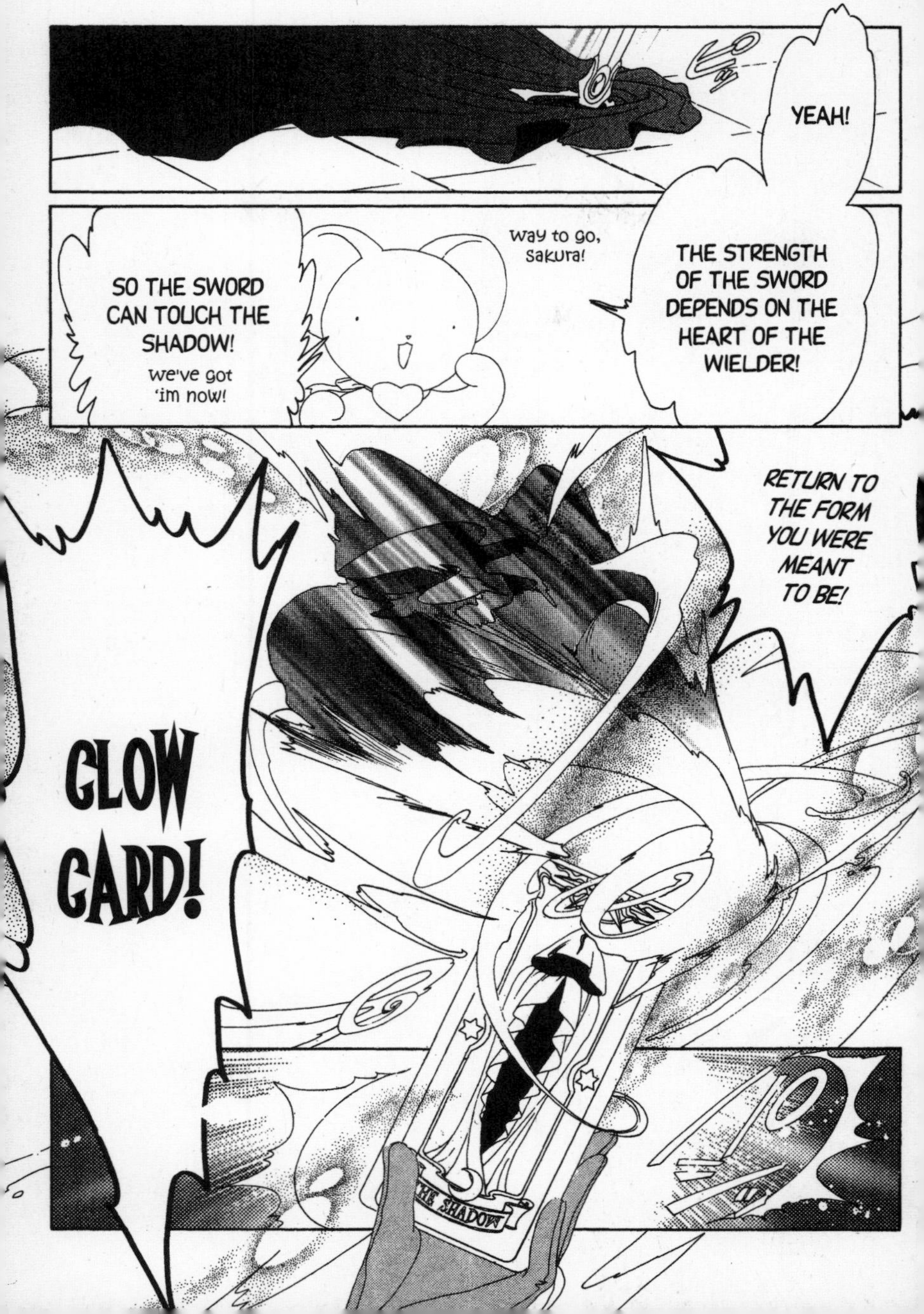
YEAH!
THE STRENGTH OF THE SWORD DEPENDS ON THE HEART OF THE WIELDER!
Way to go, Sakura!
SO THE SWORD CAN TOUCH THE SHADOW!
We've got 'im now!
RETURN TO THE FORM YOU WERE MEANT TO BE!
GLOW CARD!
THE SHADOW

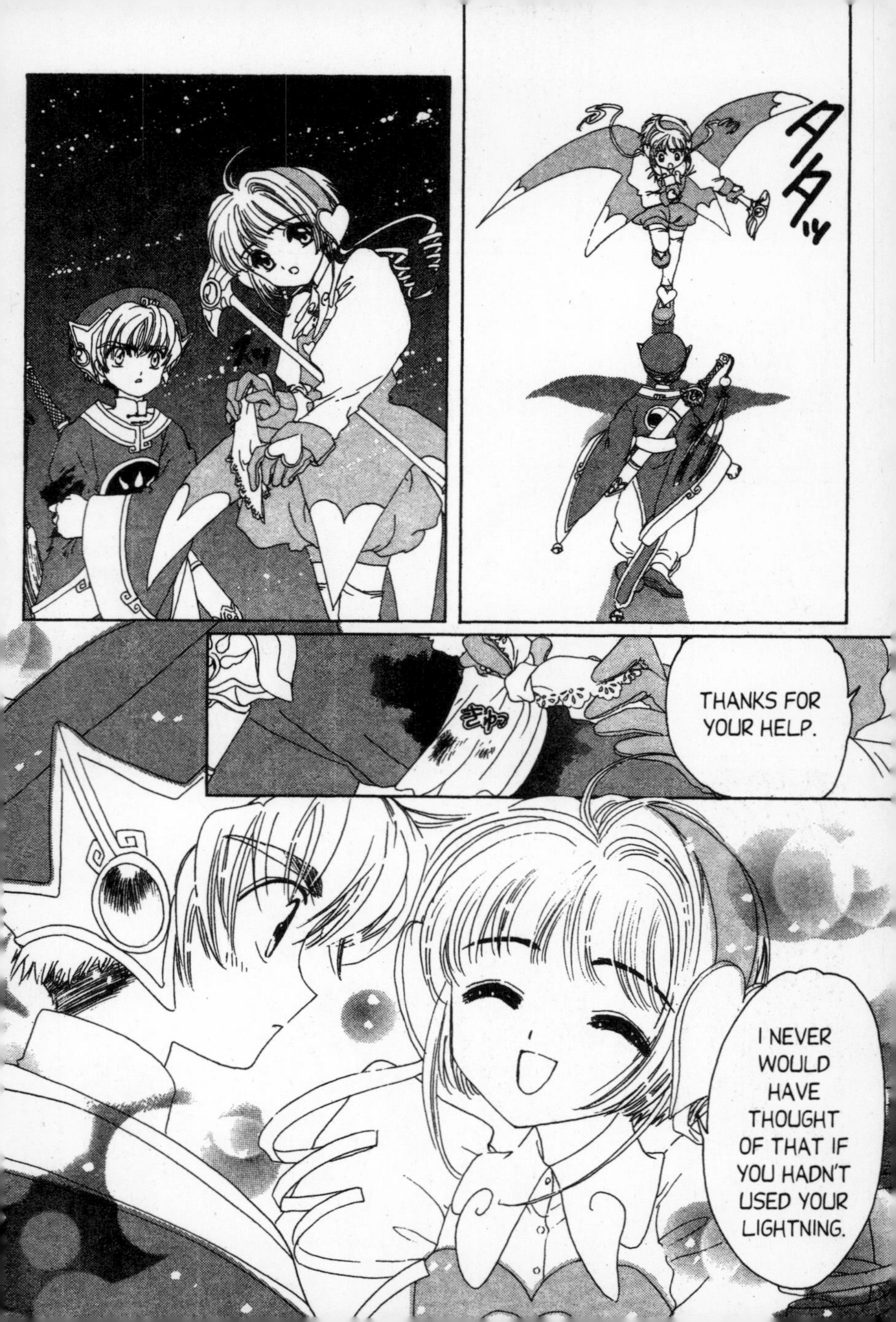
タタッ
きゅっ
THANKS FOR YOUR HELP.
I NEVER WOULD HAVE THOUGHT OF THAT IF YOU HADN'T USED YOUR LIGHTNING.

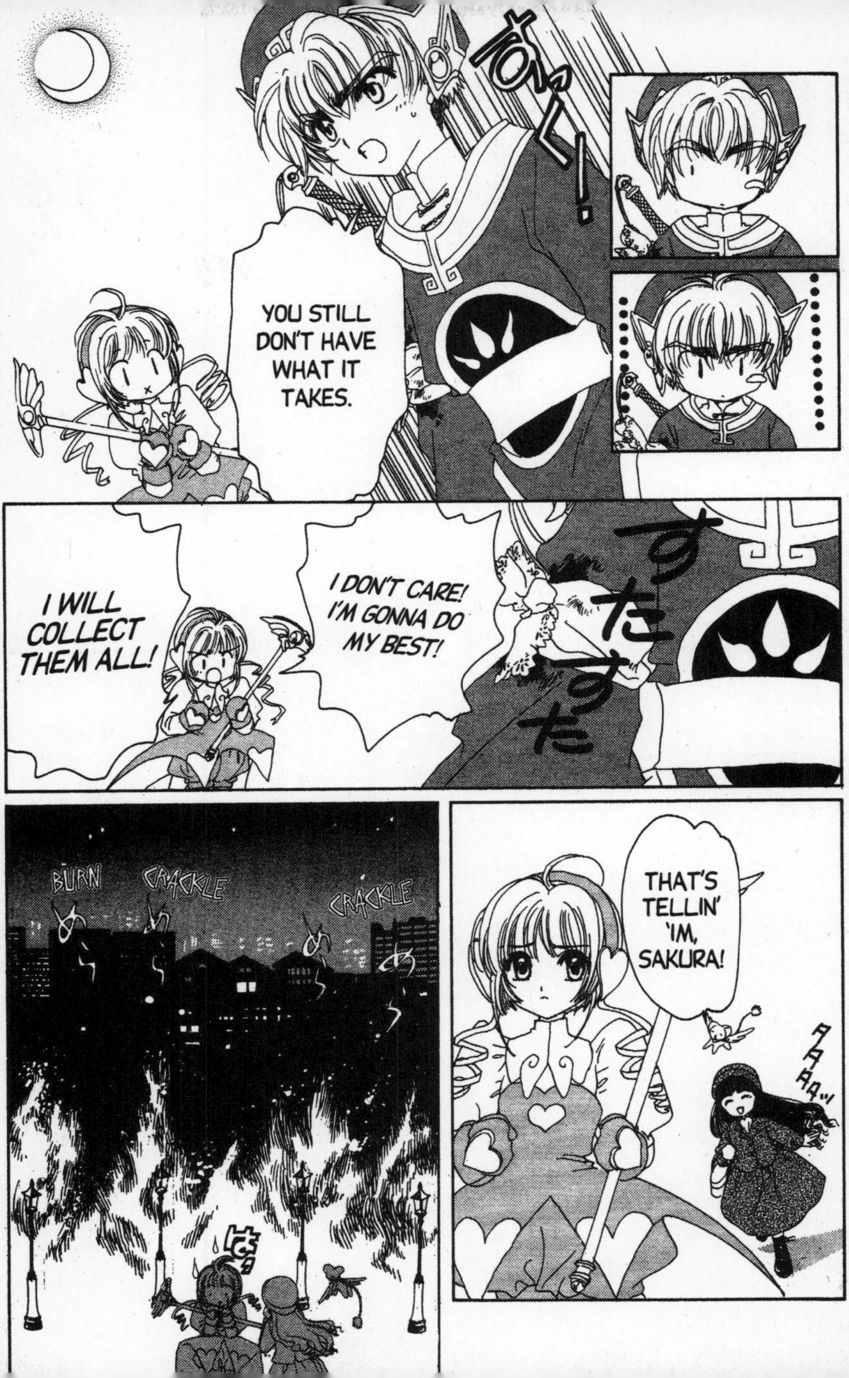
YOU STILL DON'T HAVE WHAT IT TAKES.
I DON'T CARE! I'M GONNA DO MY BEST!
I WILL COLLECT THEM ALL!
すたすたすた
THAT'S TELLIN' 'IM, SAKURA!
BURN
CRACKLE
CRACKLE

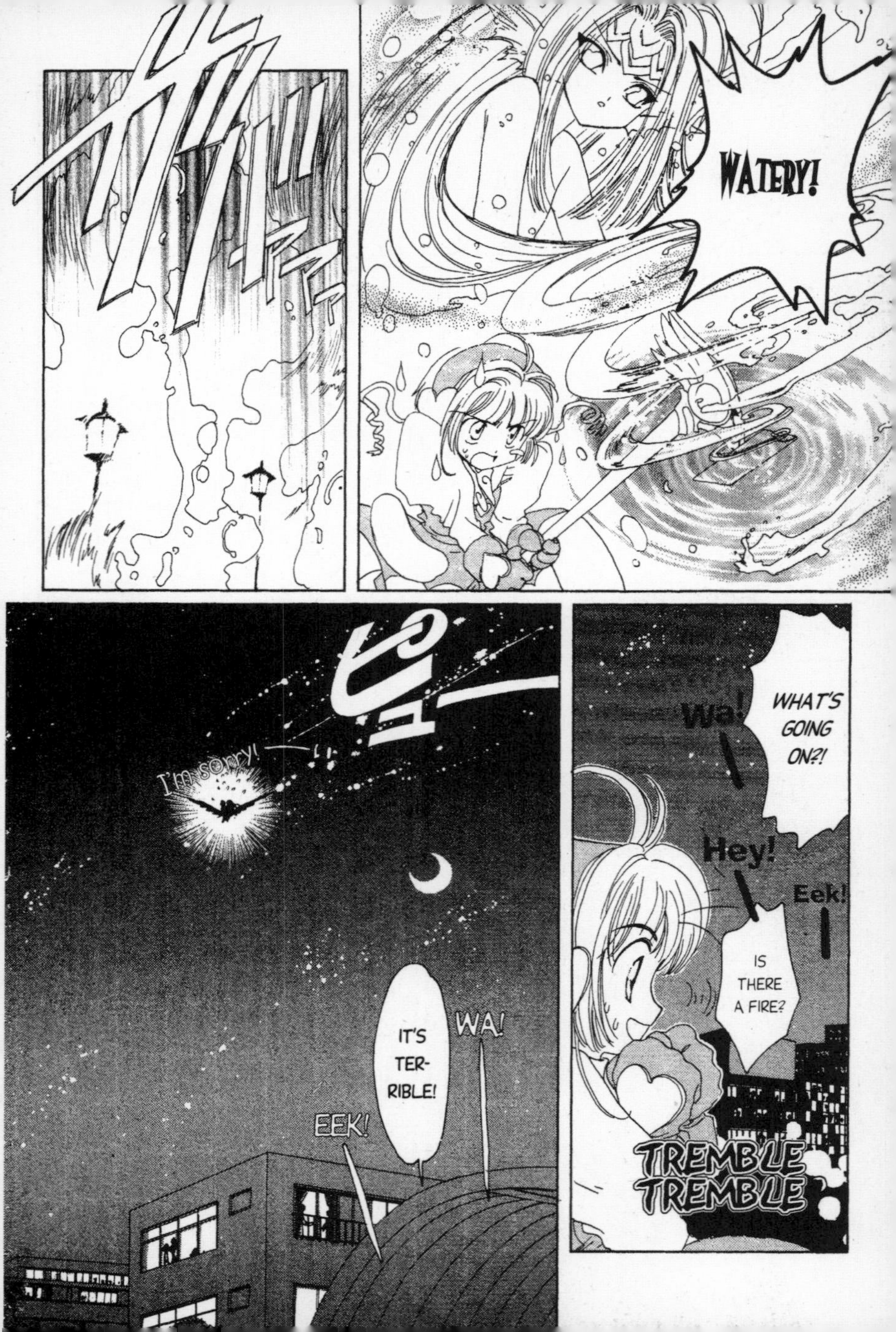
WATERY!
WHAT'S GOING ON?!
Wa!
Hey!
Eek!
IS THERE A FIRE?
TREMBLE TREMBLE
ピュー
I'm sorry!
IT'S TER-RIBLE!
WA!
EEK!

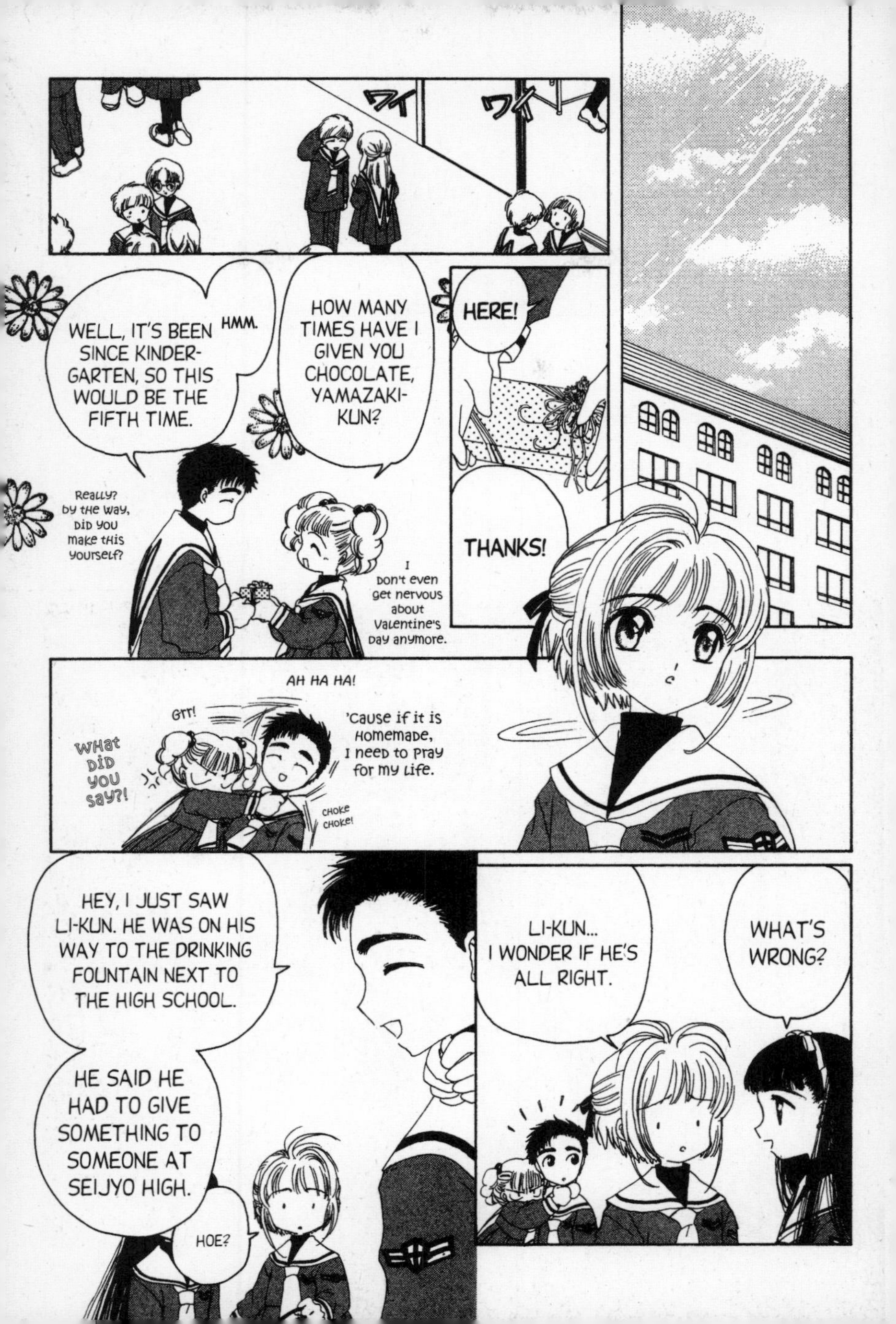
ワイ
ワイ
HERE!
THANKS!
HOW MANY TIMES HAVE I GIVEN YOU CHOCOLATE, YAMAZAKI-KUN?
HMM.
WELL, IT'S BEEN SINCE KINDER-GARTEN, SO THIS WOULD BE THE FIFTH TIME.
Really? By the way, did you make this yourself?
I don't even get nervous about Valentine's Day anymore.
AH HA HA!
'Cause if it is homemade, I need to pray for my life.
Grr!
What did you say?!
CHOKE CHOKE!
WHAT'S WRONG?
LI-KUN... I WONDER IF HE'S ALL RIGHT.
HEY, I JUST SAW LI-KUN. HE WAS ON HIS WAY TO THE DRINKING FOUNTAIN NEXT TO THE HIGH SCHOOL.
HE SAID HE HAD TO GIVE SOMETHING TO SOMEONE AT SEIJYO HIGH.
HOE?

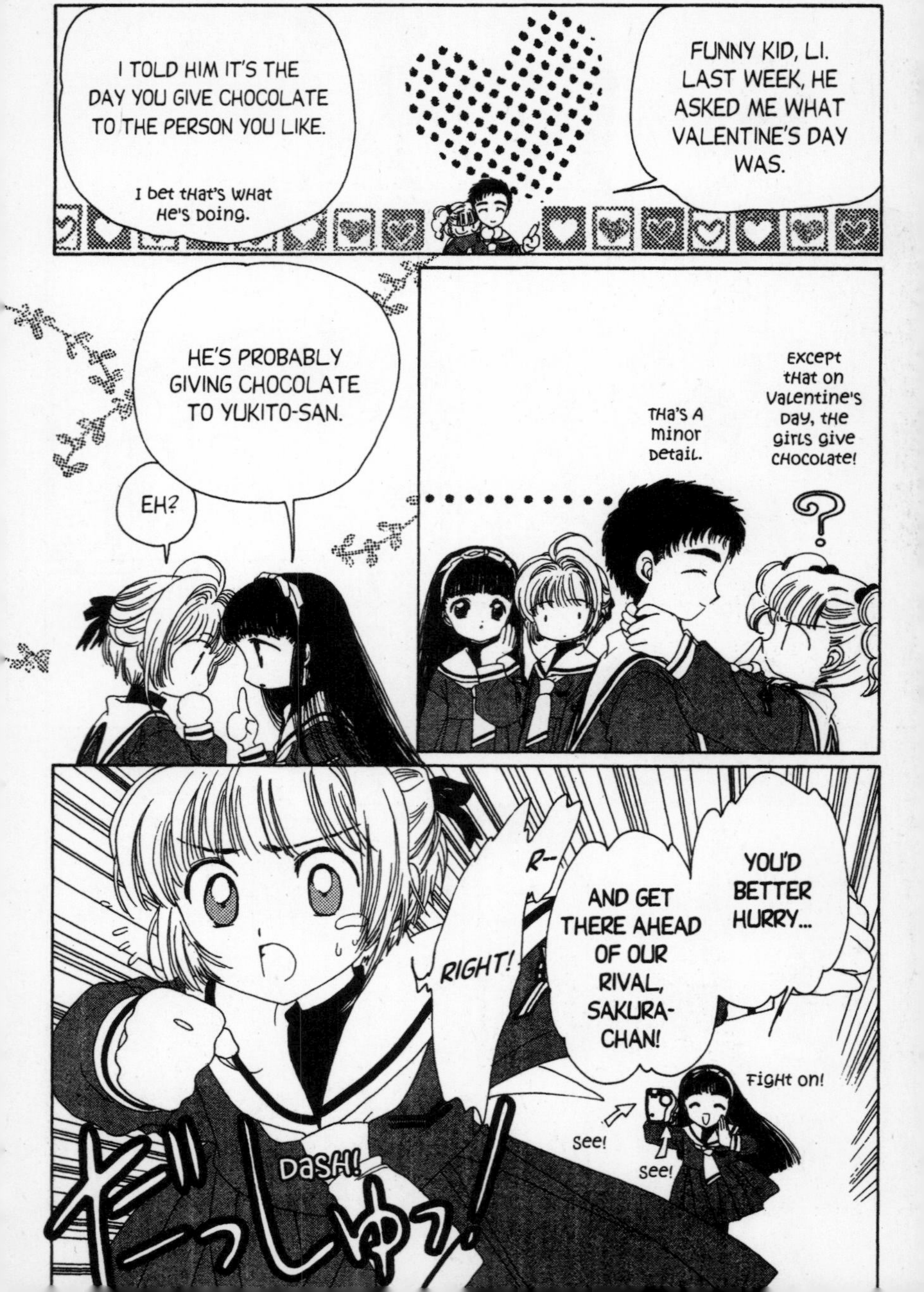
FUNNY KID, LI. LAST WEEK, HE ASKED ME WHAT VALENTINE'S DAY WAS.
I TOLD HIM IT'S THE DAY YOU GIVE CHOCOLATE TO THE PERSON YOU LIKE.
I bet that's what he's doing.
Except that on Valentine's day, the girls give chocolate!
Tha's a minor detail.
HE'S PROBABLY GIVING CHOCOLATE TO YUKITO-SAN.
EH?
YOU'D BETTER HURRY...
AND GET THERE AHEAD OF OUR RIVAL, SAKURA-CHAN!
R--
RIGHT!
Fight on!
see!
see!
DASH!

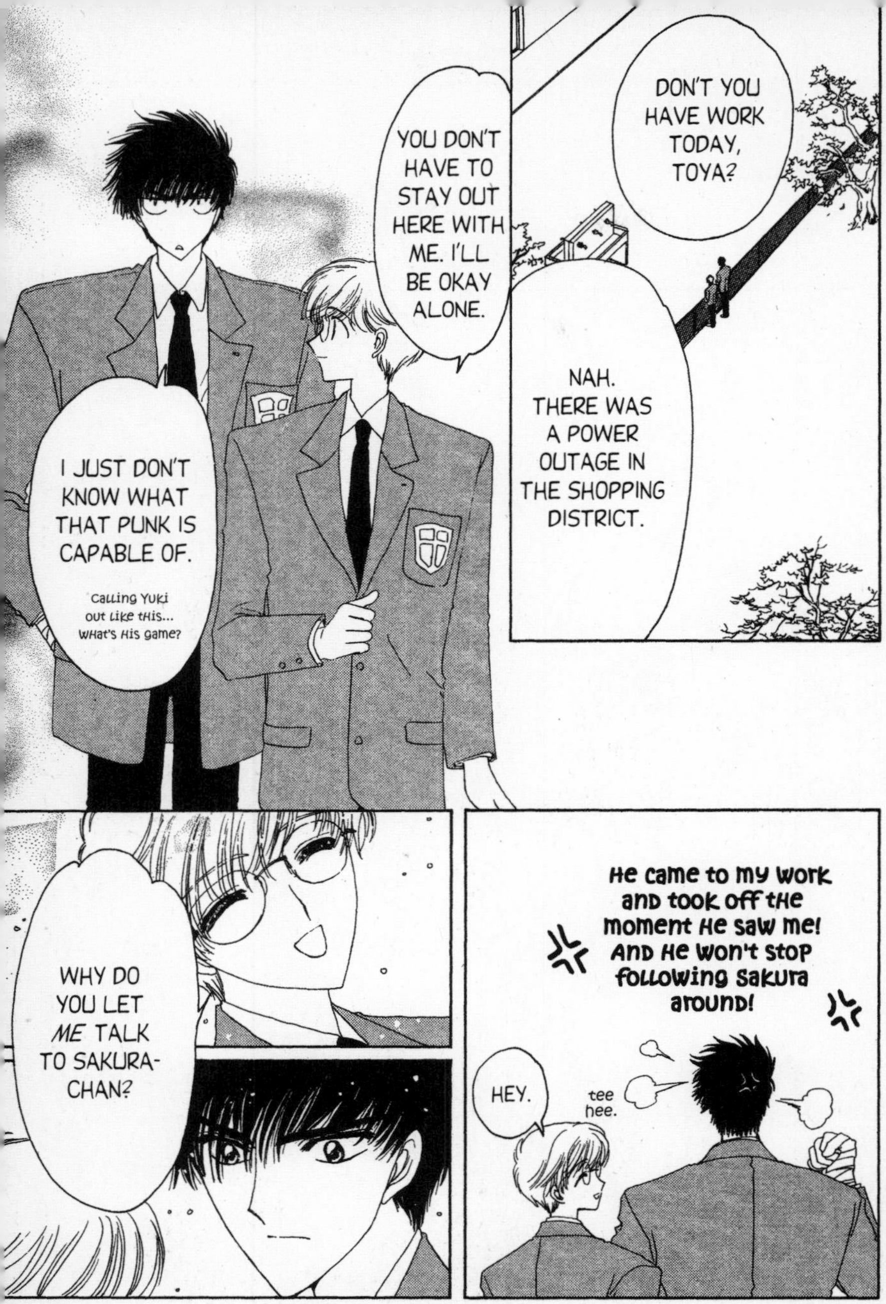
DON'T YOU HAVE WORK TODAY, TOYA?
NAH. THERE WAS A POWER OUTAGE IN THE SHOPPING DISTRICT.
YOU DON'T HAVE TO STAY OUT HERE WITH ME. I'LL BE OKAY ALONE.
I JUST DON'T KNOW WHAT THAT PUNK IS CAPABLE OF.
Calling Yuki out like this... What's his game?
He came to my work and took off the moment he saw me! And he won't stop following Sakura around!
tee hee.
HEY.
WHY DO YOU LET *ME* TALK TO SAKURA-CHAN?

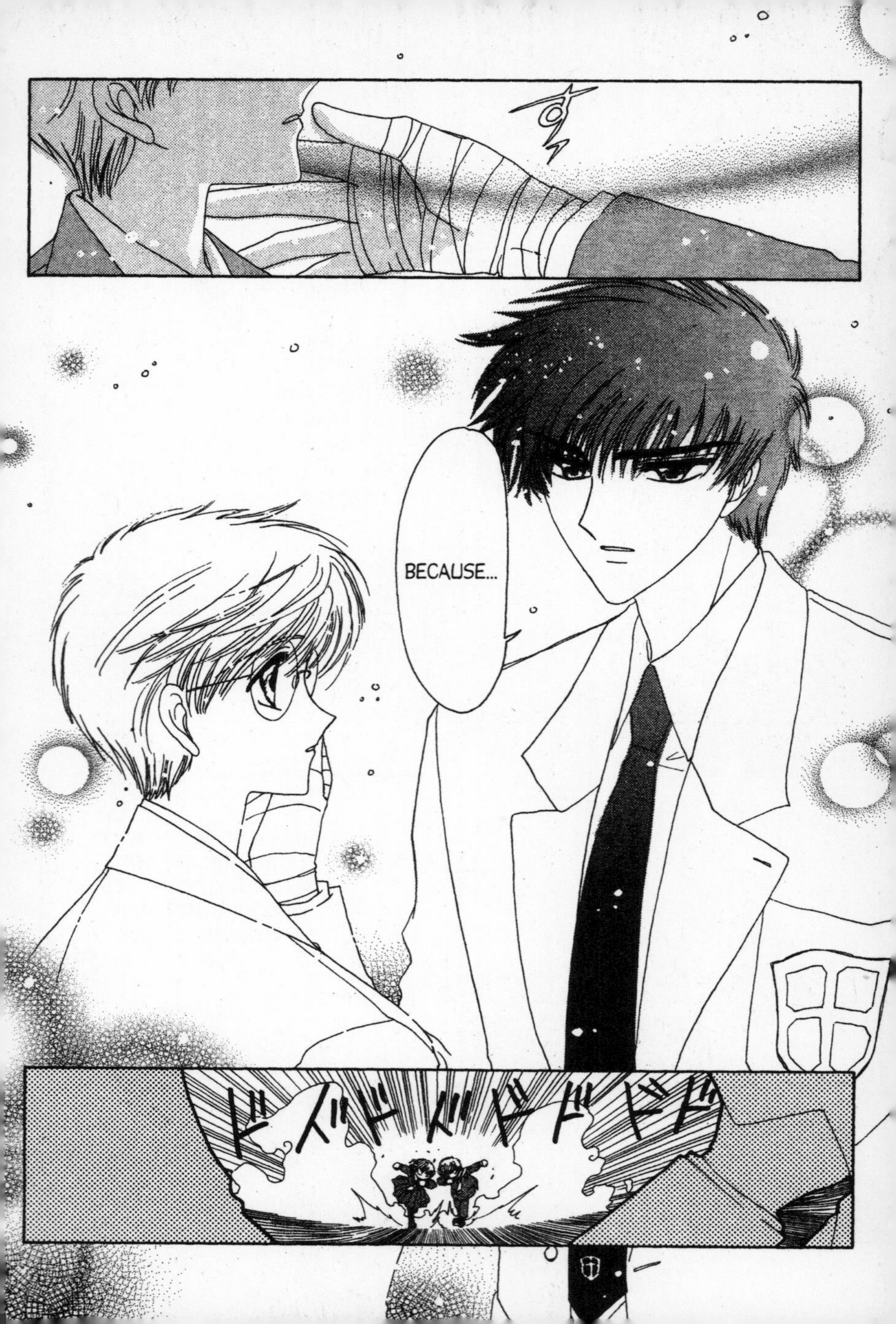
BECAUSE...

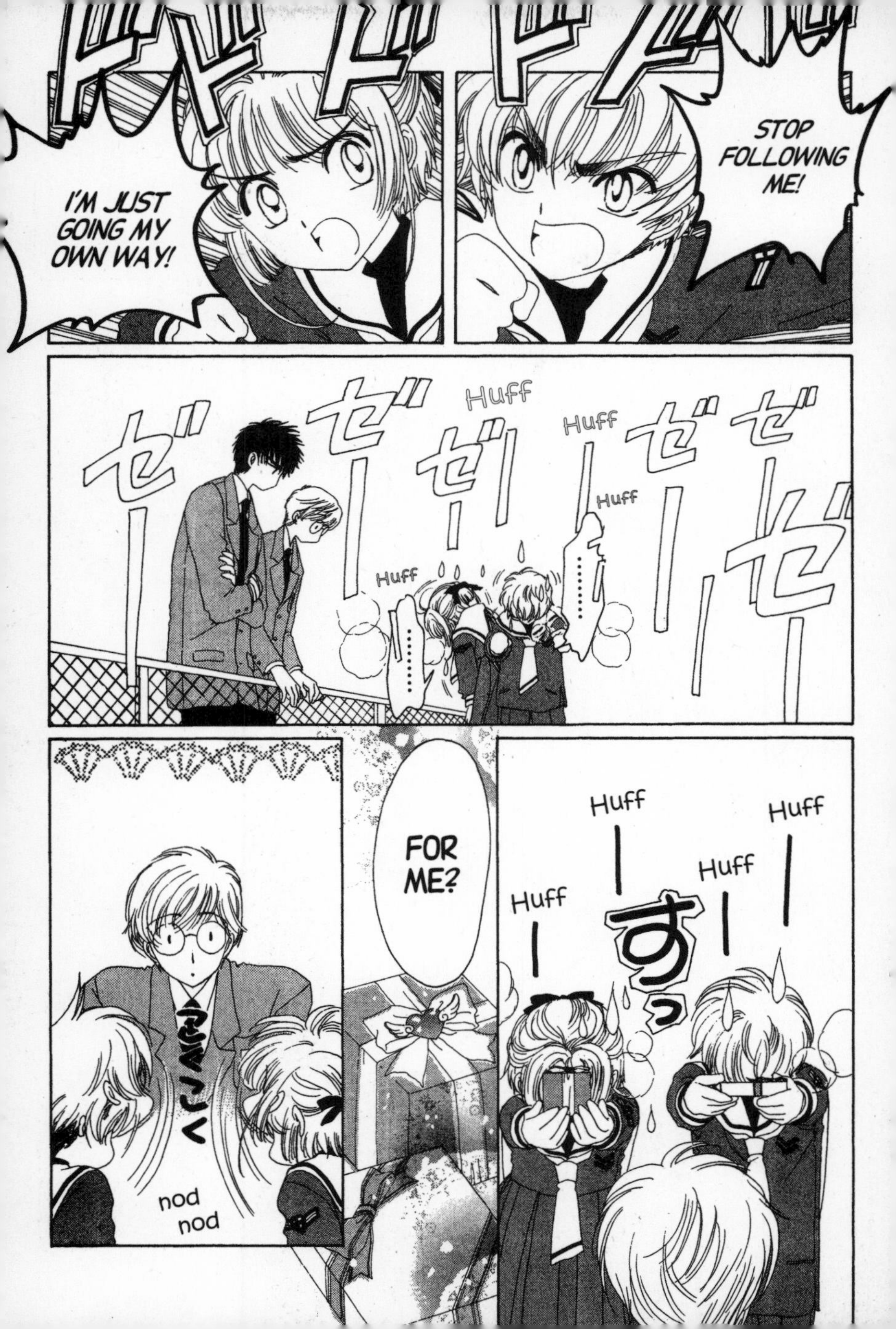
STOP FOLLOWING ME!
I'M JUST GOING MY OWN WAY!
Huff
Huff
Huff
Huff
Huff
Huff
Huff
Huff
すっ
FOR ME?
nod nod

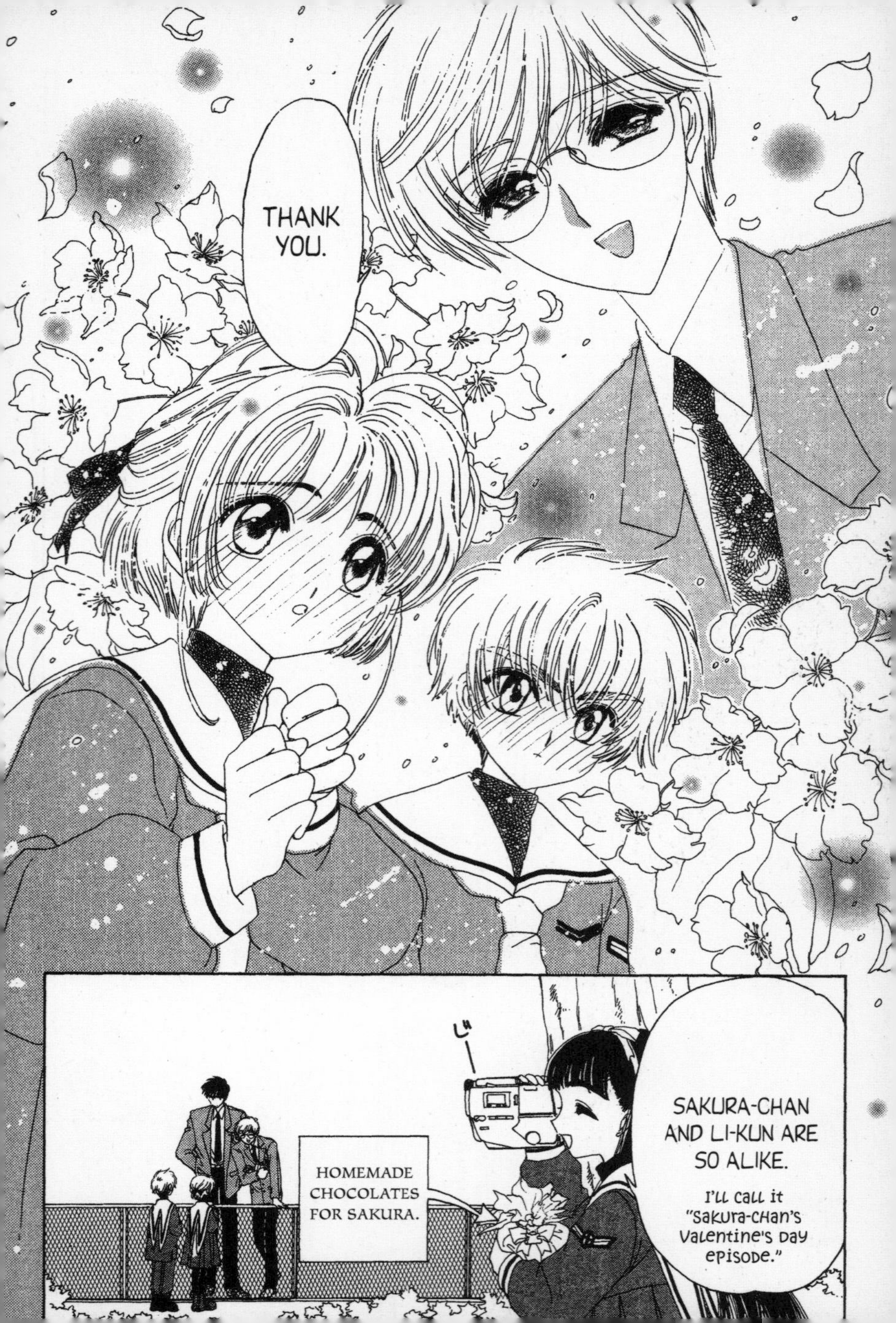
THANK YOU.
SAKURA-CHAN AND LI-KUN ARE SO ALIKE.
I'll call it "Sakura-chan's Valentine's Day episode."
じー
HOMEMADE CHOCOLATES FOR SAKURA.

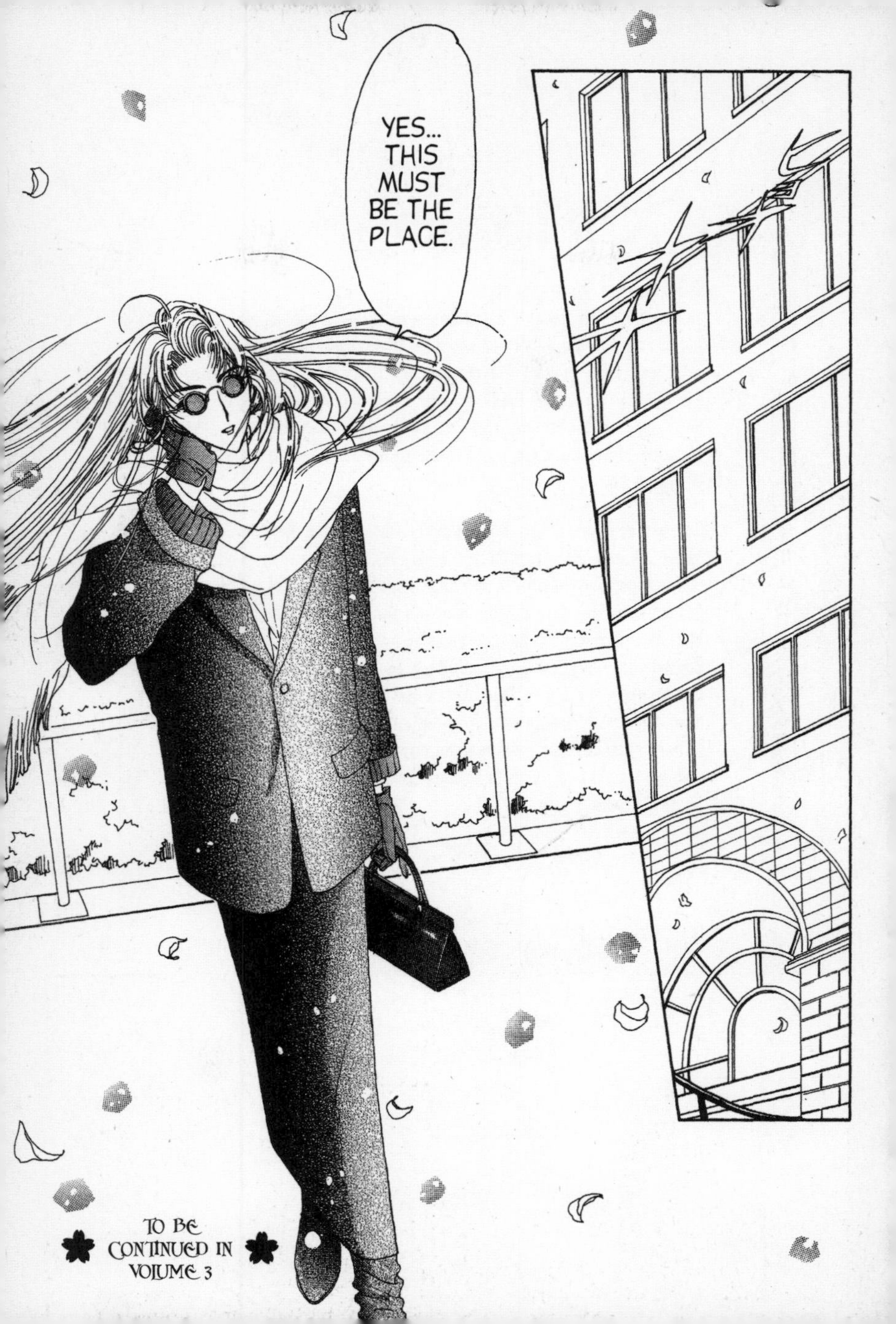
YES... THIS MUST BE THE PLACE.
TO BE CONTINUED IN VOLUME 3

NEXT ISSUE:

A Powerful Stranger...

Yo yo yo, it's K to the er-o, better known as Cerberus the Magnificent! But this isn't my story—it's all about my girl Sakura, an ordinary kid with extraordinary powers. Ever since she accidentally released the magical Clow Cards from the book I was guarding (I was guarding it! I just happened to be asleep at the time), she's been the town of Tomoeda's own Cardcaptor—and I must say, she's been doing one heck of a good job.

But she's definitely got her hands full this time. Word is there's a double of Sakura on the loose, behaving very badly. Sakura's gotta save face—especially when the double targets her brother Toya as a victim. Our friend and costume designer Tomoyo's also been having some trouble with a Clow Card in her house...who's she gonna call, I wonder? But what I'm really worried about is the strange new presence I've been feeling lately. It's as if someone with a whole lot of power has come to town...hopefully Sakura can find out what's going on while adjusting to her mysterious new math teacher, dueling with the ever-annoying arch nemesis Li and trying to cast love charms on her brother's best friend...sheesh

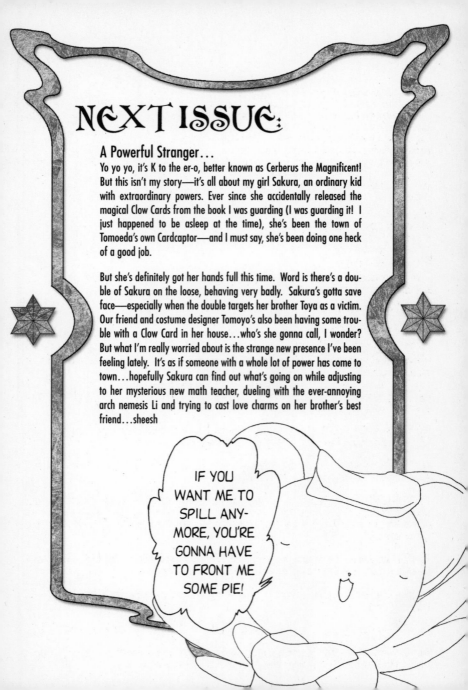

IF YOU WANT ME TO SPILL ANY-MORE, YOU'RE GONNA HAVE TO FRONT ME SOME PIE!

Glossary

Honorifics:

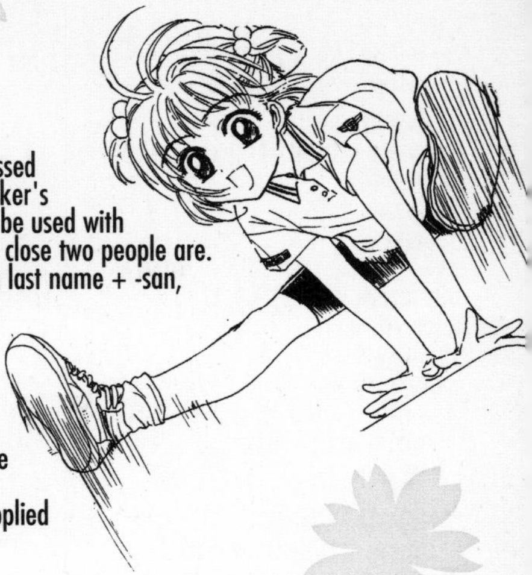

In the Japanese language, people are often addressed with suffixes on their names that indicate the speaker's relationship with that person. These honorifics can be used with first or last names or not at all, depending on how close two people are. The default for addressing someone is to start with last name + -san, so any variation from that is telling of how close two people are.

-san: The equivalent of Mr. or Mrs. It's the most common suffix in Japanese.

-chan: Indicates a friendly familiarity with someone of the same age or younger.
It's usually used towards girls, but sometimes is applied to boys as well (or magical beasts, if they're cute enough!).

-kun: The equivalent of -chan, however -kun is usually reserved for boys.

-sama: Indicates a great level of respect or admiration.

-sensei: The term for teacher.

Pg. 13—*Onigiri*. Rice balls. A Japanese snack in which plain or seasoned rice is packed into a triangular wedge and wrapped in *nori* (seaweed). Usually there is something in the middle like meat or vegetables.

Pg. 21—Bento Box. A traditional Japanese lunch box with little compartments for different types of foods. They're usually stackable and topped with a lid.

Pg. 31—Marriage Age. In Japan, the legal marriage age is 16 for women and 18 for men, hence why Sakura's mother was able to marry at such a young age.

Pg. 59—*Konnyaku*. A Jello-like food made of potato starch. It's non-fat, low in calories, almost completely tasteless and not very popular with kids.

Pg. 86—Li's Chant. As Li uses Chinese magic, his incantations were left with the Chinese kanji and phonetic readings. This spell roughly translates to: "Imperial king of Gods, thy divinity watches over all four corners. Metal, wood, water, fire, earth, thunder, wind, lighting. Whirling blade of lighting, answer my call!"

Pg. 87—Rashinban. Li's magical compass board. In the *Cardcaptors* anime, this was called a Lasin Board. This edition of *Cardcaptor Sakura* calls it by its phonetic spelling.

Pg. 91—*Oniichan*. An affectionate way of addressing one's older brother. This is how Sakura addresses Toya.

Pg. 170—Li's attack spell. This spell translates roughly to: "Thunder God, answer my call!"

Pg. 182—Valentine's Day. In Japan, on Valentine's Day girls give chocolate to boys. One month later is White Day when boys return the favor with candies.

ALSO AVAILABLE FROM TOKYOPOP®

05.26.04Y

ALSO AVAILABLE FROM ☺TOKYOPOP®

MANGA

.HACK//LEGEND OF THE TWILIGHT
ANGELIC LAYER
BABY BIRTH
BRAIN POWERED
BRIGADOON
B'TX
CANDIDATE FOR GODDESS, THE
CARDCAPTOR SAKURA
CARDCAPTOR SAKURA - MASTER OF THE CLOW
CHRONICLES OF THE CURSED SWORD
CLAMP SCHOOL DETECTIVES
CLOVER
COMIC PARTY
CORRECTOR YUI
COWBOY BEBOP
COWBOY BEBOP: SHOOTING STAR
CRAZY LOVE STORY
CRESCENT MOON
CROSS
CULDCEPT
CYBORG 009
D•N•ANGEL
DEMON DIARY
DEMON ORORON, THE
DIGIMON
DIGIMON TAMERS
DIGIMON ZERO TWO
DRAGON HUNTER
DRAGON KNIGHTS
DRAGON VOICE
DREAM SAGA
DUKLYON: CLAMP SCHOOL DEFENDERS
ET CETERA
ETERNITY
FAERIES' LANDING
FLCL
FLOWER OF THE DEEP SLEEP
FORBIDDEN DANCE
FRUITS BASKET
G GUNDAM
GATEKEEPERS
GIRL GOT GAME
GIRLS EDUCATIONAL CHARTER
GUNDAM BLUE DESTINY
GUNDAM SEED ASTRAY
GUNDAM WING
GUNDAM WING: BATTLEFIELD OF PACIFISTS
GUNDAM WING: ENDLESS WALTZ

GUNDAM WING: THE LAST OUTPOST (G-UNIT)
HANDS OFF!
HARLEM BEAT
HYPER RUNE
I.N.V.U.
INITIAL D
INSTANT TEEN: JUST ADD NUTS
JING: KING OF BANDITS
JING: KING OF BANDITS - TWILIGHT TALES
JULINE
KARE KANO
KILL ME, KISS ME
KINDAICHI CASE FILES, THE
KING OF HELL
KODOCHA: SANA'S STAGE
LEGEND OF CHUN HYANG, THE
MAGIC KNIGHT RAYEARTH I
MAGIC KNIGHT RAYEARTH II
MAN OF MANY FACES
MARMALADE BOY
MARS
MARS: HORSE WITH NO NAME
MINK
MIRACLE GIRLS
MODEL
MOURYOU KIDEN
MY LOVE
NECK AND NECK
ONE
ONE I LOVE, THE
PEACH GIRL
PEACH GIRL: CHANGE OF HEART
PITA-TEN
PLANET LADDER
PLANETES
PRINCESS AI
PSYCHIC ACADEMY
QUEEN'S KNIGHT, THE
RAGNAROK
RAVE MASTER
REALITY CHECK
REBIRTH
REBOUND
RISING STARS OF MANGA
SAILOR MOON
SAINT TAIL
SAMURAI GIRL REAL BOUT HIGH SCHOOL
SEIKAI TRILOGY, THE
SGT. FROG

05.26.04Y

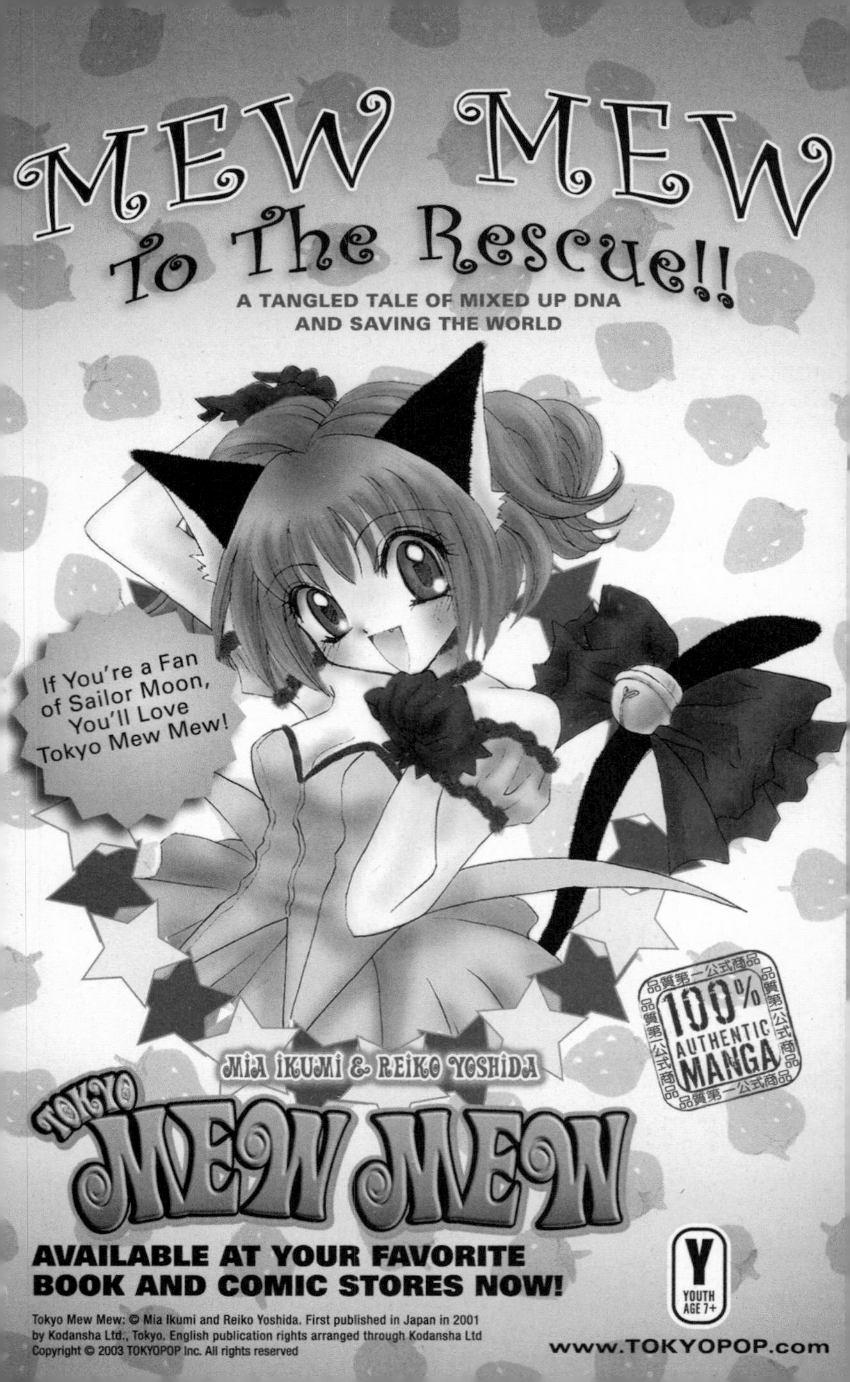
MEW MEW
To The Rescue!!
A TANGLED TALE OF MIXED UP DNA
AND SAVING THE WORLD
If You're a Fan of Sailor Moon, You'll Love Tokyo Mew Mew!
品質第一公式商品
100% AUTHENTIC MANGA
MIA IKUMI & REIKO YOSHIDA
TOKYO MEW MEW
AVAILABLE AT YOUR FAVORITE
BOOK AND COMIC STORES NOW!
Y
YOUTH AGE 7+
Tokyo Mew Mew: © Mia Ikumi and Reiko Yoshida. First published in Japan in 2001
by Kodansha Ltd., Tokyo. English publication rights arranged through Kodansha Ltd
Copyright © 2003 TOKYOPOP Inc. All rights reserved
www.TOKYOPOP.com

Zodiac P.I.

BY NATSUMI ANDO

100% AUTHENTIC MANGA

THE ANSWERS ARE IN THE STARS

AVAILABLE AT YOUR FAVORITE
BOOK AND COMIC STORES.

YOUTH
AGE 7+

www.TOKYOPOP.com

kare kano

his and her circumstances

Story by Masami Tsuda

Life Was A Popularity Contest For Yukino.
Somebody Is About To Steal Her Crown.

Available Now At Your Favorite Book And Comic Stores!

Rank	Name	Class	Points
1	???		
2	???		
3	Tomohiko Ta	B	
4	Takumi	A	
5	Mieko Ta	E	
6	Nijo Watana	C	
7	Akemi Imafuku		
8	Mizue Tanaka		
9	Yuki Honjo		
10	Reiko Yokoo		
11	Hiroki Sato		
12	Akira Oshima		
13	Eri Yugawa		
14	Aiko Yama		
15	Shogo Ka		
16	Masami H		
17	Mizuho On		

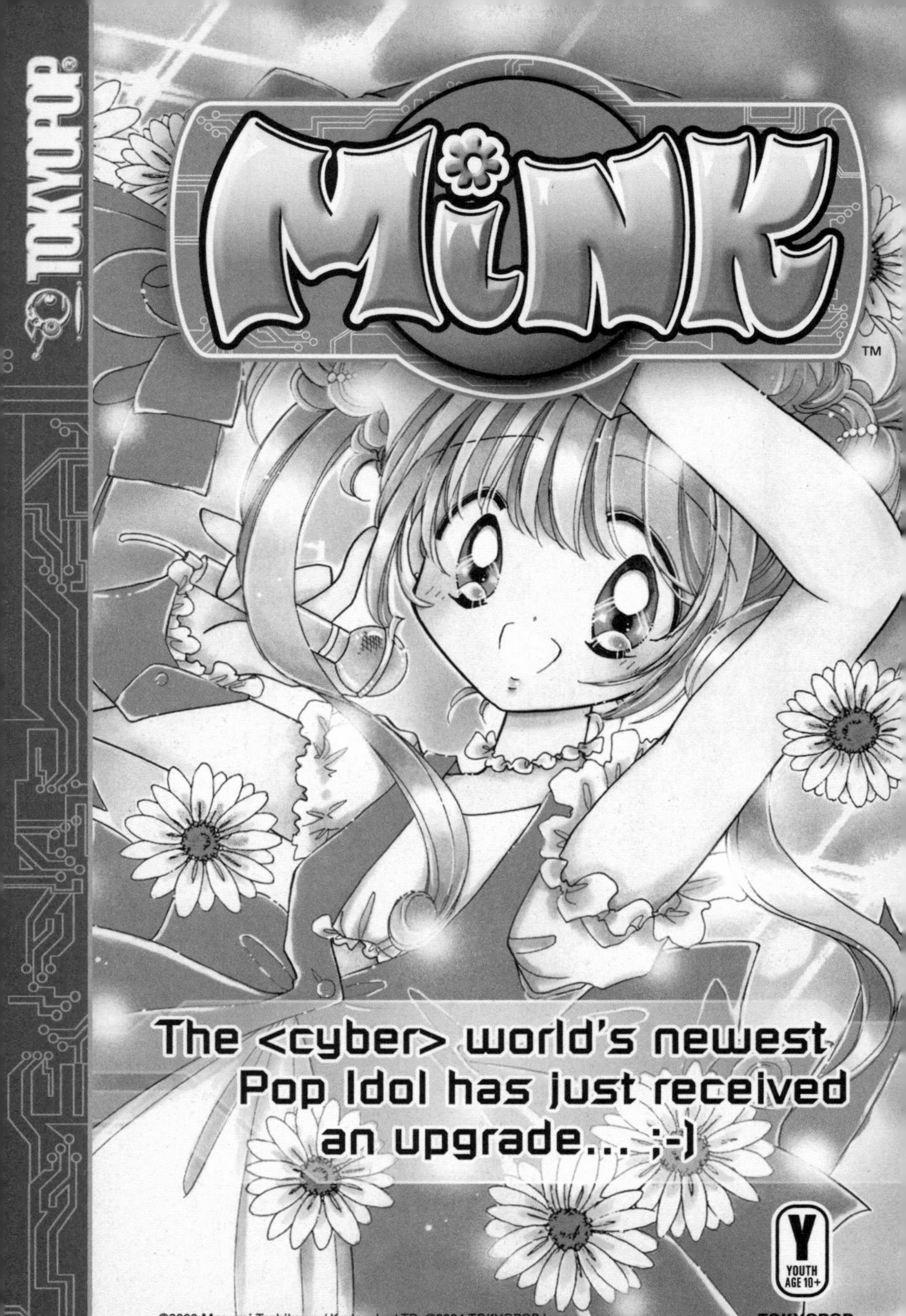
TOKYOPOP
MINK™
The <cyber> world's newest
Pop Idol has just received
an upgrade... ;-)
Y
YOUTH
AGE 10+

The One I Love

watashi no suki na hito

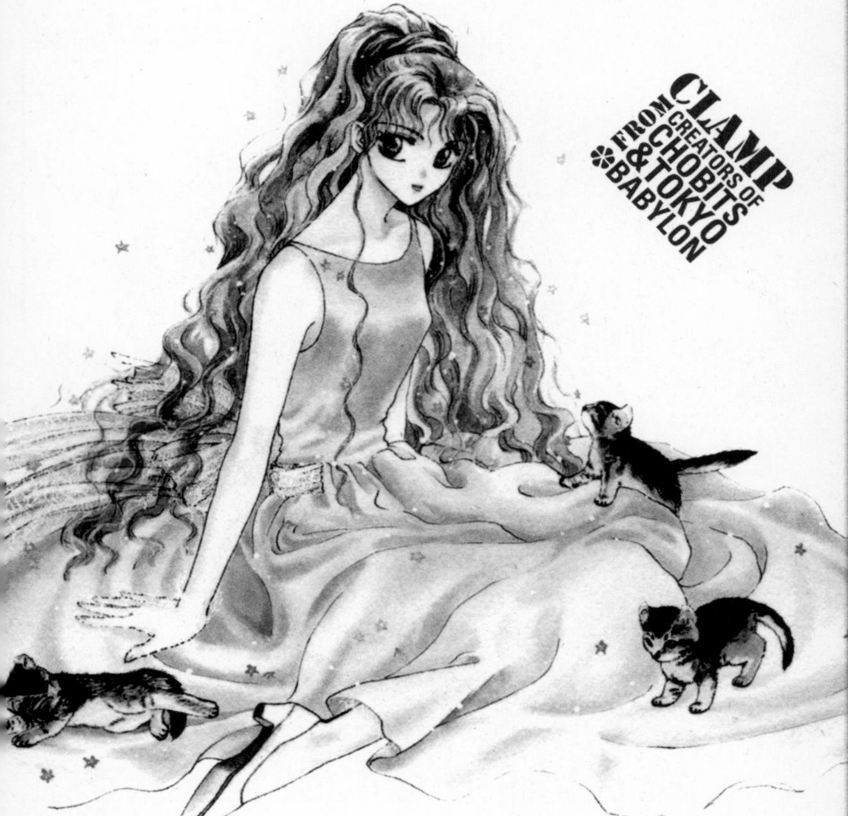
FROM CLAMP
CREATORS OF
CHOBITS
& TOKYO
BABYLON

breathtaking stories
of love and romance

T
TEEN
AGE 13+

www.TOKYOPOP.com

TOKYOPOP®

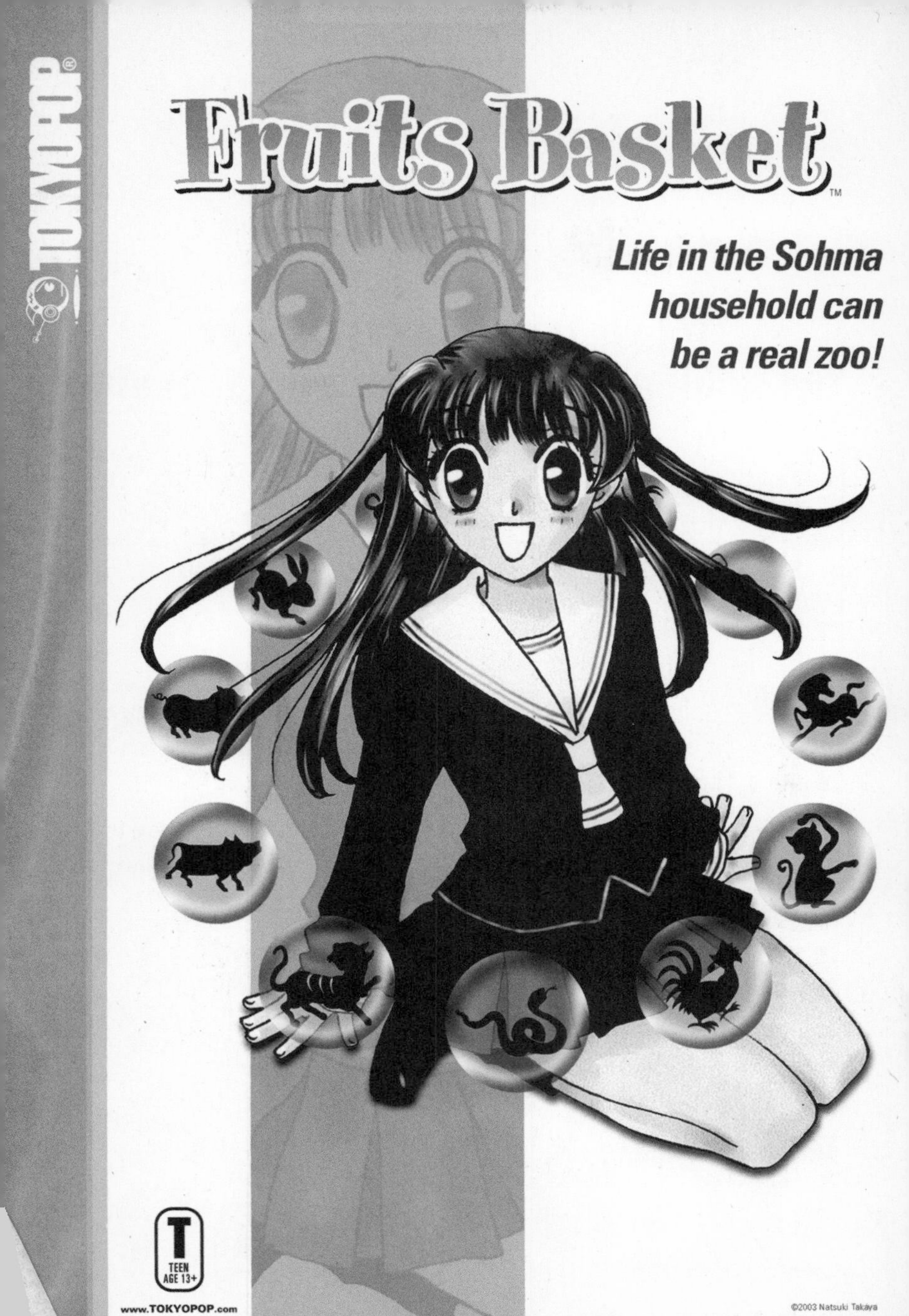
TOKYOPOP®
Fruits Basket™
Life in the Sohma household can be a real zoo!
T
TEEN AGE 13+
www.TOKYOPOP.com
©2003 Natsuki Takaya

STOP!

This is the back of the book.
You wouldn't want to spoil a great ending!

This book is printed "manga-style," in the authentic Japanese right-to-left format. Since none of the artwork has been flipped or altered, readers get to experience the story just as the creator intended. You've been asking for it, so TOKYOPOP® delivered: authentic, hot-off-the-press, and far more fun!

DIRECTIONS

If this is your first time reading manga-style, here's a quick guide to help you understand how it works.

It's easy... just start in the top right panel and follow the numbers. Have fun, and look for more 100% authentic manga from TOKYOPOP®!